BUILDING CONTRACTS

A Practical Guide

ALSO BY DENNIS F. TURNER

Quantity surveying practice and
administration 3rd edition

Building contracts

A practical guide

Dennis F. Turner
BA, FRICS, MCIOB, ACIrb

Fourth edition

Longman
Scientific &
Technical

Longman Scientific & Technical
Longman Group UK Limited
Longman House, Burnt Mill, Harlow,
Essex CM20 2JE, England
and Associated Companies throughout the world

First published 1971
Second edition 1975
Third edition 1977
Fourth edition 1983
Second impression published by
Longman Scientific & Technical 1987, 1989

British Library Cataloguing in Publication Data

Turner, Dennis F.
  Building contracts. – 4th ed.
  1. Buildings Contracts and specifications – Great Britain
  I. Title
  344.103′78′690   KD164L

ISBN 0-582-00985-5

Typeset in Lasercomp Times New Roman
Printed in Great Britain at The Bath Press, Avon

Contents

List of Diagrams

Introduction

The continuing aim of this book is to draw out the structure and key statements of the various contract forms considered, in order to emphasise their practical effects. There is now such an array of contract forms and supporting documents that to find the connecting thread between them and set it out for others has become a major operation. With each succeeding edition it has become necessary to add sections to chapters and chapters to the whole. It would therefore seem all the more useful to have a book pitched at a level somewhere between the legal treatises at the one extreme and the thumb-nail sketch at the other. In preparing this revision I have tried not to stare at the trivial, but equally not to avoid a problem by bland generalities. Where there is some doubt over, for instance, what the courts might say I have said so, while where there is a pitfall I have tried to signpost it plainly and offer a solution.

The encouragement to persevere is that what I have written before has provided some help here and there to those who have not had cause earlier to grapple seriously with this aspect of building, as well as to provide some interest for those already familiar with the subject. The range of readers is thus intended to embrace architects, surveyors, builders and others fully engaged in the day-to-day round of the industry, as well as students taking degrees or diploma and certificate courses or preparing for professional examinations and tests of competence. It is hoped that the material covered will also be of value to those undertaking continuing professional development. Others, not so directly involved in building operations, may also find the work useful in their position as clients or advisers.

The pattern followed has been to take one of the most commonly used forms (the JCT form, private edition with quantities) and consider it by way of detailed commentary. The other forms have then been considered, where suitable, on a comparative basis in relation to that form, with expanded treatment from first principles in areas of substantial difference. This pattern has made it possible to consider major problems in reasonable depth, whilst achieving a broad coverage of the whole field. It has been no part of my plan to discuss the wider issues raised by the existence of so many standard forms covering construction and overlapping as they do. The plea in the Banwell Report of a generation ago and elsewhere for one common form with variants still seems valid, and even more so than before. A problem with any range of forms is that they are likely to be revised at different times so that they will not be in step, but are busy 'leapfrogging' over one another. This must be met on a pragmatic basis, with an attempt to keep up to date even if slightly inconsistent in presentation in some chapters as a result.

Since the third edition, most of the contract forms and other documents in the JCT 1980 series have been published. Only the prime cost contract has yet to appear, so giving rise to a particular case of the 'leapfrogging' problem. These forms are the fruit of prolonged negotiations, drafting and redrafting by the Joint Contracts Tribunal and its constituent bodies, depending upon the consensus that must be reached under the constitution of that tribunal and attended by consequent delay. Several substantial issues have been grappled with and the opportunity has been taken to indulge in general tidying operations and a revision of the detailed format. Inevitably, not all of the changes have pleased everyone and it is likely that some people are pleased by none. While the JCT 1963 series was criticised throughout its life, its intended demise has been viewed in some quarters as akin to the abolition of sliced bread.

To some extent these are matters of opinion and I myself have found occasion to criticise certain aspects in the course of this volume. My special overall complaint is that nothing has been done to improve the illogical order of clauses in the main forms and that this order has been mixed with the other previous illogical order in the sub-contract forms, to give yet another such order. When so much has been changed, even down to clause numbers, why keep and confuse these frameworks? What is a matter of fact is that the forms, individually and as a system, are much bulkier and more complex than they were before. In part, this is because several documents that existed in semi-independence of the series proper (such as the warranty agreement and the 'green' nominated form) have now been brought into the series. Even the 'blue' domestic form has edged in that bit closer. But growth is also due to revision of detail and this represents a net gain in bulk, if not in clarity nor in simplicity. This tendency to proliferate appears to be an irreversible trend of modern life and is taken in this book as simply existing. That the contracts outside the ambit of the JCT have changed little is something of a relief.

It does mean though that my commentary dealing with the JCT forms has had to be recast and expanded to an equal degree. Some chapters, such as those dealing with the various forms of sub-contracting, have been entirely rewritten and most of the rest have endured considerable surgery. The structure of the commentary has been modified in an attempt to deal with the closer interdependence of the documents, while several completely new chapters have been included to deal with the extra documents that cannot now be excluded from any balanced discussion. In order to accommodate this considerable amount of additional material while keeping the book to a reasonable size, I have omitted the now unmanageably large text of the JCT main form and compacted the introductory background to the forms. A table covering a greater range of legal cases and giving direct access to published law reports has been substituted for the chapter giving case summaries. All of this means that there is now rather more 'Turner' within the volume than a simple inspection of its thickness might suggest.

I continue to express my willing thanks to the Department of the Environment, the Institution of Civil Engineers, the National Federation of Building Trades Employers, to my colleagues Messrs. J. P. Morris and D. I. Gordon, and my brother Mr A. E. Turner, for their assistance in various respects. Again my appreciation is due to my wife for her tolerating the eddying tides of paper around the house and for her typing of so much of my draft with the attendant wrestling with my writing and tape-recorded dictation, to say nothing of frequent steaming mugs of good cheer.

DENNIS F. TURNER   June 1982

PART I

General principles

CHAPTER 1

A survey of the contract forms

The purpose of this work is to examine the standard forms of contract most commonly used in the construction industry today. This chapter contains a preliminary survey of the forms, but this in turn is preceded by a few general observations.

Standard forms look in at least three directions at once. One of these is towards the wider law, be it the law of contract, be it statute law or common law, with its constant accretion arising out of decided cases. This is merely a reminder that the reader should keep the forms and hence this volume also in context. In particular, it is relevant that construction contracts modify the effect of the general law in various ways to provide for the peculiar concerns of the industry. This can be done within limits only and there are areas of the law, for instance the law of insolvency, where public policy will prevail. In addition all of the forms considered are 'entire contracts', that is contracts in which each party is committed to a single, undivided or whole consideration in exchange for that of the other: the contractor undertakes to complete the work; the client to pay for it. But they are entire contracts modified in respect of specific matters such as the introduction of variations, when payment is to be made, and who is to carry the risks; but where there are no modifications the basic concept of entirety remains in full. These points may be taken as warnings that much is assumed in the following commentaries.

If needs be, then, the appropriate authorities should be consulted on specialised aspects. All that has been done here is to include in an appendix to the book a list of relevant cases with an indication of their subject matter, so that they may be followed up if desired. These are noted in the main text if they bear strongly on the points at issue. A bibliography of parallel and background reading has also been given.

A second direction of vision for standard forms is towards the other contract documents. They attempt to define what those documents are and also, within limits, how they are related to each other, in the event of any accidental conflict or even deliberate drafting that is intended to make one document take priority over another. Thus the document may establish where the works are defined in character, quantity, specification and price. But at a higher level it is provided in the forms reviewed, with the exception of the ICE forms, that in the case of conflict between the standard contract conditions and another specially-produced document, then the standard conditions will prevail. This reverses the general legal principle of interpretation, that the special overrides the standard in divining the presumed intentions of the parties. The effect of this is that clauses inserted in, for instance, the preliminaries of bills of quantities or specifications to modify parts of the conditions will be read only as statements of intent and must also be incorporated directly into the conditions when the contract is executed. Otherwise they will fail by being construed as conflicting with the prevailing conditions.

The last direction in which standard forms look is, metaphorically speaking, over their shoulders — at the possibility of disagreement between the parties, that is between contractor and client. In the case of the more routine matters, they cater for this by giving powers of decision to various professional persons specified in the conditions. Usually their decisions will be accepted, perhaps after some modification, but if one party cannot accept a decision or if in some other way there is a major rift between the parties, then the conditions provide for recourse to arbitration in a specified way over most issues. Sometimes, indeed, the parties may face a dilemma on how to come to an agreement and may turn to arbitration as an amicable way of resolving their problem. Even this is not the last resort, as the arbitration provisions are not cast so as to preclude the possibility of one party electing to take action in the courts instead of going to arbitration, hence some of the legal cases given. This is quite apart from the limited range of situations (in England and Wales) in which a question of law arising during or out of arbitration proceedings may be submitted with consent for judicial review.

These few points made, the forms themselves may be surveyed in groups. It will be noted that here they are considered in logical families, but in the chapters that follow the forms, or part of them, may be grouped in different arrangements in the interests of extracting their meaning or comparing documents. Within the groups the pattern of collating part or sections of complete extracts into the separate documents as published is not standard. The term 'binding' has been used to indicate the separate published parts.

JCT main contract forms

This group consists of those forms issued as bindings by the Joint Contracts Tribunal which are all for use in a main contract between a client (termed the 'employer') and a building contractor, but which in other respects provide for a variety of cases.

(a) STANDARD FORM OF BUILDING CONTRACT, 1980 EDITION (NOT SO ENTITLED, BUT CONSISTING OF PART 1 AND PART 2)

This is issued in six variants (also sometimes unfortunately termed 'editions') which differ according to the type of client and the financial basis:

Private with Quantities
Private with Approximate Quantities
Private without Quantities

Local Authorities with Quantities
Local Authorities with Approximate Quantities
Local Authorities without Quantities

These contain the bulk of the requirements for an individual main contract, but need to be supplemented by one of the forms under (b) and can be supplemented by that under (c). They are also available (except in the approximate quantities variants) as 'Conditions Only' versions, that is with the articles of agreement and the appendix excluded, so that they may be used in Scotland with the Scottish Building Contract.

The first of the six listed is discussed in detail in Part 2 and Part 3 of this book along with some other forms and the plan followed is given in the first chapter of each part. The other five are then dealt with on a comparative basis in Chapter 21.

(b) STANDARD FORM OF BUILDING CONTRACT, 1980 EDITION, PART 3: FLUCTUATIONS

This is issued in two variants:
Private with, without and with Approximate Quantities
Local Authorities with, without, and with Approximate Quantities

These are therefore intended each to suit use with any one of three out of the six major forms under (a). In fact they contain alternatives to suit precisely the one with which they are used. As issued, they are also immediately suitable for use with the Scottish Building Contract. The parts of the variant for use as Private with Quantities are considered in detail in Chapter 10.

(c) SECTIONAL COMPLETION SUPPLEMENT TO STANDARD FORM OF BUILDING CONTRACT, 1980 EDITION

This is issued in one version and is a purely additional form in that the main form is complete without it. It contains all wording needed to graft it into any of the variants of the main form without direct amendment to the particular form. It is not intended for use with the Scottish Building Contract, where there is separate provision.

(d) STANDARD FORM OF BUILDING CONTRACT 'WITH CONTRACTOR'S DESIGN', 1981 EDITION

This document, discussed in Chapter 22, is issued in one version, for private use and for local authorities use. It is understood that a sectional completion supplement will also be published.

(e) ADDENDUM TO THE STANDARD FORM OF BUILDING CONTRACT, 1981 EDITION, FOR 'WITH QUANTITIES AND CONTRACTOR'S PROPOSALS'

This document has not been published at the time of writing but, on the basis of draft information, it is intended that there should be one version for use with either private or local authorities variants. It is also expected that other versions will be available to suit the 'without Quantities' and the 'with Approximate Quantities' variants of each of these. The first form only is discussed in Chapter 23.

(f) FIXED FEE FORM OF PRIME COST CONTRACT

At the time of writing the edition corresponding to the 1980 editions under (a) has yet to be published. If previous policy is followed, it will be issued in one version to suit private or local authorities use, and Scottish use, and will not need any further forms to be used with it. The distinctive features of the form are discussed in Chapter 24 on the basis of its anticipated development as part of the current series.

(g) AGREEMENT FOR MINOR BUILDING WORKS, 1980 EDITION, AND SUPPLEMENTARY MEMORANDUM

These two forms are dealt with in Chapter 25. The agreement may be used without the memorandum in suitable cases. There is one version of each to cover both private and local authorities use and they are not suitable for use in Scotland.

JCT sub-contract and related forms

This group consists of those forms issued by the Joint Contracts Tribunal which are used either before entering into or as part of a sub-contract to any of the six variants of the Standard Form of Building Contract and, it is to be expected, to the Form of Prime Cost Contract. They are not suitable for use with the 'with Contractor's Design' or the 'Agreement for Minor Building Works'. For use in Scotland, they are available in some cases as 'Conditions Only' versions, and as independent versions in others.

They provide two alternative approaches to securing a sub-contractor, and are grouped accordingly here with the group involving greater procedural complexity second. They are discussed at length in Part 3 of this volume, where they are grouped in relation to the other contract documents.

(a) NOMINATED SUB-CONTRACTS 'ALTERNATIVE METHOD'

This provides for the following forms:

Standard Form of Nominated Sub-Contract
Nominated Sub-Contract Fluctuation Clauses
Standard Form of Employer/Nominated Sub-Contractor Agreement

The last form listed is optional and the architect is left to his own devices over complementary forms for tendering and nomination.

(b) NOMINATED SUB-CONTRACTS 'BASIC' METHOD

This provides for forms with the same titles as in (a) although only the second is actually the same form, and in addition the following complementary forms:

Standard Form of Nominated Sub-Contract Tender and Agreement
Standard Form for Nomination of a Sub-Contractor

Here the architect is provided with a complete set of five forms the use of which is obligatory if the method is used.

JCT supplier forms

These forms are optional in that the architect may use them singly or together in the nomination process under the same main forms as named in connection with sub-contracts. Again there are comparable forms produced in Scotland. The two forms are:

Standard Form of Tender and Warranty Agreement
Standard Form for Nomination of a Supplier

The first of these two forms is considered in Chapter 19. The second needs no discussion.

NFBTE domestic sub-contract

Here only the Standard Form of Domestic Sub-Contract is issued and the contractor is left to devise his own complementary forms for tendering. This document is in one form only for private and local authorities use. There is no information about a separate variant for use in Scotland. The form is considered in detail in Chapter 20.

Scottish Building Contract Committee Forms

Because Scotland has a separate legal system, it is necessary for Scottish contracts to differ in a number of respects. The contracts concerned are issued by the Scottish Building Contract Committee, which is also a constituent body of the Joint Contracts Tribunal. While the forms are not JCT forms, they are identical wherever possible and otherwise equivalent. The only JCT form suitable for use in Scotland is the Form of Prime Cost Contract. Most of the forms have been referred to earlier in passing, but they may be brought together here. They are considered in Chapter 26.

(a) SCOTTISH BUILDING CONTRACT, 1980 EDITION

This is a fairly short document which sets out all the distinctively Scottish provisions and which incorporates by reference the particular 'Conditions Only' version of the Standard Form of Building Contract. This is so done that the one Scottish form is used with any of the JCT forms, except the two approximate quantities versions.

In addition to this 'straight' version there is an alternative, the Scottish Building Contract Sectional Completion Edition, which also includes the equivalent of the JCT supplement.

(b) SCOTTISH BUILDING SUB-CONTRACT, SUPPLIER AND RELATED FORMS, 1980 EDITIONS

There is a form corresponding to each of those listed under the two JCT approaches to nominated work discussed above, and an extra form for nomination. Of these, the two sub-contracts themselves are issued as Building Sub-Contracts incorporating the 'Conditions Only' versions mentioned with the JCT documents. All the rest are issued as independent forms.

(c) CONTRACTS OF PURCHASE, 1980 EDITIONS

There are two versions of this peculiarly Scottish document, the reasons for which are discussed in Chapter 26. One is for use between the employer and the contractor, and the other is for use between the employer, the contractor and the sub-contractor. They may be used in relation to any variant of the main contract or sub-contract forms introduced by one of the Scottish Contracts, and with the Form of Prime Cost Contract.

Central Government Contract Forms

A group of forms completely independent of the JCT series exists for government work. The most important forms cover the following:

(a) Building and civil engineering works
(b) Specialist works
(c) Minor works

The first of these forms is entitled General Conditions of Contract for Building and Civil Engineering Works and is the only one falling within the scope of discussion in this book in Chapter 27. Not only is it related to both building and civil engineering, but it may be used with firm or approximate quantities, or without quantities — only prime cost evades it. It is also good-tempered enough to operate all through the United Kingdom.

The government forms listed but not discussed are derived from the primary form and are very similar in all major points of principle. There is a supporting range of invitation and tender forms, supplementary conditions, etc to accompany the key forms.

Contract forms													
Family	JCT											Others	
Group	Other forms			Main forms								GC/Works/1	ICE
Sub-group	Minor	Prime cost	Design and build	No quantities		Approximate quantities		Quantities					
Variant				Private	Local authority	Private	Local authority	Private	Local authority				
Client Private													
Public													
Financial basis Firm quantities													
Approximate quantities													
Lump, no quantities													
Cost plus													
Type of work Building													
Civil engineering													

Figure 1: **Leading relationships of standard forms of contract**

The shaded portions show features that apply to a form; only the JCT 'Minor' Form indicates the scale of the work anticipated. The Scottish Contract, sub-contract forms and collateral forms have not been shown.

Civil Engineering Contract Forms

A more distant cousin to the JCT main form is the Form of General Conditions of Contract for Works of Civil Engineering Construction, issued by three leading civil engineering bodies and often referred to as the ICE Form. Here there is a third and quite different grouping of subject matter accompanied by rather more difference in the subject matter itself. The form is suitable for use by private or public clients and in this respect differs from the others except for the 'With Contractor's Design' form, the Prime Cost Contract and, oddly enough, the minor building works form. Approximate quantities are the only basis provided for and the form is not suitable for use without quantities or for a prime cost basis. Otherwise it reflects a number of practices which are traditional for civil engineering, rather than essential to it. It is discussed in Chapter 28.

There is also a sub-contract related to this form, which is not discussed in this volume.

This is the basic range of forms explored in this volume. Figure 1 shows the relationship between the key versions of the main contract forms. While over 40 documents are discussed in this volume, the total number of forms, depending on what it is finally published, will eventually be closer to 50!

It may well be thought from this outline that the differences between the various forms do not indicate a consistent pattern. The main conditioning factors are the type of client, the size and nature of the works and the basis of the financial reimbursement. Yet the forms separate, combine or even ignore these factors. The Banwell Committee's recommendation, made in 1963, that there should be a common form of contract throughout the industry would therefore seem to have substance. Such a form might need to be produced in variant forms, but in principle it seems possible. The present pattern in itself certainly does not prove otherwise.

CHAPTER 2

An introduction to the JCT form, private with quantities

The full title of the document discussed in Part 2 of this book and also in Part 3 together with other documents is 'Standard Form of Building Contract, Private With Quantities, 1980 Edition'. The usual policy is to publish a revision annually, although the amendments introduced into it may be issued separately and earlier if this is considered expedient.

The form, like all other forms of contract published by RIBA Publications Ltd, is issued by the Joint Contracts Tribunal which consists of representatives of:

Royal Institute of British Architects
National Federation of Building Trades Employers
Royal Institution of Chartered Surveyors
Scottish Building Contract Committee
Association of County Councils
Association of Metropolitan Authorities
Greater London Council
Association of District Councils
Committee of Associations of Specialist Engineering Contractors
Federation of Associations of Specialists and Sub-Contractors
Association of Consulting Engineers
Confederation of British Industries (observer status)

The philosophy of the form

Several general principles run through the form as a whole. It is, like the other standard forms, an entire contract which is modified by a number of its own provisions; these will be noted as they arise but their general effect is to reduce the severity of the contractor's obligation to complete without payment on account and without extra charge whatever happens. It also gives the employer the opportunity to introduce changes in the scheme while it is under way without the need to enter into a fresh or supplementary contract.

Financially, therefore, the contract is a lump-sum contract, but one which reveals that it is based upon priced quantities. The sum agreed may therefore be adjustable for some classes of error which come to light and also to take account of changes in the scheme. There may also be adjustment for particular sums which, while included in the main sum, were declared in the first place not to be final and also for fluctuations in market prices. None of these characteristics destroys the lump-sum form of the contract.

There are two parties who enter into the contract: the employer, who is the client, and the contractor. The employer is responsible under the terms of the contract for making all payments to the contractor and also may give a number of notices to the contractor and receive others, and may go to arbitration against the contractor, if he so wishes. Otherwise he is cast in a passive role by the conditions and his formal dealings with the contractor must be through the architect. The contractor is on the other end of this arrangement and thus has limited dealings with the employer. His overall role is anything but passive, since he is responsible for the physical construction. He thus may decide his own working methods, but will also be constantly having dealings with the architect about what he is producing and with the quantity surveyor over what he is to be paid. He therefore figures very prominently in the conditions.

Two other persons have been mentioned who have their own independent part to play, although neither is a party to the contract. One is the architect who stands between the parties, partly in a neutral way and partly to speak on behalf of the employer in professional matters. The contract assumes the traditional working arrangement of the separation of the functions of design and construction and the architect is therefore made responsible for design, for supervision to see that what has been contracted for is obtained, and for making various decisions over time and money that affect both parties. Either party may challenge these decisions by arbitration — not against the architect but against the other party. In all these matters except arbitration, the employer should remain contractually passive; his dealings should be with the architect, and not with the contractor direct. Even in his direct dealings with the architect, the employer is in some respects unable to influence the architect without the danger of infringing the provisions of the contract; the employer is entitled to what building he wants so long as he allows the architect to deal with its detailed procurement and the contractor to produce it. Should he consider his architect to have been negligent towards him, the client may take legal action against him, but this falls outside the present contract.

The other person mentioned who is not a party is the quantity surveyor. Contractually he has no controlling function and is there purely to account for the finances and to deal with the measurement and negotiation that this entails. Even aspects of this are initially the architect's prerogative and may be delegated to the quantity surveyor entirely at the architect's discretion. It is again the scheme of the contract that the employer should not enter directly into the settlements involved. If he is dissatisfied, his strict remedy within the contract is in arbitration against the contractor.

The pattern of the form

The form consists of four sections performing quite distinct functions:

Articles of agreement
Conditions
Appendix
Supplemental provisions

Of these, the first three are strictly separate contract documents, distinct from one another; the third is subsidiary to the first two, while the last supplements the rest. The conditions themselves are divided into three parts, each containing a number of clauses as follows:

Part 1: General
Part 2: Nominated sub-contractors and nominated suppliers
Part 3: Fluctuations

The whole of the form is issued in a single binding, except for most of Part 3 which is bound separately (clause 37 is in the main binding and clauses 38 to 40 are separate). The underlying logic of this presentation is unclear.

The general scheme for using the form is that the articles and the appendix provide spaces for nearly all the features that vary from contract to contract and completion of these two fairly short sections will ensure that all these features are covered. There are no gaps to complete in the conditions; there are however the following alternatives and optional clauses, all of which are indicated in the conditions by footnotes (as are several practice points):

Clause 5.3.1.2 is optional.
Clause 5.3.2 contains optional wording.
Clauses 22A, 22B and 22C are alternatives to each other and Clauses 22A and 22C contain wording that may need amendment.
Clause 32 may need amending in particular circumstances while the works are in progress, but not initially.
Clauses 38, 39 and 40 are alternatives to each other and when clause 40 is used it automatically amends clause 30.1.2.

Where other clauses make reference to any of these clauses, they are usually so worded that no amendment is needed to bring them into line. Provided therefore that all the above insertions are made and the other points are attended to, the result will be a complete and consistent contract even though it may not say what is really wanted.

The order of the clauses within the conditions follows some sort of grouping and progression but it is difficult, in the central band of clauses in particular, to trace a pattern for the purposes of commentary: why for instance completion is treated before commencement. The clauses have therefore been arranged in a different order in the present work. Any grouping or regrouping is subject to at least two difficulties: one is the standpoint from which the clauses are viewed, which will vary with the individual's purpose, and the other is that several clauses cover more than one topic or share a topic with other clauses. For these reasons several arrangements may appear logical.

The whole of the form has been taken in Part 2 of this book, except clauses 35 and 36 which constitute Part 2 of the form. These are taken in Part 3 of this book in view of their intimate relationship as part of a single scheme with the other documents for nominated work. In considering this contract form (but not necessarily the other forms considered in less detail) the plan adopted in this book has been to structure the commentary rigidly according to the major clause headings appearing within the text of the form, the subsidiary headings in the margin and usually the sub-divisions to two decimal places in the reference. In places the form departs from its basic system by introducing sub-headings within the text (not always in the same way) and side-headings against lower level sub-divisons; these have been referred to in the text. Where a marginal heading has been omitted one has been supplied and the fact noted. The headings do not strictly form part of the conditions in such a way as to affect their interpretation.

PART 2

The main contractor and the JCT Form Private with Quantities

CHAPTER 3

The articles of agreement and the appendix

Although these two sections occur respectively at the beginning and end of the document under consideration, they may here usefully be considered together. They are delineated by clause 2.1 as contract documents in their own right and they act as the slices of bread for the sandwich of which the conditions are the somewhat thick and indigestible filling. They do so by giving the standard wording of the conditions two planes of specific reference; they thus contain all the points that give the standard contract form its individuality. The articles define a number of persons and things the special titles of whom and which are regularly used throughout the conditions. The appendix as a repository of information is referred to frequently in the conditions and its nature is therefore best explored in advance.

Here the particular points of detail are considered and cryptic reference is also made to a number of clauses in the conditions. These clauses should be consulted to obtain a fuller view of the points in question.

The articles of agreement

These articles constitute the focal point of the documents in this form of contract by delineating a number of essential facts covering the persons, subject-matter and documentation of the contract. They fall into three parts, although for simplicity the article covering arbitration has been taken separately.

THE PREAMBLE AND RECITALS

These in themselves make no agreement but set out the parties and subject matter of the contract. The items to be filled into the spaces are:

(a) *The date*: This will be the date of the agreement and not the date of tender, whether this be considered as the date when the tender was actually received or the specially defined date under clauses 38.6.1 or 39.7.1 or under the formula rules referred to in clause 40.1.1.1.

(b) *The parties*: They are defined here as the employer and the contractor and these expressions are used throughout the conditions and should be used in all other formal documents.

(c) *Description of 'the works'*: This expression again becomes the formal term; the description given need outline the main contents only. Any doubt of the precise scope of the works will be resolved by viewing the contract documents as a whole. The present description identifies the works sufficiently to give them uniqueness of definition.

(d) *Site of 'the works'*: The expression 'the site' is used infrequently in the conditions and in a fairly imprecise way. Sometimes the term 'the works' is used where perhaps the site is meant. The present description is only to establish broad identity and should be backed by precise plans or other means, since the contractor obtains a full right of possession under clause 23.1.

(e) *The employer's architect*: This person is the one who has worked in the pre-contract stage; he is not necessarily the same person as the architect defined in the third article although he usually will be. The wording is wide enough to cover any consultant or quantity surveyor employed in that stage. It also makes it clear that the design work has been the responsibility of this architect and not of the contractor.

(f) *The contract drawings*: These again are formally defined and recorded by their numbers (with non-consecutive or extensive numbering systems it may be necessary to refer to the list of numbers in the contract bills). These contract drawings and contract bills should be signed to evidence them, to comply with the definitions given in clause 1.3. Often the quantity surveyor concerned will also certify the contract drawings, or else will sign the drawings which he actually used, for later evidence in dealing with variations.

The contract bills are also formally defined, although they are not dealt with by any special insertion. They will have been supplied to the employer or his advisers for examination at the tender stage.

The contract documents are described together in clause 2.1 which refers to them as 'the Contract Drawings . . . the Contract Bills . . . the Articles of Agreement, the Conditions and the Appendix'. They are all referred to in some part of these articles, if the heading itself is included.

The employer's status as being or not being a 'contractor' for the purpose of the Finance (No 2) Act, 1975 is also mentioned by reference to the appendix, which will simply say 'is' or 'is not' to govern clause 31.

Articles 1 to 4

The first four articles relate to the obligation of each party and to the identity of the two persons appointed to act between the parties. The following comments may be made on each:

1 *The contractor's obligation*: This is described in the terms used in clause 2.1 of the conditions, where the architect's 'reasonable satisfaction' is also introduced over some matters.

2 *The employer's obligation*: This introduces the definition of 'the Contract Sum' which is further treated in clause 14 of the conditions. The contract becomes an entire or lump-sum contract by virtue of this article and article 1, even though it is related to quantities and may be adjusted to give the 'such other sum' as is mentioned.

3 *The architect*: This defines the architect for contract purposes, as distinct from the person working pre-contractually and mentioned in the recital. He is the only person vested with powers of design, instruction and approval under the conditions and as such may govern the employer or the contractor alike, subject to the right of either to go to arbitration against the other over the architect's decisions. Again, any consultant is covered by the term 'the architect', although his working relationship with the contractor should be clarified by the architect. The respective duties and liabilities to the employer of the architect and any consultant under their own conditions of engagement for the services that they render and for which they are paid, are quite distinct from this standing of the architect under the conditions. The contractor has a right of immediate arbitration over any employer's nominee as successor to the named architect. Any successor is bound by the actions of his predecessor; only the agreement of the two parties or the award of an arbitrator may change their effects. Many matters are however left open to possible change until the final certificate by the provisions of clause 30.10 of the conditions, whether there is a new architect or not.

4 *The quantity surveyor*: This person is dealt with in a similar way to the architect, but he was not named in the preamble and there is no reference to binding his successor. The reason for the latter fact is that the quantity surveyor has a purely passive accounting role under the conditions and cannot change the course of events in any material way. Nothing that he does is in any case contractually final until made so by the final certificate under clause 30.9 of the conditions, except the agreement of fluctuations.

Article 5 — Settlement of disputes — arbitration

The subject of arbitration is governed by the Arbitration Acts 1950 to 1979. The present clause constitutes an arbitration agreement under the Act with provision for reference to a single arbitrator. Once appointed, the arbitrator becomes a man of considerable authority over and above the statement of this clause and his authority is irrevocable, except by leave of the High Court. Arbitration is not conducted in the public eye, but is not thereby rendered less formal in consequence.

The clause does not prevent either party going to the courts over a difference as an alternative to making a submission under the arbitration agreement and this alternative may be more straightforward where the main issue is a question of law. The clause is therefore not a *Scott* v. *Avery* clause within the decision of that case. However, if the other party wishes to hold to arbitration he may apply to the courts for a stay of proceedings; this the courts will grant and arbitration will then ensue, unless the courts have some sufficient reason to decide otherwise. The arbitrator, if appointed, and the parties themselves may wish and be permitted to seek a judicial review in the High Court over a point of law during the reference, if this is likely to reduce the costs.

Once a submission to arbitration has been made between the parties, the courts may allow court proceedings to continue instead on the application of one party, but only if it can be shown that the arbitration agreement has become ineffective in some way.

5.1 (SUPPLIED) REFERENCE TO ARBITRATION

Arbitration may be instituted only as between the employer and the contractor, but may arise out of a difference of opinion with the architect. The clause treats the latter as a difference of opinion on the part of the contractor, which is the more likely situation, but the possibility of the employer going to arbitration against the contractor because of an architect's decision in favour of the contractor is not to be excluded, in theory at least. The procedure for appointing the arbitrator is straightforward; either party may act quickly if agreement is not reached. This is so even though the reference itself may not follow until after practical completion, as set out in article 5.2.

The scope of arbitration is cast quite widely to run through the period of construction and the period following, but it does not extend into the period between contract and commencement of work. If either party wishes arbitration rather than any other method of resolving a dispute he must consider whether any such early matter can validly *not* be raised until progress has started. This may not be so, especially in a case falling under article 5.1.1.

5.1.1 The construction of the contract is quite broad, but it does not extend to matters that the courts would not themselves deal with.

5.1.2 This is written with matters arising out of the activities or inactivities of those involved during operations, or triggered off by external events, mainly in view.

Several matters are instanced, although the term 'any matter or thing of whatsoever nature arising' is sufficiently wide to cover these matters, among others. In particular, the architect's powers under the contract are open to review, as article 5.3 also makes plain. It is not necessary that the architect should have exercised his powers before a party may give notice of arbitration. A reference may arise out of the architect's failure to exercise his powers or even without him having the opportunity to exercise them. All that is required is a difference between the parties. The only matters excluded from arbitration by the conditions are those discussed under article 5.3.

5.1.3 Disputes arising under the statutory tax deduction scheme come within the scope of arbitration unless there is some other statutory means of dealing with them as clause 31.9 sets out. Any dispute over the amount of VAT chargeable under the agreement is referrable to the Commissioners and is also excluded from arbitration. Since the whole VAT agreement is supplemental to the contract, is not given as a contract document in clause 2.1 and is not brought in via the articles of agreement, it would appear that nothing else relating to the VAT agreement can be referred to arbitration either, except matters within clause 15 of the present conditions.

5.1.4. The special position of nominated sub-contractors and nominated suppliers is reflected in this provision for joint arbitration involving the employer, the contractor and the nominated persons. Similar and complementary wording is included in each of the documents and the clause referred to. The order of events envisaged is firstly that the nominated person and the employer or the contractor, as appropriate, come into dispute over a matter provided for as discussed further in Part 3 of this volume. They then take steps to ensure that the related dispute is referred to an arbitrator. If the employer and the contractor then decide that the matter in which they are in dispute and over which they are about to go to arbitration is substantially the same as or connected with that in the first dispute, they may then agree that it should be referred to the same arbitrator. This obviously allows for a more rounded view to be reached with, hopefully, an overall saving of time and expense. It will also avoid a chain of repercussions in which the intermediate parties are not ultimately liable.

Provisions similar to this article and to article 5.1.5 are made in the documents relating to nominated sub-contractors, but provisions similar to article 5.1.4 occur only in the nominated supplier clause. The effect is that, once an arbitration is set in motion somewhere in the contractual system, a party to it is obliged to permit another party to hook on via the other existing party, although this is not made explicit in any of the versions. The converse, however, is not true, an existing reference cannot be hooked on to a new one appearing elsewhere in the system. Once the employer and the contractor agree as to the similarity of the dispute and to going to arbitration, the joining of the references is obligatory. The way of avoiding this situation is to have made a prior deletion as article 5.1.6. allows.

5.1.5 It may be however that the arbitrator under the existing reference does not have the right expertise to deal with the subject matter of the present one, in spite of the overlap of issues. Since he cannot be removed by employer or contractor from his existing position, either of them may require a separate arbitration if he 'reasonably considers' this to be the case.

5.1.6. It is possible to delete articles 5.1.4 and 5.1.5 by means of the appendix and, if this is done, the other provisions leading to joint arbitration for nominated sub-contractors should be similarly treated. Clause 36.4.8 makes this provision conditional in the case of nominated suppliers.

5.2 — (SUPPLIED) THE TIMETABLE FOR ARBITRATION

The right of either party to set in motion a reference to arbitration remains live under clause 30.9.1 until 14 days after the issue of the final certificate over matters on which final certificate will be conclusive evidence, while it will then continue to apply within the relevant statutory period over other matters, including any within which the final certificate may serve its purpose as conclusive evidence. This clause regulates how early a reference may take place; in general, this is not to be until actual construction finally stops, or is alleged to have stopped. Notice of arbitration may thus be given while work is in progress, but the reference will be held over, although the preparatory work for the reference will doubtless proceed. There is, however, no requirement that notice of arbitration shall be given within any particular time of the event, if event it be, that provokes it. Either party may brood on the matter and give notice of a reference at any time within the contractual and statutory limits.

The exceptions to the enforced delay over arbitration set out in articles 5.2.1 to 5.2.3 are matters where timing runs fairly well to the root of affairs. The clause recognises that any matter whatever may be referred to arbitration without any delay if the parties agree, which would be the position even if not stated. The architect may give written consent to early arbitration on behalf of the employer, but can do this only with the employer's authority; it does not lie within the architect's discretion to do so otherwise.

5.2.1 The appointment of a new architect or quantity surveyor is regulated by the articles of agreement, and the contractor has an understandable right of objection which becomes meaningless if held over.

5.2.2 The same is true of the propriety of architect's instructions regulated under clause 4.2, which could otherwise be requiring the contractor to do that which is entirely outside his contractual obligations. Perhaps certificates are not always quite so radical in their effect, although most will be. The withholding of a certificate is the action, or rather inaction, of the architect and should be distinguished from failure by the employer to honour payment under a certificate, for which the contractor may determine under clause 28.1.1.

5.2.3 Some variation instructions under clause 13.1.2 could have radical effects and so the contractor's right of reasonable objection thereto under clause 4.1 is given here, as are matters relating to extension of time that would otherwise engender uncertainty. If hostilities or war damage affect the works it is perhaps doubtful, to put it mildly, whether there would be time to wait for the formalised procedures of arbitration to run their course over any major dispute before carrying on with site or other activity.

5.3 — (SUPPLIED) THE ARBITRATOR'S POWERS

The arbitrator has considerable powers under the Acts and this clause defines certain particular powers 'without prejudice to the generality of his powers' and must not therefore be read as limiting the arbitrator's powers under the Acts. The defined powers are in any case very extensive and may be exercised to determine all matters in dispute; the only hedge that this places about the arbitrator's activities is the self-evident limitation to what is relevant to the matters in dispute. The effect is to show that nearly all the decisions and so forth of the architect and the quantity surveyor may be challenged by arbitration, and it would seem also in the courts, and their effect amended or even reversed. In doing this the arbitrator has extensive rights of inquiry and investigation.

There are three cases to which this clause refers in which the right to go to arbitration is expressly limited:

(a) Under clause 4.2 the contractor may ask the architect to substantiate his power to issue an instruction. If the architect does so and the contractor then acts on the instruction, he precludes arbitration on whether the instruction is valid: both for himself and the employer.

(b) Under clause 30.9 the final certificate becomes conclusive evidence regarding both the works and the payment due for them, subject to a few exceptions; this becomes effective fourteen days from issue of the certificate.

(c) Under the various alternative fluctuations clauses the quantity surveyor and the contractor may come to an agreement over the amount of fluctuations adjustment, in whole or part, and this too will be binding.

In addition, clauses 19, 23 and 32 permit actions that appear not to be subject to arbitration.

5.4 — FINALITY OF THE ARBITRATOR'S AWARD

This article makes explicit what would otherwise be implied by virtue of the Acts. The statement made should, however, be read as qualified by the Acts. An appeal may be made to the High Court on a question of law arising out of the award, and therefore apparent in it, provided it is done with the consent of all parties or the court gives leave on grounds of the significance of the point at issue.

5.5 — LAW RELATING TO THE CONTRACT

This article not only governs the matter of arbitration but also, more widely, determines the general law under which the whole contract is to be interpreted in the courts if need be. It will apply automatically, unless deliberate action is taken in accordance with the footnote. The matter is considered further in Chapter 26 in relation to the Scottish Building Contract. The type of problem that can arise is shown by the case of *James Miller & Partners Ltd* v. *Whitworth Street Estates (Manchester) Ltd* which preceded the drafting of the present clause.

The attestation

The two parties will execute the contract under hand or under seal, inserting in each case an appropriate clause. Signatures of witnesses are desirable, but not a legal necessity. The most important difference introduced by executing under seal is that the limitations period for bringing an action on the contract is increased from six to twelve years.

The appendix

The purpose of the appendix is to set out in one place a schedule of the details peculiar to an individual contract, which would otherwise be inserted in a series of gaps throughout the conditions. Since such gaps are always liable to be overlooked, an appendix has much to commend it and is also easier for reference purposes.

The completion of the appendix is necessary to give the conditions full meaning and all the clauses listed in the appendix contain specific reference to it. The only other work that must necessarily be carried out on the conditions, as distinct from the articles of agreement, to make them read consistently for the individual contract is to select the appropriate alternative out of clauses 22A, 22B and 22C covering damage to the works. Any amendments beyond these are in no way necessary to the intrinsic pattern of the conditions.

There are places where amendments may be called for to make the conditions read correctly, although already consistent; such is the optional mention of the master programme in clauses 5.3.1.2 and 5.3.2, whether all the clause 22 perils are insurable for the project concerned, and whether the contractor is subject to company law for the purposes of clause 35.13.5.4.4.

Each subject referred to in the appendix is discussed under the clause concerned. There are, however, differences in principle between the treatment of items in the appendix. Some items, such as those for clause 22A (professional fees) and clause 35.2 (contractor tendering for nominated subcontract work) need not be completed to make sense although it is better, if they are not wanted, to insert 'none' in each case. Other items, such as those for clauses 1.3 and 23.1 about dates, must be completed if the clauses concerned are to have any meaning. In one case, clause 28, there is a footnote giving suggestions about insertions for the two parts, but these are only suggestions.

In each of four items provision is made for a period of time or a percentage to be read as applying if no special insertion is made. Those given are those which are most commonly inserted and so an accidental or deliberate omission of any insertion would probably give a desired result in any case. In the case of clause 30.4.1.1 (retention) there is also a recommendation in a footnote to the clause itself. The parties should be made aware of these 'fail safe arrangements', since important terms of the contract are in notes in the appendix rather than in the body of the conditions.

For clause 37 (fluctuations) a selection must be made from three alternative clauses following, otherwise clause 38 will be held to apply. Depending on which is used, one of the following two entries becomes superfluous and should be deleted for clarity. The last entry about formula rules for fluctuations requires an insertion and also a choice between alternatives. In this case the details are not referred to directly by clause 40.1.1.1 but by separate formula rules to which it refers.

CHAPTER 4

The scope of the contract

(a) Documents and instructions:
Clause 1 — Interpretation, definitions etc
Clause 2 — Contractor's obligations
Clause 4 — Architect's instructions
Clause 5 — Contract documents — other documents — issue of certificates

(b) Contract sum:
Clause 14 — Contract sum
*Clause 3 — Contract sum — additions or deductions — adjustment — interim
 certificates*

Clause 1 — Interpretation, definitions, etc

This clause brings together a large number of elements which in the main are
either self-explanatory or dealt with elsewhere.

1.1 METHODS OF REFERENCE TO CLAUSES

Any unqualified reference to a clause means a clause in these conditions, a
practice followed in this part of the commentary also.

1.2 ARTICLES, ETC, TO BE READ AS A WHOLE

The articles, conditions and appendix form a single contract when read with
the other contract documents. In relation to each other the three documents
'are to be read as a whole' and thus mutually explanatory. So there is a
warning that any part of any one must 'be read subject to any relevant
qualification or modification' in any other. This is inevitable when complex
issues interlock and it is the stuff of which contract commentaries are made.

No indication is given here as to the way in which the other contract
documents relate to those mentioned. In the case of the contract bills, clause
2.2.1 establishes them as subsidiary to the documents treated here in the event
of any attempt by the contract bills to 'override or modify'. Nothing
comparable is said about the contract drawings which are highly unlikely to
contain doubtful material. Any notion of giving information such as the
dates for phases of the works on the drawings, as distinct from showing their
extent, should be resolutely discarded. The relationship between the contract
bills and the contract drawings is considered under clauses 2.1 and 14.1.

1.3 — DEFINITIONS

To ease coping with the last problem and to save repetitious cross-referencing, a number of definitions are given here while for certain other terms the list acts as an index to where the definitions may be found. The articles, conditions and appendix do not have any further index, although the contents pages act as useful guides to where the main provisions occur, the contents being broken down in all cases into secondary clause divisions and occasionally even further. There is thus no easy way of finding every occurrence of a term in the documents, even where it is highly significant. Such a concordance would be tedious, as some of the terms occur continually, for instance 'Architect' and 'Contractor'. The terms are used throughout the document with initial capital letters in all cases and tend to stand out fairly readily. These capitals have been retained in this book only in quotations. Important instances in which a term occurs may be traced through the index to this book, or through cross-references in the text or in the conditions, etc themselves.

In general the definitions actually given in this clause are self-explanatory. Where they, and any given elsewhere, need comment this is made at the point concerned.

Clause 2 — Contractor's obligations

2.1 — CONTRACT DOCUMENTS

The contract documents are listed here and the contractor specifically undertakes to perform the works in accordance with them. Under an 'entire' contract a contractor has a very heavy obligation to carry out his contract whatever the cost of overcoming difficulties. Read alone, this clause is emphasising the point that this is an entire contract and, in so doing, reinforcing article 1. It is thus the integral philosophy of the contract that the employer pays for the finished product for which he has contracted and not for some particular necessity for achieving it. Other provisions of the contract considerably lighten the contractor's obligations here, particularly the alternative clauses 22A, 22B and 22C on insurance of the works and clause 28.1.3 on determination for *force majeure* and other matters.

The contractor's obligation to complete is discharged on the issue of the certificate of practical completion under clause 17.1. Thereafter he is not obliged to carry out any further work under the contract, other than remedial work. If he does accept further work he is entitled to negotiate special terms for it.

In delineating the works the contract documents may well impose some prior restriction over the sequence of work, construction techniques or other matters which would otherwise have been entirely left to the contractor's discretion, so long as he produced the required works at the end of the day. In general, the less the freedom of the contractor is restricted, the greater will be the potential for efficiency and economy. While the works are under way the contractor is not obliged to accept any further instruction on such matters, as may be seen from clause 4 and the related Figure 2 on page 30, except on postponement under clause 23.2 and the limited range of obligations and restrictions in clause 13.1.2, provided these latter were already specified in the contract bills.

Should the architect attempt to give any such instruction that appears *ultra vires*, the contractor may query it under clause 4.2. Even if he feels it politic to accept the instruction, he would be advised to give a notification under clause 26.1 if extra expense is involved. He may also wish to raise the question of the transfer of liability for injury which would otherwise be his under clause 20. Partial possession of some part of the works by the employer may occur under clause 18, but only by mutual agreement between the parties. Although the contractor is required to provide his master programme at an early date under clause 5.3.1.2, he cannot be instructed to change it in any particular way.

A major feature of the contract documents will inevitably be the design and quality of the finished works, and the related clauses of the conditions are considered in the present chapter. In general, matters of design, including positioning, will be shown on the contract drawings or given in the supplementary non-contract documents under clauses 5.3 and 5.4. Quality is a matter for the contract bills, as is quantity, and these aspects are established by clause 14.1. The parties thus contract for the contractor to carry out works of the quality and quantity given in the contract bills, but of the type and disposition shown on the contract drawings. The two types of document should agree where they meet. If however there is an error in the contract bills, clause 2.2.2.2 comes into play, while if there is a clash of intention between or within the documents, clause 2.3 applies.

What is contained in the contract documents will restrict the architect from asking more of the contractor or conceding less, unless a variation is given under clause 13. In turn it is neither the responsibility nor the right of the contractor to design the works in any part unless he is to do so within some performance specification (a matter not envisaged by these conditions as mentioned in Chapter 15): he is to produce what is set out in the documents. Similarly he may not deviate from the materials and workmanship specified. On the counts of both design and quality the architect should therefore be precise, and this should include the boundaries of any discretion that he is allowing to the contractor.

While this last objective can be quite well achieved in respect of design, the position is not so straightforward over quality. Some materials or points of workmanship may be of such minor importance as not to warrant detailed specification, while the standard of some workmanship is difficult to put into words. In these cases the 'satisfaction' of the architect is the standard, but such satisfaction is to be 'reasonable'. Like nearly all other matters within the authority of the architect, this satisfaction is subject to arbitration. It also has some degree of objectivity as being what other reasonable persons would accept. Either party may go to arbitration against the other if he feels that the architect's decision has been unduly biased on any point, although arbitration is unlikely over small matters.

The contract establishes no machinery for notifying satisfaction during progress. Indeed it specifically leaves all matters open, by virtue of clause 30.10, until the issue of the final certificate under clause 30.8, apart from the certificate of making good defects under clause 17.4 which, again, does not arise during progress. Otherwise the machinery is of negative character, as for example in clauses 8.3 and 8.4, and implies no final acceptance of what is not condemned at the time. The appointment of the clerk of works under clause 12 is no help here, since he has no power of approval; legally the contractor remains in suspense until the last scene of the last act.

Once the final certificate has been issued, the employer is still entitled to bring an action against the contractor within the statutory period for any breach of his undertaking under the present clause to perform the works in accordance with the contract documents. Recent cases under 'Certificates and approvals' even have the possibility that the statutory period can be interpreted more generously. Where however approval has been a matter of the architect's reasonable satisfaction, the contractor's liability is extinguished by the issue of the final certificate and the architect may find himself liable to the employer for any negligence in approval. Care is therefore needed in deciding which matters should be for the architect's reasonable satisfaction when the contract documents are prepared.

2.2 — CONTRACT BILLS — RELATION TO CONDITIONS ETC — ERRORS IN PREPARATION ETC

The contract bills are considered here in relation to the conditions etc and also in relation to their own preparation. Their relationship to the contract sum is the subject of clause 14.1. Clause 14.2 permits other adjustments of the contract bills under various other clauses.

2.2.1 If changes are to be introduced in the conditions etc for a particular contract it is necessary to amend them themselves and preferably to have them initialled in each case by the parties. Any wording set out in, for instance, the preliminaries of the contract bills will otherwise be of no effect and will be regarded only as a statement of intention that has not been implemented. Words which supplement the conditions without overriding or modifying their application or interpretation need not be inserted into the conditions. The case of *English Industrial Estates Corporation* v. *George Wimpey and Co Ltd* and other cases listed under 'Documents and measurement' illustrate this fine dividing line, but in all cases of doubt, it is better to play safe. If the clause were not present, the normal rule would apply that the specially composed document takes precedence over the standard document in contract interpretation, as has been commented in some of the cases.

2.2.2 The Standard Method of Measurement is effectively incorporated into the contract by means of the reference in clause 2.2.2.1 and the quantity surveyor must make any departures from it quite clear. This may be done either by a warning preamble in each case or by measuring and describing items in such a way as to show that a departure has been made and just what has been done. A general preamble to the effect that work is not necessarily in accordance with the Standard Method of Measurement is quite inadequate if it stands alone. (Cases that have some bearing here are listed under 'Necessary work not mentioned'.)

The contract bills may fail in the several ways given in clause 2.2.2.2. The 'method of preparation', meaning the Standard Method of Measurement and any clearly specified departures, may not have been followed precisely and so have led to misinterpretation of the bills during tendering. This will include any ambiguity in the specifying of departures, which will be construed reasonably against the writer. The bills may also be erroneous in communication: verbally, numerically or by simple omission. While the contractor may have queried any patent blemishes at the tender stage, he need not have done so and certainly should have priced the bills as they stood, unless he received a written amendment as circulated to all tenderers. Otherwise corrections are to wait over until after receipt of tenders, or even until the bills have become the contract bills.

Either the quantity surveyor or the contractor may require the rectification of the method of preparation, or of discrepancies between the contract bills and the works, and the resulting financial adjustment. On the philosophy of clause 14.1 it is necessary to give authority for a variation to achieve this; it is perhaps a little unkind, in the circumstances frequently attendant upon the production of quantities, for the clause to use the term 'error' as being, with 'omission', fully comprehensive of what happens in faulty communication. Somewhat more kindly the clause provides that the correction shall be treated quietly as a variation. At least the matter is not to be paraded too publicly. The quantity surveyor is left to his own devices over the presentation of the final account in this respect.

There is no reference here to adjustment of any error of price, which is considered and prohibited by clause 14.2.

2.3 — DISCREPANCIES IN OR DIVERGENCIES BETWEEN DOCUMENTS

'Discrepancy' and 'divergence' here have reference to uncertainty as to what is to be done in producing the works. As between the documents named there could be doubt over what materials or workmanship were to be employed or over the size of the component. In the case of an instruction, the doubt could arise where there was not a clear intention to introduce a variation and where at least the possibility of dual requirement had been introduced. If the actual quantities given for the items in the contract bills are in doubt, this clause is not relevant to their adjustment, but clause 2.2.2.2 covers the situation.

Should there be a discrepancy or divergence between the articles, the conditions or the appendix, (the contract documents not mentioned here) and the contract bills, clause 2.2.1 establishes that the contract bills will not prevail. No mention is made here of any clash of the conditions etc themselves. A clash of the articles or the appendix with a contract document is possible, if it is to be hoped, unlikely.

The procedure itself is straightforward. The contractor is obliged to give written notification on discovery of a discrepancy or a divergence and the architect equally must give instructions, which may lead to an adjustment of the contract sum. It is not clear what happens if the procedure never gets under way. Presumably if the contractor does not notify the architect in some flagrant case, he may be liable to rectify work at his own expense or to be paid some reduced amount for the undesirable work produced. The conditions are silent however on this question of default by the contractor; he is not obliged to act until he happens to find some matter and it is not always easy to establish that he had found it and simply kept quiet. In practice much discretion needs to be exercised.

The contractor may have claims under clause 25.4.5 for extension of time and in particular clause 26.2.3 for additional payment in these circumstances, if he has observed the procedure of this present clause. He may even be able to determine the contract under clause 28.1.3.4.

Clause 4 — Architect's instructions

4.1. — COMPLIANCE WITH ARCHITECT'S INSTRUCTIONS

4.1.1 The first part of the clause obliges the contractor to obey the architect's instructions to ensure that the works are produced as intended. The conditions include several references to architect's instructions and these are listed in Figure 2 on page 30. Some of these matters on which the architect must act before the works can be completed at all, such as the nomination of sub-contractors and suppliers. As distinct from these, the instructions regarding defects are designed to ensure the contractor's compliance with his basic contractual obligation under clause 2.1, while yet others introduce changes in the physical works or their timing. Other types of order and actions arise in the conditions and these are listed in Figure 3.

The contractor is provided with two lines of protection against an over-demanding architect. One is that the architect must be 'expressly empowered by the Conditions' over the matter in question, and clauses 4.2 and 4.3 give the contractor two types of safeguard here. The other is that the unfettered issue of instructions about obligations and restrictions under clause 13.1.2 could subvert the intention of the contractor by changing the fundamental working conditions. The contractor may therefore make 'reasonable objection' if matters threaten to get out of hand as he would otherwise not have adequate redress under the contract.

4.1.2 Should the contractor not comply with an architect's instruction, the employer has three remedies. One is the extreme of action for breach and another the equally drastic procedure of determination under clause 27, in

**General
provisions**

Clause	Subject
2.3	Discrepancies or divergences
6.1.3	Statutory obligations
7	Setting out works
8.3	Opening up and testing
8.4	Removal of defective work, etc
8.5	Exclusion of persons
13.2	Variations
13.3	Expenditure of provisional sums
17.3	Defects during defects liability period
23.2	Postponement of work
30.6.1.1	Documents to quantity surveyor
32.2	Protective work during hostilities
33.1.2	War damage
34.2	Antiquities

Nomination provisions

Clause	Subject
35.5.2	Change of procedure
35.8	Failure to agree details
35.10.2	Nomination by 'basic' method
35.11.2	Nomination by 'alternative' method
35.18.1.1	Nomination of substituted sub-contractor
35.24.4.1	Default of sub-contractor
36.2	Nomination of supplier

Figure 2: **Architect's formal instructions to contractor under JCT main form**
See Figure 3 for other actions and Figure 5 for certificates.

those limited cases to which it applies. The third and milder remedy avoids these final steps and is in this clause; it is to bring in other persons solely to make good the contractor's non-compliance, pay them direct and then recover from the contractor out of the contract monies 'all costs incurred', which may include additional administration and documentation. In all other respects the contract remains intact and continues. This third remedy needs to be stated here in the conditions, otherwise the employer could not encroach in such a temporary way on the contractor's right of possession of the site under clause 23.1. It is, reasonably enough, made subject to giving the contractor seven days' notice to comply with the architect's original instruction.

4.2 — PROVISIONS EMPOWERING INSTRUCTIONS

Since the architect has only such powers as the conditions give him, it is provided here that the contractor may query the architect's powers to give any particular instruction and that the architect is to state his authority. This is intended to protect the contractor against such things as the architect's interference with the contractor's site organisation. If the contractor is still not satisfied, his remedy is arbitration, which can proceed at once under article 5.2.2 but will involve inevitable delay to the extent of the works concerned. If however, he complies without reservation, he binds himself to accept the architect's power to instruct, although he may be entitled to extra payment as a result of complying and may still perhaps go to arbitration over some point within the instruction.

The words 'deemed for all the purposes of this Contract' are particularly significant; they mean that once the contractor has complied with the architect's instructions he has precluded arbitration over the basic issue of the validity of the instruction. Not only is he debarred himself but he has debarred the employer, who may not even know of the issue. The employer's only remedy, if aggrieved, may be an action against the architect outside the building contract itself. The architect will have committed the employer as soon as he writes back to the contractor to clarify his own authority. The possible consequences of this part of the clause are not at all clear; the architect should prudently warn the employer of any doubtful case as it arises.

4.3.—(CONFLATED) INSTRUCTIONS TO BE IN WRITING—PROCEDURE IF INSTRUCTIONS GIVEN OTHERWISE

4.3.1 The effect of this clause read alone is that all architect's instructions must be written and that until they are the contractor need do nothing. Reading this clause alone, the contractor need not even confirm oral instructions with the architect. The next clause modifies this.

4.3.2 The procedure stated as normal for confirmation is for the contractor to write to the architect, with a waiting period to find the architect's reaction or lack of it. (No reference is made to the time required

'Deemed' variations

Clause	Subject
2.2.2.2	Correction of contract bills
6.1.4.3	Statutory obligations
22B.2.2	Restoration after damage
22C.2.3.3	Ditto
28.2.2.2	Incomplete work at determination
33.1.4	Work after war damage

Other matters

Clause	Subject
12	Clerk of works' directions
17.2	Schedule of defects
26.1	Quantity surveyor to ascertain loss and expense due to disturbance
27.1	Notice of determination
27.4.3	Removal of plant etc
34.3.1	Quantity surveyor to ascertain loss and expense due to antiquities
35.13.1.1	Payment of nominated sub-contractors
35.26	Ditto at determination

Figure 3: **Architect's orders etc other than formal instructions to contractor under JCT main form**
See Figure 2 for formal instructions. Other duties, such as approvals are not shown here.

for the confirmation to be sent by post.) Only at the end of the procedure does the instruction take effect.

The two provisos give alternative procedures. Clause 4.3.2.1 absolves the contractor from confirmation if the architect writes first, which seems pretty obvious. It would also seem more logical for the clause to give this as the normal procedure and thus put the onus of writing on the architect in the first place. Clause 4.3.2.2 allows confirmation by the architect at his discretion of instructions given orally and acted upon at any time before finality; in this case the effect is retrospective to the date of the oral instruction, as perforce it must be to be of any value. This proviso is necessary also to cover the case in which the contractor confirms after his allowed margin of seven days. Needless to emphasise, this proviso is very valuable in the hurly-burly conditions of building work. It is not one that the architect must always act upon and he should not if he does not agree the alleged instruction. If he does not act, the contractor always has arbitration open to him. It is not clear what is intended if neither the contractor nor the architect confirms an instruction and if the contractor then does not act on it.

This procedure applies only to the confirmation of the architect's own instructions. A number of other cases of confirmation arise under the conditions. These are discussed in their places, but are summarised in Figure 4.

Clause 5 — Contract documents — other documents — issue of certificates

5.1 — CUSTODY OF CONTRACT BILLS AND CONTRACT DRAWINGS

The keeping of two types of contract documents is provided for, although the articles and conditions are not mentioned. Apart from physical care, this custody also protects the contractor's detailed prices from undue attention. Either party may see the documents, but not remove them.

5.2 — COPIES OF DOCUMENTS

As contracts are not always formally executed very promptly, the contractor may well receive these copies, or some of them, earlier so as to allow him to proceed. Strictly of course, copies of contract documents cannot be supplied until the contract is executed, but the practical intention is clear. JCT Practice Note 7 suggests that the contractor should pay for additional copies.

5.3 — DESCRIPTIVE SCHEDULES ETC — MASTER PROGRAMME OF CONTRACTOR

5.3.1 Provision is made here for a mutual exchange of documents for information between the architect and the contractor. The nature of the information is different. The architect is required by clause 5.3.1.1 to provide copies of schedules etc, 'for use in carrying out the Works'. These should only be explanatory over what is already included in the contract bills but not shown in the contract documents and, for example, might be positional

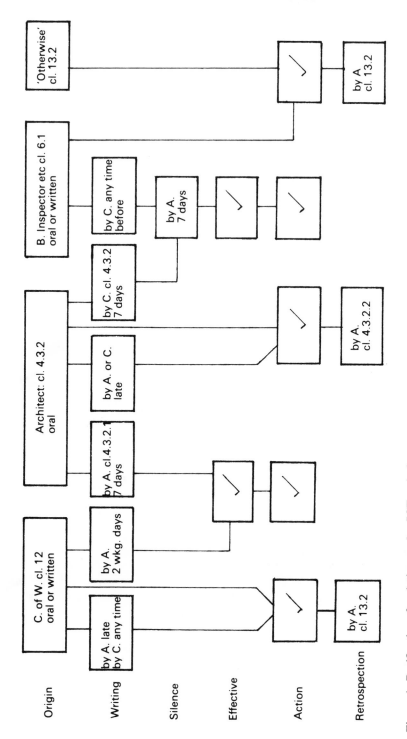

Figure 4: **Ratification of variations under JCT main form**
The above shows cases other than variations instructed in writing under clause 13.2. The contractor may act before or after the variation becomes effective. Variations immediately effective arise under clause 13.2. Clause 2.3 matters may lead to variations.

information as in a finishings schedule. As such it is information without which the contractor cannot operate at all in the areas concerned.

The contractor is required by the optional clause 5.3.1.2 to provide the architect with copies of his master programme, prepared for his own purposes in carrying out the works. This may help the architect to form an opinion of when he will need to prepare information and perhaps even aid him or the quantity surveyor to gauge the employer's cash flow profile on the project. If the architect considers the programme to be unrealistic, at any point, the most he can do is to remark on this to the contractor, he cannot insist on any change. There is no requirement for the contractor to keep the programme up to date, if he chooses to modify it within the same overall contract period or even if he is expecting to finish early or late for his own reasons. Only if he is granted an extension of time, under one of the two clauses mentioned, is he specifically asked to amend and reissue it. The original and amended programmes may well be useful evidence if there is a loss or expense claim under clause 26, although that clause is silent over any form of evidence.

5.3.2 Any schedule or equivalent document is excluded by this clause from any contractual significance. If it seeks to 'impose any obligation', then the obligation concerned should also be the subject of an architect's instruction and thus lead to variation. If, however, the information is conveyed by annotation of the contract bills it will form part of the contract unless specially qualified to the contrary.

The master programme, if provided, is also debarred in the optional parenthesis from having any formal significance over contractual obligations. At most it will have an evidential value if things go wrong, although it need not be accepted at its face value. It will not be a detailed enough vehicle for the request of information by the contractor in relation to, say, clause 25.4.6.

5.4 — DRAWINGS OR DETAILS

The contract drawings are normally only those necessary to indicate the general arrangement of the works for pricing and perhaps may be adequate for this alone. The 'drawings or details' referred to here are working drawings and are those necessary to fill in the picture, broadly in the same way as the specification. This present clause and clause 5.3 could be more similar in wording, it seems. In neither case does the architect have to provide the information as soon as the work starts, although the specification is expected in one piece. Delay in providing drawings or details can lead to a claim under clauses 25.4.6 or 26.2.1 or to action under clause 28.1.3.5, none of which mention the specification.

5.5 — AVAILABILITY OF CERTAIN DOCUMENTS

This is a simple administrative provision for documents to be readily available to the architect on the works. The quantity surveyor would also, in practice, hope to be allowed access, although he is not the architect's representative.

5.6 — RETURN OF DRAWINGS ETC

This is an option which the architect will often not exercise. In these days of easy photo-copying it serves a limited purpose. The quantity surveyor's documents are not mentioned, unless it be maintained that they too bear the architect's name.

5.7 — LIMITS TO USE OF DOCUMENTS

The documentary restriction is placed upon the contractor only and here includes quantity surveying documents. The employer may be having further similar work carried out and the architect and quantity surveyor have obvious reasons for making use of their own documents. The contractor is safeguarded in turn against the other three using his prices. The letter of the clause would preclude any exercise as a basis for cost planning and the like. The reasonable interpretation is not to give any unit prices in any circulated cost analysis information and, if this is to be published, then the degree of detail employed should be approved by the contractor. In negotiating prices with another contractor, it would be quite wrong to disclose even broad pricing principles or totals.

5.8 — ISSUE OF ARCHITECT'S CERTIFICATES

Figure 5 sets out the various certificates referred to in the conditions. Some are obligatory, while some are more discretionary and occasional. Both parties need to be aware of their content.

Clause 14 — Contract sum

14.1 — QUALITY AND QUANTITY OF WORK INCLUDED IN CONTRACT SUM

The contractor is already, under clause 2.1, obliged to carry out the whole of the works in compliance with the contract documents. This present clause establishes the contract bills as the sole repository of the specification of works, they set out the 'quality . . . of the work' as clause 8.1 acknowledges. Any supplementary specification outside the contract documents, such as positional information, is referred to in clause 5.3 by the term 'descriptive schedules'. The present clause also establishes the 'quantity of the work included in the Contract Sum' as that in the contract bills. If the contract bills are in error in either of these respects the obligation under clause 2.1 will stand, and an amendment to the contract sum will arise under clause 2.2.2.2 in respect of the error.

Architect's certificates

Clause	Subject
17.1	Practical completion of the works
17.4	Completion of making good defects after practical completion
18.1.1	Estimate of approximate value at partial possession
18.1.3	Completion of making good defects after partial possession
22A.4.2	Payment of insurance monies after damage reinstatement
24.1	Failure to complete the works
27.4.4	Expenses and loss and/or damage arising out of determination
30.1.1.1	Interim certificates generally
30.7	Interim certificate to pay off nominated sub-contractors (see also 35.17)
30.8	Final certificate
35.13.5.2	Failure to prove payment of sub-contractors
35.15.1	Failure of sub-contractors to complete
35.16	Practical completion of sub-contract works
35.17	Interim certificate to pay off nominated sub-contractors (see also 30.7)

Figure 5: **Architect's certificates under JCT main form**
See Figures 2 and 3 for instructions and other such actions.

Express provisions for adjustments

Clause	Subject
6.2	Statutory fees or charges
7	Amending errors in setting out
8.3	Cost of inspection and testing
9.2	Royalties arising out of instructions
13.7	Variations and provisional sum expenditure*
17.2	Making good defects
17.3	Ditto
21.2.3	Insurance of employer's liability
22B.1.3	Insurance premiums on employer's default
22C.1.2	Ditto
26.5	Loss and expense due to disturbance
34.3.3	Loss and expense due to antiquities
35.24.7	Substituted nominated sub-contract amounts†
36.3.2	Expense in obtaining nominated supply goods†
38.4.4	Fluctuations
39.5.4	Ditto
40.1.1.1	Ditto

*See also list of 'deemed' variations in Figure 2.

Clause 30.6.2 also falls under clause 3. It gives a list of final adjustments and again covers all of the above, except the two items marked †. In addition this clause covers the adjustment of prime cost sums by the substitution of amounts for accounts of:

    Contractor

    Nominated sub-contractors

    Nominated suppliers

Clause 15.3 allows for payment to the contractor of loss of credit for VAT, without falling specifically under clause 3.

Figure 6: **Financial adjustments referred to by clause 3 of JCT main form**
See Figure 7 for other financial adjustments.

Deductions or recoveries by employer

Clause	Subject
4.1.2	Work by others on contractor's non-compliance
21.1.3	Insurance premiums on contractor's default
22A.2	Ditto
24.2.1	Liquidated damages
35.24.6	Unrecovered cost of substituted sub-contracts

Miscellaneous provisions

Clause	Subject
27.4.4	Balance after determination by employer
28.2.2	Balance after determination by contractor
35.13.5.3	Reduction of future amounts to recover direct payments to nominated sub-contractors
35.18.1.2	Payment or allowance of unrecovered costs of substituted sub-contractors

Payments outside main framework

Clause 31 Statutory tax deduction scheme

Supplementary provisions   VAT agreement

Clause 15.3 refers to payment for loss of credit for VAT, without defining how this is to be made

Figure 7: **Financial adjustments arising other than by adjustment of contract sum referred to in clause 3 of JCT main form**
See Figure 6 for these.

14.2 — CONTRACT SUM — ONLY ADJUSTED UNDER THE CONDITIONS — ERRORS IN COMPUTATION

The clause states explicitly the implied term that the contract sum set out in the articles of agreement shall hold except where the conditions provide otherwise. The principle of adjustment is governed by clause 3. Its related clauses give specific authority, while clause 30.6.2 deals with the details.

No adjustment of the contract sum is permitted to rectify pricing or arithmetical errors on the part of the contractor. This holds whether they are visible on the face of the contract bills or not, and whether the quantity surveyor has examined the tender bills or not. It is as applicable in cases where the contract sum has been arrived at by negotiation, as where it has been obtained in competition.

Clause 3 — Contract sum — additions or deductions — adjustment — interim certificates

While clause 14.2 limits adjustments of the contract sum to what is covered in 'express provisions', this clause takes up the question of when the adjustment may effectively be made. It provides for this to be in the next interim certificate, but recognises that precise calculation may take some time and therefore allows the amount to 'be ascertained in whole or in part' and this amount to be included right away. This may be interpreted as the inclusion of any part that has been precisely ascertained or the inclusion on an approximate and conservative basis of the whole amount which has been partly ascertained.

Three terms are used here: 'added', 'deducted' and 'adjustment', as against two in clause 14.2: 'adjusted' and 'altered'. No substantive difference is intended and the present clause is using the terminology of the various authorising clauses, which are listed in Figure 6. Clause 30.6.2 brings together their effects in the final account and may be consulted together with the individual clauses concerned.

In many of these cases the adjustment will be the result of an architect's instruction. In other cases the clause is not explicit over how the authority to adjust is passed from the architect to the quantity surveyor, or confirmed to the contractor. A suitable letter or pro-forma is essential and must precede the initial inclusion of an amount.

Figure 7 also lists those clauses which allow or require the employer to make additions to or deductions from the contract sum as already adjusted by the quantity surveyor on the architect's authority. In these circumstances it is only the employer who may so act, and they are not covered by the present clause. The figure also lists a number of financial activities which may arise on occasions, and that do not fit into the clear categories otherwise given.

CHAPTER 5

The carrying out of the works

(a) Things applying:
Clause 6 — Statutory obligations, notices, fees and charges
Clause 7 — Levels and setting out of the works
Clause 8 — Materials, goods and workmanship to conform to description, testing and inspection
Clause 9 — Royalties and patent rights

(b) Persons involved:
Clause 10 — Person-in-charge
Clause 11 — Access for architect to the works
Clause 12 — Clerk of works

Clause 6 — Statutory obligations, notices, fees and charges

6.1 — STATUTORY REQUIREMENTS

It is the responsibility of the architect to design the works in conformity with all statutory requirements and the like. The intention of this clause is to place responsibility on the contractor to comply with these requirements also, many of which affect the process of construction rather than design, and to give the day-to-day notices involved.

6.1.1 The effect of this clause is perhaps wider than its intention. The first sentence does not explicitly limit the scope of compliance to the works, since 'which . . . the Works . . . connected' qualifies only from 'any local' onwards. Only in the case of local authorities and statutory undertakings does it limit their applicable regulations. It seems unlikely that the wording would be held to include matters beyond the works and therefore it seems that the related planning procedures could not be passed over to the contractor. But it seems likely that the wording has the effect of making the contractor liable to check in detail the adequacy of the design to meet the various regulations and thus perhaps liable to meet a claim for damages jointly with the architect. This seems unduly harsh in normal practice.

6.1.2. The contractor must notify the architect in writing (which will lead to some delay) if he discovers a divergence between the statutory requirements on the one hand and the contract drawings, contract bills, instructions of all types and documents amplifying the contract documents on the other hand.

6.1.3 The architect is required to give instructions with the status of a variation if appropriate within seven days of becoming aware of a divergence and subject to written notice from the contractor if the latter has found the problem. Possibly the architect would still 'otherwise discover' if the contractor were to tell him orally? Should the architect not give instructions in time, the intention of the clause is not entirely clear. While clause 6.1.1 requires the contractor to comply with statutory requirements, the present clause does not clear him to proceed without an instruction, or oblige him to wait for one. It will in any case depend on the nature of the statutory requirement and the timing of the discovery of a divergence whether the contractor can reasonably proceed and carry out work acceptable within the design concept without instruction, or whether the progress of the works will be delayed if he has to hold back the affected part.

A prudent procedure for the contractor, if faced with this dilemma, would be to apply for 'necessary instructions' under the provisions of clauses 25.4.6, 26.1.2 or 28.1.3.5 as appropriate and to state expressly that this was what he was doing. The remaining parts of the present clause otherwise point in different directions on the problem under discussion.

6.1.4 Here the contractor is empowered to carry out without prior instructions the minimum amount of work needed to secure compliance in an emergency, but no more. This would relate to such situations as instability of the works or existing structures or where a health hazard had arisen. Here the contractor is to inform the architect of the position quickly and therefore, if possible, orally. This will give the architect the chance to modify events if this is practicable. Provided the work has arisen within the scope of the present clause, it will become a 'deemed variation'. It will still be an advantage for the contractor to confirm in writing what has happened as soon as possible with supporting daywork or other records, to avoid the problems that can arise if there are no details at the final account stage.

6.1.5 This releases the contractor from liability to the employer, such as the liability to indemnify him against prosecution, where he has performed work that does not comply with statutory requirements. This is subject to two qualifications, one again being that the work is within the scope of this clause. The other is that the contractor gave written notice under clause 6.1.2. This would suggest that the contractor need not, and perhaps should not, either wait for the architect's instructions or, if these do not come, proceed to comply with the statutory requirements on his own initiative. In this case, he would simply proceed with work as delineated in the documents. While this paragraph releases the contractor from his liability to the employer under clause 6.1.1 to comply with statute in these ways, it will not remove the contractor's obligation to meet his direct statutory liabilities which cannot be extinguished by this or any other contract. Equally the present clause does not create any liability for the employer to indemnify the contractor in these respects.

A doubt may lie under the clause as to extent of reimbursement to the contractor when he carries out work and then has to rectify it to comply with regulation. To the degree that the contractor should reasonably check the design, he may strictly be liable for the extra element of cost in the rectification. (See cases on 'Defective work'.) There may also be a problem over work implied in the contract to comply with regulations. (See cases on 'Necessary work not mentioned') In practice this whole clause seems to offer the opportunity for broad-minded and tolerant interpretation.

6.2 — FEES OR CHARGES

The fees or charges here mentioned are 'in respect of the Works' and the uncertainty of scope under clause 6.1 does not apply. They would also appear to include the employer's liabilities: hence the use of the term 'indemnify'. The term 'rates' includes rates chargeable on the contractor's temporary structures. The term 'taxes' is difficult to interpret for 'in respect of the Works' is not wide enough to include taxes on labour, materials and goods as such, but is limited to the works as an entity. While value added tax is not excluded from the scope of the contractor's payment and indemnity (as indeed it could not be), it is here specifically excluded from being an addition to the contract sum since it is dealt with under the VAT Agreement provided for in clause 15. What other taxes can be intended on this limited interpretation is not clear. Any other interpretation would make nonsense of the contract in relation to the types of taxes referred to in clauses 38 and 39.

Whatever the nature of the change, the employer has to pay the amounts as additions to the contract sum. Interim payments are made without deduction of the retention under clause 30.2.2.1. Three classes of exception are given which will be governed by the rules for payment for their respective types.

6.2.1 If the authority or undertaker operates as a nominated sub-contractor or a nominated supplier, then the amount tendered should include for any related fees or charges, although these will not have been itemised in the contract bills, if ever there was a prime cost sum. As the amount will be in substitution for any prime cost sum or otherwise part of a nominated account, there will be no need to rely on this clause to justify inclusion. If however they somehow 'arise' during progress, clause 6.2 as a whole appears to exclude them from payment at all by its 'unless' provision. This is the case, in particular, if one body has such fees or charges 'in respect of' work, materials or goods of another who has been nominated. The fees or charges cannot be added under clause 6.2, nor are they included by virtue of clause 6.2.1. Strictly a variation instruction does not cover the situation, but it must be hoped that one will be accepted by all concerned as valid.

6.2.2 Here the contractor has priced the fee or charge when tendering. The clause appears to envisage that each such head of expenditure will be separately itemised in the contract bills. The GC/Works/1 contract in Condition 14, by a single provision, puts the whole obligation on the contractor to allow for all such matters in his tender; in the normal straightforward contract under these present conditions also this would appear quite fair. To comply here, a priceable omnibus item in the preliminaries would be sufficient.

6.2.3 Fees or charges may be 'stated by way of a provisional sum' and this again suggests separate itemisation, although a completely omnibus item would be adequate.

Subject to the gap mentioned under clause 6.2.1, the effect of the clause is that somehow the amounts of fees and charges will be reimbursed to the contractor, whether under the contract bills or by a later addition, which may or may not be balanced by a related deduction. Except when the amounts fall within nominated accounts, they will be paid usually net of discount and will attract neither profit nor attendance. This latter is irrelevant, since the fees or charges are not for work on site, which clause 6.3 covers. When the payment is in an interim certificate, the comments about retention under clause 30.2.2.1 should be noted.

6.3 — EXCLUSION OF PROVISIONS ON DOMESTIC SUB-CONTRACTORS AND NOMINATED SUB-CONTRACTORS

This clause removes certain activities of public bodies from the ambit of the normal arrangements for work covered by a domestic sub-contract or a nominated sub-contract. It is restricted by the words 'solely in pursuance of its statutory obligations', so that any other work carried out by a local authority, for example, that could be performed equally by a private firm is not dealt with here and would remain to be treated under clauses 19 or 35. This delineation is therefore keeping it in line with the scope of clause 6.2.1, although there may be problems over, say, nomination if part of a parcel of work came under the 'solely' qualification and part did not. The exclusion of clause 35 in particular means that a mass of details is left out and some of these may be worth including in the bills in particular instances, although others are inappropriate where there are statutory considerations. Among the more important may be noted:

(a) *The machinery of nomination by the architect and objection by the contractor, or other selection.* As there will be no alternative, this machinery becomes superfluous and an item in the contract bills or the giving of instructions is sufficient.

(b) *Arrangements about any discount.* There will not usually be any available, but the contract bills should clarify this, one way or the other, if they include items at all.

(c) *Agreements by the authority or undertaking about quality and such aspects of performance as indemnity and completion according to programme.* These are related to the largely unassailable position of the bodies concerned in these ways for this category of operation. Clause 25.4.11 makes this explicit over extension of time.

(d) *Protection of a body over payment.* The employer may not pay direct if the contractor is in default. This seems to be a reasonable quid pro quo in view of the generally privileged position of the body. The question of early final payment does not arise as retention is not held.

While statutory provisions will provide some element of a framework to the contract, the salient feature of this clause is its wholly negative nature so that bodies are not sub-contractors and not in any other defined relationship so far as the employer is concerned over their presence on site. The clause should perhaps close with some such words as 'Your move next'.

Clause 7 — Levels and setting out of the works

The architect has a limited responsibility for relating the works positionally to the site. Beyond this the contractor should obtain his information from the drawings or details referred to in clause 5.4. Delay in furnishing information under this present clause could again lead to claims under clauses 25.4.6 and 26.2.1 or action under clause 28.1.3.5, as happens also with clause 5.4.

The second sentence presents the inexplicable situation of the employer paying for the contractor's errors. It is possible to construe the wording to mean that the architect may relieve the contractor from amending his errors and in consequence the contract sum may be reduced to compensate the employer. For what bearing it has on the present clause, the parallel clause of the JCT Prime Cost Contract is reworded to make it clear that this latter construction is not intended in that contract. The comments on clause 17.2 of the present conditions are also relevant. Fortunately the decision is entirely at the architect's discretion and is therefore hardly likely to lead to litigation — unless an irate employer sues his architect.

One possible repercussion of the contractor's inaccurate setting out could be an action for trespass brought by an adjoining owner. If this were to arise, the contractor would be liable to indemnify the employer under clause 20.2.

Clause 8 — Materials, goods and workmanship to conform to description, testing and inspection

8.1 — KINDS AND STANDARDS

This clause, along with clause 14.1, establishes the contract bills as containing the specification of the works and thus complements the restriction in clause 5.3.2, while clause 2.1 obliges the contractor to carry out the works to these standards. The words 'so far as procurable' protect the contractor from having to obtain what may have become unobtainable in the period since tendering, but are perhaps of little value to him if he has contracted for what has been near impossible all along. The clause says nothing on what is to happen when an alternative is offered. Presumably the architect should be approached for fresh instructions, but there is nothing requiring the contractor to do so or even to offer an alternative of any given quality. The rest of clause 8 adds nothing in this respect; perhaps the preliminaries of the contract bills should do so and require a financial adjustment as well.

8.2 — VOUCHERS — MATERIALS AND GOODS

The architect has a discretionary power here that would extend to invoices, test certificates and the like. The contract bills should be explicit over anything other than incidental documentation ordinarily available. Special testing is dealt with in clause 8.3.

8.3 — INSPECTION — TESTS

The architect has powers here to open up any work whatever or to test any quantity of any materials or goods up to practical completion, after which it would appear under clause 17.2 that he can act only on 'defects, shrinkages or other faults which shall appear'. The purpose of opening up and testing is limited to checking whether the work, materials or goods are 'in accordance with this Contract'.

The contract bills may specify these matters in several ways, perhaps establishing a standard by reference to a particular test, perhaps by reference to particular chemical or physical characteristics, perhaps by both. The architect may instruct not only the carrying out of any specified test, but also any unspecified test, provided that its sole effect will be to demonstrate compliance or otherwise with the contract bills. The cost of these tests will be added to the contract sum only if it turns out that the contractor was not in default, although this provision will be sufficient to ensure that the architect acts with moderation. If however the architect instructs more stringent tests than originally specified, or tests that will demonstrate a higher quality than that given in the contract bills, he must be prepared to agree to payment for these tests and perhaps to an increased measured rate for the items concerned.

Routine tests at regular intervals or defined stages can well be included in the contract sum, provided the tests are clearly described in the contract bills and it is made clear that the contractor is to allow for them in accordance with this clause. Examples are testing pipework or concrete cube samples. A provisional sum for sporadic undefined testing under this clause may also be useful in the contract bills.

8.4 — REMOVAL FROM THE SITE — WORK, MATERIALS OR GOODS

The reasonable implication of this clause is that the contractor shall replace what is removed without charge and clause 13.1.1.3 may be compared and contrasted. There is no requirement that the architect shall have discovered the default within any particular time of its first being present; he may condemn the foundations when the internal decorations are under way and his power is even extended, by clause 17.2, into the defects liability period.

In a serious case of the contractor's non-compliance with the architect's instructions under this present clause, the employer may determine under clause 27.1.3. More gently, the procedure of clause 4.1.2 would be employed.

8.5 — EXCLUSION FROM THE WORKS OF PERSONS EMPLOYED THEREON

This provision reads rather quaintly on the end of a clause purporting to deal entirely with the inanimate. It does not specify positive reasons for exclusion, as this would be too restrictive, but possibly persistent poor workmanship is the reason for the position of the clause. The picture of a vexed contractor is intriguing.

Clause 9 — Royalties and patent rights

Two distinct but related cases are considered in this clause, with differences that need carefully noting.

9.1 — TREATMENT OF ROYALTIES, ETC — INDEMNITY TO EMPLOYER

The former case is that in which a sum is payable or a right is open to infringement by virtue of 'the supply and use in carrying out the Works . . . of any patented articles, processes or inventions'. It is not necessary to specify the articles, processes or inventions in the contract bills, which are here said to describe or refer to the works as such rather than methods of producing them. The contractor may choose some of these things as his own solution to his contractual obligations, as for example patent formwork, but in any case he should make his own inquiries. Here the contractor is held to have included the payment in the contract sum and to indemnify the employer against the consequences of infringement, actual or alleged.

9.2 — ARCHITECT'S INSTRUCTIONS — TREATMENT OF ROYALTIES, ETC

In the latter case, variations are apparently envisaged and here the amounts of payments for 'all royalties damages or other monies' are to be added to the contract sum. By implication, the employer also undertakes to meet any claims which may be preferred against him as building owner. This is in contradistinction to the position in the first sentence, where the contractor shoulders the indemnity. As worded, the sentence embraces architect's instructions other than for variations, including nominated work and making good of defects, and also variations that instruct the further carrying out of work of a character already included in the contract bills. It in no way requires the contractor to give notice of any supply or use which he is entering into as his own option to satisfy an instruction, so putting the employer at risk without the architect being aware. These cases could lead to unexpected and even drastic financial results, although some of them would be taken care of in the routine agreement of variation prices.

Clause 10 — Person-in-charge

It is reasonable and convenient to crystallise the contractor for day-to-day communication into one defined person and for that person in turn to be resident on site. The title given him here is not one normally used in the industry, and as such conveniently covers any foreman, engineer, agent, manager or the like. A travelling supervisor or area manager does not adequately satisfy the requirement that 'the Contractor shall constantly keep upon the Works'.

The person-in-charge is able to receive all instructions and directions, presumably including one under clause 8.5 for his own exclusion! The designation of the person-in-charge to receive instructions is not exclusive, and the architect may give his instructions to the contractor's head office if he so wishes, although this will not usually be expedient. He may not, however, give instructions to anyone else on the site, unless the person-in-charge specifically delegates the receiving of any class of instruction to such person. If the clerk of works gives any directions, these will usually be to the person-in-charge, but this gives rise to the difficulties discussed under clause 12. All this clause does is to establish that directions can be given to the contractor before the clause 12 procedures are set in motion.

The person-in-charge is not designated as the recipient of other documents, such as the contract documents, certificates or a notice of determination. This would be for the contractor to decide to suit his own organisation.

Clause 11 — Access for architect to the works

The purpose of this clause, among other things, is to secure quality control. Its necessity arises out of the contractor being given full possession of the site under clause 23.1 and thus having a prima facie right to exclude others from the site. While the employer possibly has an implied right of access under the contract, the architect has no such right. The term 'the Architect and his representatives' does not strictly extend to the quantity surveyor and others, but there would be no difficulty in so designating them in most cases of doubt.

The right of access secured by the architect is very wide in respect of both time and place and this needs to be read in relation to his responsibilities over quality under clauses 2.1 and 30.9.1.1. (The cases under 'Certificates and approvals' are also relevant.) This right of access aims to be as wide in respect of sub-contractors as it is regarding the contractor. The practical difficulty of enforcing the right all down the line of assorted sub-contractors is recognised by the words 'so far as possible', but these words also weaken the force of the obligation on the contractor.

In the case of a nominated sub-contractor, the right of access for both contractor and the architect is given by sub-contract clause 25, unless the architect certifies 'that the Sub-Contractor has reasonable grounds for refusing'. This obviates the need for the contractor to agree a special term as the present clause requires, but then also shifts the responsibility of decision from the contractor to the architect. In the case of a domestic sub-contractor, the corresponding clause has no such rider, although the whole clause may be deleted.

Suppliers are not specified here, since theirs is a contract of sale of completed goods and works inspection would be inappropriate. In any case, mass production will often make the right meaningless, as batches cannot conveniently be identified.

Clause 12 — Clerk of works

The clause gives the employer an option to employ a clerk of works and secures the right for him to inspect what is presumably the works. He is 'under the directions of the Architect', although not his representative. He is present 'solely as inspector' and the contractor's only responsibility to him is 'to offer every reasonable facility'.

The clerk of works can give no instructions and the clause thus debars him from exercising any direct influence on the works. If he gives 'directions' orally or in writing, including any for removal of defective work, apparently the contractor may choose to ignore them. Even if the contractor confirms them in writing to the architect they will still not be valid unless the architect in turn confirms them back to the contractor. They then become architect's instructions 'as from the date of confirmation', which effectively destroys their own substantive existence. If the architect does not confirm them, the contractor is left in even greater uncertainty by the silence.

The '2 working days' provision is very tight and also leaves doubt over what happens if the architect confirms after say six days. Are the directions still 'of no effect'? Clause 13.2 will apparently cover the position so long as the direction gives rise to a variation by virtue of its 'otherwise than pursuant to an instruction', but not otherwise. It is a pity that provisions under some earlier editions of this contract have not been reinstated. These permitted clerk of works' directions to rank with architect's oral instructions as being eligible for confirmation by the contractor and then to become deemed variations by the lapse of time. The present position is summarised in Figure 4 on page 34.

The practical problem is that the clerk of works is in close touch with the works and therefore many matters that concern him are matters that need a quick decision. The present wording attempts to achieve this by the two-day limit but, in so doing, it of necessity removes the procedure of the earlier editions, which had its automatic effect balanced by a safeguard of a longer waiting period. The result is confusing and leaves the clerk of works as a man of outwardly little substance on the scene, which is wrong. As mentioned above, the verbal anomalies can often be outflanked by the machinery of clause 13.2, unless it be held that the present specific clause overrules the generality of that clause. In addition, the architect can always designate the clerk of works as his representative in particular matters, so long as he does this very precisely.

The clause remains silent about the clerk of works' powers of approval of work, and strictly he has none. This is in keeping with the effect of the contract on the architect himself, whose only conclusive approval of work as carried out is that given in the final certificate, as clause 30.10 lays down, with even this of limited scope under the terms of clause 30.9.1. Some of the cases on 'Certificates and approvals' apply here.

Since this clause has a considerable bearing on the activities of the contractor and the quantity surveyor, they are well advised to request clarification of the status of the clerk of works in important cases, before any complication arises.

CHAPTER 6

The programme of the works

(a) Progress and delay:
Clause 23 — Date of possession, completion and postponement
Clause 24 — Damages for non-completion
Clause 25 — Extension of time

(b) Completion:
Clause 17 — Practical completion and defects liability
Clause 18 — Partial possession by employer
Sectional completion supplement

Clause 23 — Date of possession, completion and postponement

23.1 — DATE OF POSSESSION — PROGRESS TO COMPLETION DATE

This clause states two terms of the contract which would be implied if not expressly stated; failure in either respect constitutes a breach of contract. One is the giving of possession of the site to permit the contractor to carry out his obligations; the site itself is hardly ever mentioned in the conditions, but should be defined in the contract documents, by description in the preliminaries of the contract bills and by delineation on the contract drawings. The other is that the contractor shall 'regularly and diligently proceed' with the works and complete them; failure so to proceed may lead in an extreme case to determination by the employer under clause 27.1.2. Such failure would usually be demonstrated by a complete cessation of activity or a rate of progress which is bound not to achieve any reasonable completion date, let alone that given by the contract.

The clause, by defining a fixed completion date, also forms the starting point for the provisions leading to liquidated damages under clause 24.2, after taking account of any extension of time under clauses 25 and 33. The case of *Trollope and Colls Ltd* v. *North-West Metropolitan Regional Hospital Board* revolved around this clause and its amendment in a particular contract, based on an earlier edition of the conditions.

23.2 — ARCHITECT'S INSTRUCTIONS — POSTPONEMENT

Circumstances may arise which force the employer or the architect to call for delay in the whole or part of the works. This clause gives the architect power to order postponement, with or without good reason, and such an instruction in itself would not come within any reference to arbitration. The contractor's remedies are to claim an extension of time under clause 25.4.5.1 and loss and expense under clause 26.2.5. If postponement of the whole works or substantially the whole exceeds the period of delay, then the contractor may determine under clause 28.1.3.4. The period is usually relatively short, as discussed under that clause.

Clause 24 — Damages for non-completion

The clause permits the claiming of liquidated and ascertained damages from the contractor if he fails to complete the works on time in accordance with clause 23.1. The sum entered in the appendix will usually be calculated at a flat rate per week or other period and particular care should be taken to ensure the reasonableness of the sum entered so that the courts do not construe the sum as a penalty and thus unenforceable.

24.1 — CERTIFICATE OF ARCHITECT

The starting point is for the architect to issue a certificate stating that the completion date has been overrun. No date for issuing this is given, but it is reasonable that it should follow hard on the completion date to avoid uncertainty. Either party may, of course, dispute this certificate. Two essential elements are encompassed within the expression 'the Completion Date'. One is an initially defined completion date as in clause 23.1 and the other is a provision for the extension of time under clause 25 or clause 33. Some of the causes allowed in clause 25 are matters which would otherwise enable the contractor to substitute any reasonable completion date for the fixed date of the appendix, since they are breaches of contract and within the control of the employer or his architect. The contractor would thus be able to repudiate any liability for damages at all. To this degree, the provision for extension of time by maintaining a defined, if adjustable, completion date and keeping the right to damages alive is a safeguard to the employer rather than the contractor.

24.2 — PAYMENT OR ALLOWANCE OF LIQUIDATED DAMAGES

24.2.1 The contractor is not to be liable for liquidated damages until the issue of the certificate under the preceding clause. Damages cover any period between the completion date established and the date for practical completion, which may or may not have passed at the date of the certificate. It is for the employer to set about claiming damages; there is no obligation on the part of the contractor to pay them automatically. Neither the architect nor the quantity surveyor has authority here to adjust interim or final certificates to take account of them, and such adjustment is not mentioned in any part of clause 30. It is, however, prudent for the architect to advise the employer that adjustment has not been made, when issuing a certificate.

The employer's written notice to the contractor need not be given until the day of issue of the final certificate, but may not be later. The primary intention is that the contractor should pay sums progressively or, more likely, 'allow' them as deductions from payments made by the employer. If necessary, the employer may deduct the damages from the balance stated in the final certificate. If this balance is inadequate or in the contractor's favour, the employer may take the usual steps to recover the money as a debt.

While the sum may be related to the full sum stated in the appendix, partial possession or sectional completion may lead to a reduction and in these cases the employer is here to specify 'such part' as is relevant. This wording may also permit a remission of liability for some part of the period in special circumstances.

24.2.2 The completion date will not be finally fixed under clause 25.3.3 until well after the architect's certificate under this clause, if the implied sequence of the contract events is followed. It is therefore provided here that, if the completion date is finally fixed later, any excess damages are to be returned to the contractor. Nothing need be said about the date being earlier, as the employer will simply receive a bit more under the arrangements in clause 24.2.1.

Clause 25 — Extension of time

The effect of the operation of this clause is to reduce or remove the force of clause 24 in particular instances in which there is a cause of delay that, in general, is not the fault of the contractor, by permitting an extension of time to be granted. This benefits both employer and contractor, the former by keeping the right to liquidated damages alive and the latter by relieving him of their payment in the immediate instance. The clause is also drafted to avoid some of the pitfalls over granting an extension which have arisen in the past. It does this by allowing an interim extension to be given during progress and then to be confirmed or revised after practical completion.

In several places the architect is required to fix an amended completion date, usually in writing and sometimes by notifying the contractor, rather than by issuing a certificate as such. The effect of the extension is to make a modification of one of the terms of the contract and both parties should be notified. Since some of the causes for extension are matters of the architect's default, he is here acting as both judge and defendant.

A 'fair and reasonable' extension of time is the measure of the extension to be granted, which must mean fair and reasonable in relation to the cause. How fair and reasonable all the causes themselves are is another question, as is discussed. Nowhere in the clause or elsewhere in the conditions is there any power to insist that the contractor should make up lost time or accelerate the works when delay has not occurred. Clause 25.3.6 even specifically disallows the latter.

25.1 — DEFINITIONS

Three definitions are given for the purposes of this clause. 'Completion Date' includes any amended date arising from an extension, while 'delay, notice or extension' includes any further such happenings. 'Relevant Event' is the most significant, in that only events so delineated in clause 25.4 can lead to an extension of time.

25.2 — NOTICE BY CONTRACTOR OF DELAY TO PROGRESS

The initiative for obtaining an extension of time beyond the original or amended date for completion is to come from the contractor and further it is incumbent on him to give notice 'forthwith'. Such action and its promptness may permit alleviating action to be taken under clause 25.3.4.

The cause of delay may be such as to make it difficult to assess its length as soon as the delay becomes apparent. For instance, the cause may be of a continuing or intermittent nature or its interaction with some other cause of delay may be such as either to reduce their overall effect or to lead to further resultant delays. The contractor is therefore not necessarily required to state at once the length of delay occasioned, although he may well consider it prudent to give his opinion on this immediately. This clause consequently provides a three-stage approach under its three sub-clauses.

25.2.1 The contractor must set out in his initial notice 'the material circumstances', which are to include the cause or causes of delay and which, by implication, should cover any uncertainties and interacting matters. At the same time he must identify any relevant event which he intends to rely on to sustain his claim for an extension, as indicated under clause 25.1. More than one relevant event may combine to cause the foreseen delay.

25.2.2 The contractor is to 'estimate' the 'expected' delay, if possible in his notice, but otherwise 'as soon as possible', and he is to do this separately for 'each and every Relevant Event'. This is important for segregating the current events. The present delay may also overlap with some earlier delay leading to an extension or even with some other circumstances arising subsequent to the notice. This estimate is thus more critical than is required in the parallel situation of loss and expense under clause 26. In addition the contractor is to describe 'the expected effects' which will identify for example stages of the programme and parts of the works. This information will help the architect both to check the contractor's estimate of delay and to look for means of reducing the delay under clause 25.3.4.

25.2.3 Lastly it is provided for the contractor to give further notices to the architect covering changes in the estimate or delay and the associated effects. These notices may be as 'reasonably necessary', that is at the contractor's option, or 'as the Architect may reasonably require' if information is inadequate for him to keep the situation under review.

At each of these three stages the contractor is required to send copies of the documents to any nominated sub-contractor referred to in the original notice, and he should include any other firm which becomes involved as the situation develops. This serves to bring into play clause 35.14 regarding extensions for nominated firms, and it is therefore important that all affected nominated sub-contractors are mentioned and their representations are brought forward. It may be a representation from a sub-contractor that has triggered off the process, or a sub-contractor that has caused the delay under the relevant event of clause 25.4.7. While a nominated supplier may cause a delay under the same provision or be affected by any other delay here, he is not entitled to receive any copy documents and need not be mentioned in them. This reflects the fact that the nominated supplier is not involved in site activity.

25.3 — FIXING COMPLETION DATE

Like the contractor, the architect may have difficulty in making a firm early estimate of the delay, but he is under a general obligation to give an extension as soon as he reasonably can, so that the contractor is not left in doubt as to the measures he should be taking to meet the completion date. If the architect fails in this he may lose his power to grant an extension and thus may lose the employer the right to liquidated damages. But the architect in some cases may not be able to give a fair extension until after the previously fixed date for completion and the clause recognises this in its staged procedures. Figure 8 illustrates several possibilities in relation to the operation of clauses 25.3.1 to 25.3.3.

25.3.1 The basic action required of the architect is that he should decide whether there are any relevant events and then give an estimated extension of time once the contractor has put forward his estimate under clause 25.2.2.2. The architect is to exercise 'his opinion' as to what is 'fair and reasonable' both here and later on in adjusting this estimated extension. While he must be fair, it may be noted that under clause 25.3.3 he cannot finally revise his opinion in the direction of a shorter extension except on the basis of further suitable variations that have occurred and caution may therefore be advisable at this stage. Further, the architect may trim back the extension to allow for omission variations, but this does not allow him to give a 'negative' extension and so fix an earlier date. The original date in the contract appendix must be read as a 'fixing of the previous Completion Date' to allow a reduction of the first extension to be made, and this is an unlikely construction to receive judicial support. Clause 25.3.4.6 also bears on this aspect.

The architect need not negotiate the length of extension with the contractor, although clearly the information from the contractor is intended to facilitate consensus. At least some initial common view over the degree of approximation will help to reduce uncertainty over what is to be achieved in the circumstances, while agreement over the final extension will save ill-feeling or even arbitration. The architect's extension is to be in writing and is to state the relevant events and variations on which it is based. This will allow the contractor to object if he still considers that anything relevant is excluded.

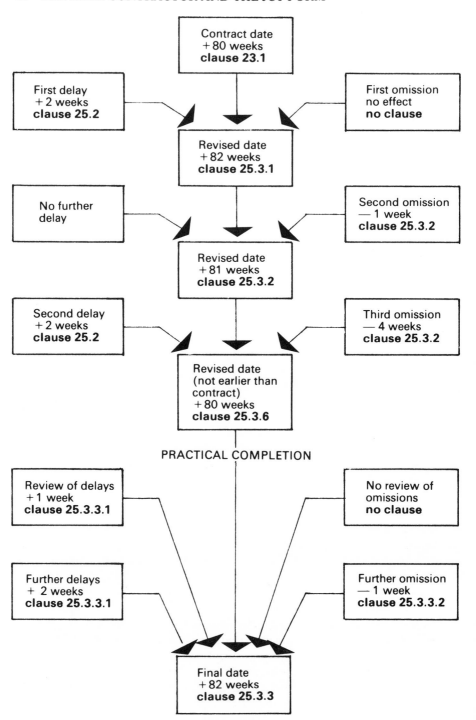

Figure 8: **Example of extensions of time by architect under clause 25.3 of JCT main form**

When such an extension has been granted, the contractor is then to amend his master programme under the optional clause 5.3.1.2, if it applies.

25.3.2 Once the architect has acted under this clause during the contract period, but not before, he may fix an earlier completion date than the already modified date on the basis that he has in the interim instructed omission variations which are quite independent of any relevant events. This revision by the architect is also quite independent of any prior action by the contractor. This again is subject to clause 25.3.4.6 and any action to mop up omission effects in this way must not occur later than the next fixing of a later date, as indicated by the words 'omission . . . after the last occasion . . . made an extension of time'. Otherwise he loses the opportunity and could well be liable to the employer for any serious lapse.

25.3.3 The final fixing of the completion date must be done within twelve weeks of practical completion. This constitutes a review of the previous date, whether original or interim, and allows for a later, earlier or unchanged final date to be fixed. It would appear that the architect must specifically confirm the original date in this way, even if there is no reason for it to have been changed.

The strict wording of the clause makes the three options mutually exclusive and also appears to allow the architect to act only once after practical completion. There may well be causes tending both to retard and to advance the date and it is only reasonable for the architect to take both into account in finally fixing the completion date.

If the architect attempts on his own initiative to have a second attempt at fixing the completion date, it would appear to be open to the party potentially disadvantaged by such action to object successfully. If however one party objects to the architect's single revised date on the grounds of its inadequate scope (quite apart from grounds of defective calculations), there would be strong reason for the other to concede a second revised date or face arbitration or other action on the grounds that the architect's decision was not reasonable. There is thus some room for manoeuvre here, rather more than the law might suggest, although the architect need take notice of no one, as in the exercise of the rest of his powers.

When fixing a later final date, the architect has a wider field than when fixing an interim date. He is not limited to those relevant events and their estimated consequences which the contractor has notified. He can thus take account of any additional relevant event in reviewing a previous decision and, further, make a decision on an extension arising from a relevant event that he has not had in view before. While this gives the architect extra discretion it also gives him the extra responsibility of clearing up any outstanding relevant events before setting in train the clause 24 procedures leading to the employer seeking damages. In this case and the next there will usually be an interval between the architect notifying the amended date and the issue of the final certificate, so that the contractor will have time to raise any complaint over the date given and the reasons.

The architect's right to fix an earlier date is more limited. It relates only to variation omissions instructed since the last extension of time was given. There is therefore no power to go back and revise any abatement of an extension already made. Only if it can be demonstrated that the previous abatement was in some way inextricably bound up with the extension to which it related and was therefore contingent upon it, is it likely that a revision could be made. In any case, if once a later date has been fixed after practical completion the power to advance the date will then have been waived by the architect.

Should the architect decide to confirm the previous date, he is to do so. Beyond this, the clause is silent. Presumably he will review all his previous decisions and the supporting data, possibly he will adduce new data, with the various elements cancelling each other out.

This clause commendably gives the power for the completion date to be finally fixed after practical completion and so overcomes the difficulties demonstrated by some of the legal decisions. It does complicate procedures though by its detail without covering all options. It also leaves open what is to obtain if the architect does not act at all within the 12-week period. Would this infer that the previously fixed date is now automatically confirmed, or is this or any revision now waived so that any liquidated damages are lost and the employer may seek only damages at large? It would appear that the latter will be the case.

25.3.4 Four provisos are given here, of which the first two may be taken together. In part these two underline the contractor's obligation under clause 23.1 'regularly and diligently (to) proceed'. In the case of delays he is to use his 'best endeavours' and take avoiding action on his own initiative, that is measures such as progressing materials orders and sub-contractors' performance, and also that of the architect. Even if delay occurs he must try to prevent it affecting the completion date and he must co-operate with the architect to reduce the effects of delay. It would be reasonable to limit the extension granted by having regard to the effect of the contractor's ameliorating action. 'All that may reasonably be required' would extend to such matters as revision of short-term programmes and relatively limited adjustments of the labour force, actions that could be taken without significant extra expense. It is in any case in the contractor's interest to save time, because time costs him money as well as the employer and he will only recover money where the cause of delay also gives rise to extra payment under clause 26.1. The contractor is not obliged under the contract, however, to work overtime or bring on extra plant or take other expensive steps to regain lost time. Should he agree to do so at the architect's request (and the word 'instruct' does not occur in this clause) he would be entitled to ask in advance for an extra payment. In its absence he may decline to take special action, just as he may decline to accelerate progress when no delay is in prospect.

The third proviso is that the architect must notify 'every Nominated Sub-Contractor' of every completion date he fixes, although he does not have to give reasons, as in the case of the contractor. This still excludes from the formal system the employer who is possibly going to act on the basis of this information. The notification requirement may involve the architect in quite extensive action, but it does reduce uncertainty. It is wider than the corresponding earlier action of the contractor under clause 25.2.

Finally no architect's decision can fix a completion date earlier than that in the contract appendix, however extensive omission variations may be, even without regard to any question of acceleration.

25.4 — RELEVANT EVENTS

The causes of delay, here called 'Relevant Events', that may lead to an extension of time will in some cases also give rise to claims under clause 26.1 for extra payment or to determination by the contractor under clause 28.1.3. This is not always so, as is shown by *Davis Contractors Ltd* v. *Fareham UDC*. The list in this present clause is the longest of all and covers all the causes in the other clauses and several more, with some slight differences in emphasis. They are therefore discussed in full below but, for convenience of comparison, the causes given in the respective clauses are tabulated in Figure 9. In addition, clause 33.1.3 governs the position where war damage occurs.

It will be noted that none of the events stems directly from the contractor's default, although there are some reservations on this over clauses 25.4.3, 25.4.7 and 25.4.10. They all arise either by the action or inaction of the employer or the architect, or through circumstances beyond the control of either party to the contract.

25.4.1 *Force majeure* is not a phrase native to English or Scots law and its meaning is imprecise, but apparently wider than act of God (an interesting theological point?). It refers to exceptional matters beyond the control of either party.

25.4.2 *Exceptionally adverse weather conditions.* The first word is important; weather may be exceptional in its degree, its timing or its persistence. Local meteorological records should be consulted where necessary to establish a norm.

25.4.3 *Loss or damage occasioned by clause 22 perils.* This is in respect of the works themselves. The contingencies may be due to the contractor's own default, as is discussed under clause 22A; it seems hard on the employer for him to lose liquidated damages in such a case. Where clause 22A applies, it is possible that clause 20.2 would carry the day against the present clause at this point. If this were so, then the indemnity of clause 20.2 would permit the employer to recover unliquidated damages for the delay, while still being obliged to suffer the delay itself. The point is by no means certain, however, and it may be noted that clause 28.1.3.2, which parallels the present paragraph in the context of determination, specifically excludes the contractor's negligence as the present clause does not. Clause 18.2 expressly excludes the risks under clause 22B or clause 22C and cannot be relied on where one of these applies.

25.4.4 *Civil commmotion (and the like).* The provision extends back to all the processes preceding the site operations, at least for the goods or materials

Cause of delay	Relief or redress available to contractor		
	Extension under Clause 25	Determination under Clause 28†	Payment under Clause 26††
Exceptional weather	Yes	No	No
Strikes, lock-outs, etc	Yes	No	No
Delay by nominated firms	Yes	No	No
Delay by statutory bodies	Yes	No	No
Inability to obtain labour, goods or materials	Yes	No	No
Exercise of statutory powers	Yes	No	No
Action on discovery of antiquities	Yes	No	No
Force majeure	Yes	Yes	No
Fire, flood, storm, etc	Yes	*Yes	No
Civil commotion	Yes	Yes	No
Lack of ingress/egress	Yes	No	Yes
Architect's variation orders	Yes	Yes	Yes
Discrepancies leading to architect's instructions	Yes	Yes	Yes
Postponement on architect's instructions	Yes	Yes	Yes
Delay in obtaining drawings, instructions etc	Yes	Yes	Yes
Delay by others engaged by employer	Yes	Yes	Yes
Opening up and testing	Yes	Yes	Yes

*   Determination following fire, flood, etc is partially covered by clause 22C

†   Clause 28 contains other grounds for determination besides those which have extensions as an alternative remedy. Others appear in clause 32 (Hostilities) and clause 33 (War damage)

††   Clause 34 (Antiquities) also makes provision for the contractor to recover losses not otherwise covered by the contract.

Figure 9: **Causes of redress under clause 25, with similar causes under clauses 26 and 28 of main form**

The precise wording of these clauses should be referred to, as in some cases this differs slightly between one clause and another. The order of the columns is not the numerical order of the clauses but gives precedence according to the number of causes covered.

directly required for the works. Civil commotion so far as it causes damage to the works is already covered in clause 25.4.3.

25.4.5 *Architect's instructions (in certain cases)*. This covers all instructions over the following matters:

(a) The resolution of discrepancies or divergences, perhaps with additional work or with resultant waiting time.

(b) Variations and the expenditure of provisional sums, that is routine physical changes and developments.

(c) Postponement, not involving physical change.

(d) Action (and inaction) on the discovery of antiquities.

(e) Nominated sub-contractors and suppliers, particularly but not only over nomination, determination and renomination.

In cases (a)–(c) as in clause 25.4.3, there is no exclusion of the contractor's negligence; clause 28.1.2.4 excludes this, and also his default. Also covered by this clause are instructions over opening up for inspection or for testing, but with the liability for the resultant delay being linked to the liability for the cost of making good under clause 8.3.

25.4.6 *Not having received in due time necessary instructions, drawings (and the like)*. In these cases 'due time' will be that necessary, for instance, to obtain materials or goods through the normal channels and also sufficient margin to assimilate all the information required for proper production planning, often a prolonged matter for today's complex building. The wording 'neither unreasonably distant from nor unreasonably close to' is intended to guard against situations in which the contractor may time his requests for information in such a way that he may embarrass the architect and himself have a lever for a claim. There seems to be no practical reason, however, why the contractor should not ask well in advance for any or all of the information he requires, provided he states the date or dates on which it is needed. This situation is excluded from the operation of this paragraph, as is the situation where the contractor does not apply at all because he does not know of his lack. It is, after all, a lapse on the part of the architect that produces the original problem and the present wording does tend to put the contractor in the position of producing the architect's check list for him, and being penalised if he does so inadequately.

The list of items repeat wording from clauses 5.4 and 7 but for some reason does not include the 'descriptive schedules or other like documents necessary for use in carrying out the Works' as given in clause 5.3.1.1. The contractor will usually be able to demonstrate that a lack here is also in fact a lack of 'necessary instructions'. This term covers the whole range of instructions given in Figure 2 on page 30. Some are instructions that the contractor will not really be looking out for, such as those concerning the removal of defective work. In the case of nomination instructions the contractor may contribute to the delay, as in his actions under clauses 35.8 and 35.9.

The architect may be delayed in issuing information, because he has not himself received design information which is the responsibility of a nominated firm. While the contractor will receive an extension here, the employer may then seek recompense from the nominated firm under Agreement NSC/2 or Agreement NSC/2a or the Warranty Agreement Schedule 3 of the Nominated Supplier Form of Tender, as appropriate. Agreement NSC/2a is optional under the 'alternative' method of nomination, but will be needed to avoid financial risk where the nominated firm assumes any design responsibility. The contractor would have no liability for design failures by these firms, even apart from the present clause, since he himself has no design responsibility under the contract.

25.4.7 *Delay on the part of nominated sub-contractors or nominated suppliers.* This clause read in isolation relieves both the contractor and nominated firms of responsibility quite unreasonably, considering that they have a direct contractual relationship, but the employer has such a relationship with the contractor only. The clause has no bearing on domestic sub-contractors and other suppliers. Its result is that if 'the Contractor has taken all practicable steps to avoid or reduce' delay, he is then granted an extension and so avoid damages. The defaulting nominated firm therefore does not have to meet the contractor's claim to be reimbursed for such damages, although remaining liable for other delay of disturbance costs, and the employer is left without redress. The defence for the nominated firm is to establish *its own* default and the fact that the contractor tried his best to overcome or prevent the default. The situation is quite farcical.

The clause is included to take account of the special position of nominated firms, with whom the contractor is obliged to sub-contract unless he can sustain adequate objections. However, as with clause 25.4.6, the various collateral agreements mentioned give the employer a direct route to approach nominated firms for redress in respect of this type of default. Agreement NSC/2a is optional and to dispense with it is once again to leave the employer open to risk.

Another three-way situation arises by virtue of a nominated sub-contractor's right to suspend work under sub-contract clause 21.8.1 and then to receive an extension of time under sub-contract clause 11.2.5.13. The discussion under the former clause should be noted. The proximate cause is the failure of the employer to pay the nominated sub-contractor direct when either Agreement NSC/2 or Agreement NSC/2a applies, a liability which arises because of the prior fault of the contractor in not paying. Although the employer is at fault and is liable to the sub-contractor himself under the relevant agreement the contractor has hardly 'taken all practicable steps' and reasonably would not receive an extension. It is to be hoped therefore that the courts will not construe his responsibilities as being abrogated when he happens to be short of cash!

More widely, the architect is required to be involved in the question of extension of time for nominated sub-contractors under clause 35.14 and sub-contract clause 11, and of certifying completion under clause 35.15 and sub-contract clause 12. (In the case of nominated suppliers' programmes the relevant clause is clause 36.4.3, but this is not the concern of the architect.)

The delay under the present clause is 'on the part of' a nominated firm and it seems likely from discussion in the case of *Westminster Corporation* v. *J. Jarvis and Sons Ltd and Another* that the courts would hold this expression to mean delay by the firm itself in carrying out its obligations, rather than delay caused after completion by poor performance such as, in that case, defective workmanship. The case is relevant in its special circumstances to other aspects of this clause. It is a nice point whether determination by the contractor against the sub-contractor under sub-contract clause 29.1 can be construed as 'delay on the part of', as is discussed under that clause. Some of the causes of determination there are delay on the part of the sub-contractor prior to determination, but they can hardly be so after the event. Clause 35.24 gives no direct help, and the contractor will need to rely on clause 25.4.5 as embracing renomination instructions.

25.4.8 *Execution of work by the employer or by those engaged by him or supply of materials by the employer.* Clause 29 deals with the overall question of work on site not included in the contract and distinguishes two categories. Clause 29.1 covers work about which the contract bills give sufficient information for the contractor to assess its effect on his overall contract obligations, while clause 29.2 covers the alternative category of work about which information is inadequate or non-existent. The reasonable concomitant under the present clause would be for the first category to lead to the possibility of extension of time only if there were an unpredicted change in its execution, but for the second to lead to the possibility of an extension by its very introduction or by its detailed execution being different from any limited information supplied. Unfortunately the clause creates the possibility of conflict of intentions by making no such distinction, so that the simple existence of work in the first category might lead to an extension. While the generality of clause 29.1 might be held to overrule the present clause, the problems encountered under clause 25.4.7 are a sufficient caution against optimism!

It is therefore advisable when setting out information in the contract bills to satisfy clause 29.1 to state that the contractor is to allow in particular for any effects on his programme, so that the question of an extension does not come into debate. This needs care in view of the issues discussed under clause 2.2.1 and possibly cannot be done in a binding manner. If there is a major question of such work, the amendment of the present clause should be seriously considered. The present clause produces a similar position over supply of materials by the employer, although clause 29 does not cover this eventuality. The effect is potentially even worse in view of the alternatives: 'the supply . . . or the failure to supply'. Any initial conditions must therefore be defined in the contract bills, and it is important to consider the effect before lightly including such 'fixing' items in the bills.

25.4.9 *Statutory powers which directly affect the availability of labour, materials or energy.* This is widely cast by the reference to 'any statutory power' but is also closely restricted so that not every action by or on behalf of government so qualifies. Firstly, it is restricted to an 'exercise after the Date of Tender' and so the contractor should have taken account of any earlier exercise with a delayed effect on the works. Secondly, it is restricted to an 'exercise . . . by the United Kingdom Government' and it does not embrace, say, the marketing actions of a national corporation unless these actions were constrained by suitably direct government intervention. Finally, the exercise must be such as 'directly affects . . . by restricting . . . or preventing . . . or delaying' the contractor, that is, it must directly impede him rather than some other firm, say his suppliers. In the case of the latter occurrence, the contractor must turn to the next clause to support his case.

25.4.10 *Inability to secure such labour, goods or materials as are essential.* This clause has the safeguard that the contractor should 'reasonably have foreseen' and provided for all likely problems of this kind — by local enquiry and the like. Acute national or even international shortages may lead to an inability to secure but often such inability is only relative and can be overcome by some degree of effort or expenditure. The wording gives no indication as to how far the contractor should go before he should ask for an extension, or what criteria the architect should apply before granting one, where labour or materials with several sources of supply are in question. Where a material has a single source of supply only, the position may be easier to establish. While this present clause covers some contingencies excluded by the narrower wording of clause 25.4.9, it is itself narrower than that clause in as much as it excludes fuel and energy.

25.4.11 *A local authority or statutory undertaker carrying out or failing to carry out work.* This parallels clause 25.4.7 and is necessary because clause 6.3 removes the bodies concerned from the scope of the nomination system where work is 'solely in pursuance of (their) statutory obligations'. In view of the difficulties of controlling such bodies, this clause may be received with rather more approbation than clause 25.4.7. Where a body is carrying out such work as, say, part of the building services and there has been a nomination, delay will fall under clause 25.4.7. If the body is acting as a domestic sub-contractor, the contractor will not be able to seek extension.

25.4.12 *Failure of the employer to give ingress to or egress from the site.* This is to be distinguished from failure to give possession of the site under clause 23.1, which is a fundamental breach as discussed under that clause and actionable accordingly. The present clause relates to allowing the contractor through adjoining property 'in the possession and control of the Employer' and by definition not part of the site, which does pass into the contractor's possession. This is at some 'due time' and may perhaps occur over only a short period. The clause provides that it may arise out of some provision in the contract bills or on the contract drawings. It may also be contingent upon the contractor giving notice to the architect, and failure to do so may defeat a claim of extension.

Alternatively the clause covers 'ingress or egress as otherwise agreed', i.e. arising during progress, perhaps by way of a variation under clause 13.1.2.1. The agreement should itself cover matters of timing and any notice and, while it refers only to the architect and the contractor, it will also need the concurrence of the employer. Since this case arises without having been contemplated in the contract, and so in the programme, it is difficult to see precisely how it can lead to extension of (contemplated) time.

Clause 17 — Practical completion and defects liability

17.1 — CERTIFICATE OF PRACTICAL COMPLETION

Practical completion is important in its own right and also for its other contractual effects, but it suffers from a lack of definition in the conditions. The inference of the term is not that the works are nearly complete, but that the architect is of the opinion that they are complete, although he will check this in detail during the defects liability period. The matter is left within the opinion of the architect and is not dependent upon any formal application by the contractor. 'The purposes of this Contract' which it affects are:

(a) The beginning of the defects liability period under clause 17.2.

(b) Liability for frost damage under clauses 17.2, 17.3 and 17.5.

(c) The ending of insurance of the works by the contractor under clause 22A, if applicable.

(d) The end of liability to liquidated damages under clause 24.2.1.

(e) The end of regular interim certificates under clause 30.1.3.

(f) The halving of the retention under clause 30.4.1.3.

(g) The beginning of the period of final measurement under clause 30.6.1.2.

(h) The opening of arbitration on most matters under article 5.

Several of these purposes are also referred to in connection with partial possession under clause 18 and in connection with sectional completion under the supplement. On the other hand clauses 2, 23, 24 and 25 all use the simple terms 'complete' or 'completion' but these appear to be referring to the same event. At this stage the contractor is no longer obliged to accept instructions requiring fresh work, even on modified terms.

17.2 — DEFECTS, SHRINKAGES OR OTHER FAULTS

This clause establishes a formal defects liability period and a procedure for dealing with defects within that period. The defects include major or minor matters and it is suggested that the term 'which shall appear' includes omissions and things which could be discerned before practical completion, but which come to the architect's notice after it. The term does not allow the architect to instruct the contractor to open up or test work irrespective of clearly observed defects as under clause 8.3, the effect of which ends at practical completion. The architect's responsibility and power is simply to specify the defect, leaving it to the contractor to decide how to remedy it in accordance with the original requirement of the contract and, if necessary, what opening up or testing is required. In specialised cases or where severe upheaval is likely, he may well be more persuasive and precise, especially if the contractor is open to action for consequential loss by the employer. It is also within the power of the architect to insist that any remedial work to nominated work should be carried out by the person originally responsible; the contractor will usually be only too pleased to concur with this. Frost is given special notice in the clause and in clause 17.3 and also takes up clause 17.5 in its entirety.

The formal period as such is in addition to, and not in place of, the common law remedy of suing the contractor for breach. It exists to allow for the contractor to be brought back to remedy defects himself. The common law remedy is governed by the Limitation Act but is somewhat reduced by the provision of clause 30.9.1.1 regarding the effect of the final certificate. The limiting time for the delivery of the schedule of defects should be carefully observed, to avoid the complication of the contractor declining to do the work and opting for a deduction from the final account instead.

The contractor is to make good defects 'within a reasonable time' of receiving the schedule. It will depend on the nature and circumstances of a particular defect as to what is a reasonable time and perhaps also on the method of dealing with it that the contractor chooses to adopt. His spur will be to secure the balance of the retention.

All work will normally be at the contractor's expense, although the clause does provide for the alternative of the employer meeting the cost. How this latter case can arise for defects which are all defined as the contractor's responsibility by the clause is not at all clear, and the architect is given no guidance by the conditions on when to exercise the power given to him. The wording does not even enjoy the ambiguity of the similar provision in Clause 7.

17.3 — DEFECTS ETC — ARCHITECT'S INSTRUCTIONS

Only one schedule of defects may be issued and its issue marks the end of the opportunity to use the defects liability period, as the last sentence of this clause lays down. There may however be defects that appear and that cannot wait until the schedule of defects before the contractor is asked to deal with them. In this case this clause allows the architect to issue instructions covering the individual defects. To avoid finality, such instructions must not be called a schedule of defects. The provisions of the clause are otherwise similar to clause 17.2 and it would seem that the two clauses could have been conflated and clarity of intention thereby gained.

17.4 — CERTIFICATE OF COMPLETION OF MAKING GOOD DEFECTS

One certificate is to be issued covering all making good. It has two effects 'for all the purposes of this Contract'; the one is to clear the way for the release of the second half of the retention by virtue of clause 30.4.1.3 and the other to help to clear the way for the issue of the final certificate under clause 30.8. In neither respect will it act to shorten the length of the defects liability period and there seems therefore no advantage in issuing the certificate of making good early. It can only lead to the missing of some defect.

The certificate means that the contractor is no longer obliged himself to return and remedy defects, but it does not end the contractor's liability for the cost of remedying them. This only comes about with the end of a period of 12 years for a contract under seal in England and six years for other contracts from the breach (or possibly longer, see cases under 'Certificates and approvals'), subject however to his release from further liability by the final certificate which, under clause 30.9.1.1, is conclusive evidence of the architect's satisfaction on some matters. The position is illustrated in Figure 10.

17.5 — DAMAGE BY FROST

This clause re-enacts in negative terms what is already stated in clauses 17.2 and 17.3. The intention is quite plain: the contractor is only liable for damage caused before practical completion. The difficulty in practice is in deciding when damage appearing after practical completion was actually caused.

Clause 18 — Partial possession by employer

It is quite common for the parties to enter into a particular contract with a defined programme of sectional completion of the works written into it, and for this purpose the Sectional Completion Supplement, dealt with in this chapter, is available. The present clause is not intended for this situation but for those cases where the employer takes early possession of some part of the works by an arrangement made with the contractor while the works are in progress. If the employer reassumes possession of any part of the site without the contractor's consent he will be in breach of his obligation to give the contractor possession under clause 23.1 and to allow him to maintain it until completion.

The broad effect of the clause is to establish practical completion of what it terms 'the relevant part' and to clarify several issues that flow from practical completion of the works as a whole but which in these circumstances become immediate for the relevant part. It is to be noted that the clause has a constrictive effect by virtue of the words 'notwithstanding anything expressed or implied elsewhere in this Contract'. Any amendment of the terms given should be made quite categorically in the clause itself and the comments on clause 2.2.1 should be noted here. There are several issues here which are qualified by the decision in *English Industrial Estates Corporation* v. *George Wimpey and Co Ltd.*

The terms of the clause apply as a series in each case that may occur during progress, and two or more series may be in force at any one time. The whole clause is numbered 18.1, so nothing is missing here in passing to consider the following.

18.1.1 An approximate estimate of the value of the relevant part is to be made; it affects only the question of liquidated damages under clause 18.1.5, and has no bearing on interim payments and the final account, any more than

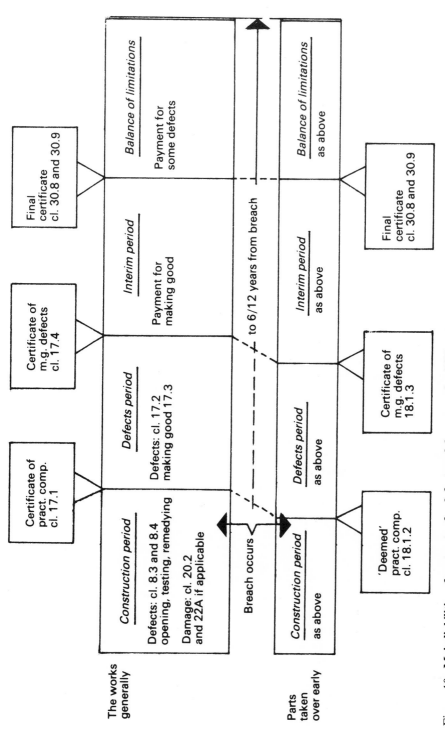

Figure 10: **Main liabilities of contractor for defects and damage under JCT main form**
Clauses considered are not exhaustive. Consequential damage is not considered, neither are materials.

has any other part of the clause.

18.1.2 Practical completion is equated with the date of possession for several purposes for which it is 'deemed to have occurred'. There is not a 'full' practical completion; this arises only with the formal certificate under clause 17.1 which is not mentioned here. Equally there can be only one final certificate with all that flows from the issue of it. Whether further work can be ordered on 'the relevant part' is doubtful.

18.1.3 An actual certificate of making good defects is however issued with an effect as indicated in Figure 10.

18.1.4 Where the contractor is responsible for insurance of the works against damage and the like he is to reduce the value insured, not by the estimated value of the relevant part but by the full value. This full value is not usually strictly known: the effect is to leave the contractor responsible for maintaining adequate insurance of the remainder of the works. In practice insurance companies take such uncertainties in their stride. What this clause does emphasise is that the relevant part must be a physically precise entity that can be identified in any insurance activities. The situation becomes virtually a mixture of clauses 22A and 22B insurance, perhaps applying to two wings of one building. The employer takes over only 'the contingencies referred to': matters not listed in clause 22A remain with the contractor.

18.1.5 The amount of liquidated damages for the remainder of the works is to be reduced in proportion to the value. The figures to be used are the estimate under paragraph (a) and the contract sum; no allowance is made for any variations and the like. Nor is provision made for the fact that the relevant part may, for the purpose of liquidated damages, be of greater or lesser importance to the employer than its construction cost might indicate. Here is a case where the introductory 'notwithstanding' of the clause might need amending on a particular contract. Payment of liquidated damages could conceivably already be under way when partial possession occurs and so the effect of this paragraph could be to reduce the payment during its currency.

Sectional Completion Supplement

Clause 18 provides for the possibility of the employer taking possession of some section of the works before practical completion of the whole by an agreement made with the contractor during progress, rather than forming part of the original contract. To cover the cases in which phased completion with clearly defined dates, possibly associated with phased possession, is envisaged in the contract the JCT issues separately the Standard Form of Sectional Completion Supplement. This has the pattern of a set of articles of agreement, an appendix and a list of alterations to be incorporated in the JCT form, either by direct amendment or by appending the supplement to the articles of agreement and endorsing by way of cross-reference in places affected elsewhere. The supplement is so drawn as to suit the with-quantities editions, either private or local authorities. With slight change it suits the with-approximate-quantities editions, and there is a variant of the Scottish Building Contract that takes account of it. It is not intended for the without-quantities editions.

No cross-references to the supplement are made elsewhere in the present volume, since there are over 90 changes introduced and in the main these are minor drafting points to include a simple mention of a section of the works, rather than of the whole works. Comment is made below on each alteration that is central to the scheme of things under the supplement, although the full wording does not need to be given in each case. The clauses affected are as follows, giving a distribution heavily loaded towards the later part of the contract as might be expected: Clause 1; Clause 2; Clause 17; Clause 18; Clause 22A; Clause 23; Clause 24; Clause 25; Clause 26; Clause 29; Clause 30; Clause 32; Clause 33; Clause 38; Clause 39; Clause 40.

ARTICLES OF AGREEMENT

The drawings and bills of quantities are qualified as 'showing and describing both the work to be done and the division of the Works into Sections for phased completion' and this links with clause 2.1. Arbitration may be opened after practical completion of any section, provided the appropriate alternative in the appendix has been selected.

CLAUSE 2: CONTRACTOR'S OBLIGATIONS

A definition of 'Section' is given to tie in with the articles and for further use. Clear sub-division of the documents is necessary to show the physical limits of, and quantities of work within, the sections and also to allow suitable sub-division of the contract sum. There is no question of several contracts with several contract sums, or of any provision akin to a 'break clause' permitting either party to opt out of any section.

CLAUSE 17: PRACTICAL COMPLETION AND DEFECTS LIABILITY

Practical completion of each section is deemed to have occurred 'for all the purposes of this Contract', as it does for the whole works under the unamended clause. This is more far-reaching in effect then the provisions of clause 18.1.2 which establishes practical completion on a section for certain purposes only.

CLAUSE 18: PARTIAL POSSESSION BY EMPLOYER

While the present supplement accommodates premeditated sectional completion, there may still be some further agreement for partial possession arising during progress and overlaying the earlier arrangements in part. The present clause is therefore amended slightly to take this possibility into account and use is made of 'section values' given in the appendix to deal with the arithmetic.

CLAUSE 22A: INSURANCE OF THE WORKS AGAINST CLAUSE 22 PERILS

An additional sentence provides for any completed section to be 'at the sole risk of the Employer as regards any of the Clause 22 Perils'. The contractor is to reduce his value insured accordingly by the value given in the appendix or some other agreed amount (presumably to take account of variations and the like), while keeping his eye on the effects of clause 18.1.4. The effect of the present amendment is therefore similar to that of clause 18.1.4 itself, and the comments made there are relevant and important here.

CLAUSE 23.1: POSSESSION, COMPLETION AND POSTPONEMENT

There is provision here and in the appendix for phased possession (not mentioned in the title of the supplement, or anywhere else in the JCT forms) and phased completion, and either or both of these could be envisaged in a contract. Many of the alterations listed in the supplement would be superfluous in a case of phased possession with common completion and the drafting is clearly not intended for such a case. The main need then would be for clear delineation of the sections in the way indicated in the articles of agreement and the appendix.

CLAUSE 24: DAMAGES FOR NON-COMPLETION

Separate amounts for liquidated damages for each section are provided for, and these amounts need not be proportionate to the contract 'value' of the section. This arrangement overcomes the deficiencies in the parallel provisions under clause 18.1.5.

CLAUSE 30: CERTIFICATES AND PAYMENTS

Several changes occur here, along with some wording to clarify uncertainty that might arise. The regular specified issue of interim certificates continues until the last section has reached practical completion, and only then do certificates become intermittent, even for those sections already completed. Retention however is released by virtue of the unamended clause 30.4 in respect of the sections individually, working from their various certificates of practical completion and of making good defects. The period of final measurement and valuation may also be timed from each of these practical completions, if a special provision is agreed, but in the absence of this (and there is no special space for it in the appendix) it will start only after the last practical completion. In any case, only one final certificate is to be issued, related to the timing of the last practical completion amongst other things, which accords with the principle that the contract is still one despite its sections.

CHAPTER 7

Disturbance of the programme

Clause 26 — Loss and expense caused by matters materially affecting regular progress of the works
Clause 27 — Determination by employer
Clause 28 — Determination by contractor

Clause 26 — Loss and expense caused by matters materially affecting regular progress of the works

26.1 MATTERS MATERIALLY AFFECTING REGULAR PROGRESS OF THE WORKS — DIRECT LOSS AND/OR EXPENSE

The broad purpose of this clause is to reimburse the contractor in certain cases of direct loss and expense, usually called claims and not covered by 'any other provision in this Contract'. In particular it would seem to cover cases not provided for under clauses 2.2, 2.3 and 8.3; clause 13.5 expressly excludes matters dealt with here. It is therefore wider in its operation than any other such clause, but is however limited in two ways: firstly by the fairly tight list of matters in clause 26.2, and secondly by the stipulation that regular progress must have been materially affected to bring the clause into effect. The provisions of the clause are not however final, in view of the proviso in clause 26.6.

'Direct loss and/or expense' appears to envisage immediate extra expenditure on labour, material and plant or on overheads, such as supervision, directly associated with the works. An element of loss of profit, extra financing charges and inflation allowance may be allowable in particular circumstances, as suggested by the cases under 'Disturbance, determination and loss and expense'. Any claim that disturbance of the works has so committed the contractor as to prevent him taking on other work might be too remote to fall within the ambit of this clause.

The criterion that regular progress must be materially affected to allow reimbursement of the contractor has the effect of excluding from the operation of the clause any matter that may cause expense without also affecting progress. In practice there will be few cases where it cannot be shown that progress has also been affected, whether or not the overall contract period is extended. The evidence of the contractor's master programme provided under clause 5.3.1.2 may prove useful here, even though it is not a contract document; provided it was furnished to the architect in the first place and has been worked to and has kept up to date since, it will be primary evidence of what should have happened. Once evidence has been produced, a claim for extension of time will often arise under clause 25. Under that clause the contractor is to 'do all that may reasonably be required ... to proceed with the Works'. As has been suggested in discussing clause 25, the contractor is not obliged to go to additional material expense in this way, although he will obviously want to shorten the delay in those cases not covered by the present clause to reduce his own expense.

When this present clause also applies, the contractor may expect reimbursement if he simply accepts the delay and uses 'his best endeavours to prevent (excessive) delay' under clause 25. Should this state of affairs be unacceptable to the employer, the architect may quite reasonably request further action from the contractor to save time and the contractor may, equally reasonably, expect to be paid for what is involved. The contractor is however under no absolute obligation under the contract to undertake such action, even with payment.

It is left to the contractor to initiate action by writing to the architect. The 'application' need not be for any amount, it is simply 'stating' that loss or expense has occurred or is threatening. The contractor need not even given an approximate estimate at this stage. However there are three provisos that the contractor must observe carefully to ensure that his claim can be dealt with under this clause and will not be left to the other 'rights and remedies' of clause 26.6.

The first proviso is that the application is to be made as soon as the contractor is aware of actual or potential disturbance leading to loss or expense. Usually this will occur close to its commencement and thus allow recording and other procedures to be set up. The contractor should certainly give notice before major effects have been suffered, otherwise it may prove impossible for an adequate check to be kept on the financial implications. He may then be forced to accept a poor settlement on the grounds that he has permitted the loss of evidence. If commencement is still some way off, it is just possible with certain matters coming under clause 26.2 that ameliorating action could be taken by the architect to remove the causes of disturbance, even though there can be no action that attempts directly to interfere with contractor's own site organisation. While the contractor might well not be liable for breach if he delayed his application, such delay could conceivably lead to some offsetting of his claim. Under this proviso the contractor is also to apply when he is not aware of disturbance, but should be. Admirable though the sentiment may be, it is difficult to see how this feat may be performed. The provision here is additional to the requirements for establishing extension of time under clause 25.2.

The second and third provisos require the contractor to substantiate the fact of disturbance and then to provide details which allow calculation of the financial consequences. These two steps may be distinct, but they are more usually closely linked. They may each be progressively performed, even if culminating in a single claim document. Under the provisos the architect, to whom the application is to be made, is also to adjudicate on the validity of the claim and may himself settle the amount. As several of the matters listed in clause 26.2 fall largely into the category of the architect's default, the architect is placed in the position of being his own judge as well as defendant, just as he is in some cases under clause 25. For this reason, as well as others, he will usually wish the quantity surveyor to determine the amount, as the clause permits. Because the contractor's written application is a condition precedent to meeting a claim of this type, the quantity surveyor cannot deal with it for interim or final payment under clause 26.5 until the contractor has applied and the architect has referred it on to the quantity surveyor.

The procedure under the clause for initiating a claim is rather similar to that for obtaining an interim extension of time and the two matters may be pursued together when the clause is common, as clause 26.3 infers. The subject of the whole of clause 26 is one of some importance and presents difficulty on a practical level. In particular the persons concerned should ensure that adequate working arrangements are set up under this part of the clause to deal with the resulting records, negotiations and settlement.

26.2 LIST OF MATTERS

Seven 'matters' referred to in clause 26.1 are listed. They are a selection of the 'Relevant Events' in clause 25.4 under which heading they are discussed. They are shown in outline in Figure 9 on page 60, but in some cases correspond to parts only of the paragraphs of that clause:

26.2.1 Not having received in due time necessary instruction, drawings.

26.2.2 Opening up for inspection or testing — depending on liability.

26.2.3 Discrepancies or divergences — here, the mere existence of one of these is a possible ground of claim, whereas in clause 25.4 it is only the architect's instructions regarding them that give rise to extension of time. This is a fair, if fine, distinction since the contractor may face disturbance of progress by virtue of having already acted on incorrect documents and having to put right the consequences.

26.2.4 Execution of work by the employer or by those engaged by him, or supply of materials by the employer.

26.2.5 Postponement — not involving physical change.

26.2.6 Failure of the employer to give ingress to or egress from the site — it may not always be easy to distinguish this from some change introduced under clause 13.1.2.1 and so valued as a variation under that clause. There the change is signalled by an architect's instruction and affects something imposed on the contractor; under clause 26.2.6 the employer has lapsed in providing a positive facility to the contractor. Here again the subject may be some matter not given in the contract bills.

26.2.7 This would cover only the effect of the execution of work under the architect's instructions on the programme: all costs of performing the work itself, including any working piecemeal or out of sequence, should be accounted for in the measured prices of the work under clause 13.5.1 or of other affected work under clause 13.5.5. In practice this distinction is not always easy to maintain.

While clause 25.4 covers extension of time due to antiquities, the aspect of loss and expense is treated under clause 34 along with the main question of antiquities.

26.3 — RELEVANCE OF CERTAIN EXTENSIONS OF COMPLETION DATE

As already noted, loss and expense is usually bound up with extension of time. Extra time may mitigate the disruption by allowing steadier working, but it may also be linked to additional supervision, standing time and other unproductive costs. The architect is required here to state to the contractor the extensions already granted in respect of particular relevant events. While under clauses 25.2 or 25.3 he will give a total extension and identify which events he has taken into account, he is not required to analyse the extension. This becomes important when dealing with a claim, since other relevant events will not attract payments, but it needs care as the two categories of event are often difficult to separate.

The cross-reference to parts of clause 25.4 give the same list as that for matters under clause 26.2, but in a different order. In practice the confusion of events will often necessitate an analysis of the whole pattern of extension of time to enable a proper assessment of loss and expense to be made.

26.4 — NOMINATED   SUB-CONTRACTORS — MATTERS   MATERIALLY   AFFECTING REGULAR PROGRESS OF THE SUB-CONTRACT WORKS — DIRECT LOSS AND/OR EXPENSE

26.4.1 Sub-contract clause 13.1 contains provisions corresponding to those in the present clause in its various parts and with the causes of loss and expense relating to disturbance of both the contractor's and the nominated sub-contractor's work. This clause links in these provisions by requiring the contractor to pass a nominated sub-contractor's application on to the architect, and then requiring the architect or the quantity surveyor to ascertain any amount for loss and expense. The sub-contract investigations and negotiations are to be conducted through the contractor and in most cases the claim will be presented as an integral part of the contractor's own documentation. While extension of time for a sub-contractor usually results in an extension of time for the contractor, it is quite possible that disturbance of the sub-contractor's work will be self-contained and not affect the contractor.

26.4.2 Although there are no sub-contract provisions corresponding to clause 26.3 here, this clause does produce an equivalent provision by requiring the architect to notify both contractor and sub-contractor of any revision to the sub-contract period or periods dependent on particular matters. These are the same matters as in the present clause 26.3, if references to the sub-contract are corrected.

26.5 — AMOUNTS ASCERTAINED — ADDED TO CONTRACT SUM

Clause 3 provides that additions to the contract sum may be taken into interim payments 'as soon as . . . ascertained in whole or part', so that amounts under the present clause in general may be included. Not only this, but clause 26.1 refers to an 'amount . . . which has been or is being incurred', so that inclusion relates to both progressive incurring and progressive calculation. In practice this allows for the inclusion of provisional amounts prior to final calculation.

26.6 — RESERVATION OF RIGHTS AND REMEDIES OF CONTRACTOR

Having said all that it does, the clause ends by reaffirming the right of the contractor to further action by way of arbitration or in the courts. It thus provides machinery for less formal settlement and for payment, but without prejudicing the contractor's wider position through using this machinery. The other rights and remedies will not be restricted by, for instance, the terms of this clause and may therefore be resorted to for the satisfaction of wider issues, or where the contractor is dissatisfied with the settlement offered by the architect or the quantity surveyor.

Clause 27 — Determination by employer

The action contemplated by clause 27, under which the employer can 'determine', and by clause 28, where it is the contractor who determines, is referred to several times as determining 'the employment of the Contractor under this Contract'. This is to be distinguished from 'determining the Contract', when the ending of the contract itself ends all its machinery and the aggrieved party must proceed against the other for breach.

The two clauses on determination in these present conditions set out the procedures to be followed after determination of employment and the rights and liabilities of the two parties until the final settlement. These two clauses therefore determine only the employment of the contractor while leaving the contract itself in being, and they thus maintain the clauses themselves in operation — and also others which will still be required for final settlement and, if necessary arbitration. Except in clause 27.2 there is no mention of reversing the procedure and reinstating the contractor's employment. In the event of a reconciliation the parties would need to make their own arrangements and agree terms to suit.

27.1 — DEFAULT BY CONTRACTOR

The procedure for determining in each of the cases given requires only two registered or recorded letters. The basic timetable is as follows: (i) The architect writes specifying the default; (ii) A waiting period of 14 days is allowed for the contractor to cease his default and (iii) if he does not, then the employer may determine within a further 10 days.

It would appear that the employer may determine within his 10-day period even if the contractor ceases his default immediately after the 14-day waiting period. If the employer does not act within his period he will apparently have lost his right to determine, if the contractor has resumed work. If however the contractor continues in default beyond the 14 days, it would then seem reasonable for the 10 days not to run until and if the contractor ceases default and for the employer to be able to determine at any time during the extended period of default or for 10 days after. This is illustrated in Case 1 of Figure 11.

Another element is woven into the basic timetable and is shown in Case 2 of the same figure. It would be possible for the contractor, if negligent or unscrupulous, to cease default within the 14 days and then to resume it later. If the architect had to serve a fresh notice on the contractor and initiate the timetable again, it would be possible for the contractor to be continually going into default and coming out again and yet for the employer to be unable to determine. It is therefore provided that if the contractor repeats a default for which he has already received an architect's notice, the employer may determine within the 10 days and without any waiting period to see whether the contractor is going to continue in default. For this quite severe procedure to take effect the default must be a repetition of the original default in the sense of falling within the same category, out of the four listed categories, as did the original default. A default in another of the four categories would require a fresh procedure to take place.

It is possible to see that either party could abuse this clause by playing close to its letter and there are therefore two safeguards given. One, for the employer's benefit, is that determination is 'without prejudice to any other rights and remedies', a phrase commented on under clause 26.6. The other, for the contractor's protection, is that determination shall not be brought about 'unreasonably or vexatiously', that is on grounds of a quite minor but strict default or perhaps by a too harsh operation of the timetable in a particular case. The contractor may thus give notice of arbitration and, if the determination still proceeds, arbitration would ensue at once under article 5.2

Four ways of defaulting are given, any of which would be a breach of contract in any case:

27.1.1 'Wholly suspends' represents a complete withdrawal of manpower from the site; the presence of equipment alone will not be a sufficient defence since nothing is being carried out.

27.1.2 'Fails to proceed regularly and diligently' represents a fitful approach and falling behind the programme without cause; it will put the contractor in breach of clause 23.1.

27.1.3 Refusal or wilful neglect in removing defective work or the like must be such as to have serious effect. A less drastic remedy here is to employ other persons under clause 4.1.2 to carry out the removal in question. Where it is impracticable for such persons to carry out the work while the contractor is in possession, owing to its extent or serious nature, then the alternative of determination is available here.

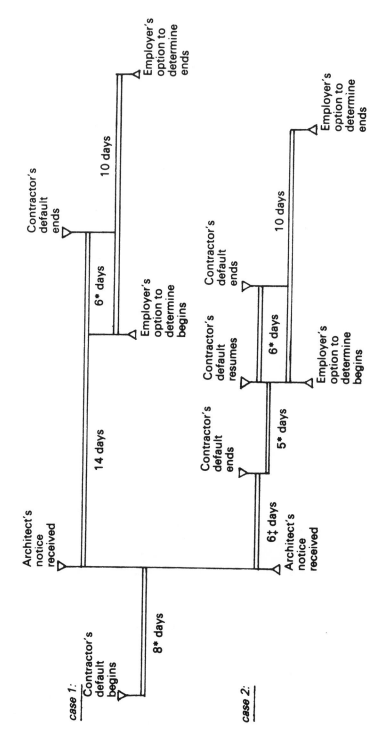

Figure 11: **Timetable for determination procedure under clause 27.1 of JCT main form**

Two of many variant cases are shown — a break in default in case 2 leads to earlier determination. Periods marked * could be of any duration, shorter or longer. The period marked ‡ is too short for the employer to act during its currency.

27.1.4 Assignment or sub-letting in themselves would not be causes for determining at common law. They are regulated under clause 19 and are therefore able to be brought within the scope of this present clause.

27.2 — CONTRACTOR BECOMES BANKRUPT ETC

The provisions of bankruptcy and company law are beyond the scope of this discussion. However, there is some doubt as to whether the present clause would be valid if tested in the courts. Where there is a receiver or a manager on behalf of debenture holders it is likely that the clause will be upheld. Where there is actual insolvency it would seem that the basic principle of the law would prevail, which is that the trustee or liquidator could choose whether or not to disclaim the contract in the interests of creditors as a whole. The weakness of the clause in principle is that it endeavours to put one particular creditor, the employer, in an advantageous position compared with the rest.

This clause differs from clause 27.1 by making determination automatic as soon as bankruptcy or the like actually takes place. The aim of this is to seek to avoid the trustee or other person having any period in which to elect to carry on with the works when it would be better for the employer to employ another contractor. It is still desirable, however, to write to the trustee, as soon as he is known, and obtain confirmation that he accepts determination; otherwise the legal doubt mentioned will remain.

The clause also mentions the possibility of an agreed reinstatement of the contractor's employment. This would be possible in any case and the clause gives no terms or procedure. Whether it is wise to reinstate the contractor will depend on the stage of the works, among other things. Fairly early in the programme it may be difficult for the contractor to carry on with hope of finishing and the employer may wish to change; the contractor will have less retention money at stake and more work to do to release it, and may thus be willing to go. At a later stage these considerations will work in the opposite direction and continuance may be better for both parties, although obviously the employer then has more retention money available and may wish to make the change. If the contractor's employment is reinstated, however, there is always the risk to the employer that the trustee or the like may exercise his continuing right to disclaim later on, if and when the financial state is more advantageous to the creditors as a whole.

This is not a very satisfactory position, but then determination never is. The clause has its snags, but will often be accepted in practice as the basis for settlement.

27.3 — (NOT USED)

This clause appears only in the local authorities edition of the contract, with the heading of 'Corruption'. It is discussed in Chapter 21.

27.4 — DETERMINATION OF EMPLOYMENT OF CONTRACTOR — RIGHTS AND DUTIES
OF EMPLOYER AND CONTRACTOR

Whatever the cause of determination, the same procedures are given for finishing the works and coming to a settlement. Their effectiveness will be affected by the considerations mentioned under clause 27.2 where this is relevant. They do not apply if the contractor's employment is reinstated.

27.4.1 *Employment of others.* This is the clear sequel to the preceding steps. No restriction is placed on the employer as to the type of contract or contracts that he may enter into to secure completion. Much will depend on how piecemeal the balance of the works is; the employer does not need the approval of the contractor or of any trustee to his commercial dealings, but he will be expected to use such economy as is consistent with progress. Subject to the adequacy of the contractor's title, where the cases listed under 'Insolvency of contractor and title to goods' are relevant, whatever lies on the site may be used for the works and whatever else is needed may be purchased. In the case of materials and goods, some of these will have become the employer's property under clause 16.1; there is here no restriction to these or to the contractor's property and the materials and goods of sub-contractors will also be included. Whatever is used will come into the final reckoning under clause 27.4.4. In the case of plant and the like, the employer has no right of ownership under these conditions, but only a right of free use; he will have to account for these items under clause 27.4.3. He will not be able to retain hired items free of charge, although he may keep them on under clause 27.4.2 if the hirers so agree.

27.4.2 *Suppliers and sub-contractors.* The scope is not restricted to nominated firms only but is perfectly general. The first main provision under clause 27.4.2.1 is that in any case where the contractor remains in active business, the employer has an option within 14 days of determination to ask for an assignment of agreements. This is of value where continuity is required. Normally the employer will wish to reassign to the incoming contractor and there will therefore have to be a subsidiary provision in the assignment for the supplier or sub-contractor to object to a further assignment to the as yet unknown contractor. Clause 19.4 and sub-contract clause 31.1 are in conflict with this provision by giving a subsidiary determination with no provision for assignment of the sub-contract and reinstatement of employment, and should be compared here. The same problem does not arise under clause 36.4.5.

The second main provision under clause 27.4.2.2 is that the employer may pay such firms any monies not already paid by the contractor, except where there has been insolvency. It is general in regard to the timing of work in relation to the determination. This covers the practical situations where firms go on working past determination due to uncertainty about what has happened to the contractor. The subsidiary provision here is that the option conferred is over and above any duty or option about direct payments under clause 35.13.5 that may already have been made to nominated sub-contractors in particular.

It is made clear that all direct payments may be charged to the contractor in the final reckoning. The value of this to the employer will be quite adequate where there is a determination under clause 27.1 and the contractor is still solvent at settlement. It will be reduced in all other cases according to what settlement the contractor or his representative is able to offer, except in the unlikely case of the employer owing money to the contractor. The making of direct payments for any or all outstanding amounts under this clause is entirely at the employer's option. Expediency in initially securing the goodwill of the firms will probably be balanced against the financial outcome at the end of the day.

27.4.3 *Removal of plant and the like.* This is to take place 'within a reasonable time' of the architect's written requirement; the wording permits more than one such requirement to be served, as plant becomes progressively superfluous. The reference to removal of plant hired by the contractor would cover cases where the latter was responsible for removal under his hire agreement and the hirer has agreed to the plant remaining on site under an assignment: it does not and could not imply any right for the employer to retain the hired plant without the hirer's agreement.

If the contractor removes items when required, then the employer will be responsible for any loss or damage outside the category of fair wear and tear. If the contractor fails to carry out removal, the clause relieves the employer of this responsibility. It does however leave the employer liable to pass the whole of the net results of sales over to the contractor, by the words 'holding . . . to the credit of the Contractor'. This is in keeping with the fact that ownership of plant and the like at no time passes to the employer and its value cannot be set directly against any debt of the contractor to the employer under clause 27.4.4. Where the contractor is proved insolvent this could mean a substantial sum to be paid over in its entirety and, in effect, only recovered in part in the final settlement, as shown in Figure 12. This could be galling to the employer, but is unavoidable under this clause.

27.4.4 *Final settlement.* It is provided that this shall take account of three items on the employer's side:

(i) *The employer's 'direct loss and/or damage' due to the determination.* A most likely head of claim here would be delay in completion of the works; a basis similar to that of liquidated damages would probably be suitable, although clause 24 as such would be suspended by the determination, since clause 24 rests on clause 25.

(ii) *Expenses properly incurred by the employer.* These would include retention monies held on nominated sub-contractors before determination, temporary measures following determination, and the amount paid for work and materials to achieve completion. These latter would in turn include additional professional fees and insurances. These expenses could only be called in question if it could be shown that the employer had proceeded with gross lack of commercial reasonableness.

(iii) *Monies paid to the contractor before the date of determination.* This is the total of all interim certificates actually met by the employer. It is not

Position as it should have been

Contract sum	£100,000
Value of variations, etc (net additions)	£2,000
Hypothetical final account	£102,000

Position at determination, and payments eventually made

Value of work executed		£40,000
Interim certificates	£38,000	
Less five per cent retention	1,900	
	36,100	
Nominated sub-contractors paid before determination (including retention)	1,000	
Nominated sub-contractors paid after determination (including retention) and already in the £38,000 above	1,600	
Payment of retention on nominated sub-contracts actually paid by contractor and already in the £1,900 above:		
Five per cent on £12,000	600	
		£39,300
*Margin on work up to determination		£700

Position at final settlement

Paid at or about determination	£30,300
Paid for completion contract	69,000
Employer's loss and expense	5,000
	£113,300
Less hypothetical final account	102,000
Net indebtedness of contractor	£11,300

If the contractor is still solvent this debt will be met in full. If he is insolvent and only able to pay his creditors, say fifty per cent, then the position could be as follows:

Payment due to employer (50 per cent of £11,300)		£5,650
Payment due to contractor for plant sales (not in figures above)†		
	Gross realised	£1,400
	Less expenses	200
		1,200
Payment made by contractor		£4,450

*The margin of £700 is 'absorbed' in the final settlement and in effect is kept by the employer.

†The full benefit of plant sales goes to the contractor; the employer cannot retain the £1,200 nor even deduct it from the £11,300 and thus benefit by fifty per cent of £1,200.

Figure 12: **Example of financial results of a contract determined under clause 27 of JCT main form**

required that the exact value of work before determination shall be calculated. The 'monies paid' may include payments in respect of nominated sub-contractors which the contractor has failed to pass on and which the employer may or may not subsequently have paid direct.

These three items are to be set against 'the total amount which would have been payable on due completion', that is to say against a hypothetical final account prepared on the basis of the contractor's own prices or other terms throughout. The resultant difference is to be a debt payable by the one party to the other as appropriate, after the issue of a certificate.

In the nature of the items involved, the final settlement can hardly be reached until completion of the works. The clause specifically states that until such completion and the 'verification within a reasonable time of the accounts' the contractor is not entitled to any further payment, which is only reasonable in the circumstances. Possibly even the last interim certificate may not have been honoured at determination and it will lapse at that date and should therefore not be paid at any time. But equally the payment of the debt as between the parties is conditional on settlement and this could place a heavy burden of additional bridging finance on the employer in some cases.

There is the not unlikely possibility that the contractor, while solvent at determination, may become insolvent later and before final settlement. In such a case the employer may find that certain recovery from the contractor has slid away into the mists of receivership or the like and in the main will never reappear. The clause also presupposes that the employer will in fact wish to complete the works and not abandon them. However, under clause 27.1 at any rate, the employer may invoke the clause 'without prejudice to any other rights or remedies' and thus may be able to repudiate the contract and sue accordingly. Clause 27.2 is naturally silent on the point and leaves the employer at some disadvantage.

To amplify the discussion, a financial example is given in Figure 12. The figures are fictitious, but not inconceivable, and show incidentally that the employer may be outstanding for quite a proportion of his original commitment, at least until settlement and perhaps even thereafter in a case of insolvency.

Clause 28 — Determination by contractor

28.1 — ACTS ETC GIVING GROUND FOR DETERMINATION OF EMPLOYMENT BY CONTRACTOR

This clause brings together all the causes for determination by the contractor. Insolvency in this case does not warrant separate procedures and is included here, but there are also included several causes which are in no way the fault of the employer. The same two safeguards apply as discussed under clause 27.1 and they are enshrined in the same words 'without prejudice to any other rights and remedies' and 'shall not be given unreasonably or vexatiously'. The roles of the two parties are reversed in the present clause, and the safeguards therefore operate in reverse also. It may be observed that several provisions of this present clause are more severe on the employer than the corresponding provisions of clause 27 are on the contractor. The discussion on determining the employment of the contractor under that clause is also relevant here.

The procedure for determination in all the cases below is simply that the contractor may 'forthwith' determine his own employment. In the case of clauses 28.1.1 and 28.1.3 'forthwith' operates at the end of a waiting period, but only under the former clause need the contractor indicate that he is intending to determine. All of which is quite harsh.

28.1.1 *The employer does not pay on any certificate.* This clause operates after 14 days or more of default, followed by a seven-day warning period. The reference is to 'the amount properly due to the Contractor on any certificate'. Here 'properly' is included to take account of clause 30.1.1.2 entitling the employer to make deductions from 'the amount stated as due' by the architect under clause 30.2. It would be clearer and avoid any attempt to determine solely when such deductions have been made, if the further words 'subject to any deductions authorised by the Conditions' were added after the words 'any certificate' as is done in clause 30.8 to give complete clarity. If the employer wishes to make deductions for other reasons than those expressly provided in the contract, then he cannot safely make them from a certificate, but must initially pay and then recover, if need be, at arbitration or the like.

The payment of any amount in respect of value added tax alongside contract payments is due under the VAT Agreement (provided for in clause 15) at the same time as the corresponding interim certificate is honoured. It is an amount calculated by the employer on the basis of the contractor's provisional assessment and it is not therefore 'due . . . on any certificate'. On this basis it perhaps strictly need not be mentioned as excluded from the scope of default under the present clause, but the mention avoids any doubt. It is in any case subject to objection by the employer under the VAT Agreement clause 1.2.2 and delay in paying it could not be intended to lead to default.

28.1.2 *The employer interferes with or obstructs the issue of a certificate.* The employer and the architect will perforce be in direct association in many ways throughout the progress of the works; at no point must this operate to influence the impartiality of the architect and this may be a fine point of distinction. It is the action of the employer only that is here envisaged and must be demonstrated, not the inefficiency or even obstructiveness of one of his professional advisers. The case of *R. B. Burden Ltd* v. *Swansea Corporation* bears on this whole matter, although decided on an earlier form of this clause. The discussion under clause 30.1 also relates to the present clause.

28.1.3 *The carrying out of the uncompleted works is suspended.* This may come into play for a number of causes which are named in clause 25.4 as 'Relevant Events' and under which they are discussed individually. Some of them also occur as 'matters' in clause 26.2. A comparison of their broad scope is made in Figure 9. Determination is the most drastic remedy provided for them and, unlike the other remedies, can only be implemented after a 'continuous period' of delay and where 'the whole or substantially the whole of the uncompleted Works' is suspended. The period of delay is to be inserted in the appendix, but in default of any insertion it is provided in the appendix that it will be one month, with one exception. This period may well be considered too short in some cases.

Where less than substantially the whole is suspended, the contractor must continue with those parts of the works that are unaffected, otherwise he will be in breach of clause 23.1 that he shall 'diligently proceed'. In such a case he cannot acquire a right to determine, unless he first works himself to a halt. Indeed if he does not proceed he may much sooner provide cause for the employer to determine under clauses 27.1.1 or 27.1.2.

Only four of the causes of suspension call for particular comment here. One is clause 28.1.3.2 with its reference to the clause 22 perils, which are events requiring a delay of three months according to the appendix, unless some other period is stated. Clearly one month would be too short here and three is more balanced. Some of the causes may arise out of the contractor's negligence and this is excluded accordingly, although for some odd reason his default is not excluded as it is in clause 28.1.3.4. (Neither negligence nor default is excluded in the comparable clauses 25.4.3 and 25.4.5 regarding extension of time.) The reference to clause 22 perils introduces whichever of the variants of clause 22 applies. If the contractor determines when clause 22A applies, the insurance monies would pass to the employer by virtue of the joint cover of the policy. Clause 22B needs no comment. Clause 22C also contains its own provisions for determination to meet its particular circumstances of frustration and scale of work, rather than delay which is in view here. It may thus come into operation distinctly earlier than the present clause.

The second cause that calls for special comment is in clause 28.1.3.3, where 'civil commotion' is mentioned alone and its direct effect is not qualified as in clause 25.4.4. It is already covered by clause 28.1.3.2 so far as physical damage to the works is concerned but not otherwise.

The third such cause is in clause 28.1.3.4, where negligence and default of the contractor may lead to action by the architect and here both are therefore excluded. Clauses 28.1.3.4 to 28.1.3.7 will all have a clear effect in deterring the employer of the architect from undue dilatoriness or delay. Even where the contractor is at fault under clause 28.1.3.4 the architect should act with reasonable promptitude.

The fourth cause to mention is 'delay in the execution of work' not part of the contract under clause 28.1.3.6. This is different from simply performing work as in clause 25.4.8.1, where the problem is mentioned of the distinction between work under clause 29.1 given in the contract bills and that, under clause 29.2, not so given. This ceases to be a problem here by virtue of the way that delay is defined. There may be delay due to the introduction of unexpected work, but the contractor should secure agreement about this before consenting to it happening. If it were likely to lead to prolonged suspension, he might be able to withhold his consent.

28.1.4 *The Employer becomes bankrupt (or the like).* There is no provision for automatic determination here as there is when the contractor becomes bankrupt, since the contractor will obviously stop in his own interest. Under clause 27.2 he could conceivably try to carry on in some circumstances. The same legal doubt hangs over this clause as over clause 27.2, although the contractor should be in the position here to obtain security of payment before proceeding. If the employer does default in payment, the contractor may then determine under clause 28.1.1.

28.2 — DETERMINATION OF EMPLOYMENT BY CONTRACTOR — RIGHTS AND DUTIES OF EMPLOYER AND CONTRACTOR

This clause governs a number of particulars, but states that what is provided is without prejudice to two overriding considerations, the first being 'the accrued rights or remedies of either party', which may exist as contraclaims to modify the amounts otherwise payable under clause 28.2.2. These may be due to statutory fees, liquidated damages, insurance premiums, claim settlements, direct payments to nominated sub-contractors or quite a number of other causes provided throughout the conditions. For instances see *Lintest Builders Ltd* v. *Roberts.* The second consideration covers matters of injury and indemnity arising under clause 20 and it is provided that the effect of that clause is extended to cover such of the contractor's activities on site as he is still required to carry out after determination. In this case the term 'without prejudice' is uncertain in meaning. It clearly covers, as with the rights and remedies, the survival of whatever liabilities may have arisen during the truncated carrying out of the works. Any action or the like will still be pursued. The term does not appear able to take the weight of extending liability on the part of both parties over into the period following determination. At determination, the contractor stops 'carrying out the Works' as clause 20 describes it and so his indemnity stops, so that in turn there is nothing left to which the present clause may stand 'without prejudice'. Clause 28.2.1 treats clause 20 as a thing of the past and gives its own definition of liability, which it seems must stand, in view of the inapplicability of the 'without prejudice'.

The respective rights and liabilities of the parties are broadly that the contractor is to clear the site and that the employer is to pay the contractor any outstanding amounts for the works and unfixed goods and materials and also the cost of removal and any loss incurred through determination. Here, as distinct from clause 27.4.4, there is no requirement for payment to depend on the architect's certificate, although both he and the quantity surveyor would be deeply involved in reaching an agreement, which would in part at least be related to the basis in the contract bills.

28.2.1 The contractor's right of removal of all that is his is here made an obligation as well, so that the employer may reassume possession of the site free of all temporary items and materials mentioned. Many of these might be of great use to the employer if he is going to complete the works, but unless he makes an attractive enough offer to the contractor outside the contract, they will go. Payment for this removal follows under clause 28.2.2.5.

The contractor is to act expeditiously, but not as a matter of urgency; he must not penalise the employer though by delay. In substitution for the clause 20 indemnity the present clause gives a simple contractual obligation to exercise care and the employer could proceed against him if, and only if, he were negligent. This is more limited than an indemnity, as the discussion under clause 20 indicates.

The contractor is to remove 'all his . . . materials and goods'. For materials and goods 'his' must reasonably be interpreted as applying to those items which the contractor owns, or at least to which his title is no worse than that of the employer. If the employer has paid the contractor for them, the employer will prima facie have a better title but may not have an adequate one, as mentioned under clause 16. Removal is made subject to clause 28.2.2.4 under which the employer purchases items, so that they are 'his' rather than the contractor's. Once the employer has paid the contractor he cannot remove; they are no longer his items. But until the employer has paid, the contractor may remove what is 'his' even if the employer is bound to pay for them in due course, punitive though having to pay for such action might be considered to be. To avoid this expense the employer needs to pay quickly, but then may not be acquiring an adequate title until the contractor in turn pays. The risk here is significant only if there is an immediate likelihood of the contractor becoming insolvent.

28.2.2 The contractor is to be paid for work carried out under clauses 28.2.2.1 and 28.2.2.2 as in an interim certificate. This will rely on measured rates from the contract bills and rates derived from these. In the case of partially completed work this will produce rates which would not occur in the normal final account. However in this situation there will of course be a final and therefore firm calculation of all the sums concerned, rather than an approximation. While clause 30.1 is the authority given here, it in turn depends on clause 30.2 which sets out in full the categories to be taken into the reckoning. There would be an overlap with the subsequent elements, but this is excluded by the qualifications at the end of the two clauses.

Clause 28.2.2.3 refers to loss and expense other than that due to the determination itself and therefore caused earlier, as clauses 26 and 34.3. Clause 28.2.2.6 covers the loss and expense due to determination and, curiously enough, specifically mentions losses caused to nominated sub-contractors. In the rest of the clause these persons are inferred, as they often are throughout the conditions, so that the addition here appears unnecessary. Loss and expense under both clauses carries the same broad meaning as in clause 26, and in the case of that due to the determination itself, it extends to include the loss of profit on work not carried out because of the determination (see *Wright Ltd* v. *P.H.T. Holdings Ltd*).

The cost of materials or goods covered under clause 28.2.2.4 includes 'those for which the Contractor is legally bound to pay'. This will often include items which have not been delivered at the date of determination. If there may be doubt over the adequacy of the title which the contractor can pass to the employer for all items which are on or off the site, the employer should not himself pay for these items until he is assured of the contractor's title, by whatever documentary proof may be necessary. This is subject to the comments under clause 28.2. By the time settlement is achieved this will usually be a matter of history. The main point of the 'legally bound' provision in most cases is that it draws a line up to which the employer must pay. Whatever else may be agreed in the interests of expediency cannot be enforced by law.

The cost of removal under clause 28.2.1 is the reasonable expense of dismantling the site organisation. It will include some costs which will have been allowed in the preliminaries of the contract bills for ultimate removal, but the 'total value of work completed' will have been calculated under clause 28.2.2.1 on the basis of what has been done prior to determination only, and this will not in the main cover any removal.

28.2.3 In keeping with the absence of any certificate as such, it is here provided that the employer himself shall notify the contractor and each nominated sub-contractor of any amounts due to each such firm as a result of the determination settlement. At this stage there is no attempt to see that payments are made, or indeed that any payments outstanding at determination have been made. Clause 35, like so much else, is cut off by determination.

CHAPTER 8

Injury during progress of works

Clause 20 — Injury to persons and property and employer's indemnity
Clause 21 — Insurance against injury to persons and property
Clause 22 — Insurance of the works against clause 22 perils

Clause 20 — Injury to persons and property and employer's indemnity

The broad pattern of the contract with regard to injury is firstly to provide that the contractor will indemnify the employer in respect of a wide range of contingencies arising out of the progress of the works. Indemnity here carries its normal meaning of the protection which one party to an agreement affords to the other against some category of loss or against the claims of a third party. As such, the indemnity here is not only wide in scope, but is also unlimited in the potential liability of the one party to the other within that scope. The effectiveness of the protection offered will therefore depend on the substance of the contractor to meet the liability. The contractor may be driven into insolvency to meet his liability to indemnify, but this will be cold comfort to the employer if the result is quite inadequate to meet his loss or afford him protection.

As a background to this indemnity, it must also be borne in mind that a plaintiff can often move against either party or against both as joint tortfeasors. The present clause aims to ward off the effects of such action from the employer and on to the contractor in the class of matters covered. If however the indemnity is exhausted by the insolvency of the contractor, then the plaintiff may carry on against the employer for the remainder of his claim.

Largely because the substance of the contractor may be inadequate to meet his responsibility to indemnify, the contract provides for insurances to be effected under clauses 21.1 and 22A in respect of some matters of indemnity. These insurances often provide a greater depth of financial protection than the indemnities which they support, but in most cases are cast more narrowly in scope. While the insurances are intended to reinforce the indemnities, they in no way take the place of the indemnities. Thus, should an insurance fail for any reason the indemnity under the contract will still have to stand alone to meet the situation or to carry on where the insurance leaves off. Diagram (a) of Figure 13 illustrates the broad position.

The interaction of indemnity, negligence and insurance may be complex, as illustrated by cases under 'Injury to persons, property and indemnities'. There

(a) Contractor's overall responsibility

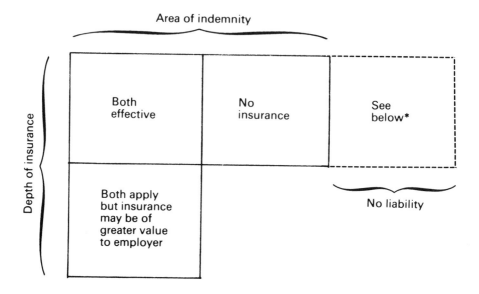

(b) Indemnity afforded by contractor and employer to one another

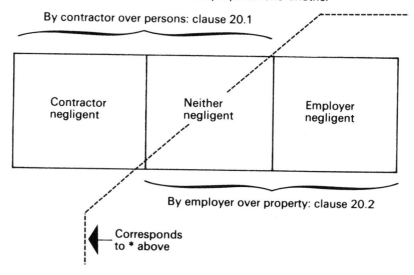

Figure 13: **Diagrammatic representations of indemnity and insurance under JCT main form**

is also the interaction of the various insurances under the various clauses mentioned in this chapter and this is a good reason for obtaining cover with one insurer so far as possible.

There are some contingencies with regard to which indemnity is not called for, but there is a responsibility under the contract for one party or the other to insure against risks. These are covered by clauses 21.2, 22B and 22C, and are also shown in Figure 13. There are also some contingencies with regard to which neither indemnity nor insurance is required, these being covered by clause 21.3.

20.1 — LIABILITY OF CONTRACTOR — PERSONAL INJURY — INDEMNITY TO EMPLOYER

The contractor here indemnifies the employer in respect of personal injury or death of any persons for which claims may arise in a number of ways. The indemnity is limited in two ways, the first being a natural limitation to those persons who would be able to sustain a claim at all; thus in most cases a trespasser would be unable to claim. The matter is limited secondly to those cases where the employer is not responsible by his own act or neglect or by that of any persons for whom he is responsible; this latter term includes persons employed by the employer under clause 29 and would presumably cover the architect, the quantity surveyor and any consultants. If the contractor wishes to avoid liability under this clause, then effectively the onus of proof is upon him, as the comparison at the end of the comments on clause 20.2 shows.

While the clause secures protection for the employer by way of indemnity in those cases where responsibility can be shown to rest with the contractor, it is quite silent where the opposite situation applies. The employer is not bound to indemnify the contractor against claims brought against the latter as a joint tortfeasor. The contractor would probably have to meet the claim and seek contribution from the employer under the Law Reform (Married Women and Tortfeasors) Act 1935.

20.2 — LIABILITY OF CONTRACTOR — INJURY TO PROPERTY — INDEMNITY TO EMPLOYER

The range of risks embraced in this clause is quite general and the range is wide enough to cover the works themselves under the term 'any property real or personal'. The contractor is already prima facie bound to carry out and complete the works under clause 2.1 and in so doing to remedy any damage, so there is a degree of overlap here, so far as the indemnity provided extends. Where clause 22A is used, and this is the most commonly employed alternative for insurance of the works under this edition of the conditions, there is joint insurance by the employer and the contractor and in consequence a further overlap, which is considered under that clause. It may also be that the present clause may prevail against clause 25.4.3 in circumstances which are considered there, when clause 22A is used. Where either clause 22B or 22C is used, the risk and insurance of the contingencies listed is with the employer alone and to that extent damage to the works, and any resultant delay, is excluded from the present clause. However, the range of risks is not unlimited in these cases and the contractor is still bound to indemnify the employer regarding the works in other respects. Some limitations to the range of risks over the works and other property, for which indemnity is required, is introduced by clause 21.3.

The indemnity provided for the employer here is narrower than that under the preceding sub-clause in that it covers only those cases where there is negligence, omission or default of the contractor or of the classes of persons for whom he is responsible. There is a whole area of responsibility that lies between these cases and those mentioned in the parallel provisions of clause 20.1 as involving act or neglect of the employer. In this area will lie those cases where one or both parties must take responsibility in law for what flows from his/their actions however blamelessly these have been performed. Some of these cases are to be covered by insurance under clause 21.1. They leave, so far as the present clause is concerned, a gap in the protection afforded the employer that does not exist in clause 20.1. This may or may not be considered a fair principle, but the employer should be advised of it so that he may seek any cover that he thinks appropriate.

The effect of the present clause is to place the onus of proof of the contractor's negligence on the employer if he wishes to avoid liability to a third party. This is the reverse of the position under clause 20.1 and arises from the way in which the boundary is defined. The two definitions may be compared as follows:

In clause 20.1 all liability is the contractor's, except where there is 'any act or neglect of the Employer' or certain other persons. The contractor must therefore prove the employer's liability.

In clause 20.2 liability is the contractor's only where there is 'any negligence, omission or default' by him or certain other persons. The employer must therefore prove the contractor's liability.

The scope of the two is illustrated in Diagram (b) of Figure 13. It may be noted that the two definitions are not precisely the same and they may be compared with the further versions in clauses 28.1.3.2 and 28.1.3.4. In general any event or non-event may be expected to be covered by any of the versions, but there may be the breeding ground for further legal ingenuity here.

Clause 21 — Insurance against injury to persons and property

As discussed in introducing clause 20, the pattern of the contract is to require insurance for certain of the matters of indemnity and thus to provide protection for the contractor and, indirectly, for the employer against the contractor's inability to satisfy the indemnity completely. The present clause deals with all such matters under clause 21.1, other than the works themselves which fall under clause 22A when that clause is used and the contractor is liable for the risks. In clause 21.2, it goes further and deals with certain third party claims which are not the subject of indemnity under clause 20.

21.1 — INSURANCE — PERSONAL INJURY OR DEATH — INJURY OR DAMAGE TO PROPERTY

21.1.1 The clause ensures by its opening words that the contractor's indemnity is in no way diminished in principle. It then requires not only the contractor but also his sub-contractors of all kinds to maintain insurances to support the two categories of indemnity in clause 20 protecting the sub-contractors themselves and also extending the protection of the employer and the contractor down the line of responsibility. For instance sub-contract clause 7 requires nominated sub-contractors to be so insured. Without insurance the collapse of a sub-contractor under claim could have serious effects.

The subject matter of the insurance is set out in the same terminology as in clause 20 and the comments under that clause, as to both scope and exclusions, apply equally here. In the case of responsibility to employees and the like, clause 21.1.1.2 simply reminds the contractor of the statutory requirements that he and his sub-contractors must in any case meet. In the case of other responsibilities over both persons and property, the minimum amount of insurance cover is to be given in the appendix. This amount is a matter over which the employer must seek careful advice, and regarding which the contractor may well wish to maintain his third party policies at a higher level in any case. In each of these cases the contract bills will require the contractor to include his own sum for the costs incurred — which is different in principle from the procedure for clause 21.2.

21.1.2 The architect may require 'evidence' to assure the employer that the insurances exist and that they are up to date. The employer himself may also reasonably require sight of the policies, for details of coverage and also of receipts. Here, as distinct from clauses 21.2.2 and 22A.2, there is no requirement for the architect to approve the insurers.

21.1.3 If there is any lapse, the employer may act to remedy the position, since he has a strong interest in the insurance under this clause. The amount recoverable if the contractor defaults is the amount paid by the employer rather than some other amount that may have been inserted in the contract bills. The right to recoup is not limited to deductions from monies under the contract, but may also be by action for debt. Any deduction is more likely to arise early in the contract under this present clause and would then be adequately and most conveniently made by deduction from amounts due under interim certificates. This is subject to the possible problem arising under clause 28.1.1 and discussed there.

21.2 — INSURANCE — LIABILITY ETC OF EMPLOYER — PROVISIONAL SUM

This clause is concerned with a very limited range of liabilities as is noted below in more detail. Its broad aim is to provide for occasions where damage is caused to property, usually adjoining the works, by the carrying out of the works and when the contractor is working in a proper manner and without negligence. The case *Gold* v. *Patman and Fotheringham Ltd* is relevant here and the present clause exists to deal with the issues that it raised.

21.2.1 It comes into operation if and only if the contract bills provide a provisional sum or sums to cover the cost of the insurances in the contract sum and to define the extent of the cover to be provided. In turn, the architect will have to give instruction under clause 13.3 to set the procedure in motion. In itself the clause has the nature of a practice note, as part of it at one time was, by reminding the parties of certain risks and precautions to be taken, rather than establishing any contractual position. Even any provisional sum in the contract bills will serve as little more than a declaration of intention and as a means of ensuring that the contractor is obliged to effect an insurance under the contract. What will really count will be the terms of the policy entered into after the contract is signed, which may embody the terms of this clause, but in so doing will inevitably qualify them. The clause itself, by some of its limitations, recognises that it is edging into fields where insurance is not always obtainable at all, or if obtainable may be so heavily qualified or carry such a heavy premium as to be of little value. It is because of these uncertainties that the provisional sum approach is inevitable; the contractor is in no position to assess in advance the cost of insurance which in fact is very expensive and also difficult to obtain.

The direct reference of the clause is to 'damage to any property other than the Works'. As such it excludes injury to persons that may occur in the same incident; this is already covered under clauses 20.1 and 21.1.1.1. It is wide enough to cover property owned by the employer or otherwise. The causes of damage given would usually result in a structural failure, but arise where the contractor is carrying out his operations in an efficient and reasonable manner. Provided that in so doing, he is doing what is necessary to produce the finished result for which he has been engaged, the contractor will not be liable to indemnify the employer under clause 20.2, where he is liable only for his own negligence and the like. The effect of the insurance being in the joint names of the employer and the contractor is to prevent the insurance company proceeding against one of them, as it might if that one had not been included in the policy.

The giving of specific causes of damage excludes any wider unspecified matters that may also be the employer's responsibility. In addition, five specific exclusions are made and may be noted as follows:

(1) This emphasises the purpose of the clause and also excludes matters already covered by clause 20.2 and perhaps also by clause 21.1.1.1.

(2) These matters would lead to an action against the architect for professional negligence.

(3) This is a risk which no insurance company is likely to take on in advance. It may also arise while the work is still in progress and the parties will lose their insurance cover if they proceed in such circumstances.

(4) Clause 22C, like the present clause, has reference to property other than the works in the existing structures; 'unfixed materials and goods' are also distinguished from 'the Works' in the two clauses here mentioned. The present exclusion is needed to avoid an overlap of insurance for these liabilities.

(5) This is a common exclusion under insurance policies.

21.2.2 The procedure for effecting the insurance is that the architect is to approve the insurers and have custody of any policy and receipt. The latter is reasonable in that a single premium will probably apply for each policy. At the approval stage the architect is likely to be deeply involved in agreeing the precise risk or risks to be covered and the terms of cover.

21.2.3 As the insurance provisions are dealt with by the expenditure of a provisional sum, there appears to be no need for this clause requiring the amounts then to be 'added to the Contract Sum'. Clause 6.2.3, for instance, is drafted on a contrary assumption.

21.2.4 The employer again has a right to insure if the contractor defaults. In this case the simple omission of the original provisional sum in the final account will tidy up the financial position.

21.3 — EXCEPTED RISKS — NUCLEAR PERILS ETC

This clause removes certain matters from the scope of both the indemnity and the insurance that the contractor is to provide. The statutory position is that those who carry on activities involving a nuclear risk are bound to compensate any persons who may suffer as a result, thus making any undertaking of the contractor superfluous. In the case of aerial pressure waves it is not possible to obtain insurance cover and so the impossible is not demanded. In view of the insurance problem the contractor is also released from his indemnity obligation under clause 20.2 and the earlier parts of the present clause, so that the risk reverts to the employer. Whether the employer can still rely on clause 2.1, regarding completion of the works themselves, to override the effect of the present clause on this second matter is a nice point of law, but this clearly is not the intention of those drafting it.

The clause 22 perils definition contains wording producing a similar exclusion to the present clause over its own subject matter.

Clause 22—Insurance of the works against clause 22 perils

Three alternative clauses are provided here and, in accordance with the footnote to the conditions, the two not required must be deleted in any particular case. The three alternatives must be considered in many details quite distinctly and are:

Clause 22A — Insurance of entirely new work by the contractor.

Clause 22B — Insurance of entirely new work by the employer.

Clause 22C — Insurance of work of alteration or extension and of the existing structures and contents by the employer.

Where a project consists of two physically distinct portions, the one being new work and the other alterations and extensions, it is quite possible to use the first of the alternatives along with the third, qualifying them as each applying to their respective part of the works. The only physical confusion likely would arise from a common stock of materials for the whole of the works, although the costs of preliminaries may also be a problem. From a procedural point of view, events would be governed by the alternative invoked when a particular incident occurred. While clause 22C must be used where existing structures are concerned, it is desirable to use clause 22A wherever possible for reasons given below. If therefore the new work is a major element in the whole, the use of both clauses should be considered. Clause 22B is not so desirable, as is discussed below.

There are several broad points that should be noted about these alternatives as a group. Their reference is to loss and damage to the works themselves, with some extension in the case of clause 22C, and not to any injury flowing from the carrying out of the works, which is the subject of clause 20. In each case the same list of risks is provided against and, while the range is wide, the clauses do not require a strict all-risks cover. There are therefore a number of possible risks to the works that remain with the contractor — for example, theft and vandalism.

What each alternative is doing is to relieve the contractor, to some quite considerable degree, of what would otherwise be the full burden of his contract, that is to restore the works at his own expense in the event of their partial or complete destruction by any of the causes named. This is the basic obligation assumed by the contractor to complete the works under clause 2.1. It is reinforced in clause 20.2 since that clause is wide enough to cover the works. The present clauses, however, oblige one party or the other to enter into insurance against the most common risks and thus make it obligatory on the employer to pay for such insurance, either directly or in the contract sum. The effect is to protect both parties: the contractor against possible crippling if a major disaster were to occur and the employer against the resultant loss that he would suffer at a determination. Insurance in these circumstances has much to commend it; whether a contract should insist on it is a matter of philosophy. More radically, clauses 22B and 22C transfer the risk as well as the insurance to the employer.

There are a number of matters of detail common to the alternatives. These are considered under clause 22A and reference is then made to them under the other alternatives.

22A.1 — INSURANCE IN JOINT NAMES OF EMPLOYER AND CONTRACTOR

This clause is the most commonly used alternative and suits most new work.

Unless the employer has some specially favourable arrangement it will be cheaper and more convenient to use this clause. It also leaves with the contractor the contractual risk that the insurance is intended to cover and this seems far more appropriate than what happens under clause 22B. Most contractors will then effect an endorsement of the employer's interest on their running all-risks policies.

The insurance is to be in the joint names of the employer and the contractor. The insurer thus cannot pay out to one party as insured and also proceed against the other party, if that other party has been negligent. An insurance in the name of one party only would mean the possibility of an action by the insurer against the other as a joint tortfeasor. An insurance in the name of the employer alone would thus mean the possibility of proceeding against the contractor under the indemnity of clause 20.2 as worded. If for some reason the joint insurance here provided were to fail, then the contractor would still be liable to the employer direct under his indemnity; the insurance is the first, but not the only port of call. Being in joint names, the insurance will fall to the employer should the contractor determine under clause 28.1.3.2 after loss or damage has occurred, provided that the endorsement has been made in the specific way provided. If however, determination occurs under any part of either clause 27 or 28, the employer should check as soon as possible that the insurance is being maintained to avoid doubt.

The causes of loss and damage are described in current insurance terms, which have been inserted bodily into the list of clause 22 perils set out in clause 1.3. This bodily insertion is not without difficulties in the case of building work. Several of the causes may arise directly out of the building work, such as fire, explosion, and bursting or overflowing. Others, particularly storm, tempest and flood are matters against which the contractor may be required to take certain precautions under the contract bills. Possibly the contractor could adopt a less than careful attitude, knowing that he was covered even against his own negligence. This is a common feature with insurance, and becomes critical for the employer under clauses 22B.1 and 22C.1. The position is confused here since nothing in the present clause suggests that it is without prejudice to clause 20.2 and that clause does not exclude any of the risks mentioned in this present clause from its scope. On the other hand, the insurance required does not cover for the costs of delay which the contractor would have to bear unless he made special provision.

Several causes of loss and damage are excluded in the list, these being those excluded for other purposes under clause 21.3 where they are discussed. The footnote to the clause recognises that there may be further causes that should be excluded in the peculiar circumstances of a particular contract, owing to the lack of available cover. While it is desirable that the employer should make enquiries on this aspect in any doubtful case where inviting tender, the contractor certainly should do so before contracting to do the impossible.

The question of delay may be more pressing for the employer. The causes given in the present clause may lead under clause 25.4.3 to an extension of time and so to the employer losing a right to liquidated damages; he would need a special and separate insurance if he wished to guard against this possible loss. But further, under clause 28.1.3.2 the contractor may even be able to determine if the same causes lead to a protracted, but quite possible delay to substantially the whole of the works. The appendix provides for three months' delay unless some other period is inserted. If the particular cause is beyond the control of the parties then these provisions may well be equitable. If the contractor has contracted to stave off certain contingencies and these have occurred, then the position seems quite unfair to the employer. The latter may have an avenue of redress under clause 25.4.3, as discussed there, but under clause 28.1.3.2 he appears to be without escape, except on the ground of the contractor's negligence.

The subjects of insurance are 'all work executed and all unfixed materials and goods' and a percentage addition may be made to these insured items for the amount of additional professional fees that will be incurred during restoration. The property in all materials and goods passes to the employer as soon as they are fixed or, if unfixed, on inclusion in an interim certificate. The insurance cover is wider than this and includes all materials and goods intended for the works and duly delivered, even if they have not been paid for or fixed. The cover is not wide enough to include off-site materials and goods and clause 16.2 specifically makes the contractor responsible for these until delivered. Also excluded from the insurance is all property of the contractor or sub-contractors temporarily on site; this property will usually be insured by them, but this is of no immediate concern to the employer under the joint insurance.

The insurance will be in respect of an increasing value as work proceeds although the policy will take care of this on a fairly flexible basis, as is the way of insurance. The cover is to cease on practical completion, at which stage the contractor has fulfilled his basic contractual obligation under clause 2.1 and the employer may take possession and also must assume responsibility for any insurance required. If partial possession of the works takes place then a corresponding transfer of risk occurs at the same time and the contractor ceases to provide insurance cover for the portion completed, under the terms of clause 18.1.4.

22A.2 — INSURERS APPROVED BY EMPLOYER

In view of the joint insurance, the insurers are to be approved by the architect. Similar provisions to those under clauses 21.1.3 are made for the custody of the papers, and for action and recovery if the contractor defaults in insuring.

22A.3 — USE OF POLICY MAINTAINED BY CONTRACTOR

22A.3.1 If however, the contractor maintains a running all-risks policy, this may be accepted as an alternative to the special policy envisaged under 22A.2 and is what is commonly provided. It is subject to the endorsement of the employer's interest on the policy and to a regulated right to call for documentary evidence of this endorsement or even to call for the policy and receipts. Since the policy and receipts of the larger firms of contractors will have reference to many contracts, they will not be called for lightly. But precise definition of terms is necessary or otherwise some doubt may lead to production.

22A.3.2 Not unreasonably, the arrangements of clause 22A.2 are also brought in here if the contractor is at default in the insurance. No right to approve the insurer is imported, since the contractor's running policy will be serving all manner of contracts and employers and the mere existence of one is presumably assumed to be adequate demonstration of the character of the insurers.

22A.4 — ACCEPTED INSURANCE CLAIMS — CONTRACTOR'S OBLIGATION — USE OF INSURANCE MONIES

22A.4.1 The contractor is required to carry out whatever is necessary to make good the loss and damage incurred and then to proceed to completion in keeping with clause 2.1. He may delay work on the damaged portion only until the insurer has accepted the claim and then must proceed with 'due diligence', although if prudent he will ensure that all evidence needed for settlement is made available to the insurer before it is removed or covered up. He must proceed with 'due diligence', bearing in mind that the extension of time granted by the architect under clause 25.4.3 is subject to a provision of similar significance. The contractor should not suspend activity on any undamaged parts of the works not subject to claim, otherwise he will be in breach of contract, as outlined under clause 28.1.3. It seems reasonable for him also to carry out emergency work at once, although the clause does not require this. Whether the claim is settled at once or progressively is not relevant to the contract machinery, although it will affect the details of its certification according to the method of valuation used.

22A.4.2 Payment to the contractor for the work of restoration is to be made under interim certificates as for any normal payment, but will not be subject to retention since this has already accrued under the original payments for the damaged work. These certificates will be issued at the same times as the main series and could be combined with them, if convenient for all concerned.

The clause is quite silent about the whereabouts of the insurance monies between settlement of the claim and their progressive payment to the contractor. They are monies 'received' which then 'shall be paid'. Some form of joint holding account is needed to satisfy the joint nature of the insurance. This is particularly important if the delay is pushing either party to insolvency; otherwise the monies might be lost in the resulting confusion.

22A.4.3 The contractor will receive the whole of the insurance monies, except the percentage for fees, and no more. Whether the main monies are adequate is a matter that he alone must see to in settling the claim and, earlier, in securing adequate cover. The employer, as having a smaller interest, will not have been able to influence the overall settlement to any degree, as this will have been between the contractor and insurer primarily. He will therefore receive a sum for fees which will fluctuate with the rest and which may be quite unrealistic in relation to his expenditure, which will be governed more by the nature of the restoration than its value. Where there is complete destruction the architect may well have to give the insurer corroboration of the extent of work destroyed, although this service would not be chargeable to the employer.

22B.1 — CLAUSE 22 PERILS — SOLE RISK OF EMPLOYER

The greatest difference between this alternative and clause 22A.1 is not that it makes the employer responsible for insurance, but that it transfers the normal contractual risk under an entire contract (to complete the works whatever happens) from the contractor to the employer in respect of the clause 22 perils. To line up with the phrase 'at the sole risk of the Employer' used in clause 22B.1.1, clause 20.2 removes the employer's right to indemnity under that clause when this present clause applies. The reason for this root difference is not clear and it is even harder to see why the employer should ever wish to accept it. It offers him no protection against the contractor's negligence or other default even if the insurance fails and it is to that degree weaker than clause 22A.1. By apportioning the physical risks of building between the two parties it may also open the way to disputes as to whether a happening comes within the defined list or not.

It is understandable that if, for instance, an insurance company is itself the employer it may wish to be its own insurer by carrying risks not due to the contractor's negligence, without effecting an outside insurance. This philosophy is built into the corresponding local authority edition clause, which does not require the employer to insure. But both that and the present clause achieve their object at the expense of removing the entire right to indemnity and it is this aspect that seems both unnecessary and undesirable.

Along with this major difference, the clause presents several points of relationship with clause 22A.1, as may be noted.

22B.1.1 The list of causes of loss and damage and exclusions is the same and insurance against them by the employer merely serves to intensify the points just made. Also the subjects of the insurance and the exceptions to it are the same, except that the employer is not required to insure professional fees. This is understandable, since they are not amounts which would be reimbursed to the contractor.

22B.1.2 The insurance will again be related to an increasing value and contractually it need not extend beyond practical completion. It may be assumed to run thus far from the employer's obligation to produce evidence of its currency 'at any time' under clause 22B.1.3. The policy is to be 'proper', but the contractor has no right to object to the insurers as such. Some form of running policy would be acceptable here, with an endorsement relating to the specific contract.

22B.1.3 The contractor may take out insurance in lieu of the employer if the employer fails and may recover the cost in interim certificates and in the final account. If the contractor were not to take up his option to insure he would stand to lose little: he has already been paid for his work to date and the determination terms under clause 28 are generous to the contractor, to say the least. In addition, the retention monies are at least intended to constitute a trust fund as provided by clause 30.5.1, in the event of the employer's insolvency resulting from a disaster.

22B.2 — LOSS OR DAMAGE — APPLICABLE PROVISIONS

Not unreasonably the contractor is required to give notice of any loss or damage since neither architect nor employer may otherwise know of it until it is too late to claim under the insurance. If the contractor fails in this notice, at least in a case where only he could reasonably know of the occurrence, he would find himself liable under this clause to bear the cost of any reinstatement already carried out. The provisions for restoration and payment are straightforward and reflect the fact that the employer has taken the risk.

22B.2.1 The contractor is to be paid for the works themselves as though no loss or damage has occurred.

22B.2.2 He is also to be paid for all extra work 'as if . . . a Variation' which will be valued in accordance with clause 13 and paid through interim certificates and the final account. Here the interim payments will rank for deduction of retention monies; this is distinct from the position under clause 22A.4.2. Extension of time and the possibility of determination for protracted delay still apply, although limited in the latter case if the contractor has been negligent, but the contractor is still to proceed with due diligence as is the case with clause 22A.4.1. The employer may find himself paying out before the insurers are ready to pay him in this case, although normally some interim arrangement will be made. Whether the insurer's basis of payment is the same as the contract basis is a matter which must remain at the employer's risk.

22C.1 — EXISTING STRUCTURES — CLAUSE 22 PERILS — SOLE RISK OF EMPLOYER

This alternative stands with clause 22B against clause 22A by placing the same contractual risk and its insurance with the employer. While it may be regretted that the indemnity of clause 20.2 is again removed, the broad philosophy of the clause is otherwise easier to accept in the present case. Where alterations and extensions are being carried out, not only they but the existing structures and their contents fail to be considered for insurance purposes; two separate insurances, one by each party, can easily give rise to complications in the event of loss or damage occurring. The works may be so small in value, by comparison with the property being altered or extended (and on occasions its contents) or may be so intimately related to it that it is more rational for the insurance to be effected by an extension of the existing insurances than by some fresh cover, even if it is possible to obtain such. In addition there is the element of loss of use of premises to be considered in any insurance. The contractor should not be required to fathom all these depths in the course of his own quite distinct line of business.

22C.1.1 The clause proceeds accordingly and follows quite closely the structure and detailed wording of clause 22B.1.1, but includes the existing structures and their contents, whether owned by the employer or not, as matters for obligatory insurance by him. As a result a difference is introduced: 'adequate insurance' is substituted for 'a proper policy of insurance' and a footnote recommends further modification if complete insurance is not obtainable. Intentions should preferably be set out in the contract bills so that the contractor is informed when tendering, though since he is not at risk the matter is hardly vital.

22C.1.2 Another difference is the right of entry and inspection to produce a survey and inventory if the employer then defaults in insuring. If a right of entry is needed to insure on the employer's behalf it would seem equally necessary to have the same right to check the adequacy of the insurance where the employer does effect it, but this is not stipulated. Again the contractor is not at risk, unless an incident drives the employer into insolvency, and there seems to be little real reason why the contractor should take up his option to enter or even insure when the case arises. He has the same general protection as under clause 22B, except that the special determination provisions in the present clause are not quite so much in his favour.

22C.2 — LOSS OR DAMAGE — APPLICABLE PROVISIONS

The clause, in dealing with loss or damage, requires the contractor to give notice in the same way as under clause 22B.2, the comments on which also apply here. If loss or damage occurs, their extent or character may affect considerably the future position of either party and therefore the provisions of this clause which may apply are considerably more involved than those under the alternative clauses. In particular, a special option of determination by either party is introduced; this is illustrated by Figure 14. These provisions have direct application only where there is loss or damage affecting the works; if lightning, for instance, damages some part of the existing structures without affecting the works, the clause will not be invoked. Conversely if only the works are damaged, then clearly the clause will apply. If the same incident affects both parts, then the clause will apply to the works but not to the existing structures as such, though it may be impossible to restore the works without restoring parts of the existing structures at the same time.

22C.2.1 Again the contractor is to be paid for the works as though no loss or damage has occurred. If there is a determination under clause 22C.2.2, then this present provision must be read for the uncompleted works in conjunction with clause 28.2, as mentioned there.

22C.2.2 Restoration of the existing structures may be quite incidental and

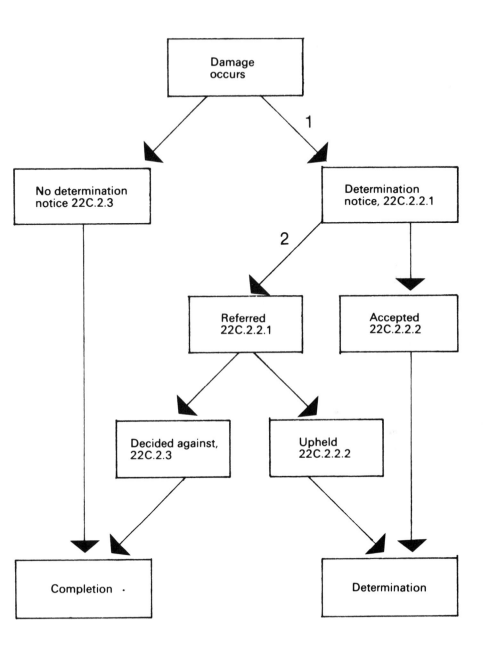

Figure 14: **Optional determination procedures under clause 22C.2 of JCT main form**
The maximum duration at (1) is 28 days. The maximum duration at (2) is seven days. No other durations are given in the clause.

the contractor may therefore be prepared to take it in his stride, but it may be so great as to be out of all proportion to the original works and perhaps of a scale or character for which the contractor is quite unsuited. He might therefore wish to determine under this clause or possibly the employer would wish to do so to secure a more suitable contractor.

Alternatively the employer might find himself faced with his existing structures substantially destroyed. In such a situation he might prefer to demolish what remained and rebuild in a different form, or even on a different site. He would not want the works to proceed and would wish to determine: this he could seek to do under the present clause, provided that the works had been damaged. If the existing structures had been heavily damaged while the works remained unscathed it would seem that the employer could not strictly utilise the provisions, but an arrangement related to them would seem reasonable. Frustration could well arise and lead to such a position.

Whether a determination can be effected on these or similar grounds depends on whether it would be 'just and equitable'. This phrase is not defined and if the parties differ an arbitrator is to be appointed to settle the matter on whatever principles he can adduce. A timetable for the determination procedure is laid down and both time limits must be held to by the parties concerned if they variously wish to achieve determination or secure a reference to arbitration. If the determination is secured, the contractor will be paid off on the terms of clause 28.2, except that he will not be reimbursed for any loss of profit or the like. In addition clause 22C.2.1 will apply and this secures that there will be no deduction for the damage or loss to the works already carried out.

22C.2.3 Unless a determination occurs, the provision of clause 22C.2.1 will be read with this clause and will give a position which is the same as that in clause 22B.2 in all respects, except that the architect has an option whether to instruct the contractor to clear debris or not. In the case of excessive damage to the existing structures it may not be appropriate to ask the contractor to remove debris.

CHAPTER 9

Variations of the works

Clause 13 — Variations and provisional sums

Clause 13 — Variations and provisional sums

The first three sub-clauses of clause 13 are concerned with the instructions to be given and their scope, while the latter four deal with the financial adjustments that result.

The conditions throughout assume firm quantities and this clause in particular is affected by this conception. Provisional quantities forming part of otherwise firm bills would, it is suggested, come within the term 'provisional sums' under this clause and be treated accordingly. Only in clauses 30.6.2.2 and 30.6.2.12 is there a reference to 'work described as provisional', presumably by endorsement of the quantities. Bills consisting entirely of approximate quantities should be related to the approximate quantities edition of the JCT form, discussed in Chapter 21.

13.1 — DEFINITION OF VARIATION

13.1.1 The first part of the definition of 'Variation' makes it plain that a change in the tangible works is intended in this clause, while other issues may come under clause 13.1.2. The list given is illustrative but not restrictive as shown by the word 'including'. The subject of 'removal from the site' is clearly distinguished from the same activity under clause 8.4. When the nomination of a sub-contractor occurs under clauses 35.4 to 35.12, this may lead to changes in attendance or in cognate matters due to an exchange between the 'basic' and the 'alternative' methods of nomination. The effects may be charitably embraced as relating to 'any work' and being 'in the Contract Bills', although it may well not be shown 'upon the Contract Drawings'.

The clause does not attempt to define how extensive a variation may become and still be binding. To increase the size of a contract five-fold or to change the character of a substantial part of the works drastically would hardly be a valid variation, despite the last sentence of clause 13.2. To do this would go beyond 'the alteration or modification of the design, quality or quantity of the Works', the reasonable interpretation of which is in terms of incidental parts of the whole. The works should still, after variation, be the same 'Works as shown upon the Contract Drawings and described by or referred to in the Contract Bills'. Otherwise the contractor is entitled, under clause 4.2, to decline the variation as being outside the architect's powers or to agree to it only on terms that would constitute a fresh contract.

This clause shows the necessity for a comprehensive set of contract drawings and an adequate description of the works in the contract bills, while both should permit a reasonable flexibility. Any undesigned parts of the works should be delineated as far as possible on the contract drawings and be covered by a specific provisional sum in the contract bills, to be dealt with under clause 13.3.

The borderline between variations *on* a contract and the variation *of* the contract in a major part of its essence is hard to define. Often when the former position is still held to by the parties, there will be adjustment of preliminaries and of units prices over and above the adjustment envisaged by clause 13.5, so avoiding a radical variation of the whole basis of the contract.

13.1.2 The continuing definition of variation in this clause covers several matters which will not affect the state of the works as they will appear after completion. The definition embraces variations in obligations and restrictions set out in a limiting list, but then only variations of those actually 'imposed by the Employer in the Contract Bills'. The power to instruct a variation in these respects is therefore circumscribed, rather than kept wide as over design and similar changes in clause 13.1.1. It is also limited by the contractor's right of reasonable objection under clause 4.1.1.

The list sets out four cases in which the employer may affect the contractor's activity under the contract, in all cases at least by implication on the site. These matters may overlap to some extent so that, for instance, access or use of parts of the site may be inseparable from limitations of working space.

Again working space may be restricted only at certain times of day, say to allow passage of the employer's workpeople or plant, effectively causing a restriction of working hours at those times. It is conceivable that this interaction could interfere with the operation of the present clause. An attempt to instruct a variation in one restriction (say access) could lead to the introduction of another (say working space, by sealing off some part of the site) that was not in the contract bills, and such an effect would invalidate the variation. These instances, drawn from the first three cases, all affect the contractor's programme for the works negatively by setting bounds to his activities.

The fourth case, 'execution or completion of the work in any specific order' may also overlap with the other cases, but presents aspects that are more particularly its own about how to perform the works. Thus it covers positive dictation to the contractor in advance about the sequence (but not the timing) of his programme. The contractor's master programme supplied under clause 5.3.1.2 will be prepared in the light of these obligations. A variation of such an obligation may be a radical affair, but in passing it may be observed that there is still no power here to affect technological matters of production directly, although an instructed change of work sequence may lead the contractor himself to make a change of plant for example, to suit the revised circumstances.

None of these obligations or restrictions is specifically related to timing in the progress of the works, although the contract bills may so relate them, and so this clause gives no authority to instruct change in timing, although timing may be affected indirectly. The architect may instruct postponement of any packet of work or even the whole, under clause 23.2, but there is no opposite power to instruct an acceleration of the programme. This power would need to be express to override the position created by an entire contract. Its absence is underlined by the nature of the provisions about extension of time discussed under clause 25.

While the list in this present clause is in itself limited, its operation in a particular contract is further limited to such of the matters in the list as are 'imposed . . . in the Contract Bills'. The wording does not stretch to cover such matters of these types as might have been imposed in the contract bills, but have not been. Thus 'alteration or omission' of any of the matters actually imposed and described is reasonable enough to interpret, although extreme alteration might be held to strike at the root of the contract. The 'addition . . . of' such matters is difficult to interpret logically if they are already imposed — presumably 'addition to' them in the sense of supplementing them is what is intended and what the words 'addition' and 'alteration' might be held to embrace at law. An item in the contract bills attempting to reserve to the employer the right to impose any of the obligations or restrictions later but without any prior definition would probably fail by its vagueness. Any employer who is not sure precisely what he will want would be advised to have inserted in the contract bills as exact an item as possible to keep his right alive.

The whole of the subject matter of this clause is well known and occurs frequently in practice, but it is still an area in which the contractor need not be co-operative even upon favourable terms if the contract is not explicit.

13.1.3 After the preceding two parts of the definition of 'variation', this final part narrows it by excluding any right to introduce a nominated sub-contractor to do work already priced by the contractor in the contract bills. This exclusion applies where 'the measured quantities have been set out' for work of the type concerned. It does not prevent, for example, a variation omitting an area of granolithic flooring by the contractor and adding for the same area terrazzo flooring by the nominated sub-contractor for terrazzo work covered by a prime cost sum in the contract bills, the change in specification being for a relatively incidental area. If there is no prime cost sum for terrazzo, the position is more complex. The positive side of this provision is dealt with by clause 35.1 under which heading there is further discussion. Clause 35.2 deals with the reverse case of the contractor performing work against a prime cost sum.

This clause does not exclude nomination of a supplier as it does a sub-contractor. Such a 'nomination' would not fall within clause 36.1, but should be treated as a change of 'quality' under clause 13.1.1 with any resulting change in price, since no site work by the supplier is involved.

13.2 — INSTRUCTIONS REQUIRING A VARIATION

Without the words 'may issue instructions requiring a variation' here written into this entire contract, neither could the employer have a variation as defined in clause 13.1 introduced into the works, nor could the contractor enforce payment based on any instruction of the architect. It would be necessary to execute a supplementary contract for any and every variation, with the same formality as the original contract. Here the normal form of written instruction, signed by the architect alone, is sufficient.

Authority is also given to the architect to sanction variations other than those which he has instructed. Examples would be any direct orders from the employer (who should always be discouraged from such activities), emergency work initiated by the contractor and cases in which there has been a failure to follow the contract procedure laid down in say clause 6.1. Perhaps clause 12 comes under this last umbrella, although this is questionable. In all such cases the architect is permitted but not compelled to give his sanction, although if he did not the contractor could resort to other remedies in suitable cases.

The clause does not cover confirmation of the architect's own oral instructions, which are dealt with under clause 4.3. A summary of the various provisions for ratification is set out in Figure 4 on page 34. Matters that are deemed to be architect's instructions leading to variations are listed in Figure 3 on page 32.

Instructions under this clause may give rise to claims for extension of time under clause 25.4.5, for loss and expense under clause 26.2.7 or even to determination under clause 28.1.3.4.

13.3 — INSTRUCTIONS ON PROVISIONAL SUMS

The conditions are distinctly vague and nowhere give a definition of a provisional sum. Clauses 6.2.3 and 21.2.1 refer to provisional sums for fees, charges and insurances, while the present clause envisages their use for undefined work executed at least in part by the contractor. Clause 30.6.2 then deals with the adjustment of the contract sum to take account of the expenditure of provisional sums. All sums are as set out in the contract bills. This is in line with general practice and consistent with clause A.8.1.a of the Standard Method of Measurement, which offers the following definition in the absence of any other in a contract:

> The term 'provisional sum' is defined as a sum provided for work or for costs which cannot be entirely foreseen, defined or detailed at the time the tendering documents are issued.

13.3.1 The architect has to give instructions over the expenditure of provisional sums in the contract bills and also over prime cost sums crystallising out of such provisional sums. These prime cost sums are mentioned in the footnote to the clause and are to be dealt with under clause 35 or clause 36 as appropriate.

13.3.2 Provisional sums within a sub-contract, domestic under clause 19 or nominated under clause 35, are mentioned separately here as requiring instructions, although these are strictly 'included in the Contract Bills'. The first will be expressly written in, while others will be contained within the prime cost sums.

13.4 — VALUATION OF VARIATIONS AND PROVISIONAL SUM WORK

13.4.1 This clause provides for variations and work arising from provisional sums (presumably both related to the contractor's own direct work and to that of domestic sub-contractors) to be valued by the quantity surveyor. It is one of the only clauses that reserves functions for him alone to deal with, subject to the usual recourse to arbitration by the parties. Specific rules for valuation are listed and are to apply 'unless otherwise agreed by the Employer and the Contractor'. This expression presumably covers the acceptance of a special quotation from the contractor for a parcel of work or some special terms for changing an obligation or restriction, or something similar. The contract does not give either the architect or the quantity surveyor authority to conclude any such agreement and it is necessary to obtain the employer's approval at least in principle and preferably also as to the amount.

The clause then states the obvious by extending the provision along the contractual chain to nominated sub-contractors and making the provisions in the relevant sub-contract apply. These provisions give rules which are identical in substance with those of clause 13.5 here, and also make the quantity surveyor responsible. If there is no quantity surveyor (as under the without-quantities edition) then the architect assumes the responsibility. The side-stepping of the rules when 'otherwise agreed' is between contractor and nominated sub-contractor in this case, but is subject to approval by the architect and not the quantity surveyor.

The way in which domestic sub-contractors appear to flit from attachment to contractor here and to nominated sub-contractor in the preceding clause presents no problems contractually, it is just untidy.

13.4.2 While part or even all of a particular provisional sum may turn into prime cost work to be nominated as the footnote to clause 13.3.1 recognises, the work may be channelled back to the contractor for direct execution because he tenders for it successfully under clause 35.2. Since his tender should contain its own term over variations and complete valuation, the present clause channels the work into the notional sub-contract for these purposes. This somewhat perverse procedure could conceivably continue in ever decreasing circles if there were a suitable provisional sum within the contractor's tender for prime cost work.

13.5 — VALUATION RULES

This clause spells out the traditional method of valuing variations with some supplementation. It is a clause which the quantity surveyor may well call his own; indeed it is doubtful whether anyone would want to wrest it from him.

The scope covers variations defined in clause 13.1 and arising under clause 13.2, and the expenditure of provisional sums under clause 13.3 when these do not become any form of prime cost work. Expense beyond what this clause contemplates is to be dealt with under clause 26 by the architect, or the quantity surveyor on his behalf.

The procedure is that the quantity surveyor shall measure and value the variations and ultimately present them in 'a statement of all the final Valuations' as provided for in clause 30.6.1.2. No requirement as to the form of this document is imposed by the conditions.

13.5.1 The listed rules for valuation of additional or substituted measured work are to be applied successively as one or another fails to fit the case concerned; the results are what are generally termed bill prices, pro-rata prices and star prices or something similar. No distinction can be found between rates and prices in this clause or in practice. These rules depend for their application on the degree to which it is work of similar character executed under similar conditions and there is not a significant change in quantity. These are wide terms and imply that they may be treated widely to permit suitable flexible pricing, but also the words 'similar' and 'significantly' used call for restraint against conjuring up subtle distinctions. In the normal presentation of bills of quantities fairly broad give and take applies and the same attitude should apply to the settlement stage. (The case set out under 'Necessary work not mentioned' should be noted.) Certainly the wording does allow account to be taken of more difficult working conditions, unfavourable timing of work, less economical plant, small deliveries and special visits, for example. It also allows for lower prices in suitable cases.

The prices in the contract bills are the starting point in valuation. There is no authority to go behind these to determine whether they were economical prices in any particular case or whether the profit element has been unevenly distributed between items. If this is the case, the variation prices must nevertheless be at the level of the original prices, even for star prices, and must not be used to adjust the position. The contractor, having chosen the original dispositions of his costs and profits, must hold to them. This will apply particularly when it is suggested that all profit is in the preliminaries or that most of the preliminaries have been spread over the measured prices. Preliminaries may rank for adjustment in their own right under clause 13.5.3.3. However, for the valuation that these clauses envisage the adjustment should be self-contained and must not extend to restructuring of the pricing of the contract bills.

13.5.2 When work included in the contract bills is omitted by a variation, the contract prices are to be used in valuing the work actually omitted. But the omission may have repercussions on the cost of performing the remaining work, so that clause 13.5.5 should also be consulted.

13.5.3 When measured valuation is performed by way of addition or omission, this clause provides three supplementary rules. Firstly, the measurement is to follow the same principles as that for the contract bills, as is necessary if prices applied to the resulting quantities are those in the contract bills or related to them. But secondly the unit prices may have been adjusted in some overall way at the end of a section or on the main summary of the contract bills, for instance to take up an arithmetical tendering error or to add a profit margin on a domestic sub-contractor. Any such adjustment is also to be made in pricing variation quantities, whether the adjustment be up or down.

While measured quantities and prices are related to each other, they are jointly related to the subject matter of the third rule — preliminaries. These are defined to tie with the type of items usually under just such a heading in the contract bills, some of which are by way of site overheads. One particular variation or the cumulative effect of several may sometimes justify an adjustment of some part of otherwise 'fixed' preliminaries. This rule permits such adjustment 'where appropriate', although these will not usually by a directly proportional adjustment of preliminaries related to a change in measured value. What is permitted here is something strictly related to the varied physical work carried out in an orderly way, as with all other variation assessment. Preliminaries are especially likely to be caught up in questions of disturbance, perhaps involving prolongation or intensive supervision, but this must still be taken under clause 26.

13.5.4 When work cannot be properly dealt with by measurement either because there is no practicable way of analysing it or because the resulting quantities cannot reasonably be given unit prices, this clause requires daywork to be used; that is for the contractor's direct expenditure to be recorded and priced on a cost basis. The clause relates such work to standard definitions of prime cost of daywork, variously for builder's work or for specialist's work.

In each of these cases the definitions are to be those current at the specially defined date of tender, which is ten days before receipt of tenders. The definitions lead to the payment of rates current when daywork is performed and so daywork is excluded from fluctuations adjustment either by clauses 38.5.1 or 39.6.1 or by the formula rules referred to in clause 40.1.1.1, whichever happens to apply. Since these definitions suggest that overheads be dealt with as a percentage addition to the other costs in each case but do not state any percentage figure, it is required that these percentages should be given in the contract bills. The words 'where . . . have agreed and issued a definition' recognise that the standard definitions do not cover all trades. Special terms would have to be agreed for any missing cases, preferably as part of the contract by inserting special terms in the bills or the contractor requesting them at the time of tendering.

It is quite normal to make the clerk of works the architect's authorised representative for signing daywork records; he will sign sheets as a record only, as they will be subject to the quantity surveyor's decision on whether to measure the work in question. The clause gives no guidance as to what happens if the records are not delivered within the time stated. Late records may be suspect or hard to check, but the contractor has to be paid somehow. Any doubtful sheets may be endorsed accordingly and the quantity surveyor will then feel entitled to reduce them at his discretion. A clause in the preliminaries in the contract bills, warning the contractor of this, may be of assistance. Other forms of contract provide for this as a standard arrangement.

13.5.5 The rules so far have dealt with the valuation of the variation itself. Sometimes a variation will have cost effects beyond its own direct boundaries by changing the physical conditions of working. This clause requires the effect of 'substantially (changing) the conditions under which any other work is executed' to be taken up by revaluing that work, using such parts of clause 13 as are suitable. Omissions in some part of the works may affect what remains quite seriously, so that perhaps plant is used less efficiently or a subcontractor coming from a distance has less work to set against his travelling time. Both additions and omissions may change things like congestion and accessibility, the utilisation of scaffolding and the sequences of working. Like other elements in clause 13, the cost effects are to be assessed independently of the disturbance aspects that may be involved, sometimes a fine distinction.

13.5.6 Clause 13 admits that not every eventuality can be covered by explicit rules, and that in some cases a 'fair valuation' must be made. These cases may be variations of obligations and restrictions under clause 13.1.2 for which measured valuation or daywork are seldom going to provide an answer, although some analysis based on them may be needed. Otherwise they may be elements of variation under clause 13.1.1 as indicated by the expression 'liabilities directly associated'. The financial consequences of changes in the nomination procedure under clause 35 would also be accommodated here as the effects will be commercial rather than physical.

Following this clause comes the proviso already alluded to that the disturbance effects and other loss and expense due to variations are to be excluded from operations under the present clause and come within the ambit of clause 26, or possibly elsewhere in the conditions.

13.6 — CONTRACTOR'S RIGHT TO BE PRESENT AT MEASUREMENT

The clause wording seems to envisage measurement on site: this will often not be the case, but at any rate the contractor is entitled to be present and, in quaint echoes of a lost era, passively to take 'such notes and measurements as the Contractor may require'. The contractor's perusal of the resultant valuation is apparently not anticipated by the conditions until the period of final measurement and valuation under clause 30.6.1.2. Nowhere do the conditions suggest that the contractor would have any objections to raise, although he has a period of grace between receiving the final certificate under clause 30.8 and its taking effect under clause 30.9.1 in which it is inferred he may have the odd comment to make. In practice, there is much lively cooperative anticipation of this stage from the earliest days of the works onwards.

13.7 — VALUATIONS — ADDITIONS TO OR DEDUCTION FROM CONTRACT SUM

The result of any addition or deduction is that, in addition to the final certificate, interim certificates will be adjusted by virtue of clause 3. As interim certificates are themselves approximate, so the adjustment may also be approximate.

CHAPTER 10

Fluctuations of costs and prices

Clause 37 — Choice of fluctuation provisions — entry in appendix
Clause 39 — Labour and materials cost and tax fluctuations
Clause 38 — Contribution, levy and tax fluctuations
Clause 40 — Use of price adjustment formulae
Formula rules for use with clause 40

The order followed in this chapter is that given above; the centre two clauses are reversed in an attempt to break up a rather indigestible diet. As clause 38 is substantially a verbatim repetition of parts of clause 39, taken from it selectively, it is easier to consider the fuller clause first and then pick out differences in the shorter one. Clause 40 proceeds on a quite different basis and only leads to reference back to clause 39 on a few points. It may therefore be studied independently if required without too much turning over of pages.

While clause 37 is printed in the same document as the rest of the conditions, the other clauses considered in this chapter are published separately in a document entitled: *Part 3: Fluctuations.* These other clauses are among the longest clauses in the conditions and are possibly the most tedious. All of these clauses are inconsistent in relating marginal headings to first level divisions of clauses, so that it is difficult to use the same rigid system here as in other chapters.

Clause 37 — Choice of fluctuation provisions — entry in appendix

This clause appears as Part 3 of the main conditions where it is a signpost to the appendix which identifies which of the three alternative substantive clauses applies in the contract. It makes allowance for clause 38 to apply if the appendix entry is left blank, as this gives the least measure of fluctuations adjustment out of the three clauses. It is clear from the wording and the footnote that deletion of the whole fluctuations element from the contract is not contemplated, although it produces no drafting complications if this is done. It is assumed, apparently, that the parties will regard the legislating and derived activities of governments of any persuasion as sufficiently unpredictable at all times as to require due arrangements in the contract, with which assumption one may well sympathise. Whenever economic conditions are in themselves uncertain then a leaning to full fluctuations will be evident, to put it mildly.

A variant way of providing for limited fluctuations would be to delete either the labour or the materials provisions from the alternative chosen. For that matter, there is no difficulty in drafting to prevent the use of labour provisions from one alternative and the materials provision from the other. Whether there is any virtue in any of these possibilities at any time is beyond the scope of the present discussion, but in an economic climate of inflation it is undoubtedly necessary to use either one of clauses 39 or 40 without qualification.

Clause 39 — Labour and materials cost and tax fluctuations

The main divisions of this clause deal with labour, materials and finally with a number of subsidiary issues. Before taking up the two divisions on labour, it is useful to set out in the next paragraph a few distinctions and relate them to a tabulation. While the points made here may not be of immediate value, it may help to refer back to them as some sort of grid reference scheme in the gloomy tracts that follow.

For labour adjustments clause 39 embodies a number of provisions which give 'layers' of payment or allowance, in this paragraph viewed solely as increases. While the details of these provisions are mentioned as they occur, it is useful to summarise them in advance as the interrelationships are not all self-evident.

Table 10.1

Category	Base amount	Consequential increase	Rate increase
(a) Wages etc, workpeople	39.1.1	—	39.1.2
(b) Ditto, non-workpeople	—	—	39.1.3 (M/L)
(c) Employer's insurances, workpeople	39.1.1	39.1.2	— (L)
(d) Ditto, non-workpeople	—	39.1.3 (M/L)	— (L)
(e) State pensions and other taxes, workpeople	39.1.1 39.2.1	39.1.2	39.2.2
(f) Ditto, non-workpeople	39.2.1	39.1.3 (M)	39.2.3 (M)
(g) Contracted out, workpeople	39.1.1 39.2.7	39.1.2	39.2.7
(h) Ditto, non-workpeople	—	39.1.3 (M/L)	39.2.3 (M/L)

In Table 10.1 'Category' is indicative of the emoluments and expenses concerned, while 'Base Amount' is a reference to the clause which introduces them as a basis for the contract sum. On to this original layer for some elements, such as pension contributions, there may come a layer for the rate of 'Consequential Increase' in the amount of the elements due to an increase in other elements, such as wages, to which they relate as a percentage or sliding scale. Then there may be a 'Rate Increase' in any of these elements themselves, so that the rate, percentage or scale goes up. This may be quite independent of the other increase, or the two may be compounded. As a 'deemed' basis is used in some cases, the two increases allowed do not necessarily add up to the real total in every case, they may come to more or less as indicated by (M) or (L) in the Table, or even by (M/L).

39.1 — DEEMED CALCULATION OF CONTRACT SUM·—RATES OF WAGES ETC.

The opening paragraph introduces the subsidiary clauses considered below in which a general pattern is followed of giving first the original deemed basis of calculating prices so that the next clause or clauses then give the events leading to adjustment. No other adjustment may be claimed by either party. The method of making any resulting adjustment is dealt with in clauses 39.5 to 39.7.

These fluctuations are restricted to those arising out of clearly identifiable national negotiations and their related regional variations and take no account of any private bargaining that may go in a particular locality or on a single site. This gap and others referred to below are intended to be bridged by the provisions of clause 39.8.

39.1.1 *Payments forming the basis of prices.* This applies to the prices in general, but the words 'including . . . insurance' are placed immediately after 'prices' to show that it applies also to these insurances which are included in many cases within prices since the insurances are a percentage of the total of the other prices. The main elements needing comment are as follows:

(1) *'Rates of wages and the other emoluments and expenses'.* These are to be in accordance with the rules or decisions and the terms specified, which are those of the named council and agreements and also of corresponding bodies and agreements for trades not covered by those named. The wording of the clause taken with the definition of 'workpeople' in clause 39.7.3 excludes all salaried employees and employees without a negotiating body, and these are dealt with by clauses 39.1.3 and 39.1.4. It also excludes payments, such as transport and fares, which are not determined by these bodies, and these are covered in clauses 39.1.5 and 39.1.6.

(2) *'Payable by the Contractor to or in respect of workpeople'.* It would appear that this wording is intended to mean what is payable as emoluments to the contractor's own workpeople or as expenses in respect of them, since only they are paid by him under 'the rules or decisions' of clause 39.1.1.3. It is at least not intended to mean in respect of self-employed persons and workpeople of domestic sub-contractors, the latter coming within the orbit of clause 39.4, although it would be read as overlapping with that clause. The categorising of workpeople in the present clause into two sets does nothing to

clarify matters, useful though the two sets may be in other respects. These sets are both 'engaged upon or in connection with the Works', in the one case 'either on or adjacent to the site' and in the other 'neither on nor adjacent to the site', so that the definition is comprehensive. In the latter case only there is a limitation to those 'directly employed by the Contractor' to avoid drawing in workpeople of other firms. Either this is unnecessary or it should be extended to cover the former case as well, and thus remove doubt.

(3) *'The rules or decisions of (wage-fixing bodies) ... and the terms of (holiday agreements) ... promulgated at the Date of Tender'*. Since promulgation may take place some while before an alteration becomes effective, this means that the tender may have to allow for an increase, as it will usually be, that may become payable only when the contract has been under way for some time. 'The Date of Tender' is specifically defined under clause 39.7.1.

(4) *'Any incentive scheme and/or productivity agreement'*. While the 'rules or decisions' referred to in the last paragraph include for such schemes and agreements, they do not make them obligatory upon contractors as, for instance, rates of wages are obligatory. The present wording is needed therefore to bring them within the scope of fluctuations adjustment, since they would otherwise be excluded by the decision on this issue in the case of *William Sindall Ltd* v. *North West Thames Regional Health Authority*.

(5) *'The rates or amounts of any contribution, levy or tax ... calculated by reference to the rates of wages (etc)'*. These items are defined for the purposes of this and other clauses in clause 39.2.8. The wording at the end of this present clause brings them within the basis, so that they are related to the rates of wages etc, as are the two types of insurances at the beginning of the clause. The wording differs in position and detail, as the contribution, levy or tax may be calculated on a graduated or other basis that is not a constant percentage of the wages and so forth.

39.1.2 *Increases or decreases in rates of wages etc — payment of allowance.* Adjustment is to be made when an alteration causes an increase or decrease and the wording refers back to that of the preceding paragraph in all appropriate places. The net amount is to be paid or allowed, i.e. it is to be without any allowance for overheads, profit or the like. Profit is specifically ruled out by clause 39.5.6. Adjustment of the two insurances is restricted to what is consequential. Clause 39.1.1 defines these as being 'based upon' the rates and wages and other matters and thus a 'consequential' proportional adjustment is permitted, but this will not extend to adjustment arising out of a change in the rate of premium. In addition, a similar adjustment of any contribution, levy or tax is covered here, thus permitting adjustment where these are directly related in volume to wages and the like. Where such contribution, levy or tax changes in rate, the resultant adjustment is dealt with under clause 39.2.

39.1.3 *Persons employed on site other than 'workpeople'.* This clause deals with the first of the two excluded categories mentioned under clause 39.1.1, i.e. those who are employed by the contractor but who are not workpeople under clause 39.7.3. It extends fluctuations adjustment to such others only if they are 'engaged . . . either on or adjacent to the site' and so still does not take in those corresponding to workpeople off-site under clause 39.1.1.2. This means that it covers site supervisory personnel, site office and visiting staff within limits, but excludes those working at head office for instance. One limit is that those on site on a visiting basis must achieve certain attendances defined in clause 39.1.4.1; they are then to be counted in proportion to their attendance in the week concerned. The other limit is that adjustment is at the rate applying for a craftsman rather than the rate actually applying to the employee, be it higher or lower, and clause 39.1.4.2 defines this further.

The contractor's craftsman used as a benchmark will probably be in an occupational pension scheme covered by a wage-fixing body, this case being the exception to clause 39.2.7, which clause refers it to here. If the craftsman is so covered, adjustment for both consequential and the change of rate aspects are covered in one place. Otherwise authority for adjustment is split between this clause and clause 39.2.3.

39.1.4 *Supplement to last*. Three facets of clauses 39.1.3 and 39.2.3 are defined here. Firstly, in calculating adjustments for non-workpeople only whole days in batches of at least two in the same week may be taken into account, but these need not necessarily be consecutive. Secondly, if there is a choice, the rates, etc applied to these days are to be those for the most highly paid craftsman. The references to 'a craftsman employed' and, in the previous clause, to an 'amount as is payable or allowable' make these top levels actually applying on site or off site for the works and not top levels under the rules at large. It is therefore conceivable that the levels will change as various trades perform their parts of the works. The reference in brackets to a domestic sub-contractor brings his tradesmen into the range of those considered here in calculating an adjustment for the contractor himself. Lastly, non-workpeople are defined in terms which make them also direct employees.

39.1.5 *Workpeople — wage-fixing body — reimbursement of fares*. The second excluded category mentioned under clause 39.1.1 was expenses: those of transport and fares. The basis given here for transport is a 'basic transport charges list' attached to the contract bills and which would cover the contractor's own or hired transport. In the case of fares the datum is the same 'rules or decisions' as in clause 39.1 and again they are as promulgated at the date of tender, while the employees covered are workpeople as defined by that clause. There is therefore no opening to make adjustments for transport or fares of other employees. Clause 39.1.3 does not refer directly to the present clause, while this clause does not make a proviso as does clause 39.2.7 to place any part of its subject matter under the umbrella of clause 39.1, and so get back to clause 39.1.3 that way.

39.1.6 *Increases or decreases in last*. The net adjustment of the expenses defined under the last clause is permitted here. No rules are given here to cover transport and the list in the contract bills should contain them. In the case of fares, adjustment may arise in either of two ways: the national negotiating bodies may agree to change the rules and decisions on reimbursable fares, or the actual fares themselves may change quite independently.

39.2 — CONTRIBUTIONS, LEVIES AND TAXES

The opening paragraph performs a similar function to that in clause 39.1. The subsidiary clauses cover matters stated in or resulting from an Act of Parliament, whether payments by or refunds to the contractor.

39.2.1 *Payments forming the basis of prices.* These are defined in wide terms to cover any such sum payable by a person in his capacity as an employer, and are again related to 'workpeople' by the following clause, provided that they were payable at the date of tender. There is thus no element of anticipation in the tender, as under parts of clause 39.1. The aim is to provide not only for alterations in the 'rate' of existing items, such as national insurance and state pensions, but also for the emergence of some new 'type' as yet unknown. These are in addition to alterations in amount under clause 39.1.1.

39.2.2 *Circumstances of adjustment of last.* This refers closely to clause 39.2.1, using the two definitions there for this purpose, and provides for a net adjustment on the pattern of clause 39.1.2. The term 'pays or will pay' allows for cases where the payment is actually made after the contract period. Alterations in the rate of levy under the Industrial Training Act as a tender rate are excluded from the scope of the paragraph, but if the levy happened to be abolished it would presumably rank as a tender type under the clause! The definition of 'workpeople' in clause 39.7.3 restricts the employees to whom the present adjustment applies but the next clause makes up this deficiency.

39.2.3 *Persons other than workpeople.* The provision here allows for non-workpeople by wording similar to that of clause 39.1.3. It refers specifically to clause 39.1.4 to bring in the detail of that clause.

39.2.4 *Refunds forming the basis of prices.* This follows closely the structure and philosophy of clause 39.2.1, to take account of any refund of what was there referred to as payable (as for instance the one-time selective employment tax which was refunded for a manufacturing establishment) and also to take account of any premium receivable over and above a refund. A refund must be directly of what was paid and does not cover training-board grant or other irregularly occurring amounts.

39.2.5 *Circumstances of adjustment of last.* This inevitably follows clause 39.2.2, but needs to make no exclusion of the Industrial Training Act.

39.2.6 *Definition of premiums.* It is made clear that the term is unimportant; it is the characteristics of the payment which render it eligible.

39.2.7 *Inclusion of occupational pension schemes.* If the employment of workpeople is 'contracted-out' for pension purposes so that state pension contributions are not made, this allows an adjustment to be made 'as if that employment were not contracted-out', that is to say at the same rate. The contributions under the other recognised scheme will be at least as high as under the state scheme. This is subject to the proviso that if the other scheme is established by the rules of one of the wage-fixing bodies mentioned in clause 39.1.1.3, then it falls within the operation of clause 39.1 in general. This means that the level of adjustment is then at the actual level of the scheme concerned and not at a 'deemed' state scheme level. The clause refers only to 'workpeople', but clause 39.1.3 allows a measure of adjustment for non-workpeople in respect of pension contributions, as it does for other expenses.

39.2.8 *Definition of contributions, levies and taxes.* The same approach is used here as in clause 39.2.6.

39.3 — MATERIALS, GOODS, ELECTRICITY AND FUELS

In this case the two causes of fluctuations, market and statutory, are not separated since they will not show separately on any quotation, price list or invoice.

39.3.1 Payments forming the basis of prices. For two reasons it is necessary to have a list of basic prices attached to the contract bills, although the term 'attached' may itself reasonably be interpreted loosely, if the observation be permitted. One reason is to restrict the materials and goods eligible for direct adjustment to a manageable list containing only items which occur in quantity in the works or which are particularly unstable in price. Further materials and goods are covered in effect by the percentage additions under clause 39.8. The other reason is to record, as part of the contract, actual prices which are the market prices current at the date of tender. This is necessary since many materials and goods have no clearly identifiable market prices and the parties must therefore agree their own basis while the tender is still under consideration, usually in relation to quotations received while preparing to tender. Electricity does not present quite the same uncertainty, but inclusion of the particular tariff avoids doubt. In the case of other fuels the same considerations apply as for materials and goods. They may be included only if the contract bills allow them, so that inclusion in the present list without support from the contract bills would lead to no adjustment occurring.

No attempt is made in this clause or the next to introduce any element of prediction of fluctuations. These are seldom known sufficiently in advance for very much to be at stake on this score. Thus if the contractor were notified on the day before the date of tender of an increase taking effect one week later he would not be required to take account of it in his tender and in the interests of his competitiveness he should not.

39.3.2 *Circumstances of adjustment of last.* Adjustment is restricted to the above list and to fluctuations in market price. Thus a change of supplier would not in itself call for an adjustment unless it was accompanied by a demonstrable change in the market price. If there is no change of supplier, it is difficult to establish that any change of price is not a market fluctuation, although any increase made that is flagrantly out of step with other suppliers should be resisted by the contractor or, even if he should pay it, by the quantity surveyor on behalf of the employer. It is in the case of materials, goods and fuels that clause 39.5.1 is of most service in resisting exploitation, by requiring written notice of any event producing a fluctuation. The term 'payable by the Contractor' restricts the effect of this paragraph to direct purchases by the contractor and thus excludes sub-let work which must be dealt with under clause 39.4, if at all.

39.3.3 *Definition of duty or tax.* No attempt need be made to analyse the statutory element at any stage. Fluctuations due to this element are allowable so long as the materials and goods are purchased directly by the contractor. There is again no restriction as to whether the changes were foreseen and, as usual, the effect of value added tax is excluded. Accordingly the clause lists them right back along the chain of supply.

39.4 — FLUCTUATIONS — WORK SUB-LET — DOMESTIC SUB-CONTRACTORS

The effect of clauses 39.1 to 39.3 is to limit the area of adjustment to labour, materials and so forth for which the contractor pays directly. The present clause provides for similar adjustment where the contractor pays indirectly, by way of a domestic sub-contractor, for sub-let work. There is no reference here to nominated sub-contractors or suppliers and they are expressly excluded from the present provision by clause 39.6.2.

39.4.1 *Sub-let work — incorporation of provisions to like effect.* The contractor is obliged to incorporate fluctuations provisions in all domestic sub-contracts and there can be no adjustment for him here if he does not. Since the trend of prices is almost invariably upwards, there seems little need to force the contractor to do what will usually be in his interest, as the sub-contractor will be looking for adjustment anyway. It is unlikely that the employer will be the loser. Strictly, the contractor is in breach of contract if he fails to include the provisions in any sub-contract and presumably could be liable for damages if the employer failed to recoup the result of the occasional decrease. Where there is an increase the breach becomes a technicality and the contractor carries the loss. These provisions are to be 'to the like effect as' the clauses named. Some differences in detail of the wording are needed to avoid any circularity of reference (since clause 39.5.1.6 refers back to the present clause) and to deal with the three-tier relationship of the quantity surveyor, contractor and sub-contractor in settlement. None of these matters present problems.

39.4.2 *Sub-let work — fluctuations — payment to or allowances by the contractor.* For the contractor, adjustment follows as a 'net amount' when he pays more or less under the sub-contract. There is thus no addition for profit as such and no general addition is permitted by clause 39.8.1. Adjustment is limited to the net adjustment of the price payable under the sub-contract. The contractor should therefore ensure not only that the provisions are included, to comply with clause 39.4.1, but that any sub-contractor bases his quotation on the level of prices applying on the date of tender for the main contract. If the level at the date of the sub-contractor's quotation is used, the contractor will be limited to recovering any increase after that date and will have to bear any increase occurring between that date and his own earlier date of tendering.

39.5 TO 39.7 — PROVISIONS RELATING TO CLAUSE 39

These clauses are principally concerned with setting out machinery for adjustment. In so doing they make explicit what may be implied in other clauses in the conditions and also introduce some definitions.

39.5.1 *Written notice by contractor.* This clause is closely linked with the following one. The wording avoids the necessity of deleting the inapplicable items in the list.

39.5.2 *Timing and effect of written notices.* Notice is to be of events producing a fluctuation and not of the later fluctuation itself. The purpose of this is presumably to give the architect the opportunity to counter any large increase by substituting a cheaper material or, even where this is neither desirable or possible, to warn the employer of what is coming. Payments may be made to the contractor only where the notice has been given. Absence of notice however is no bar to the employer recovering any decrease, as there is no reference to 'allowance'.

39.5.3 *Agreement — quantity surveyor and contractor.* The traditional method of evaluating fluctuations has been by detailed calculations based on time sheets and invoices, although the conditions do not explicitly ask for this. This may often be the most suitable method, but it may incur labour costs out of all proportion to the sum of money concerned. There are also circumstances where it could conceivably be open to abuse. The present clause gives a complete discretion to the quantity surveyor and the contractor as to the method used in calculating adjustments, and as to which adjustments to treat by a particular method. Any agreement is related to an amount in respect of the occurrence of any event. It would therefore be possible, for example, to change the method of labour adjustment part way through the contract or to adjust for two materials by differing methods, although consistency of approach will usually be preferable. It is beyond the scope of the present discussion to consider detailed methods, but some form of analysis of the measured quantities or use of interim valuations with some adjustment could act as a basis. Clause 40 provides for this on a quite sophisticated basis, but that clause used alone must be included in the contract initially and it is not possible to change over to it in mid-stream.

The result is to stand for all the purposes of the contract and will therefore not be subject to arbitration. This is reasonable enough from the contractor's point of view, since the two sides have already agreed the amount. Whether the employer will always be so happy at irrevocable commitment without prior knowledge may be questioned.

39.5.4 *Fluctuations added to or deducted from contract sum.* Effect is to be given to fluctuations by adjustment of the contract sum in the case of normal completion or in the final settlement where the contractor determines. When the employer determines, the adjustment will be taken into consideration under clause 27.4.4 in calculating the total amount which would have been payable on due completion, although here it is not a direct adjustment of the final payments to the contractor and so is not mentioned in this clause. In any of these cases, the adjustments will have already been reflected in interim certificates and materials need not be fixed to qualify.

39.5.5 *Evidence and computations by contractor.* As the present approach to fluctuations adjustment is based on the contractor's costs, this clause requires him to furnish the necessary data as soon as is reasonable in the form of 'evidence and computations', as required by the architect or the quantity surveyor. Evidence is more the concern of the architect who receives notice of causal events under clause 39.5.1 and it would include anything needed to substantiate the notices, but it would also include signed sheets, invoices, receipts and the like that are more the concern of the quantity surveyor. Computations are based on this evidence. How far they go towards helping the final 'amount . . . to be ascertained' will depend largely on what is agreed between the quantity surveyor and the contractor, relating to the latter's costing system and the term 'may reasonably require'.

A further requirement is added about amounts deduced indirectly, that is in respect of the contractor's non-workpeople and those of domestic sub-contractors. The contractor is made responsible for certifying that the evidence required, and by implication produced, is valid. This is necessary in the absence of wage sheets or allocation sheets in most cases in the case of the two-day rule in clause 39.1.4.

39.5.6 *No alteration to contractor's profit.* This clause underlines the frequent earlier reference to the net amounts of increase, decrease or difference. Even where there is sub-letting, there is no adjustment of the contractor's profit.

39.5.7 *Position where contractor in default over completion.* The essence of this clause is to restrict adjustment for fluctuations, upwards or downwards, to 'the amount . . . otherwise payable . . . or allowable', once the completion date has been reached. It does not stop adjustment altogether. The operative condition is 'if the event' leading to adjustment 'occurs after the Completion Date', so that any adjustment caused by a preceding event will continue to be applied for work overflowing beyond the completion date, but any adjustment due to a later event will not be made. Adjustment, whether an increase or a decrease, then levels out. What the clause does not permit is any abatement of the amount accruing in the period before the completion date when, for instance, the employer may be forced into making excess reimbursement because an undue amount of work has been performed late and at expensive rates. The converse may also occur simply as a result of variations in the contractor's progress over which neither employer nor architect has any contractual control.

The completion date under clause 24 means the original date or the adjusted date after extension of time and so the provision is made subject to the next clause here dealing with extension of time.

39.5.8 *Rider to last clause.* The provision over completion is made subject to two points. Under clause 39.5.8.1 it is not to operate unless clause 25 is used in its entirety; according to a practice note this is because of the principle adopted in pegging fluctuations amounts. This may be a desirable arrangement to protect the contractor (but see the comments under clause 25 on some of its provisions in terms of protecting the employer) but it does not follow as a logical necessity that it must happen and the clause here could be deleted to permit modification of clause 25.

Further, under clause 39.5.8.2 the operation depends on all extensions of time being granted by the architect in response to the contractor's notification (and presumably his particulars and estimate), and thus in due time. Here, there may be grounds for confusion in the expression 'as he considers to be in accordance with that clause' which introduces the architect's interpretation of the clause as a ground for identifying what he has not yet done but should do. But there will also be grounds for review of fluctuations because the contract date remains provisional until it is finally fixed, up to 12 weeks after practical completion under clause 25.3.3. If there is a change, some event as defined in clause 39.5.7 may be pushed into or out of the reckoning.

39.6 — WORK ETC TO WHICH CLAUSES 39.1 TO 39.4 NOT APPLICABLE

Four cases are explicitly excluded from the operation of the clause. In the first and third of these cases it will be necessary to make deductions of hours and quantities which they embrace and which may be on the main time sheets and invoices, to arrive at the fluctuations under the various parts of clause 39.

39.6.1 Daywork will be valued at current rates where the Definition of Prime Cost of Daywork or a similar basis is used; any source of conflict in any other proposed daywork terms should be avoided when drawing up the contract documents.

39.6.2 Nominated work will be subject to its own terms and is not covered by clause 39.4 over purely domestic sub-contractors.

39.6.3 A tender under clause 35.2 should be made on the same terms as competing tenders by other firms so that there is direct comparability and this makes the contractor's position for fluctuations equivalent in this case to that of a nominated firm.

39.6.4 Value added tax is excluded from the contract sum by clause 15 and the whole of any tax payable by the employer is dealt with through the VAT Agreement provided for under that clause.

39.7 — DEFINITIONS FOR USE WITH CLAUSE 39

Several terms widely used throughout clause 39 are defined.

39.7.1 The early timing of the date of tender is intended to avoid last-minute detailed adjustment of prices. Quotations for materials and sub-trade quotations will often be received by the contractor after this defined date of tender, but in any case should have been related to it in the inquiries sent out.

39.7.2 While formwork is not incorporated in the works, where timber in particular is used its fairly high wastage rate differentiates it from all other temporary items. The clause allows this timber to be considered as materials, or if one is so inclined as goods, although any residual value would be credited. It also differentiates electricity and other fuels (where applicable) from consumable stores.

39.7.3 This definition of 'workpeople' has the effect of excluding certain employees' wages etc and payments to self-employed persons from fluctuations adjustment, as is mentioned under clause 39.1.1, which it is here reinforcing by partial repetition. Clause 39.1.3 then partly relieves the position.

39.7.4 The definition of 'workpeople' depends on that of 'wage-fixing body' which is here made stringent by excluding the same persons as does clause 39.7.3.

39.8 — PERCENTAGE ADDITION TO FLUCTUATION PAYMENTS OR ALLOWANCES

This clause is quite clear as to what is to be done, although it gives no explanation as to why. The use of the various foregoing clauses leaves the contractor short of adequate reimbursement for fluctuations since they do not cover a number of items, such as the complete extra cost of labour and staff paid under other negotiating arrangements or under none, plant other than transport, overheads, and materials not included in the basic price list. This clause allows the gap to be bridged in whole or in part on the basis that these items will vary in broadly the same proportion as the directly calculated items and can thus be expressed in percentage terms. Ideally the percentages inserted in the appendix should accord as closely as can be assessed with the margin of value excluded from the explicit provisions of the conditions, so that the contractor's need to make an allowance in his tender is correspondingly reduced. The clause refers to 'the percentage stated', whereas the appendix could give percentages. The stating of various percentages on the several elements may give a more accurate adjustment.

While clause 39.5.6 under its own terms, does not allow profit to be adjusted, there would seem to be no reason for not including a profit margin on the fluctuation amounts calculated on the net basis of clause 39. In fact it is very difficult to insert so precise a percentage as to permit a categorical statement that profit has either been included or excluded.

Clause 38 — Contribution, levy and tax fluctuations

38.1 — DEEMED CALCULATION OF CONTRACT SUM — TYPES AND RATES OF CONTRIBUTION ETC

This clause permits adjustment due to a change in rates or the introduction or abolition of a contribution, levy or tax in the same way as does clause 39.2. It does not however lead to any adjustment consequential upon changes in wage rates and the like which give rise to a proportionate change in the volume of contribution or the like, quite independently of any fluctuation in the rate of the latter. Clause 39.2 has clause 39.1.2 with it to take care of the adjustment related to volume, but the present clause stands alone and adjustment cannot be made.

This clause needs little separate comment, as it consists in essence of material which has been discussed under clause 39. It is almost sufficient just to list the clauses which correspond, subject to necessary editorial differences, as follows:

Clause 38.1.1 corresponds to clause 39.2.1
Clause 38.1.2 corresponds to clause 39.2.2, with the inclusion of clauses 39.1.1.1 and 39.1.1.2
Clause 38.1.3 corresponds to clause 39.2.3
Clause 38.1.4 corresponds to clause 39.1.4
Clause 38.1.5 corresponds to clause 39.2.4
Clause 38.1.6 corresponds to clause 39.2.5
Clause 38.1.7 corresponds to clause 39.2.6
Clause 38.1.8 corresponds to clause 39.2.7
Clause 38.1.9 corresponds to clause 39.2.8

Clause 38.1.8 does not include the proviso at the end of clause 39.2.7, so that occupational pension schemes established by the rules of wage-fixing bodies as defined in the proviso do not, in clause 38.1.8, attract the possibly higher actual reimbursement level. They attract only the 'deemed' state scheme level.

38.2 — MATERIALS — DUTIES AND TAXES

In step with the labour provision, causes of fluctuations for materials, goods, electricity and fuel are restricted. This clause covers more items than the heading would suggest, but this is in line with clause 39.

In this case it requires new clauses in comparison with clause 39, with a different philosophy. The result is reasonably clear in meaning but particularly hard to apply.

38.2.1 *Payments forming the basis of prices.* This clause requires the establishment of a list of materials and so forth for which price fluctuations will be admitted, but without any prices being included in the list. Thus far the clause follows clause 39.3.1, but in other respects it follows clause 39.2.1 with the same use of 'type' and 'rate'. The incidence of duty or tax again runs through the chain of supply.

38.2.2 *Circumstances of adjustment of last.* As would be expected from the structure of the preceding clause, this clause closely follows clause 39.2.2. The term 'what the Contractor actually pays' limits adjustment to the contractor's direct purchases. Any adjustment to the permitted items will fall under clause 38.3.

38.3 — FLUCTUATIONS — WORK SUB-LET — FOR SUB-CONTRACTORS

38.4 TO 38.6—PROVISIONS RELATING TO CLAUSE 38

38.7 — PERCENTAGE ADDITION TO FLUCTUATION PAYMENTS OR ALLOWANCES

All of these clauses follow their equivalents in clause 39 and differ only in numbering internal cross-references so that no further comment is needed.

Clause 40 — Use of price adjustment formulae

This clause represents a departure from the approach of clauses 38 and 39, which are based on the more traditional system of analysing changes in the contractor's costs to arrive at the adjustment for fluctuations. These costs could have been incurred efficiently or otherwise, but only in the case of some gross divergence would there be any serious reassessment of the level of reimbursement proposed. The present clause gives a method of adjustment which is related to the contract value of the work instead of its cost. It is thus in line with the philosophy of the contract in not paying for cost as such, although it may be objected that it is a comparatively blunt instrument in that the adjustment made may differ to a fair extent from the change in cost. It is not intended by the JCT that the method should be used for work such as involved alterations where it is not possible to categorise fully and clearly the work that is envisaged. However where it is suitable, it aims to eliminate a lot of the detailed grinding work that is done in the application of the other method, although to do this it depends for its operation on a fairly elaborate set of rules, partly algebraic.

In addition to the clause itself, a separately published document entitled 'Standard Form of Building Contract Formula Rules' is incorporated into the contract by reference, and the clause is heavily dependent on it for its own application and even intelligibility in places. The document is defined in the clause by the short title of 'The Formula Rules' and contains the technical and accounting, as distinct from the legal, elements of the procedure for adjustment. It therefore covers much ground that is outside the scope of this volume, but those aspects of it which are essential to the discussion of this clause are set out later in this chapter, particularly the definitions of terms. To bring the whole discussion together, some preliminary points may be made about the system:

(a) Fluctuations in price are allowed for by adjustment of the prices for measured items and the like in the contract bills in accordance with published indices, whether the actual costs of the contractor vary by a greater or smaller amount. No attempt is made to exclude a profit element as in the alternative approach.

(b) Calculation requires an analysis of the contract bills, accepted by the contractor as standing for the purposes of this clause, and with any resulting financial discrepancy in the final reimbursement taken up in the contract sum by implication. A running system of calculation occurs as each interim valuation is made, based on the additional amount of work included since the previous valuation and not necessarily on the amount of work performed since then. Any overall final discrepancy revealed by the settled account is to be spread at the various index levels prevailing throughout on an 'averaging' basis.

(c) The basis for calculations is to be the formula rules already alluded to and discussed hereafter, together with monthly index bulletins published nationally.

(d) A disciplined timetable of valuations is essential, related to certificates at equal time intervals (almost inevitably monthly) and not to stage payments.

40.1 — ADJUSTMENT OF CONTRACT SUM — PRICE ADJUSTMENT FORMULAE FOR BUILDING CONTRACTS — FORMULA RULES

40.1.1 By contrast with clauses 38 and 39, this clause does not define any deemed basis of calculation of the contract sum, since the formula rules defined in clause 40.1.1.1 cover what is needed. In accordance with the remainder of the conditions value added tax is not to be dealt with here, while clause 40.1.1.2 states that the fluctuations provisions will not affect the VAT Agreement (a side comment that is not made in quite the same way elsewhere in the conditions).

40.1.2 The definitions referred to are used primarily for the operation of the rules, but they also govern several terms in this whole clause. In particular the date of tender used in clause 40.1.1.1 is defined in the same way as in clause 39.7.1, that is as 10 days before the date for receipt of tenders. Also there are several definitions affecting clause 40.1.3. Most of the definitions are summarised later in this chapter.

40.1.3 All certificates, other than those purely to release retention, are to be used for the assessment of fluctuations amounts with the gross values forming the basis of calculations. The mechanics of doing this are covered by the rules, rules 20 and 28 being of particular relevance to this clause. Their combined effect is that, in interim certificates before practical completion and in the one immediately following it, the current index numbers are to be used, while in all subsequent certificates an 'averaging' system is to be used based on the various preceding index numbers. This is to allow for the fact that work first taken into the valuations during settlement will actually have been carried out with the rest at earlier dates.

40.1.4 The corrections to be made under this clause are quite limited in scope as will be seen from the list in the last part of this chapter. They particularly exclude any correction for the use of a measured quantity which proves on closer calculation to be high or low. While such a quantity will be automatically corrected by a later valuation for interim payment purposes, the inclusion of an incorrect quantity in the earlier valuation in relation to the then prevailing index number will result in an 'incorrect' financial adjustment for fluctuations which is to stand. This clearly means that a closer assessment for valuation is needed than might otherwise be considered necessary on a purely interim basis.

40.2 — AMENDMENT TO CLAUSE 30 — INTERIM VALUATIONS

This clause introduces a modification into the system of interim certificates given in clause 30.1.2 by making the preparation of valuations obligatory before all certificates, since without these it is impossible to operate the present clause at all. The period during which regular interim certificates are to be issued under clause 30.1.3 is such as to include one after practical completion. This is to allow the last parts of work carried out to be included at the current level of adjustment under the rules for the month concerned. Otherwise these parts would fall to be valued under the averaging provisions of the rules which are only intended to be applied to marginal amounts of work throughout the whole contract period, and not to a complete section performed within a short period.

The effect of clause 30.2.1.1 is to make all fluctuations amounts subject to retention by adding them to the list of elements in the certificates which are so subject. This is a distinct change of principle from clause 30.2.2.4 which leaves other fluctuations amounts clear of any retention adjustment.

40.3 — FLUCTUATIONS — ARTICLES MANUFACTURED OUTSIDE THE UNITED KINGDOM

The principle underlying clause 40 as an entity is that adjustment is by reference to price trends throughout the United Kingdom for work similar to that included in the contract. Rule 4(ii) however excludes from this method of adjustment imported articles which the contractor can incorporate into the works without processing, since these articles may be subject to price trends which are quite out of step with those prevailing in the UK. These articles are likely to be individual components, but the rules do require them to be 'specifically identified in the Contract Bills' in any case. Where no such identification is given, the articles will remain to be treated under the rest of the rules. Where it is given in the list required, the articles are to be dealt with under a similar procedure to materials covered by clause 39.3, phrases of which are embodied in the present clause. The system of formula adjustment is not therefore carried into this difficult area and the older system of market adjustment is retained where it is quite appropriate.

40.4.1 — NOMINATED SUB-CONTRACTORS

So far as this contract is concerned, this clause simply says that any nominated sub-contract is to contain its own provisions for fluctuations or else no adjustment will be made. This may be gleaned from the words 'the Sub-Contract . . . shall provide if required for adjustment', the inference being that if nothing is required and embodied in the sub-contract then nothing will be available to permit adjustment. It would appear that a clause similar to clause 39.6.2, saying this and directly excluding nominated sub-contracts from the operations of clause 40, would have been adequate and clearer. The three alternatives given for the sub-contract basis do not add anything to the main contract and they are in any case open-ended. The term 'some other method' allows for a method equivalent to that embodied in clauses 38 or 39 if desired and this would not involve any clash in itself with the present method. Sub-contract clause 34 referred to is simply the umbrella clause leading to selection of a specific later clause in the particular sub-contract.

Nominated suppliers are also excluded from the scope of clause 40 by virtue of the formula rules themselves.

40.4.2 — DOMESTIC SUB-CONTRACTORS

This clause sets out an option for the contractor and any domestic sub-contractor to agree between themselves to operate fluctuations under the formula rules, on a similar basis to clause 40.4.1, except that the last open-ended alternative is not given. It is an option by reason of the words 'unless . . . otherwise agree' and leaves the possibility of agreeing to no basis and therefore to no fluctuations, but not to another basis as would be possible under clause 40.4.1. This optional arrangement is also different from the mandatory position under clause 39.4.1 where the contractor 'shall incorporate' without qualification. As was pointed out under that clause, this is so because clauses 39.1 to 39.3 limit adjustment to the contractor's direct payments to employees or for materials and goods and clauses 39.4.1 extends the arrangements to cover sub-let work. The present clause leaves matters optional, presumably because the formula rules do not limit adjustment as between the parties to the contractor's own work so long as work is set out and identified in the contract bills. This being the case, there would seem little point in having the present optional requirement at all so far as the financial position between employer and contractor is concerned. The contractor for his own purposes will need to ensure however that any agreement with a sub-contractor is related to the appropriate date, as discussed under the corresponding position under clause 39.4.2.

40.5 — POWER TO AGREE — QUANTITY SURVEYOR AND CONTRACTOR

This clause parallels clause 39.5.3 in giving a discretion to the quantity surveyor and the contractor to settle some area of the fluctuations by modifying the rules in some way, and in then making such settlement to stand 'for all the purposes of this Contract', that is to say not to be subject to arbitration or court action. The parallel is distorted in two respects, however.

40.5.1 Any alteration must be 'reasonably expected' to give 'the same or approximately the same' result as the original. 'Reasonably' puts the matter back into the arena of arbitration or the courts, at least so far as the alteration goes if not the actual calculation flowing from it.

40.5.2 A sub-contractor is not bound to accept any such agreed amount as settling his own entitlement, whereas under clause 39.5.3 the position is not explicitly covered. However, on general legal grounds, the sub-contractor would not be affected in either case by the agreement under the main contract and would be entitled to hold to the formula in his own contract with the contractor as determining his own settlement. On the other hand if he wished to settle on the amended basis agreed in the main contract, he could seek to do so, and would usually be brought in on the negotiations at the time.

40.6 — POSITION WHERE MONTHLY BULLETINS ARE DELAYED ETC

The operation of the whole formula concept is obviously dependent on the data contained in the bulletins, the preparation of which is entirely beyond the control of either party to the contract. This clause provides the outline for what is to happen when there is a temporary or even permanent lapse in the issue of bulletins.

40.6.1 To cover the most pressing question of cash flow, this clause requires adjustment to continue to be made according to whatever is a suitable means of calculation.

40.6.2 When it is expected that publication of bulletins will be resumed before the final certificate is to be issued, the calculation may be of a relatively approximate nature, since this clause requires the substitution of the corrected figures when the back numbers of the bulletins become available.

40.6.3 To prepare for a resumption, the procedures of the clause and the rules are to be kept going so that the necessary detail is to hand when the bulletins are issued.

When it is not expected that bulletins will be issued before the final certificate is due, it may be suggested that the parties have two paths open. One is to agree to wait until the bulletins do appear, although this would not prevent the architect from exercising his duty and option to issue the certificate at the due time, leaving it with the parties to accept it subject only to the adjustment of the fluctuations element. The other is to agree that the quantity surveyor and the contractor shall settle a final amount, using such precision as is possible to come close to the levels anticipated. The quantity surveyor and the contractor could perhaps force this settlement by acting under clause 40.5, although here the employer would have the right of action provided only for him under clause 40.6.3 and might even be able to hold that the absence of the bulletins undermined the use of the other clause at all.

When it is not expected that bulletins will be resumed in time and then they are, the parties may wish to review any agreement in the light of the new facts. Much will depend upon timing and the amount at stake, and the conditions themselves give no lead on this — wisely enough.

40.7 — FORMULA ADJUSTMENT — FAILURE TO COMPLETE

This clause legislates for a more commonly anticipated problem than its immediate predecessor: that of failure to complete. In so doing, it produces a similar effect to that of clauses 39.5.7 and 39.5.8.

40.7.1 If the contractor overruns the original or amended completion date, work included in all certificates issued after that date is to be pegged at the level applying at that date. This means that the contractor is to bear an excess amount of fluctuations expense caused by the late completion for which he is contractually liable, subject to the same limits as clause 39.5.7. Again, this present clause does not allow any abatement for work carried out late but before the due date for completion. It also means that if there should be any reduction in the index numbers, the contractor will retain the saving — which may well be considered equitable.

The strict wording of the clause abrogates not only the use of later index numbers, but also the use of all preceding (and possibly lower) index numbers, under the 'averaging' system for work already executed but not yet included in certificate valuations. This is presumably not intended by wording that is given to deal with another situation, but is at least open to doubt as to how it might be interpreted by the courts. Meanwhile a realistic approach in practice would be to continue the averaging system for certificates following the one after practical completion, while following this clause earlier. The final certificate is exempt from the problem under the wording used here.

It is not clear what clause 40.7.1.2 is about. If it is spelling out that any error in applying the delay provision is to be corrected, this sort of point is usually taken as read in interpretation and is superfluous. Presumably it will mainly be used to cover cases where an extension of time under clause 40.7.2.2 is granted after the due date for completion, although this is strictly the reverse of what it envisages.

40.7.2 This replicates the provisions of clause 39.5.8 and needs no further comment.

Formula rules for use with clause 40

As mentioned in the introduction to the discussion of clause 40, a separate document called 'Standard Form of Building Contract Formula Rules' contains the detailed rules for operating the clause. The notes that follow aim only to summarise those parts of the rules that are relevant to an understanding of the clause and not to comment closely on the precise wording and the effect of this wording in using the rules. To do the latter would be to go beyond the scope of this volume in looking at contract matters and to enter into areas of technicalities and accounting. This limitation means that the summary is of parts only and therefore selective.

There are several definitions set out in the rules, both for their own purposes and also for the understanding of the clause, where a number of the terms are used. The most important are as follows:

(a) *Date of tender*: this is defined in the same way as in clause 39.7.1 which is deleted when clause 40 is used.

(b) *Index numbers*: numbers contained in the monthly bulletins and used in the calculation of fluctuations amounts by applying the ratios of the base month numbers and the valuations period numbers to the contract values of work executed, duly analysed. The combination of these and other elements produces the 'formula' which is the distinctive feature of the whole system.

(c) *Monthly bulletins*: these are issued by the Property Services Agency of the Department of the Environment and form an independent source for the contract basis and for subsequent adjustment.

(d) *Base month*: the month for which the published index numbers are used as the contract basis, this being recorded in the contract appendix and normally being the calendar month before the date when tenders are due to be returned. This date is later than the defined date of tender by 10 days and in particular cases this difference may affect which is the relevant base month.

(e) *Valuation period*: this needs to be regulated closely in view of the relating of fluctuations to the monthly bulletins and there is a further definition to establish the mid-point of the period to cover marginal cases.

(f) *Work categories:* the more detailed of two classifications of the contract work which may be adopted as the divisions to which the index numbers are applied. The rules give categories such as insitu concrete and hardwood joinery. In addition specialist work of the contractor is treated. Some clarification by annotation of the contract bills is also needed.

(g) *Work groups*: the less detailed classification which may be used instead of the previous form mentioned in (f). It operates by aggregating work categories into larger units defined in the contract bills. It makes for more simple working but must be used with caution for suitable cases only.

(h) *Balance of adjustable work*: some sections of the contract bills, such as the preliminaries, are excluded from the work categories and are valued for fluctuations by an 'averaging' method based on the index numbers for all other categories used in the contract.

(i) *Non-adjustable element*: a proportion of the value of work may be excluded from the operation of the formula under the local authorities edition of the JCT form as discussed in Chapter 21.

In addition to these definitions the rules also list elements of value that will be excluded from adjustment:

(a) Daywork and work priced at a 'fair valuation' under clause 13.5, loss and expense payments under clauses 26.1 and 34.3, and any other sum related to actual costs incurred.

(b) Imported articles not needing processing before incorporation in the works.

(c) Nominated sub-contract and supply accounts and related profit, which have their own adjustment mechanisms.

(d) Unfixed materials and goods, although these will enter into the system as they become part of work executed in later valuations.

The other matter of importance for present purposes is a clause dealing with the adjustment of errors in using the formula method, this being referred to in clause 40.1.4. Adjustment is limited to correction of errors of arithmetic, allocation to work categories and use of index numbers. The bulletins giving index numbers themselves give numbers as provisional in the month of issue and confirm them or amend them to firm numbers in the following month, or as soon as possible; alteration will follow here as though there had been an error. This clause and the specific rules for adjustment that follow underline the comment made under clause 40.1.4 that no adjustment can be made to the ascertained sum for fluctuations to take account of any error in allocation of the quantity of work in one monthly valuation as against any other.

This section has dealt briefly with what constitutes only the smaller part of the rules. The rules themselves are followed by a Section 2 and Appendices which give much detail that may be very important in particular contracts, but which falls outside present consideration.

CHAPTER 11

Payments and settlement

Clause 16 — Materials and goods unfixed or off-site
Clause 30 — Certificates and payments

Clause 16 — Materials and goods unfixed or off-site

16.1 — UNFIXED MATERIALS AND GOODS — ON SITE

The clause relates to unfixed materials and goods intended to be fixed in the works. When fixed they will pass to the employer in any case. (The general position is shown in Figure 15.) Before they are fixed this clause is effective, but only provided that the contractor has obtained adequate title to the goods which he can pass on to the employer. This is a difficult area, as is shown by such cases as *Aluminium Industrie Vassen BV* v. *Romalpa Aluminium Ltd*, and *Dawber Williamson Roofing* v. *Humberside County Council*. Plant and material for temporary works are not treated here, leaving the employer with less protection if he has to determine than other forms of contract provide. (See pages 341 and 366.)

Two main provisions are included. The first is that no such unfixed materials and goods may be removed without the architect's consent. This is a useful weapon in times of shortage, or where perhaps a replacement consignment might not completely match what is already on site. The second provision is that when the contractor has been paid for them under an interim certificate, the materials and goods shall become the property of the employer. These latter are thus a more restricted group of materials and goods, although when determination arises and the issue of ownership becomes important clause 27.4 extends its scope to all materials and goods, whether paid for or not. The contractor remains liable for loss and damage, except to the degree that the employer has assumed the risk under either of the optional clauses 22B and 22C.

If the employer has failed to pay some part of an 'amount properly due', and thus is in breach of contract, property in materials and goods newly included in an interim certificate would not pass to the employer. This would be so at least to the extent of the underpayment, but on a strict reading to the full value included, since the passing of title is dependent on proper payment of the amount due as such.

While the employer becomes the true owner of the materials and goods

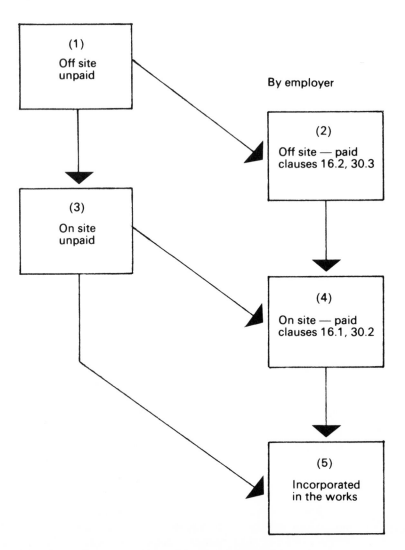

Figure 15: **Ownership of materials and goods under JCT main form**

A.   Where no clause is given the general law applies.
B.   At all stages (1) to (5) the contractor is responsible for loss or damage, subject to the provisions for insurance under clause 22 in its various parts.
C.   Determination by the employer for any reason gives him a right to use materials at stage (3), subject to paying for them at final settlement.
D.   Insolvency of the contractor, if he is a private individual, may lead to 'reputed ownership' problems at stage (2) on determination and may defeat the employer's title.
E.   Other complex problems of title to goods may also arise if the supplier does not pass a good title to the contractor.

concerned, the contractor's insolvency would raise the question of whether the contractor was the reputed owner; under the Bankruptcy Act 1914 this would give the trustee in bankruptcy the title to them. It has been held in *Re Fox ex parte Oundle and Thrapston RDC* v. *The Trustee* that unfixed materials on the works are usually not in a contractor's reputed ownership, but that materials in his yard usually are. The present clause is therefore satisfactory in this respect for materials and goods clearly on the works and paid for by the employer.

The material and goods are those delivered to, placed on or adjacent to the works; 'adjacent' has been held to be wide enough not to be restricted to 'adjoining' but to depend on circumstances, which is not very illuminating. Comparison may be made with clause 16.2 which deals with materials and goods 'off-site'. That clause relies for definition on clause 30.3, which defines its scope as embracing 'materials and goods before delivery thereof to or adjacent to the Works'. This takes matters full circle which, in turn, would not matter apart from the doctrine of reputed ownership referred to above.

There are thus two grounds for uncertainty in insolvency: whether a particular consignment of materials or goods is adjacent to the works or off-site and, if it is adjacent, whether it is in the reputed ownership of the contractor or not. In addition, there is the wider question of the adequacy of the contractor's title which assumes such significance in these circumstances. If determination occurs by reason of the contractor's insolvency, clause 27.4 mentioned above also falls to be considered in deciding this particular ownership problem. If the contractor determines under clause 28, matters should be resolved without problem over a period.

16.2 — UNFIXED MATERIALS AND GOODS — OFF-SITE

The materials and goods referred to under this present clause are off-site in 'the premises where they are' which are defined in clause 30.3.3. The effect is that where the architect has exercised his optional powers under clause 30.3 and the contractor has been paid, the materials and goods in question become the property of the employer, the clause having been drawn up to guard against reputed ownership and inadequate title of the contractor. Irrespective of which insurance clauses apply to the works, the latter remains responsible for the materials and goods and for insurance under clause 30.3.9. This is reasonable since those clauses deal only with materials and goods on the works. This responsibility extends also to the transport of the materials and goods; upon delivery they come under the provisions of clause 16.1.

Clause 30 — Certificates and payments

This clause deals with all certificates that regulate payments under the contract. The main subjects covered may be grouped as follows:
   (a) Interim certificates and retention: clauses 30.1 to 30.5.

(b) The final adjustment of the contract sum: clauses 30.6 and 30.7.

(c) The final certificate: clauses 30.8 to 30.10.

There are other certificates, referred to elsewhere in the conditions, which do not have a direct financial effect although they will set in motion events that will lead to payments. (A list of all certificates is given in Figure 5.) Also, numbers of clauses govern the amounts of payments in various ways; it may be necessary to consider several in respect of any one matter. The present clause serves as a clearing house for the main issues, several of which are summarised in Figure 16.

30.1 — INTERIM CERTIFICATES AND VALUATIONS

30.1.1 Clause 30.1.1.1 obliges the architect to issue interim certificates in accordance with the programme given here both before and after practical completion and he may not decline to do so on the grounds that an inadequate value has accrued since the previous certificate.

The employer, in turn, is obliged to meet the amounts of certificates within 14 days. This he must do in full, subject only to the few deductions allowed by the conditions, and listed under clause 30.6.2 as being sums not to be deducted by the architect in advance of certifying. If the employer does not pay, subject to deducting these sums and his right of set-off mentioned below, the contractor has a right of determination under clause 28.1.1.

While the general right to make these deductions is given elsewhere in the conditions, clause 30.1.1.2 gives the particular right to make deductions from retention money when being paid to the contractor or through him to a nominated sub-contractor 'by the operation of clause 30.4'. This is necessary since the retention has been held with trust status and otherwise is inviolable by the employer, or by his liquidator or the like. The employer still cannot draw from the retention while it is held in trust; this does not appear to be the significance of 'deduction from monies . . . to become due' and in any case such drawing would only reduce the available retention to the employer's detriment. It does mean, though, that contractual deductions may be made while retention is passing through the interim certificate mechanism.

Provided that the part of a payment which is not retention is at least as great as the deduction, the whole matter is a technicality. The present provision deals with the remaining situation in which a deduction erodes the retention. It is limited by its last sentence to deduction from the contractor's own retention. The retention of a nominated sub-contractor can be touched only if the aim is to recover from that firm.

Whatever the reason for a deduction, the employer is to notify the contractor of it under clause 30.1.1.3. This information should be given when the payment is made or would otherwise have been made, and so accompany the statement of the amount of deduction required under clause 30.5.4. Here he must distinguish clearly between deductions from the contractor's own monies and those of any nominated sub-contractor. This keeps everyone informed and allows any protests to be registered.

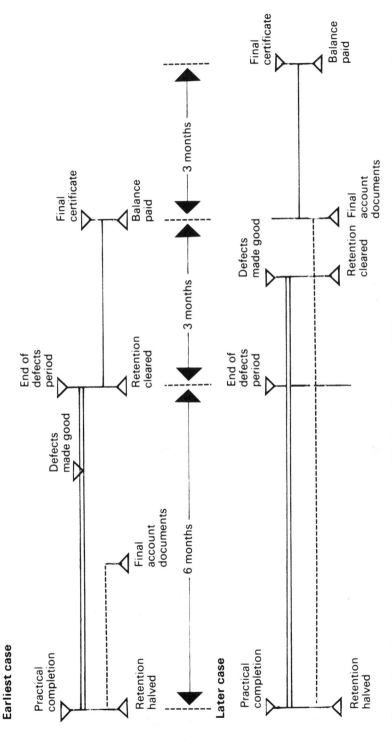

Figure 16: **Actions between practical completion and final certificate under JCT main form**

A. Defects period is fixed in length; period before final certificate is a maximum; intervening period may be of any length.

B. Final account documents do not affect retention payments but do affect payment of final balance.

C. Partial possession advances some matters (see Figure 10).

The employer's obligation to pay is subject to his common law right of set-off as the case of *Gilbert-Ash (Northern) Ltd* v. *Modern Engineering (Bristol) Ltd* underlined in passing. He must however be sure of his grounds for taking this action, as has been demonstrated by *Killby & Gayford Ltd* v. *Selincourt Ltd*. The contractor in turn must not determine too hastily, since this remedy only applies against the employer's default after presentation or prior interference, as decided in *R. B. Burden Ltd* v. *Swansea Corporation*. If the contractor wishes to take issue with the architect over a certificate before presentation or over the lack of one at an earlier stage he may take the employer to arbitration at once under article 5.2.2. The permitted time-lag produces a further, if invisible, margin of retention while the works are in progress.

30.1.2 The issue of certificates and the computations that lie behind or are apparent in them are the architect's responsibility and he is obliged to take counsel with no one, subject to the possibility of arbitration. Normally the quantity surveyor will prepare valuations for every certificate, which is when the architect usually 'considers them to be necessary'. This becomes mandatory when formula fluctuations are in operation and clause 40.2 deletes these words. The quantity surveyor will recommend the amount to the architect with any detail as to what is due to nominated sub-contractors so that the architect can inform the contractor of these amounts as required by clause 35.13.1.

It will usually be quite clear to the quantity surveyor what should be included in a valuation, but he should take up doubtful items with the architect before the valuation is prepared, or else include and then comment on them when forwarding the valuation. If the architect is in doubt over what is included he should confirm this before he issues his certificate, since the valuation does not lessen his responsibility. The position will not usually be irrecoverable in any case, since in view of clause 30.10 no interim certificate is final. (See several cases under 'Certificates, payments and set-off' and 'Certificates and approvals'). However, the architect and the surveyor each risk liability for negligence if there is any gross error and this may be serious if the contractor becomes insolvent during progress. (See several cases under 'Certificates, payments and set-off' and 'Certificates and approvals'.)

30.1.3 Before practical completion the contractor is entitled to certificates at intervals. It is possible so to complete the appendix as to relate the certificates to stages of value or to physical stages of the works, but this is comparatively unusual although it is envisaged by clause 30.2. By far the most common arrangement is to follow the appendix and to insert 'one month'. In accordance with normal legal practice this is one calendar month. It has not been common to make any stipulation as to the time of month at which certificates are to be issued, although this can have some importance to the contractor in the extent to which the credit available from merchants can be used to finance his operations. When clause 40 is included in the contract, the formula method for fluctuations depends on the accuracy and timing of interim certificates. These provisions give added force to the architect's obligation to issue certificates 'from time to time as provided'. The contractor for his part may not decline the issue of a certificate.

After practical completion it is not intended that there should be any large sums outstanding to the contractor, other than the second portion of the retention monies. In the following period such matters as the final evaluation of variations or the settlement of an amount for loss or expense (a frequently protracted business) or of a nominated account may however throw up additional sums. Further, final payment to a nominated sub-contractor under clause 35.17 may become due, leading to a reduction in the retention monies themselves. Interim certificates are to be issued to cover such instances but are not required to conform to a regular timetable. It will often be the contractor who sets affairs in motion and this he may do subject to at least a one month interval between certificates.

Such certificates may occur right up to the issue under clause 30.8 of the final certificate, which will take up any remaining slack in the payments and which is not necessarily subject to a one month interval between itself and the last interim certificate. However if it is still necessary to make final payment to nominated sub-contractors under clause 30.7 in the last month, the last interim certificate will be displaced to 28 days before the final certificate and perhaps closer than usual to the preceding interim certificate.

30.2 — ASCERTAINMENT OF AMOUNT DUE IN INTERIM CERTIFICATES

The first part of the clause defines 'the amount stated as due' at the contract intervals as having three elements. These are first a gross valuation based on additions as clauses 30.2.1 and 30.2.2 and on deductions as clause 30.2.3, and then two deduction elements, one of retention as clause 30.4 and one of amounts previously certified.

Two qualifications are given. Any agreement about stage payments will override the provisions given here; such an agreement needs to be carefully drafted to establish just how it relates the present clause to avoid ambiguity or conflict. The gross valuation is to include amounts up to a date not more than seven days before its issue. It may include more recent work and materials, but need not. Obviously a day or two will normally be needed to complete documentation and perhaps for postage as well. Seven days is a helpful margin in this way, but still allows the inclusion of nearly all recent work and materials.

30.2.1 Some amounts on the additions side of the gross valuation, usually the bulk, are subject to retention. The routine value of work, materials and goods figures here.

The major element as in clause 30.2.1.1 of the total value in most certificates will be the work properly executed and the normal basis of calculation will be the contract bills, although this is not expressly provided. The term 'properly executed' gives the architect authority to exclude any work considered to be defective, but this cannot be taken to mean that all the work included has necessarily been properly executed and that some part may not be condemned later. (See *Newton Abbot Development Company Ltd v. Stockman Bros.*) Additional work valued under clause 13.5 is to be included here. If work is omitted under that clause it will simply not be included. If formula fluctuations under clause 40 apply, the adjustment up (or conceivably, down) is authorised here making the sums subject to retention, which they will not be when calculated on the alternative basis.

A further category included is the value of the materials and goods including the value of those provided by nominated suppliers. These are defined in clause 30.2.1.2 in the same terms as in clause 16.1, under which latter clause they will usually become the property of the employer once paid for, although the points discussed there should be noted. The proviso protects the employer against having to find finances for items which have been brought to site far too early. 'Not prematurely' needs generous interpretation in times of steeply rising prices (for the benefit of whichever party has to pay any increase) and also where delivery dates are uncertain. Again, it may be best to bring such materials as facing bricks on site in one consignment to avoid the risk of differences in shade between consignments. The proviso does protect the employer against the possibility of being faced with materials that are found to have deteriorated or to have been stolen at the time of a determination.

Materials and goods off-site are covered in clause 30.2.1.3, but may only be included when the architect has chosen to operate clause 30.3. While ownership should pass to the employer under clause 16.2 (but see that clause) once he has paid, various liabilities remain with the contractor. These include transport to site and the amount calculated here should allow for this being still a future cost.

The amounts for nominated sub-contractors referred to in clause 30.2.1.4 are interim amounts for work, materials and goods only and the clause defines them in similar terms to those in the previous clause. There are several other points arising in connection with payments to nominated sub-contractors and the comments on clause 35 and on sub-contract clause 21 should be noted.

Lastly, all the contractor's profit on nominated amounts is included here and is thus subject to retention, whether the nominated amounts are completely so or not.

30.2.2 Other amounts in the additions side of the gross valuation are not subject to retention.

Several assorted and usually incidental amounts are brought together in clause 30.2.2.1. The clauses quoted relate to statutory fees and charges, setting out, opening up and testing, royalties and patent rights, defects liability, special insurance regarding property, and insurance of the works and existing property on the employer's default. The only problem arises with fees and charges payable under clause 6.2, because of the restricting effect in the present clause of the term 'in accordance with clause 3', that is to say a restriction to those amounts under clause 6.2 which 'are added to the Contract Sum'. While these amounts will not be subject to retention, other amounts listed in clauses 6.2.1 to 6.2.3 presumably will be. These other amounts are not identified separately under clause 30.2.1 but clause 30.2.1.4 subsumes the clause 6.2.1 cases and clause 30.2.1.1 must read as covering the rest in 'the total value of work' as being what is in the contract bills.

The frequently larger loss and expense amounts are referred to in clause 30.2.2.2. These comprise both the general amounts and the amounts due to antiquities. No amount results from an adjustment of the physical works as such and there may be nothing extra to show for the expenditure, so that the normal contingencies of default and the like against which retention is accumulated do not arise. In a number of instances, the amounts are due to a lapse on the part of the employer or the architect, making any deduction of retention even less reasonable.

After these come two matters of more regular character. Clause 30.2.2.3 relates to final payments to nominated sub-contractors which clause 35.17 requires to be made ahead of the final certificate. Clause 30.2.2.4 covers fluctuations additions based on costs, giving a different result from that for formula fluctuations.

Lastly, clause 30.2.2.5 brings in the corresponding nominated sub-contract provisions. These are more restricted in scope, maintaining silence over, for instance, amounts due to royalties and antiquities.

30.2.3 The amounts on the deductions side of the gross valuation comprise any sums for fluctuations omissions when fluctuations are based on costs, for both the contractor and the nominated sub-contractors. Corresponding with the position over additions, these amounts are not subject to retention.

30.3 — OFF-SITE MATERIALS OR GOODS

The effect of clause 30.2.1.2 is to make it obligatory on the architect to include in his certificates the value of the materials and goods properly on site. Clause 16.1 provides for ownership of them to pass to the employer on payment of the certificate first including them. If a determination occurs the ownership position will usually be quite clear when the employer reassumes possession of the site and of what stands or lies on it under clause 27.4.1. If however the employer were to pay without safeguards for materials or goods off-site he might find that in the event of a determination his legal title was overthrown by the doctrine of reputed ownership, despite the words 'shall become the property of the Employer' in clause 16.2. This and wider dangers are signalled strongly by several cases under 'Insolvency of contractor and title to goods'.

The present clause therefore sets out the safeguards and gives an option to the architect to certify their value at his discretion as parts of the amounts stated as due under clause 30.2, i.e. subject to retention. Since it is an optional power, the provisos laid down do not of themselves entitle the contractor to claim interim payment as of right. Rather they are limitations of the architect's discretionary powers within the terms specified and act as a practice note of what is to be observed in such a procedure. They may be grouped as follows:

(a) The physical condition of the materials and goods:
clauses 30.3.1 to 30.3.3 and 30.3.7.

(b) The legal status of the materials and goods:
clauses 30.3.4 to 30.3.6.

(c) The contractor's substantiation of the foregoing:
clause 30.3.8.

(d) The nature of the insurance referred to but not defined in clause 16.2:
clause 30.3.9.

The provisos may still leave the employer at some risk where the contractor is not a limited company, but are otherwise quite sound except in Scotland. The legal position rests partly on *Re Fox ex parte Oundle and Thrapston RDC* v. *The Trustee.*

As drafted, the clause envisages some decision, while the contract is under way, to pay in this manner, apart from any other consideration this may well be useful to keep the contractor in credit in some circumstances. Off-site fabrication is increasing and so is the desirability of specifying in the contract bills particular materials and goods to which the clause will apply as of right for the contractor. A suitable clause will accomplish this without the necessity of amending the present clause. The provisos will then assume greater regulative force, since they will govern the contractor's right to insist on payment and the architect's obligation to certify it.

30.4 — RETENTION — RULES FOR ASCERTAINMENT

30.4.1 The right of the employer to deduct retention is conferred by clause 30.2, which goes further and defines 'the amount stated as due' as that resulting after the deduction of retention. The present clause deals with the calculation of the retention in such a way that on the one hand it builds up broadly with the work under the contract, and on the other it reduces as the contract passes through successive phases. Three rules are given, of which the last two share a footnote explaining the effect of the rules. While the effect would be produced by following the rules carefully if blindly, presumably the authors sense that they are not entirely self-luminous in intention, however precise in meaning. The footnote therefore, while not forming part of the contract for interpretation, may reassure the weary pilgrim that he is still on course!

The retention percentage is defined in clause 30.4.1.1 as 5 per cent or any lower percentage entered in the appendix. A further footnote here recommends 3 per cent or less for contract sums of £500,000 or more. This retention percentage acts as the base figure and clause 30.4.1.2 applies it direct as the deduction from the value of work prior to practical completion and from the value of materials and goods, for both the contractor and nominated sub-contractors. The percentage is then halved under clause 30.4.1.3 as the deduction from the value of work between practical completion and the certificate of completion of making good defects, or between their equivalent when there is partial possession or final payment of a sub-contractor. As these are the only positive authorities for deduction, the further silence of the conditions means that no retention is to be held on work between the making good of defects or its equivalent and the issue of the final certificate. A 'release' of retention is achieved therefore by calculating a smaller total retention in a later certificate, by applying the lower percentage or none at all to given sections of work.

As different parts of the work may be in any of the three stages, work falling within the terms of clause 30.2.1 may be subject to full, half or no retention in any one interim certificate in the later stages of a contract.

30.4.2 For later conciseness, the parts of the retention are distinguished as 'Contractor's retention' and 'Nominated Sub-Contract retention' respectively, although the latter in turn is to be calculated again for each sub-contractor under clause 30.5.2.1.

30.5 — RULES ON TREATMENT OF RETENTION

The previous clause gives rules for building up and whittling away the retention; the present deals with what happens to it in the interim. It gives no authority to the employer to have recourse to the retention while it rests in his trusteeship over any default of the contractor or of a sub-contractor. The right to deduct from the retention is however discussed under clause 30.1.1.2.

30.5.1 The trust status of the whole retention is established, whether or not it goes into a separate account under clause 30.5.3. The employer is not obliged, separate account or no, to invest the retention. If there is any interest it remains with the employer under that clause. The wording here and the reference to retention in sub-contract clause 21.6 creates a direct trustee position for the employer with each nominated sub-contractor, as well as with the contractor. No such trustee position is established for the contractor over sub-contractor's retention or other amounts when transmitted through him to them.

30.5.2 The various retention amounts on the contractor and nominated sub-contractors are to be stated for each interim certificate, usually by the architect on the quantity surveyor's advice. These should be expressed as the total to date, rather than the increase or reduction for the particular certificate, as this is the most relevant figure. While the employer and the contractor should receive the master statement, normal commercial practice dictates that each sub-contractor should receive only the statement for his own retention in spite of the exact wording of the clause.

30.5.3 The creation of a trust fund in a distinct bank account is a provision peculiar to the private editions of the conditions, although the wisdom of this limitation might well be questioned! Even so, it is optional in that it only comes about if the contractor or any nominated sub-contractor requests it. As the requirement is to place 'the Retention' in the account, it would appear that a request by even the smallest sub-contractor, in terms of value of work, is enough to force everyone's retention into the account. Usually if the account is opened, it will be tidier to use it like this anyway. Here the employer certifies, unusually, to the architect that the retention is in the account. While the contractor receives a copy of this certificate, there is no express right for any sub-contractor to receive this or even an obligation for the contractor to certify that it exists.

The general question of investment of the retention is discussed under clause 30.5.1. The particular matter of any interest accruing in the separate account is covered here, so that the employer may retain any such interest.

30.5.4 If the employer does deduct under clause 30.1.1.2 for any contra-amounts, he must give the contractor details in relation to the current statement under clause 30.5.2.1. Otherwise the contractor will face an unexplained discrepancy in reconciling the previous and present retention totals and any increases and reductions. This ties with the requirement of clause 30.1.1.3 to give a reason for the deduction.

There is not a requirement for the employer to tell the architect of his action (although the architect will probably have precipitated it by his advice) and the architect does not need to show the deduction in his next interim certificate to keep accounts in order. Reasonably, he and the quantity surveyor will be fully informed.

30.6.1 — FINAL ADJUSTMENT OF CONTRACT SUM — DOCUMENTS FROM CONTRACTOR — FINAL VALUATION UNDER CLAUSE 13

(The three parts of clause 30.6 are each accorded a heading and this pattern is followed here.)

The requirement in clause 30.6.1.1 is that 'the Contractor shall send . . . all documents necessary' for the final account that he has, and this is quite general and will cover time sheets and invoices relating to fluctuations, for example. It is not limited in time either, except by the word 'reasonable'. If the contractor held up a substantial amount of vital information until the end of the period of final measurement and valuation or beyond and then released it in a mass, it would then be unreasonable for him to press for the final certificate within three months under clause 30.8. The architect is to receive all these documents unless he specifically routes them to the quantity surveyor, which he will usually be happy to do. He may wish to comment on points of principle in them or need to raise variation instructions for instance, but the detail he will usually leave with relief to the quantity surveyor.

'The statement of all the final Valuations under clause 13' in clause 30.6.1.2 covers all measured work and daywork related to variations and provisional sum expenditure. This is the work which the quantity surveyor is specifically assigned to value and which to a large extent he can deal with independently of the contractor's participation in principle, whatever may actually happen in practice. The statement is also limited to this work, since the contractor will need to supply and therefore know about virtually all information for the other additions elements of the final account under clauses 30.6.2.6 onwards. This and all the other elements will come together as the final account under clause 30.6.3. Before this, the architect is to send a copy of the statement to the contractor and a relevant extract to each nominated sub-contractor. Nominated suppliers are not included, as there is an element of replacement of breakages which does not concern the employer's settlement. The extracts are necessary before clause 30.7 can be operated to settle nominated sub-contract accounts, and this in turn must precede clause 30.6.2.6 as part of the whole final account process.

In practice, these matters tend to occur and agreement to be reached in whatever order is most conducive to progress, but this does give a regulating framework if needed.

A time limit is set on the period of final measurement and valuation and the appendix gives this as six months, the same as the defects liability period, unless some special insertion is made. It is subject to the supply of information from the contractor, but then certainly cannot be much longer, because the final certificate may be due within a further three months under clause 30.8 and the statement of valuations is to precede this. While no time interval is specified between the two, all that is needed is time enough for the contractor to voice any complaints he may have in fairly broad terms and thus either obtain a stay of the final certificate or make it quite clear that he will go to arbitration on it. In practice the contractor is usually in close negotiation with the quantity surveyor during the drawing up of the final account and knows in advance whether such action is going to arise.

30.6.2 —ITEMS INCLUDED IN ADJUSTMENT OF CONTRACT SUM

The preceding clause having given rise to exchange of documents required for the preparation and perusal of the final account, the present clause lists the elements in the account. The starting point is the contract sum, which may only be adjusted 'in accordance with the express provisions of the Conditions' as clause 14.2 puts it. There are therfore two lists giving respectively the major and most common deductions and additions permitted by the conditions. Discussion here follows the classification of the clause: and the authorising clauses in numerical order are given in Figure 6 on page 38.

Among the deductions in clause 30.6.2.2 are the inevitable deductions of prime cost sums for sub-contractors and suppliers, and other amounts for sub-contractors with related profit. Attendance does not automatically rank for adjustment because of a change in these amounts as such, and will only be adjusted if there is a change of scope affecting the incidence of attendance. This latter could happen with even marginal adjustment of the main amount.

The first four additions in clauses 30.6.2.6 to 30.6.2.10 also relate to prime cost sums. These are nominated sub-contract amounts (including those arising from provisional sums and defined by reference to clause 30.7 under which an anomaly is mentioned), amounts for work performed by the contractor himself, amounts for materials and goods from nominated suppliers and profit related to each set of amounts. In the case of nominated suppliers, there is specific mention of the inclusion of cash discount and the exclusion of value added tax as input tax. This is unnecessary in the case of nominated sub-contractors, as the references to the sub-contracts spell out the corresponding terms.

Profit is defined in the case of nominated sub-contract amounts as being 'upon the amounts referred to in clause 30.6.2.6.' These are the gross amounts under the appropriate sub-contracts and (despite the anomaly noted under clause 30.7) are not to be reduced before the profit is calculated by any credit under clause 30.7 for direct payments by the employer to nominated sub-contractors before nomination. Since the sub-contract amounts *are* gross, the contractor will still receive profit on any sums which the employer has paid direct to sub-contractors and which are not to be deducted in the present settlement. Views on the fairness of this may vary. However the contractor loses the discount on the sums.

Also inevitable are the deductions in clause 30.6.2.2 of provisional sums expended in accordance with clause 13.3.1, or not used at all, and of provisional work in the contract bills. Provisional work is not covered in clause 13.3.1, but is discussed below in respect of what is substituted. Deductions due to variations are of two kinds: work physically omitted and work which remains physically as intended, but which is being revalued because of a change in the circumstances of its execution. These categories are discussed under clause 13.5. The corresponding additions in clauses 30.6.2.11 and 30.6.2.12 for variations and expenditure on provisional sum work occur in the reverse order.

The last specified deductions in clause 30.6.2.4 are the amounts of any fluctuations adjustments which reflect reductions in costs to the contractor, these costs being embodied as parts of various prices in the contract bills. These deductions are therefore calculated, as are the corresponding additions in clause 30.6.2.15, rather than amounts taken directly from the contract bills.

A group of miscellaneous additions in clause 30.6.2.10 receive blanket authority from clause 3 and their references relate to the following:

Clause 6.2.	Statutory fees and charges.
Clause 7.	Errors in setting out.
Clause 8.3.	Opening up and testing.
Clause 9.2.	Royalties, damages, etc.
Clause 17.2.	Making good defects.
Clause 17.3.	Making good defects.
Clause 21.2.3	Special insurance of property.

The fairness of the employer having to pay for several of these is discussed under the clauses concerned. It is possible to construe clause 7 in such a way as to regard a deduction as a credit for a condoned error; although no credit is mentioned in the present clause it could fall under clause 30.6.2.5. The mention of special insurance is strictly not necessary, since this is a provisional sum and would not fall under the clauses discussed earlier.

The other specific additions in clauses 30.6.2.13 and 30.6.2.14 cover loss and expense, both generally and in the case of antiquities, and insurance of the works and existing property paid for by the contractor on the employer's default. Oddly, where the employer pays for similar insurance on the contractor's default under clause 22A this becomes one of the items that may not be dealt with in the final account and is included in the list below.

The deductions and additions lists both end with a provision in clauses 30.6.2.5 and 30.6.2.16 for 'any other amount which is required by this Contract'. The only items that appear to fit here are extra expenses in renomination of sub-contractors under clause 35.24.7 and those related to nominated suppliers' materials or goods under clause 36.3.2, unless the credit over setting out is introduced under clause 7. Even the correction of errors in the contract bills under clause 2.2.2.2 falls elsewhere to be treated like variations. The items that do not clearly belong here or in the next paragraphs are the VAT related loss discussed under clause 15.3, and the statutory tax scheme deductions and adjustments under clause 31.

The conditions deal with several situations where the contractor defaults by allowing the employer himself (and no one else) to make deductions from 'monies due or to become due' or to recover amounts as debts, so that he is reimbursed for expense or is in receipt of damages. These amounts are thus to be ignored in the final account and will not be reflected in the final certificate either, as they would otherwise be deducted twice. However the employer should be notified of them as they arise and be reminded of them when the final certificate is issued. These cases are the contractor's default over:

Clause 4.1.2.	Performing work when instructed.
Clause 21.1.3.	Insuring third party liability.
Clause 22A.2.	Insuring the works.
Clause 24.2.1.	Completing the works on time.
Clauses 35.13.5.3.	Paying nominated sub-contractors.
Clause 35.24.6.	Nominated sub-contractors' determination.

Defects in nominated sub-contract works after final payment may also lead to payment by the contractor of an allowance in favour of the employer under clause 35.18.1.2 and it would appear that this does not operate through the final account either.

When the employer under clause 27 determines the employment of the contractor, the present clause does not come directly into play, but it will still be necessary to prepare a hypothetical final account based on its principles. When it is the contractor who determines under clause 28, the requirement is to settle under the arrangement of an interim certificate valuation, as in clause 30.1. As that clause depends on clause 30.2 however, many of the present principles will still be relevant. The essential differences will be in the valuation of partly complete work.

30.6.3 — COMPUTATION OF ADJUSTED CONTRACT SUM — CONTRACTOR TO RECEIVE COPY

The results of clause 30.6.2 are to be made available to the contractor 'before the issue of the Final Certificate' without any margin being given. This is not too critical usually since, as has been discussed over clause 30.6.1.2, the contractor will be well aware of the preparatory steps. The quantity surveyor has supplied the statement of valuations, the contractor himself has supplied most other detail (as distinct from necessarily knowing whether it is agreed), while nominated sub-contract amounts must be cleared at least 28 days before the final certificate.

30.7 — INTERIM CERTIFICATE — FINAL ADJUSTMENT OR ASCERTAINMENT OF NOMINATED SUB-CONTRACT SUMS

All nominated sub-contractors are to be paid off before the issue of the final certificate, so that proofs of payment can be obtained under clause 35.13.3 (subject to the issues discussed there). To permit this, an appropriate interim certificate covering all nominated sub-contracts amounts without deduction of retention is to be issued 'as soon as practicable'. It need not be the last interim certificate and in fact the sub-contractors may be paid off in several certificates by virtue of clause 35.17. Its issue holds off the final certificate for 'not less than 28 days' and for this reason it may be issued closer than one month to the preceding interim certificate to reduce delaying the issuing of the final certificate. This may occur even if it is not the last interim certificate, as long as it includes the last nominated sub-contract amount.

The amounts are 'sums . . . as finally adjusted or ascertained' under the sub-contracts. 'Adjusted' refers to deductions from and additions to an original sub-contract sum, while 'ascertained' refers to computation of a final sum from a schedule of rates, for example. These terms are following the principles in sub-contract clauses 15.1 and 15.2 respectively. The sums are to be 'reduced by any amounts to be credited', these being payments made by the employer direct to any sub-contractor before nomination, but originally included in the sub-contract tender, and presumably within the prime cost sum in the contract bills. The payments will have been in respect of design, fabrication and the like, made under the terms of either Agreement NSC/2 or NSC/2a, whichever has been used.

The 'amounts . . . to be credited' are not mentioned in clause 30.6.2.6 in referring to the final account settlement, although that clause mentions the provisions of the sub-contracts as does the present clause. Clause 30.6.2.6 would be better if, in referring to the present clause, it mentioned both or neither. As it is there is an anomaly, so that strictly the contractor will be paid in the final account for work for which sub-contractors have already been paid direct. It is suggested that this should not be done and that the courts would not uphold the opposite absurdity if it were pressed, despite the further anomaly mentioned in the next paragraph, which might be adduced in support.

While either of these collateral agreements covers the position between employer and sub-contractor, the agreements have no bearing on the contractor's own position. There therefore is no direct authority under these conditions for work to be omitted from the contract and to be paid for direct.

This is what has happened in this case. However by the operation of the agreements in this way a part of the work has been omitted from the contract even though it is a part done before nomination of the sub-contract and so not included within the scope of the nomination. It may well be argued that the contract does not embrace any design and so this work was not covered by the prime cost sum, but this argument is more precarious in the case of fabricated work. Strictly it would seem the contractor could stand on his rights and insist that work should not be omitted from his contract and given to another, even if that person is also to be his sub-contractor. The question of liability for defects in the fabricated work may also arise and the position is unclear.

If such direct payment is made, the contractor in any case will be entitled to profit upon the sums before reduction, as discussed under clause 30.6.2.

30.8 — ISSUE OF FINAL CERTIFICATE

The clause obliges the architect to issue the final certificate within three months of the happening of the latest of three events. One of these, the ending of the defects liability period, is at a fixed interval from practical completion. The other two are determined mainly by the actions of the contractor, who can thus advance the issue of the final certificate by his own promptitude. This timetable is one of the least observed features of the contract, usually due to delays in agreeing the final account, and the three persons principally involved often share responsibility. The architect's issue of instructions in proper written form may have lagged during progress and confirmations from him under clause 4.3.2 or clause 13.2 may be hard to obtain. Even when he has this information, the quantity surveyor may not be advanced in his measuring and valuing. Sometimes he may be too concerned with obtaining the contractor's agreement, desirable though it is, to every minor point before supplying the architect with figures for the final certificate. The contract does not necessarily call for the agreement of the final account, but simply that the contractor shall have had opportunity to see its contents. If the final certificate is issued on that basis and the contractor is dissatisfied his remedy lies in arbitration. The occasional operation of the strict procedure might be beneficial to all, while also involving some possible embarrassment and some certain expense. Lastly, the contractor may be dilatory in producing the essential information in his possession. Usually there is enough delay by each to obscure any clear responsibility of any one person.

The effect of the final certificate is the subject of the next clause. Here the architect is required to notify each nominated sub-contractor of its date of issue, as the sub-contractors' residual liabilities to the contractor and the employer change at that date. This change is in accordance with clauses 35.17 and 35.18 of these conditions and also ties in with clause 5.3 of Agreement NSC/2 or NSC/2a.

The present clause stipulates the monies to be shown in the final certificate. These are simply the final cost of the works, the total amount certified on account and the difference becoming a debt due. The contractor's right to any outstanding interim amounts is preserved by the words '(without prejudice ... by the Employer)', while the next clause deals with the status of the certificate if arbitration or any other proceeding is looming. Normally there will be a balance in favour of the contractor which will be due 14 days after the issue of the certificate.

The final certificate must take account of 'the Contract Sum adjusted as necessary'. It should not, however, make the 'deductions authorised by' the conditions but should simply be 'subject to' such deductions. The employer should therefore make — and if necessary be advised by the architect to make — any such deductions from the final balance whether or not already allowed for by deductions from the interim amounts certified by the architect. If these deductions reverse the direction of indebtedness the employer should advise the contractor at once. The matters leading to such deductions are listed in the discussion on clause 30.6.2.

30.9 — EFFECT OF FINAL CERTIFICATE

30.9.1 Here are set out those matters in which the final certificate provides 'conclusive evidence' 'in any proceedings', that is in actions in the courts or in arbitrations, and the ways in which this function is restricted. By providing a positive and closely limited statement of the matters on which it is conclusive evidence that the contractor has carried out all his obligations properly, the clause thereby excludes all other matters. These matters of conclusive evidence are as follows:

(i) Materials and workmanship under clause 30.9.1.1. These are limited to those cases in which quality and standards are to be to the 'reasonable satisfaction of the Architect', a phrase which has been discussed in relation to materials and workmanship under clause 2.1. The architect is therefore not stating in the final certificate his satisfaction with what is usually by far the greater bulk of the construction specified precisely in the contract documents. The contractor remains liable to the employer for any breach in complying with what has been specified during the period provided under the Limitation Act, that is 12 years for a contract under seal and six years in other cases. In the cases defined in clause 2.1 in which the architect expresses his reasonable satisfaction by issuing the final certificate, any continuing responsibility is however effectively transferred from the contractor to the architect. In passing it should be noted that, while this is the position under this present clause between employer and contractor, the terms of the contract between employer and architect may widen the responsibility of the architect over supervision. The cases on 'Certificates and approvals' which were mostly decided on contracts not including the present wording, indicate some of the possibilities and may indicate a lengthening of the period of liability under the Act. The position of nominated sub-contractors is modified by Agreement NSC/2 or NSC/2a, as noted under clause 30.8.

(ii) Adjustments of the contract sum under clause 30.9.1.2. Here con-

clusiveness that all adjustments have been made and are indisputable is limited by 'any accidental inclusion or exclusion'. This extends into the processes of quantities and pricing in the final account and is widely enough worded to go back to the contract bills by way of clause 2.2.2.2, to which even clause 14 is subject. This should give any quantity surveyor cause for solemn thought. Any inclusion or exclusion that was foregone in negotiation of the final account in consideration of some other matter is not envisaged here; it will not be 'accidental'.

Once conclusiveness has been eroded in this way, with accident excluded at one end of the spectrum and fraud at the other, perhaps all that is left is some category of negligence that does not merge into either and that in itself might give the employer (if not the contractor) a right of action against his professional advisers. While it may be thought desirable for the employer, who is usually passive during settlement, to have the door kept open in this way, it hardly seems appropriate for the contractor who is usually anything but passive and who is often responsible for providing information that might otherwise be excluded. Again the period of the various rights and liabilities will be governed by the Limitation Act.

Clause 30.9.1.2 does not affect other financial matters that may lie between the employer and the contractor and that are referred to in the contract otherwise than as leading to adjustment of the contract sum. Some of these are recognised in clause 30.8 as 'deductions authorised by these Conditions' which the employer may make from the amount certified by the architect. The other main category will be actions for breach of contract by either party, including matters arising from disturbance of progress which are hinted at darkly in clause 26.6 in the phrase 'without prejudice to any other rights and remedies'.

Two overriding qualifications to all that has been mentioned so far about conclusiveness are referred to in the opening words of clause 30.9.1. Fraud is mentioned without amplification, but could relate to fraud on the part of the architect in drawing up the final certificate or on the part of the contractor in presenting to the architect or to the quantity surveyor on his behalf the various physical and financial elements covered by the final certificate.

'Arbitration or other proceedings' constitute the other qualification. The conditions make no attempt to limit when legal proceedings may be initiated and they could start at any stage. In the case of arbitration the position is regulated by article 5. On a few matters only article 5.2 permits arbitration to take place before practical completion without mutual agreement between the parties (which would allow any matter to be referred to arbitration at any time), while on other matters it may have taken place later but before issue of the final certificate. On still other matters of dispute the arbitration machinery may already have been set in motion and, even if not, either the employer or the contractor has 14 days from the issue of the final certificate to request arbitration on any matter governed by the certificate. Thereafter the limitation period applies to any type of proceedings as already discussed.

30.9.2 This provision deals with proceedings started before the issue of the final certificate. Clause 30.9.2.1 takes the tidier case in which proceedings are concluded with no more than the expected degree of protraction. Here there will be two possibilities: that conclusion is reached before or after the issue of the certificate. In the former situation the certificate simply becomes subject to the result of proceedings. In the latter situation, while the issue of the certificate will not and must not be delayed, its effect will be uncertain until the proceedings end, when again the certificate becomes subject to them. As worded, this clause as a whole appears to make all matters covered in the final certificate remain in suspense in this latter case until proceedings end, and not just any elements in it which comes within the scope of the proceedings. There are no words equivalent to 'save only . . . relate' as in clause 30.9.3. It may be questioned whether this is really what is intended, but it would seem that the courts could take this interpretation. The importance of this is that the limitation period for instituting proceedings runs from the date at which the final certificate becomes conclusive evidence over any particular matter. Under clause 30.9.3 this is a progressive matter, while here it is apparently not.

Clause 30.9.2.2 is also affected by the point just noted, but presents its own further peculiarity. It legislates for the situation in which proceedings have started but then both parties run out of steam and there is a hiatus of 12 months. The position is not explicitly covered in which the courts or the arbitrator cause such a delay. When this hiatus has occurred, presumably by the implied consent of the parties, the final certificate becomes conclusive evidence on any matters which figure in the proceedings, which may or may not then be worth reviving. Thus far the clause represents a commendable route to progress. What is not rigorously defined is the timing of the 12-month period. If it is a period following the issue of the final certificate in whole or in part, and perhaps with a gap between the certificate and itself, then a likely intention will result (although maybe not that in mind when the wording was drafted, which may have been better served by the insertion of 'after the issue of the Final Certificate' after '12 months'). If it can be construed as a period entirely before the issue of the certificate, then some consequences could flow that are most unlikely to have been intended, especially when the words 'whichever shall be the earlier' are taken into account.

30.9.3 This clause is happily clear after its predecessor. It deals with proceedings begun in the 14 days available to either party for this purpose immediately after the issue of the final certificate. The certificate is suspended in its effects on the points at issue until the proceedings are completed, but only on these points as distinct from the position noted under clause 30.9.2.2. It then becomes subject to the results of the proceedings, as is reasonable. There is no provision for a hiatus occurring in this case, but in view of the limited range of matters over which the limitation period is extended by the proceedings and any delay in them, this is likely to be of little consequence. Since the 14 days' grace relates solely to the subject matter of the final certificate, it in no way curtails the rights of the parties on other matters throughout the limitation period.

30.10 — EFFECT OF CERTIFICATES OTHER THAN FINAL CERTIFICATES

This clause makes the already implied legal position an explicit one in the contract, and has particular importance in regard to the certificate of practical completion under clause 17.1, the certificate of completion of making good defects under clause 17.4 and interim certificates under clause 30.1. The architect has full power to defer or review any approval right up to the issue of the final certificate, while clause 30.9 places severe limits on how conclusive it will then be. Several cases are relevant. Not all certificates relate to work materials or goods, as Figure 5 shows.

CHAPTER 12

Contingent matters

Clause 32 — Outbreak of hostilities
Clause 33 — War damage
Clause 34 — Antiquities

Clause 32 — Outbreak of hostilities

This clause assumes fairly passive conditions that allow its provisions to be put into effect in an orderly manner. In the event of war damage occurring, clause 33 may be superimposed upon the present clause. There remains the distinct possibility that hostilities could so change circumstances that — not to put too fine a point on it — the contract could become 'frustrated' and this could lead to a different basis of settlement, as the footnote to the clause recognises.

32.1 — NOTICE OF DETERMINATION OF THE CONTRACTOR'S EMPLOYMENT

Hostilities under this clause are to be of major character, but need not involve the United Kingdom as an actual theatre of war. Their existence alone is sufficient to justify determination, no direct effect on either party need be demonstrated and arbitration on the act of determination itself is not therefore possible, as it is in the somewhat similar case of clause 22C. Determination may be effected by either party and is purely optional, since the parties may both wish to carry on.

32.1.1 Notice of determination may be served at any time after the early limit of 28 days.

32.1.2 The late limit is practical completion or war damage, with determination taking place at once, subject to the provisions of clause 32.2. The purpose of this clause is to keep alive the contractor's liability to make good defects, unless war damage occurs and probably throws doubt on what are defects under clause 17.2 and 17.3.

32.2 — PROTECTIVE WORK

Although the determination is immediately effective, it might be unreasonable for the contractor to cease his operations at once. A short period is thus allowed in which the architect may instruct work necessary to achieve such things as stability, weathertightness and enclosure of the works. Such instructions could well include the leaving in position of scaffolding and other supports. A limit is placed on how long the contractor need go on with such work if he is hindered by reasons beyond his control, bringing affairs to a maximum of three months and 14 days from notice of determination.

The inference of this is that the architect should not instruct the contractor to carry out work that is expected to take more than three months, but the clause is open at this point. The term 'continuation . . . up to points of stoppage' relates to the minimum amount of work necessary and in the circumstances envisages that both sides will adopt a reasonable attitude over the extent and time. Otherwise the usual remedies are available.

32.3 — PAYMENT

This clause, like clause 22C, relates itself to the provisions of clause 28.2 which govern the contractor's removal from site and his final payment. As in the case of clause 22C, the contractor is not entitled to reimbursement for loss of profit or similar matters arising out of the determination. Work instructed under clause 32.2 is to be valued as a variation and this will be a case where the term 'not . . . under similar conditions' in clause 13.5.1.2 must be kept well in mind when valuing measured work. Clause 13.5.6 may also be applied to this post-determination work.

The clause comes into effect when the contractor has carried out or duly abandoned any work instructed under clause 32.2, or otherwise within fourteen days of determination, and he should then commence removal of whatever he is entitled to remove. He may well already have been removing superfluous items while carrying out work under clause 32.2.

Clause 33 — War damage

If there is an outbreak of hostilities coupled with war damage to the works, several situations may arise. There may have been completion or determination under clause 32.1 before the war damage occurs; in neither of these cases does the present clause apply and the contractor's liability to carry out work (other than remedying his own defects) is discharged, even if the damage occurs while he is still carrying out protective or other work under clause 32.2 The present clause operates only when war damage occurs before completion or determination, but it recognises that either of these may follow on war damage.

The clause has an effect somewhat similar to that of clause 22C where the employer takes the risk of damage to the works from certain causes. The contractor is reimbursed by the employer for all work that he carries out, while the employer has to look elsewhere to recoup his expense. Either party may determine as a result of the damage.

33.1 — EFFECT OF WAR DAMAGE

This clause is to operate notwithstanding anything expressed or implied elsewhere in the contract and thus overrules such matters as the contractor's responsibility for materials or goods under clause 16.1 or the indemnity of clause 20.2 so far as the works or materials or goods are concerned. It even overrules the 'entire contract' obligation of clause 2.1.

33.1.1 This provision allows for the contractor being paid for all that he does or supplies in the course of the works before or after the war damage, and here and later the pattern follows that of clause 22C.

33.1.2 The architect has the power to instruct what shall be removed as being beyond repair and also to instruct on work which he may consider necessary to avoid further deterioration and which the contractor might not otherwise perform.

33.1.3 Following on from this the contractor is to perform all this work and replacement and any other making good, at his discretion it seems, to achieve required standards. He is then to proceed to completion, unless he invokes clause 32.1. If he proceeds, he also receives an extension of time without giving notice or following any other procedure under clause 25.

33.1.4 Any of these instructions or any other work which the contractor carries out as extra to the works must be treated as 'deemed' variations to be valued under clause 13.2, as with work instructed under clause 32.2.

The contractor will not be paid for his own plant and the like, nor for off-site materials and goods unless paid for on an interim basis by the employer under clause 16.2, if any of these is lost or damaged.

33.2 — RELATION WITH CLAUSE 32

Either party may determine under clause 32.1 without the other being able to prevent it at any time after the outbreak of hostilities, and a severe piece of war damage seems a very likely way of precipitating such action. While the contractor will then be relieved of the obligation to reinstate damage and carry on and complete the works, it is reasonable that he should still leave them in a condition that will not lead to undue deterioration. The present clause secures this by defining that in this situation clause 32.2 shall cover any outstanding instructions already given under clause 33.1.2 and thus keep them alive.

Since the effect of clause 32.2 is in no way diminished by the occurrence of war damage, it would seem that the architect could in any case give instructions under that clause if the present clause were not in existence.

33.3 — USE OF COMPENSATION FOR WAR DAMAGE

Since the employer has reimbursed the contractor, the employer not unreasonably receives compensation as and when it materialises, leaving the contractor to collect anything in respect of plant or other of his property.

33.4 — DEFINITION OF WAR DAMAGE

The definition in the Act is cumbersome, but has a wide scope.

Clause 34 — Antiquities

34.1 — EFFECT OF FIND OF ANTIQUITIES

This clause deals with objects previously unknown that may be discovered during the contractor's operations. They need not be historic or prehistoric and the term 'of interest or value' gives the clause wide scope. If the contractor is in any reasonable doubt over an object, he should observe the precautions of this clause rather than destroy the object as unimportant; provided he did not act capriciously, he would be entitled to any consequent reimbursement under clause 34.3 without the need of an architect's instruction. Whatever the objects they become the property of the employer, although he in turn may have to deal with them as treasure trove.

34.1.1 The requirements laid upon the contractor are designed to ensure that objects are not displaced or damaged through inexpert attention, although this clause appears to recognise the possibility of an accident occurring in the act of discovery itself.

34.1.2 This clause takes account of the fact that the position occupied by an object may be as important to the expert as its character.

34.1.3 This is the only reference to the clerk of works outside clause 12. Where objects of value are accessible the quickest route to the employer via his representative is needed!

34.2 — ARCHITECT'S INSTRUCTION ON ANTIQUITIES FOUND

This provision is cast in very general terms, as is emphasised by the portion in brackets. Where discoveries may range from a dinosaur's kneecap to a heathen temple this is quite understandable: expert persons may be brought on the site and will be in a position equivalent to that of those working for the employer under clause 29. In keeping with this position, these experts and specialists are excluded from the scope of the contractor's indemnity of the employer under clause 20. Work by the contractor himself may also fall within the instructions and will be valued as appropriate.

34.3 — DIRECT LOSS AND/OR EXPENSE

34.3.1 This clause follows the wording of clause 26.1 closely and provides the contractor with the same opportunity for reimbursement as does that clause. Since the architect will be aware of the situation and how it has developed, the contractor is not required to make written application to establish his right in principle to payment. Otherwise matters will take a similar course and the comments on clause 26.1 should be considered here also. In this present case there is no question of any lapse on the employer's side and there is no wording corresponding to clause 26.6. The contractor must therefore ensure that reimbursement under this present clause is adequate, since he can bring no action for breach in the circumstances, although arbitration is still possible on the amount. This reimbursement is to cover the loss and/or expense which the contractor may incur by his own working or stopping work under clause 34.1, or resulting from the architect's instructions under clause 34.2 that cannot come under the valuation rules of clause 13.5.

34.3.2 When this financial reimbursement is possible and the contractor is also entitled to extension of time, the architect must state the amount of extension if it is relevant to the reimbursement, as happens also under clause 26.3. The contractor however may not determine under clause 28.1 if his progress is impeded. It is conceivable that circumstances could arise which would lead to the contract being frustrated.

34.3.3 This is the routine provision allowing payment under interim certificates and in the final account.

CHAPTER 13

Financial legislation

Clause 15 — Value added tax — supplemental provisions
Supplemental provisions (the VAT agreement)
Clause 31 — Finance (No 2) Act 1975 — statutory tax deduction scheme

Presumably even the drafters of forms of contract (to say nothing of commentators) must wilt at the steady flow of assorted legislation that leads to the distortion of what was once a tidily planned document. Much legislation is taken account of fairly indirectly in the present conditions, but this chapter brings together items which have arisen because of statutes requiring specific reference in the conditions, and which have financial consequences. While clauses 15 and 31 are clauses in the conditions in the usual way the supplemental provisions are simply attached to the conditions.

It may be noted that the collection of tax moves in opposite directions in the two cases, creating a slightly odd situation. The possibility of any interaction between these cases has not been considered. Formula fluctuations is just mentioned at one stage — bring that in as well and the scene is set for the insoluble. But perhaps we are becoming frivolous.

Clause 15 — Value added tax — supplemental provisions

15.1 — DEFINITIONS — VAT AGREEMENT

Solely for its own purposes and those of the supplemental provisions, this clause defines three short titles. The term 'value added tax' is used in full in several other clauses, however, rather than 'tax' alone as here.

15.2 — CONTRACT SUM — EXCLUSIVE OF VAT

The contract sum is defined in the articles of agreement and clause 14.2 establishes its general integrity, while the present clause sets out that the contract sum is exclusive of value added tax. Adjustments to the contract sum will also be exclusive of the tax and the conditions specifically provide that value added tax shall not be dealt with under or affect the contract itself, in the following clauses:

Clause 6.2	Statutory fees and charges
Clause 28.1.1	Default in paying certificates
Clause 30.6.2.8	Adjustment of contract sum
Clause 38.2.1	Fluctuations
Clause 38.2.2	Fluctuations
Clause 39.3.3	Fluctuations
Clause 40.3	Fluctuations

The contract sum having been circumscribed in this way, the clause goes on to provide that the contractor is to charge his output tax to the employer quite separately under the VAT Agreement, which has been given a collateral status under clause 15.1 and which is discussed later in this chapter. The only other clause dealing with VAT transactions is clause 35.13.5.3, where the reference is to the distinct question of input tax chargeable otherwise to the contractor.

15.3 — POSSIBLE EXEMPTION FROM VAT

One of the basic principles of value added tax is that when goods and services are taxable, whether at standard rate or zero rate, then the supplier of these goods and services may recover from the Commissioners any input tax charged to him earlier in the chain of supply. If the goods and services which he supplies are exempt from the tax, it is equally a principle that any input tax borne by him is not recoverable from the Commissioners. This clause takes account of the possibility that some element of the works might be transferred from taxable to exempt status after the date of tender, with the result that the contractor would find that input tax which he had expected to recover would no longer be recoverable, while still being payable. The employer is to pay 'an amount equal to the loss' to the contractor, apparently by addition to the contract sum in this case even though the term is not used. The VAT Agreement is concerned solely with the contractor's output tax, and had it been intended to reimburse by that channel, presumably the present clause would have been there. No mention is made of payment in interim certificates, although this would be equitable where much money was involved, on the analogy of clause 3.

The reimbursement is limited to tax on entities which 'contribute exclusively to the Works' and thus excludes such items as head office expenditure and plant, which contribute to several projects in principle at least.

Supplemental provisions (the VAT agreement)

This agreement is printed not as part of the conditions themselves, but as an additional section following them, and it is not listed among the contract documents under clause 2.1. It is the intention that it should be used in every contract, since construction work is not tax exempt even though much of it is zero rated. The possibility of a change of rating producing a liability to pay tax must therefore always be in the background. At the same time the agreement is to be operated in a semi-detached relationship to the conditions as will be apparent so it is kept as the distinct section that it is. It is considered under the headings that are used in the agreement, which sometimes cover a whole clause and sometimes only a part, but often cover several parts. This untidy division will be taken as it is found.

The agreement is closely related to clause 15 of the conditions and as a result it is executed at the same time as the contract proper. The broad purpose is to secure that the contractor receives from the employer by payments outside the main contract itself the tax which he is required to account for to the Commissioners as output tax on his supplies to the employer. (Both 'tax' and 'Commissioners' are defined in full in clause 15.1.) Clause 15.2 of the conditions leaves the contract sum as exclusive of any of the tax, while the conditions provide in places listed in discussing that clause that no tax will be added to the contract sum in the final account. Only in clause 15.3 of the conditions is there a provision for input tax chargeable to the contractor to be recovered from the employer in unusual circumstances and apparently by an addition to the contract sum.

There are a number of reasons why this financial framework has been chosen. These include the problems of identifying in advance in tenders those items that would carry tax with certainty at zero and other ratings, the difficulties associated with changes in tax rates during progress, and other factors of a fiscal nature. In addition, to have included the arrangements within the contract would have meant that the architect would have been responsible for certifying tax sums for payment. This would have conflicted with the principle that the contractor is responsible for assessing and collecting the tax on behalf of the Commissioners and that the employer then needs a channel of appeal through the contractor to the Commissioners if he is aggrieved.

1 — INTERIM PAYMENTS — ADDITION OF VAT

This part of the agreement covers the central point that the employer is to pay tax, which is clearly output tax under the wording given. Input tax will be recovered in normal circumstances by the contractor from the Commissioners. The overall position should thus be that he will not be out of pocket, at least so far as the tax itself is concerned, whatever his expenses of administration may be.

1.1 — WRITTEN ASSESSMENT BY CONTRACTOR

This clause and the next then provide for the action to be taken by the contractor and the employer respectively over interim amounts. Alongside interim certificates and other financial certificates, the contractor is to give a 'written provisional assessment', not of the tax but of the supplies subject to tax and the applicable tax rates. This may apply alongside the final certificate if necessary, since clause 1.3.2 allows for later final settlement of the tax. This assessment from the contractor should not be treated as a tax invoice (which is dealt with under clause 1.4) and he should endorse it accordingly. It is to be for sums after retention deduction or for retention releases.

1.2 — EMPLOYER TO CALCULATE AMOUNT OF TAX DUE — EMPLOYER'S RIGHT OF REASONABLE OBJECTION

1.2.1 The employer's part will usually be to calculate the tax on the data provided and pay it with the monies due on the contract. If however there is some adjustment of tax rates between receiving assessment and making the payment, then the employer is due to pay a correspondingly adjusted amount (although the wording of the sub-clause is silent on the point), as the date of receipt by the contractor is the key date. If the employer's payment is in transit when the rate changes, book-keeping intricacies are required to get matters back into balance.

1.2.2 A more complex situation arises if the employer disagrees with the assessment he receives. Here he has a right of objection and the contractor has to reply, either changing or confirming his assessment. Both parties are bound here to a tight timetable and there may not be another round of objection and reply. The employer should therefore pay any amount at this stage and reserve his final appeal until the stage set out under clause 3.1. If he pays an amount as the total of the contract payment and the tax which is smaller than the contractor is expecting, then the contractor is to treat the total as inclusive of a proportion for tax at the rate that he holds to be correct, remit this sum to the Commissioners and issue a receipt to the employer. This will mean that the sum he has received for the contract payment has been effectively reduced. To avoid the possibility of the contractor seeking to determine under the contract on this score clause 28.1.1 of the conditions excludes action here as a ground.

1.3 — WRITTEN FINAL STATEMENT — VAT LIABILITY OF CONTRACTOR — RECOVERY FROM EMPLOYER

1.3.1 This clause gives the timetable and procedure for tidying up the provisional assessments and payments. The timetable takes the certificate of completion of making good defects as the earliest date for a final statement. In terms of final account settlement this may well be optimistic; it is the time for the final release of retention and may therefore be the earliest time when the last amounts of tax will fall due and, on this reckoning, is a reasonable date. It is however only an earliest date and the clause simply requires the contractor to prepare his statement 'as soon as he can'.

1.3.2 This provision then allows it to be issued 'before or after' the contract final certificate. This appears to reflect the somewhat elastic arrangements for settlement that the various taxation authorities are wont to operate — and here the contractor is acting as the agent of one of them!

1.3.3 When once the statement has been issued and unless the employer challenges it under clause 3.1, there is a quite short timetable for settlement of indebtedness in whichever direction it turns out to exist.

1.3.4 If the debt is reversed the same timetable applies. The whole procedure given is straightforward and rounds off the interim procedure under clause 1.1.

1.4 — CONTRACTOR TO ISSUE RECEIPT AS TAX INVOICE

The heading of this clause reads a little oddly. The reason is that a tax invoice is to have specific information for the benefit of the person taxed (the employer in this case). Since a detailed prior invoice is not available under the procedure of this agreement, and because of the particular nature of construction and its accounting, it is necessary to define the receipt as an invoice. It is obligatory on the contractor to issue one after every payment he receives, otherwise the employer has a redress under clause 7.

2 — VALUE OF SUPPLY — LIQUIDATED DAMAGES TO BE DISREGARDED

2.1 Since liquidated damages deducted by the employer are not a reduction in the value of goods or services supplied, except in so far as they represent an assessment of reduction in value due to lateness, this clause is giving expression to the ruling of the Commissioners that a deduction for such damages is not to reduce the taxable amount that would otherwise arise. This accords with clause 1.1 which relates tax calculations to the amounts of certificates. These are themselves the amounts before deductions as is discussed under clause 24.2 of the conditions and clause 30.8 but the present clause avoids any special interpretation here.

2.2 This clause sets this same matter out from the viewpoint of the contractor.

3 — EMPLOYER'S RIGHT TO CHALLENGE TAX CLAIMED BY CONTRACTOR

The contractor is not very concerned with the amounts of output tax, in that his function is to charge them to the employer and then to pass on what he receives to the Commissioners. Only if he makes some error that fails to be adjustable under the procedure of clause 4 when once he has discharged the employer will he stand to gain or lose. The employer on the other hand has a real interest since he pays the tax ultimately, even though he may be able to recover it either as input tax or on account of his status.

3.1 The employer is therefore given a right of challenge here. The interested party at the other end of the transaction will be the Commissioners, but the employer cannot appeal directly to them as they are levying the tax on the contractor and he must appeal, while having only his passing interest. The solution adopted here is that the contractor is obliged to ask the

Commissioners for their decision over any disagreement between himself and the employer and, if the employer remains dissatisfied, to make any appeal then to the courts on the employer's representations. The employer in turn agrees to meet the contractor's expenses and indemnifies him accordingly.

There are several riders to this procedure. Under this clause it must be initiated 'before any payment or refund becomes due under clause 1.3.3 or 1.3.4', that is within 28 days of the employer receiving the contractor's final statement of tax.

3.2 Next the employer must pay the tax assessed before the Commissioners will consider the appeal.

3.3 Lastly there is introduced a short timetable for settlement after the employer has accepted the Commissioners' verdict at the appropriate stage, this timetable having the same frame as that in clauses 1.3.3 and 1.3.4.

4 — DISCHARGE OF EMPLOYER FROM LIABILITY TO PAY TAX TO THE CONTRACTOR

When matters have run their course in a straightforward fashion, as they usually will, or have taken a more tortuous course under the previous clauses, then the employer is to be released from further liability to the contractor, who will therefore carry any error of his own. There remains the possibility of the Commissioners re-opening matters to the financial detriment of either party, and here it is provided that a further adjustment will be made, subject to the employer's right to revive clause 3 and set an appeal in motion.

5 — AWARDS BY ARBITRATOR OR COURT

Clause 6 excludes any arbitration over the present agreement and clause 3.1 refers to the statutory right to appeals to the courts. There is also the possibility that similar action over the contract itself may vary the amount of consequential tax falling due. This could occur if some part of the works were revalued for instance and payment by the employer is covered here as it does not arise over a certified amount that is covered by clause 1.1. It would not occur if there were an award of damages or the like that did not change the value of the works, but rather compensated for some lapse or misdeed. The principle in this latter instance would be the same as that made explicit in clause 2.

6 — ARBITRATION PROVISION EXCLUDED

In view of the statutory position of the Commissioners and the further rights of appeal to the courts over the subject matter of the agreement under clause 3.1, it is clearly inappropriate to retain the contract arbitration as well for this matter. It would appear that if some dispute arose over any other aspect of the agreement then arbitration under the conditions would still be available.

7 — EMPLOYER'S RIGHT WHERE RECEIPT NOT PROVIDED

The provision here given as a remedy to the employer is quite drastic, amounting as it does to the right to suspend all payments under the contract proper, and not just the agreement, until a piece of paper is provided by the contractor. It may therefore only be invoked in drastic situations and so the two provisos are given, both of which must apply at any one time. These are the employer's needs for a receipt for tax recovery and that he has paid tax properly to the contractor. Any counter-right that the contractor might otherwise have under the contract, such as determination, is suspended by virtue of this clause.

8 — (SUPPLIED) ADDITIONAL TAX INCURRED BY EMPLOYER AFTER DETERMINATION

When the employer determines the employment of the contractor due to the contractor's default, the provision of clause 27.4.4 is that the employer is to recover from the contractor the 'direct loss and/or damage' that he sustains. This will include any higher cost of completion of the works. Since the conditions exclude any reimbursement of tax under the contract (except in clause 15.3), the employer would stand to be out of pocket by the amount of any tax payable on this higher cost. The provision here allows this tax to be recovered from the contractor by adjustment of the amount arising under clause 27.4.4. This is in addition to the amounts certified by the architect, but would be dealt with under the contract calculations by the employer rather than under the agreement calculations.

Clause 31 — Finance (No 2) Act 1975 — statutory tax deduction scheme

The purpose of the legislation referred to in this clause is to deal with the problems of tax evasion to which the labyrinth of sub-contractors, the 'lump' in the industry, gave rise. It gives an arrangement by which a 'contractor' collects tax on behalf of the Inland Revenue and accounts to them for it in cases in which a 'sub-contractor' of his does not have a tax certificate evidencing that he is paying tax direct. There exists what may be described as a PAYE system for firms.

Under the legislation a 'contractor' is so defined as to cover a contractor in the sense in which broadly these conditions use the expression; but in addition 'contractor' is to include 'any persons carrying on a business which includes construction operations' and 'any local authority' and the range of statutory development corporations and cognate bodies — that is many who will be employers under some editions of these conditions. It is in the case in which the employer is a 'contractor' that the present clause operates: the contractor in turn becomes a 'sub-contractor' for statutory purposes. The clause makes no reference to any case in which the employer is not a 'contractor', nor to the very common cases in which the contractor is himself a 'contractor'!

While an employer will automatically be a 'contractor' by virtue of his wider statutory position in many instances, and particularly under the local authorities editions of these conditions, the criterion for a private employer is whether he is engaged in 'construction operations' which are defined very widely under the legislation. The critical point is whether the employer carries on such operations as part of his business. This will include cases in which the employer does work entirely on his own premises, as well as those where the work is a direct component of some contract with another.

Should the employer be a 'contractor', the guiding principle is that he must then make the statutory tax deduction from any payment to his 'sub-contractor' unless the latter has a current valid Inland Revenue tax certificate. The statutory onus of checking on whether there is a certificate is placed on the employer and he must make a deduction if he is not satisfied, but not before he has attempted to obtain evidence. If he fails to make the deduction he may find himself liable to the authorities for the tax.

There are several potential hazard areas in the detailed operations that are needed and the clause is mainly concerned with steering a safe path through these. The clause is not necessary simply to make the scheme apply to the contract: the parties are obliged to operate it by law without any provision here. Discussion is largely centred on the ways in which contractual and statutory obligations intermesh. It may be questioned whether the legislation is entirely satisfactory in its operating principles. In several respects it requires one party to act for the Inland Revenue and for or in relation to the other party in some way, but this is enacted without giving that other party any redress for the default of the first. The present clause therefore includes a number of provisions to create a contractual obligation to make redress possible. This is fine for persons using these conditions, but it seems a pity that it has to be done and it is no help to those contracting without their benefit.

31.1 — DEFINITIONS

This clause incorporates for contract purposes a number of key terms. Those of significance for the present discussion have been considered in the preceding introduction.

31.2 — WHETHER EMPLOYER A 'CONTRACTOR'

31.2.1 This is the cross-roads of the whole clause and provides for definition of the employer's initial status in the appendix and therefore for later parts of the clause to be read as applying or not.

31.2.2 While the employer may not be a 'contractor' initially, this clause allows for the contingency that he may become one before payments are finalised and that it will then become necessary to revive the provisions. The onus is on the employer to notify the contractor, so that he in turn may act under clause 31.3.

31.3 — PROVISION OF EVIDENCE — TAX CERTIFICATE

31.3.1 Here starts the section of the whole clause that applies only if the employer is or becomes a 'contractor'. The employer in such a position has to avoid at least three pitfalls: if he does not deduct but should, the tax authorities will still present him with the bill; if he does deduct but should not, he will be in breach of contract; if he defers a due payment because the contractor has not clarified his own position, he will still be in breach of contract. Under the legislation the contractor need not notify the employer until just before payment is due and this could cause operating complications. It is therefore to avoid these problems that a contractual procedure is set up here so that the contractor must act well ahead of the first payment or within a similar margin of the employer becoming a 'contractor'. If the latter is the case it will still not always avoid difficulties; the time limit is not related to the timing of any payment.

31.3.2 When the employer is dissatisfied with the contractor's tax certificate or other evidence that tax should not be deducted, the employer is entitled to make a deduction provided he notifies the contractor of his reasons for dissatisfaction, of his intention to make a deduction and of the need for the contractor to provide information as a basis. Again the combined timescales of the present clause and clause 31.6.1 may not prevent difficulty in all cases.

31.4 — UNCERTIFICATED CONTRACTOR OBTAINS TAX CERTIFICATE — EXPIRY OF TAX CERTIFICATE — CANCELLATION OF TAX CERTIFICATE

31.4.1 The contractor's status, as well as that of the employer, may be subject to change: he may obtain a tax certificate and cease to be liable to deduction by the employer. The obligation is on the contractor to notify the employer.

31.4.2 Alternatively a current tax certificate may or may not be renewed on expiry: either way the contractor (who will know in advance) is to notify the employer, while again the contractor's status will change if there is not a renewal.

31.4.3 Lastly the contractor may have his tax certificate cancelled in mid-flight and again the employer must be told. The obligation on the contractor to notify in these various cases is not statutory, but is here made contractual. When a change occurs, suitable parts of clause 31.3 are invoked.

31.5 — VOUCHERS

While the employer is under statutory obligation to the tax authorities to forward vouchers, he is under no obligation to the contractor if he does not. A contractual obligation is therefore introduced, to protect the contractor from the consequences of losing his tax certificate status owing to the vouchers not being forwarded by the employer.

31.6 — STATUTORY DEDUCTION — DIRECT COST OF MATERIALS

31.6.1 When the employer is required to make the statutory deduction, he must exclude 'the direct cost . . . of materials' in making his calculations. As the clause operates only when the contractor does not have a tax certificate, it includes the words 'and [to] any other person' when referring to the cost of materials. Thus the employer must obtain the cost of materials for any firms employed by the contractor, as their tax will be included in the total deduction made by the employer. In the relatively unlikely event of a firm which has a tax certificate being employed by the contractor who does not have one, due adjustment will be needed. When the contractor has a tax certificate but a sub-contractor of his does not, the employer has no interest as the contractor is a 'contractor' under the legislation and collection stops at his level.

    31.6.2 The contractor is the obvious person to have precise information for the purposes of clause 31.6.1 and he is here made liable for supplying it to the employer, who in turn is indemnified against the consequences of 'incorrect statement', such as being himself liable to the Inland Revenue for any deficiency of tax.

    31.6.3 If the contractor fails to provide the information after being notified of the need, then the employer may make a 'fair estimate', which will be acceptable to the authorities.

31.7 — CORRECTION OF ERRORS

Here again correction of error or omission is made a contractual obligation because the legislation imposes no obligation as between the parties. A 'statutory obligation on the Employer not to make such correction' relates principally to time acting as a bar.

31.8 — RELATION TO OTHER CLAUSES

Since the present clause is so entangled with legislation it must prevail in the way stated. Matters of timing of payments or adjustments of their amounts are presumably in mind: the wording reflects the only lack of confidence in the conditions! The wording is not necessarily such as to debar either party from his right of recompense where some other provision is overridden by its operation. While the present clause will take precedence, because its effects will be unforeseen, there must remain access to an adjustment.

31.9 — APPLICATION OF ARBITRATION AGREEMENT

There are various rights of appeal over taxation matters and so it is necessary to exclude the usual arbitration avenue in these respects. It remains in force in all other respects, though.

PART 3

Nominated and other persons and the JCT Form, Private with Quantities

CHAPTER 14

Other persons employed on the works or on the site

An introductory survey
Clause 19 — Assignment and sub-contracts
Clause 29 — Works by employer or persons employed or
engaged by employer

An introductory survey

There are several ways in which persons may come to be employed on the works or on the site, or possibly on both, despite the contractor's right of possession under clause 23.1 and his obligation to carry out and complete under clause 2.1. These may be identified as follows:

(a) *Assignment*: The contractor passes over his performance of the whole of the works and rewards for so doing to another, while not being relieved of his contractual liability over performance. This act, and also assignment by the employer, are considered in this chapter under clause 19.1.

(b) *Domestic sub-contracting or sub-letting*: the contractor passes over a part only of the works and rewards as in (a), while remaining directly related to the employer and continuing to deal with the architect and the quantity surveyor. This is usually on his initiative and is considered in this chapter under the rest of clause 19.

(c) *Nominated sub-contracting*: this is similar to (b), but the contractor has no option about whether to sub-contract and little option about to whom to sub-contract, as the architect's nomination will usually have to be accepted. This is considered in Chapters 15 and 16.

(d) *Work by the employer directly or by persons under direct contract to him and with no contractual relationship with the contractor*: this can arise in the particular circumstances prescribed in clause 29 considered in this chapter.

(e) *Statutory obligation being fulfilled by public bodies*: this may or may not be work paid for by the contractor, but because of its statutory nature he must permit it. This is considered under clause 6.3 in Chapter 5.

In addition to the above there are also likely to be suppliers whose obligation extends no further than delivery to the site. These may divide into domestic suppliers (a term not used in the conditions) equivalent to and perhaps included within domestic sub-contractors, and nominated suppliers equivalent to but distinct from nominated sub-contractors and considered under clause 36 in Chapter 19. The exact position of domestic suppliers is unclear in terms of the conditions and is discussed under clause 19.2 in this chapter. Figure 17 provides a basic summary of the main relationships that are produced.

Clause 19 — Assignment and sub-contracts

19.1 — ASSIGNMENT

Assignment is not a simple matter at law and neither party would be permitted by law to assign his whole contractual relationship with its rights and liabilities unilaterally. This would amount to substituting a new contract with one of the parties changed, such a substitution being known as novation. The present clause adds to the wider law on assignment the requirement of the other party's consent, which is apparently not subject to arbitration.

The clause has less procedural importance when the employer assigns, since his role under the contract is less complex. More importantly this clause is concerned with situations in which the contractor may himself wish to arrange for others to do all or part of the works which he has contracted to do with his own direct organisation. Assignment in the case of the contractor appears to mean here the passing over of the whole performance of the works by the contractor to another. The employer may well have chosen the contractor partly on the basis of certain qualities of organisation and workmanship and may not wish to agree to an assignment. His consent is therefore required.

19.2 — SUB-LETTING — DOMESTIC SUB-CONTRACTORS — ARCHITECT'S CONSENT

Sub-letting relates to some part of the works which the contractor may wish to sub-contract. This clause regulates it when it is proposed entirely on the contractor's initiative, while clause 19.3 legislates for a variant situation. It legally embraces labour-only sub-contracting, although seldom will it be practicable or reasonable to press this so far. Here the contractor retains overall organisation and it is the quality of the sub-let work that is in question. Hence it is the architect who is most intimately concerned and his consent is required rather than that of the employer. His right to withhold consent is qualified and therefore open to arbitration, but it seems likely that the contractor must be able to prove loss of consequence if a firm of adequate quality is excluded. A sub-contractor so obtained is termed 'domestic' to distinguish him from the 'nominated' sub-contractor, also mentioned in clause 19.5.

It is probably correct to interpret 'Domestic Sub-Contractor' as applying only to someone who works on the site, in order to exclude a person who merely supplies for the contractor to fix. The conditions as a whole (see for instance clause 11) and the definition in clause 1.3 in particular appear to take

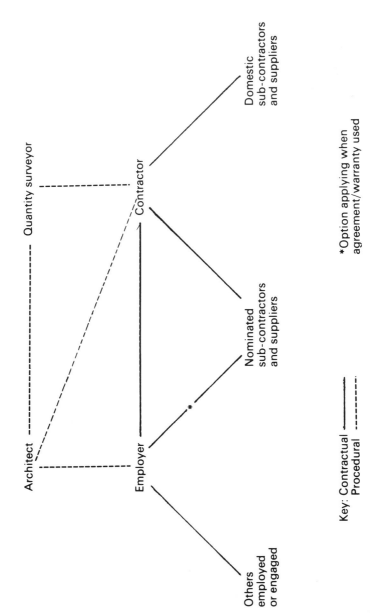

Figure 17: **Contractual and procedural relationships created or implied by JCT main form**
Some are formalised by other forms in the series. Contracts of professional advisers and relationships of clerk of works and statutory bodies are not shown.

'the Works' as the construction as an end-product, so that any part of them must include the relevant fixing element. If so there is strictly no power to disapprove of a domestic supplier as such in the conditions, but only to disapprove of work produced by one. In the case of a domestic supplier who supplies such ready-fabricated articles as ironmongery or pipes it would also be almost impossibly restrictive to classify him as a domestic sub-contractor under the present clause. But in other cases, such as precast concrete cladding and specially-manufactured windows, the critical element may be the manufacture rather than the fixing and the architect's consent is highly desirable from the employer's angle. Provided the architect has a suitable shortlist of available firms, one precautionary approach would be to name domestic sub-contractors in the contract bills under clause 19.3 and then allow the sub-contractor to 'sub-let' fixing back to the contractor, thus becoming a domestic supplier. Once sub-letting properly occurs, the architect will usually have a right of access to workshops etc. under clause 11. In the case of a sub-contract for a major building element, failure to secure this agreement in advance would be valid ground for not approving a proposed sub-letting.

If the contractor attempts to ignore the clause, the employer may determine under clause 27.1.4. This is an extreme remedy and not one to be applied lightly; it is in any case qualified by 'not ... unreasonably or vexatiously'.

Whether assignment or sub-letting occurs, the employer will be entitled to have the works completed under the same terms and conditions, including those of time and price. If in tendering the contractor bases his price on those contained in a particular sub-quotation, he must do so at his own risk, knowing that approval to sub-let to the quoting firm may later be declined on some reasonable grounds. This and similar difficulties may be avoided if the contractor asks for approval before signing the contract, so long as the sub-contractor remains available to him when needed. Architects will often ask for proposals over sub-letting to be forwarded with the tender or soon after. Difficulties may arise with finishing trades or other work late in the programme, where firms may be loathe to commit themselves a long way ahead.

19.3 — SUB-LETTING — LIST IN CONTRACT BILLS

19.3.1 This clause provides a middle course between the one extreme of including work in the contract bills and waiting to see whether the contractor will seek consent for sub-letting, and the other extreme of the architect instructing the acceptance of a single nominated sub-contractor against a prime cost sum. Work is included in full in the contract bills and is priced by the contractor, but with the rider that it 'must be carried out by persons named in a list', from which the right to select a domestic sub-contractor is at 'the sole discretion of the Contractor', who is to be paid only the sum in the contract bills whoever performs the work. The list is to be 'in or annexed to the Contract Bills' which suggests the possibility of the persons being named before tendering by the architect, or being agreed by the architect and the contractor between tender and acceptance.

19.3.2 In any case the list under clause 19.3.1 is to contain 'not less than three persons' and, once it is in being, it may be added to by either the employer, 'the Architect on his behalf' or the contractor, subject to consent in each case. This consent may be of little concern to the contractor in that he may ignore persons added by others, unless they are so numerous as to block his escape route under clause 19.3.2.2. On the other hand the employer, or more particularly the architect, will be interested in additions proposed by the contractor as one of these persons is very likely to be chosen by the contractor. Their efficiency and quality of work must be carefully investigated. This process of adding agreed persons may go on right up to the execution of a sub-contract.

Instead of the list burgeoning it may wilt away 'for whatsoever reason' as clause 19.3.2.2 puts it, which might include the persons being heavily committed elsewhere, not liking the contractor or being lured away by competitors. If less than three persons are on the list 'at any time' and this may occur early in the selection process, two primary options are available. One is for the employer (but not 'the Architect on his behalf') and the contractor to add agreed extra names, a process which is likely to favour the contractor. The other is for the contractor to agree to perform the work, reserving the option to put forward his own domestic sub-contractor under clause 19.2.

Clearly this clause is seeking to provide for the indeterminate, but it does rather shilly-shally at this last point. It is not clear how it is decided which of the two options will prevail. If the employer first proposes a name or names to which the contractor cannot reasonably withhold agreement, does he prevent the contractor from performing work? Or if the contractor first gets on with the work or sub-lets it, or even notifies his firm intention to do one of these things, does he abrogate the other option? Some indication that the contractor may only gallop away after the other option has been tried and agreed to be found wanting may be considered reasonably necessary. No question of extension of time or loss and expense arises if there is delay in obtaining a domestic sub-contractor here, so that excessive delay on the employer's side should be avoided wherever possible.

So far as the architect's concern for quality and so forth is concerned, clause 19.3 still leaves him with the power to exclude from the original list or its supplements any persons to whom he reasonably objects, and the more critical the requirements of quality etc the more likely he is to be able to object successfully. One fairly remote possibility would be if the employer put forward someone unsatisfactory under clause 19.3.2.2. A more troublesome question arises under this clause if the contractor establishes his position to carry out the work himself and lacks the expertise. The architect appears to have no way round this problem unless it is possible to omit the work as a variation; but the contractor too is caught if all suitable persons drop out of the running, the 'then work shall be carried out by the Contractor', as with any domestic sub-contractor's work under clause 19.2.

19.4 — SUB-LETTING — DETERMINATION OF EMPLOYMENT OF DOMESTIC SUB-CONTRACTOR

The clause provides for automatic determination of any sub-contract for sub-let work by an embodied condition similar to that required for nominated sub-contractors under sub-contract clause 31.1. The aim is to set the sub-contractor free to enter into any fresh contract with the employer or to sub-contract with a new contractor and thus secure continuity of work in what could otherwise be a period of uncertainty. One side-effect of this is that it conflicts with the right of the employer to receive an assignment under clause 27.4.2.1, since there will be no surviving agreement to assign. This will be no bar to making fresh arrangements.

Another problem arises further down the contractual chain in respect of controlling the powers of a domestic sub-contractor, whatever the means of his selection, to assign or sub-let under Sub-Contract DOM/1 and the discussion under clause 26 of that form should be noted. The present clause is silent about what happens if the sub-contractor's employment is determined. It would appear that clause 19.3 has been extinguished by its once-for-all operation and that there must be a reversion to clause 19.2 if the contractor wishes to sub-let again. The architect has neither the right nor the duty to name another person and apparently cannot even insist that the contractor must sub-let again.

19.5 — NOMINATED SUB-CONTRACTORS

19.5.1 This is a simple cross-reference to clause 35, nominated sub-contractors being no concern of the present clause.

19.5.2 While the contractor can go through the convolutions of clauses 19.2 and 19.3 over domestic sub-contractors, he cannot be obliged to perform nominated sub-contract work. The architect must nominate, or if needs be re-nominate, under clause 35. The contractor will only be involved if he elects to tender and is allowed to do so under clause 35.2. But, equally, the contractor cannot have measured work, priced by him, taken away and made the subject of nomination. Clause 13.1.3 protects him against this eventuality.

Clause 29 — Works by employer or persons employed or engaged by employer

The purpose of this clause is to regulate the position between the contractor and those who may perform work without having any contractual relationship whatsoever with him. These persons are defined in clauses 29.1 and 29.2 as 'the Employer himself or . . . persons employed or otherwise engaged by him', so that all of them (except obviously the employer) have some contract with the employer. They are to that extent possibly to be distinguished from the 'third party' dealing with antiquities under clause 34.2 or statutory bodies under clause 6.3. Otherwise there are the similarities that their actions or inaction may lead to the contractor obtaining extension of time under clause 25.4.8.1, extra payment under clause 26.2.4.1 or even a right to determine under clause 28.1.3.6. In these clauses, the provisions run parallel to those regulating the supply of materials and goods by the employer, which are not appropriate here as they relate to off-site activity.

This clause is needed to allow the person, including the employer, to enter the site and work on it, as clause 23.1 otherwise gives the contractor unimpeded possession. At this point there is a lack of precision, in that the site is not mentioned, although the expression 'the Contractor shall permit' is meaningless in the absence of such an inference.

This clause relates only to 'work not forming part of this Contract' to permit its concurrent execution. It gives no power to the employer to require the architect to issue a variation instruction to omit work from the contract, so that the employer may then enter into a separate and perhaps more advantageous contract with another for the same work. If the work is instructed to be omitted it must be left out at least until practical completion. This position is rooted in the general law and is parallel to that under clause 13.1.3 where the substitution of nominated sub-contract work for contractor's work is expressly excluded.

29.1 — INFORMATION IN CONTRACT BILLS

Two cases are distinguished. In this clause the reference is to that in which the contractor is warned in the contract bills about what is to be done by others. This is 'as is necessary' to enable him 'to carry out and complete the Works in accordance with the Conditions', which includes completion on time. The phraseology here for pre-contract information is uncomfortably close in its demands to that used for post-contract information in clauses 5.3.1.1 and 5.4. To give the contractor enough information it is most likely that the contract drawings will also have to embody suitable detail. Provided that the information required by the present clause is given, 'the Contractor shall permit execution of such work'. The information may be more than is strictly required for arriving at the contract sum and other than will sensibly go between the covers of the contract bills. To avoid later argument that work has been inadequately described and should therefore fall under clause 29.2 with the effect there mentioned, agreement should be confirmed at the contract stage (perhaps in an appendix to the contract bills) that the information given is adequate for present purposes in whichever document it is presented, even though the details are yet to be made available or perhaps even decided.

What is more properly and narrowly needed at the tendering stage and to be enshrined in the contract bills is enough information for the contractor to assess the financial implications of what is intended; that is the nature, extent and duration of the work as it will affect his operations. The contractor should then price the organisational effects against the items giving the information. Over and above this, there should be included any further priceable items by way of facilities and attendance that the contractor is to provide for these other persons, as required by the Standard Method of Measurement and similar, where suitable, to the provisions for nominated sub-contractors discussed under sub-contract clause 27. These priceable items will therefore form part of 'the Works'. The question of the contractor's programme needs special care, in view of the problems raised by the inadequate wording of clause 25.4.8, under which the point is discussed.

29.2 — INFORMATION NOT IN CONTRACT BILLS

This is the second case distinguished. Here no information is given in the contract bills, even if the mere possibility of the work is mentioned; or alternatively the information given is inadequate. Such work may be performed only with the contractor's consent, which is not to 'be unreasonably withheld'. The intention of this provision is to prevent the employer bringing in persons whose activities would completely disrupt those of the contractor, so that the basic conditions under which the works would be performed are effectively changed.

If such work is permitted by the contractor he will be entitled to be paid for attendance and other costs as a variation under clause 13.1.1.1. The conditions are not specific about organisational effects, but the contractor is entitled to regard the cost of these as an item to be agreed before his consent is to be construed as 'unreasonably withheld'. In the case of persons working under clause 29.1, the contractor should only be entitled to extension of time and loss and expense payment if they fail to meet their programme; but the comments under clause 25.4.8.1 should be noted. Under the present clause the simple introduction of these persons may lead initially to such an entitlement, although the contractor must under the relevant clauses give notice of this when giving his consent. This underlines the importance of providing adequate information in the contract bills to satisfy clause 29.1 wherever possible to avoid the contractor maintaining that he viewed the information as inadequate and so made no allowance at all when tendering.

29.3 — (SUPPLIED) RESPONSIBILITY OF EMPLOYER

The clause aligns with clause 20 in making it clear that the contractor does not indemnify the employer against the activities of these persons. Clause 20.1 uses the same expression 'person for whom the Employer is responsible' to exclude such persons from its scope, while clause 20.2 limits the contractor's responsibility to a defined group of persons. The present clause excludes its own subjects from that group by declaring them not to be sub-contractors. On the other hand, if the contractor injures them or damages their work he will be liable to indemnify the employer under clause 20.

CHAPTER 15

An introduction to the nomination of sub-contractors

The documents related to nominated sub-contractors
The bearing of the parts of the document

All of the persons dealt with in the present part of this volume referred to in the main contract and the relevant clauses are discussed mostly in chapter 14 and the following chapters. But in addition there are several other documents in the JCT series that are to be used for particular categories of persons and these must also be discussed to give an overall view. Only in the case of persons employed or engaged directly by the employer and referred to in clause 29 are there no further documents provided in the series, and the employer must make such arrangements as are appropriate.

The plan adopted is to take one category of persons and to discuss the main contract provisions together with related documentation. The first category, nominated sub-contractors, however, has a complex set of documents and so this chapter establishes a frame of reference for the following chapters, without itself discussing the contents of any documents. This is done by relating the documents to each other in the following section and then looking at the parts of each document which apply at succeeding stages. The framework may also be considered as applying in simplified form to nominated suppliers in Chapter 19.

The documents related to nominated sub-contractors

While reading the JCT main contract as a whole may occasionally give a sensation akin to riding on a big dipper, at least it tends to progress in some direction. In the case of the JCT nominated sub-contract related documentation, the feeling is more akin to being on a roundabout; whichever animal one has mounted one might wish to have started by riding another. There are several documents in historical sequence, but cross-referencing to each other so often and so closely that there is no indisputable starting point for examination. Further, there are two sets of procedures for nomination, both of which are possible under main clause 35. One of these is generally termed the 'basic' method and is the more complex and rigid, while the other, known as the 'alternative' method, is more simple and flexible. Neither of the terms 'basic' and 'alternative' is used in any of the documents, but they are culled from the JCT Guide. Equally the documents do not indicate specifically when either method is to be used, although it may fairly be inferred that the scale and intricacy of sub-contracts are relevant criteria. It is thus not mandatory to use a particular method, but one or the other must be used to give a workable apparatus and the contract bills must state which is to be used for a particular nominated sub-contract so that the contractor can include for his related obligations accordingly.

In the light of these remarks, the documents may be classified as follows:

(a) Used always with the 'basic' or the 'alternative' methods:
Main clause 35: Nominated Sub-Contractors

(b) All used always with the 'basic' method:
Tender NSC/1: Standard Form of Nominated Sub-Contract Tender and Agreement
Agreement NSC/2: Standard Form of Employer/Nominated Sub-Contractor Agreement
Nomination NSC/3: Standard Form for a Nomination of a Sub-Contractor where Tender NSC/1 has been used
Sub-Contract NSC/4: Standard Form of Nominated Sub-Contract

(c) Used optionally with the 'alternative' method:
Agreement NSC/2a: Agreement NSC/2 adapted for use where Tender NSC/1 has not been used

(d) Used always with the 'alternative' method:
Sub-Contract NSC/4a: Sub-Contract NSC/4 adapted for use where Tender NSC/1 has not been used.

The bearing of the parts of the documents

The essence of nomination is that it gives the architect an unusual measure of control in respect of a person who works on the site as a sub-contractor under the contractor's general control. While the act of nomination occurs at one point, it is part of a chain of the architect's activities (in some cases undertaken in co-operation with the quantity surveyor and the contractor), of which the more important are listed below. Under each activity is given the salient parts of the documents already listed (other than the 'a' suffix variants) which broadly relate to the various activities in at least some respect as noted. In some cases the 'a' suffix variants differ in points of detail such as clause number order.

Activity	Reference	Requirement or stage
(a) Selecting one or more potential sub-contractors for the parcel of work on criteria of quality of work and performance and perhaps design ability	Main clause 35.1	Definition of nomination and reservation to architect
	Main clause 35.2	Contractor himself tendering for nominated work

Activity	Reference	Requirement or stage
(b) Obtaining a tender that isolates one person as the most desirable	Main clause 35.3	List of sub-contract related documents
	Main clause 35.5	Use of 'basic' and 'alternative' methods
	NSC/1, Schedule 1	Tender and stipulations Particulars of main contract and sub-contract
	NSC/2, whereas 1 clause 9	Reference to tender Reference to tender Conflict between documents
	NSC/4 Articles/recitals clause 2.2	Reference to tender Conflict between documents
(c) Setting up a collateral agreement between the employer and the sub-contractor, unless this is not required under the 'alternative' method	Main clause 35.6	Use of NSC/2
	Main clause 35.11	Use of NSC/2a
	Main clause 35.20	Disclaimer over employer's liability to sub-contractor
	Main clause 35.21	Disclaimer over contractor's liability to employer
	NSC/1	Stipulation over when NSC/2 effective
	NSC/2, whereas 4	Disclaimer over architect's liability to sub-contractor
(d) Obtaining or setting in motion and then approving any design or specification work by the sub-contractor	NSC/2 clause 2	Sub-contractor's warranty over design, specification and performance
	clause 3.2	Promptness of information to architect
(e) Introducing the contractor and the proposed sub-contractor, so that they may agree any commercial, technical or operational points about the work that affect them both	Main clause 35.7.1	Architect to send tender etc to contractor
	Main clause 35.7.2	Contractor and sub-contractor to agree particulars in NSC/1
	Main clause 35.10.1	Contractor to send agreed NSC/1 to architect
	NSC/1, Schedule 2	Particular conditions to be agreed between contractor and sub-contractor
	NSC/2, clause 1	Sub-contractor's undertaking to settle last and then notify architect
(f) Allowing for objections at this stage from the contractor or sub-contractor to be	Main clause 35.4	Contractor objects to proposed sub-contractor
	Main clause 35.8	Contractor and sub-contractor

Activity	Reference	Requirement or stage
resolved, or for another sub-contractor to be found		disagree over particular conditions
	Main clause 35.9	Sub-contractor withdraws offer
	Main clause 35.23	Proposed nomination does not proceed
	NSC/1	Stipulations regarding: identity of main contractor, agreeing particular conditions, no charge to employer
	NSC/2, clause 2	Various matters about design, etc before or after any nomination
(g) Nominating the sub-contractor, so that he and the contractor enter into a binding contract	Main clause 35.10.2	Architect issues NSC/3 under 'basic' method
	Main clause 35.11.2	Architect issues equivalent instruction under 'alternative' method
	Main clause 35.12	Contractor acts under last Reference to nomination
	NSC/2 Whereas 3 clause 3	Not liable for delay due to late nomination
	NSC/3	The nominating document
	NSC/4, Articles/recitals	Reference to nomination
(h) Issuing information and instructions, inspecting and approving the sub-contractor's work and generally acting in the same ways over the physical work as towards the contractor, but acting in all matters through the contractor	Main contract, in general	On appropriate matters
	NSC/4, in general and clause 4	Architect's instructions, contractor's directions
(i) Agreeing and certifying interim payments to the sub-contractor through the contractor, but operating safeguards for the sub-contractor	Main clauses 30.2 to 30.6	Main payments
	Main clauses 35.13.1 and 35.13.2	Normal procedure
	Main clauses 35.13.3 to 35.13.5	Procedure for direct payment
	NSC/2 clause 4 clause 7	Architect to operate normal procedure Architect and employer to operate direct payment

Activity	Reference	Requirement or stage
	NSC/4, clauses 21.2 to 21.9	Interim payments
(j) Agreeing and certifying final payments to the sub-contractor, as last	Main clause 30.7	Final payment of sub-contractor
	Main clause 30.8	Date of final certificate notified to sub-contractor
	Main clause 35.17	Final payment of sub-contractor
	NSC/2, clause 5	Architect to operate final payment
	NSC/4, clauses 21.10 and 21.11	Final accounts
(k) Instructing contractor on what extensions of time may be granted to the sub-contractor	Main clause 25	Main contract extensions
	Main clause 35.14	Sub-contract extension
	Main clause 35.15	Sub-contract late completion
	NSC/2, clause 3	Sub-contractor not to cause main contract extension
	NSC/4	
	clause 11	Sub-contract extension
	clause 12	Sub-contract late completion
	clause 21.8	Suspension of work by sub-contractor
(l) Exercising some control over threatening determination of the sub-contractor's employment by the contractor, if determination occurs in any way (including if the sub-contractor himself determines) nominating another sub-contractor	Main clause 35.24	Determination and re-nomination
	Main clause 35.25	Architect's instructions over determination and payment
	NSC/2	
	clause 3	Sub-contractor not to provoke a determination
	clause 6	Sub-contractor to indemnify employer over re-nomination loss and expense, caused by sub-contractor
	NSC/4	
	clause 29	Determination of sub-contract by contractor
	clause 30	Determination of sub-contract by sub-contractor
	clause 31	Determination of main contract by employer (not strictly relevant under present heading, but noted for completeness)
(m) Seeing that any residual liabilities of the sub-contractor affecting the employer are settled through the contractor	Article 5.1.4	Arbitration involving sub-contractor
	Main clause 35.16	Sub-contract practical completion
	Main clause 35.18	Defects after final payment

Activity	Reference	Requirement or stage
		and before final certificate
	Main clause 35.19	Loss or damage after final payment and before main practical completion
	Main clause 35.22	Restrictions in contract of sale, etc
	NSC/2	
	clause 5	Defects after final payment and before final certificate
	clause 5	Defects after final certificate
	clause 8	Sub-contractor to warn of restrictions in contracts of sale, etc.
	clause 10	Arbitration
	NSC/4	
	Article 3	Arbitration
	clause 2.3	Restrictions in contracts of sale, etc
	clause 14	Sub-contract practical completion

It may be noted that all parts of main clause 35 are given here and that this is the clause which holds the documents together by setting out the procedures most explicitly, so that discussion of procedures is centred on Chapter 16. Also all but two activities have parts of that clause listed. The one exception is activity (h) over instructions and supervision for which the sub-contractor 'is' the contractor so far as the architect is concerned. The other is activity (d) over design and the like which occurs outside the main contract and also outside the sub-contract, under which the sub-contractor receives all design information from the architect, including that which the sub-contractor himself has prepared but which has then been approved and incorporated by the architect. The sub-contract is therefore also silent, but so too is the tender under which this point is discussed. Beyond these instances, the omission of a reference to part of a particular document under any activity is for a fairly evident reason, usually related to the timing of the activity.

CHAPTER 16

Nominated sub-contractors in the main contract

Clause 35 — Nominated sub-contractors

Clause 35 — Nominated sub-contractors

This chapter together with Chapter 19 deals with one aspect of the JCT main form, the rest of which is treated in Part 2 of this book. Here it is considered with the various other documents to which it is related. An outline of the overall relationships is given in Chapter 15 and for simplicity cross-references in this chapter have been limited. References outside the present clause to the main contract and sub-contract have been made as 'main clause' and 'sub-contract clause'. In general the 'a' variants of the several sub-contract documents have not been mentioned, as the content is the same.

An outline analysis of this lengthy clause 35 is as follows:

(a) Clauses 35.1 to 35.12. Prior to a sub-contract: general matters and nomination procedure
(b) Clauses 35.13 to 35.19. During a sub-contract: payments and programme.
(c) Clauses 35.20 to 35.26. Appended matters: provisos, renomination and determination.

In the special case of public undertakings solely fulfilling their statutory obligations, clause 6.3 excludes them from the class of sub-contractors in general and so from the provisions of this clause, *inter alia*. Where a public undertaking is also a nominated sub-contractor, as clause 6.2.1 recognises to be possible, some care is needed in segregating these two activities.

GENERAL

35.1 — DEFINITION OF A NOMINATED SUB-CONTRACTOR

The basis of the definition given here in the latter part of the clause is that a nominated sub-contractor is 'a sub-contractor to the Contractor', but with whom the architect has a special concern. In the first instance the architect has 'reserved to himself' rather than delegated to the contractor 'the final selection and approval' of such a person after the contract has been placed, either by providing for a prime cost sum or by naming the sub-contractor in the circumstances set out in clauses 35.1.1 to 35.1.4 which are considered individually later.

This summary of the clause structure indicates that it permits either a prime cost sum or naming to be used in any one of the circumstances given above to lead into an individual nomination. The obvious combinations are either a prime cost sum and an entry in the contract bills as clause 35.1.1 (the two being in fact synonymous) or a naming and one of the post-contract options in clauses 35.1.2 to 35.1.4. However main clause 30.6.2.1 mentions naming in the contract bills and so upsets this tidy apportionment. It also mentions 'amounts in respect of sub-contractors named' as distinct from prime cost sums and provisional sums, while main clause 19.2 excludes domestic sub-contractors from the present grouping. The conditions thus appear to envisage naming in the contract bills affixed to a sum which is not a prime cost sum (but which must allow the addition of profit as main clause 30.6.2.1) and in which, in practical terms, is a sum entered by the quantity surveyor in advance of tendering rather than the result of the contractor obtaining a quotation from the one sub-contractor and including that amount (singly or against quantities) increased by his own profit. There seems nothing to be gained by using this method rather than entering a prime cost sum and the name of the sub-contractor in the contract bills for such a case.

What is clear is that under the remaining options the reservation can only be made by naming the person, since they occur at the post-contractual stage when a prime cost sum is no longer appropriate. It is then perhaps necessary to have the 'notwithstanding' proviso to override the requirement of the Standard Method of Measurement that all nominated sub-contractors are to be indicated by a prime cost sum in the contract bills. Main clause 2.2.2.1 can be read at 'specifically stated' so as to make the present proviso little more than a practice note.

The procedure for nomination, in so far as it affects the employer, the architect and the contractor appears in various parts of clause 35. A number of provisions relevant to the special relationships between architect, contractor, and nominated sub-contractor, and in places also the employer, are covered in various parts of the clause. These topics can only be seen in their totality when the other documents, listed in clause 35.3 and considered in various chapters, are consulted.

Since the contract sum is based upon the concept of an entire contract, two factors are introduced to take up the uncertainty which nomination would otherwise produce. One is the involvement of the contractor at particular stages of the selection process to agree that relevant terms fit into his contract, or to negotiate amendments to contract, sub-contract, or both. This occurs within the nomination procedure under later parts of clause 35. The other, set out in the earlier part of this clause, is a mechanism permitting financial adjustment of the contract as well as reserving the right of nomination to the architect solely for work annexed within the categories of this clause. The parts of this mechanism may be taken in order.

35.1.1 Provision for nominated contractors may be by an initial statement made in the contract bills. This is best done by way of a prime cost sum as has already been discussed. Whether the proposed sub-contractor is named as well is not material contractually, although this may help the contractor when tendering. A prime cost sum instructs the contractor when tendering to include a sum of money in his tender (from which the contract bills and contract sum are derived) to represent the as yet unsettled nominated sub-contract amount, inclusive of a cash discount to him to comply with sub-contract clause 21.3.1.1. He also allows in his tender for profit and attendance. When the nomination has been made based on the actual tender amount and the final account for the nominated sub-contract has been agreed, this amount is substituted for the prime cost sum under the provisions of main clauses 30.6.2.1 and 30.6.2.6, and an adjustment is made to the contractor's profit.

35.1.2 A provisional sum may be included in the contract bills for a more or less defined parcel of work, without it being indicated that all or any of the work will fall to a nominated sub-contractor to perform. In this case the resulting instruction may produce contractor's or nominated sub-contractor's work, apparently without any limitation as to what work is to fall to one or the other. This is out of step with the next clause.

35.1.3 A straightforward variation may be instructed and part of the work may be executed by a nominated sub-contractor, provided two conditions are met: the work must be additional to that given in the contract, and it must also be similar to work for which the contract bills provide for nomination. Both of these positive conditions relate to the negative provision of main clause 13.1.3 that a variation cannot substitute nominated work for contractor's measured work of identical type given in the contract bills. The difficulty about the first condition is that it is restricted to additional work, which appears to mean 'further work' and not 'the additions element or substituted part of the varied work'. It excludes by definition what main clause 13.1.3 permits by silence, the relatively incidental 'ebb and flow' between contractor's and nominated work, and this leaves a gap in the wording.

35.1.4 Lastly a nomination may arise by agreement between the parties, the architect acting for the employer. This makes the list open-ended, and is intended to cope with work not envisaged in the contract and of a specialised nature. It is not qualified as to how it may arise; presumably this is to be by means of an instruction requiring a variation. If so, it provides *inter alia* a way around the problem of clause 35.1.3 whilst safeguarding the contractor.

35.2 — CONTRACTOR'S TENDER FOR WORKS OTHERWISE RESERVED FOR A NOMINATED SUB-CONTRACTOR

This clause is set apart from the mainstream of clause 35, inasmuch as it deals with a distinct situation in which the contractor undertakes work reserved for the architect's nomination.

35.2.1 The contractor may himself tender for work covered by prime cost sums which are either in the contract bills or arise out of architect's instructions regarding provisional sums. This is not entirely at the contractor's discretion and equally he cannot be obliged to tender for such work. It exists only where the following three conditions are all fulfilled:

(a) The contractor must carry out such work directly in the ordinary course of his business. This condition is reinforced by the stipulation about sub-letting which reproduces the effect of clause 19.2, but without mention of the architect's consent being 'unreasonably withheld'.

(b) The contractor's wish must have been known at the time of entering into the contract and have been recorded in the appendix. In practice the employer is hardly likely to hold rigidly to this condition if it makes commercial sense to do otherwise. If a prime cost sum arises out of a provisional sum it is deemed to have satisfied this condition.

(c) The architect must be willing to receive tenders from the contractor. This is sufficiently important for it to overshadow the preceding conditions and to be the determining practical factor. The reasonable practical step at the time of entering into the contract is for the architect and the contractor to agree those items entered in the appendix under this provision for which the architect is in fact prepared to consider tenders from the contractor. In default of this the contractor would appear to have no right to go to arbitration.

A practical point to be observed is that, while such a tender will be deemed to include any allowance in lieu of cash discount, this should be stressed when the tender is invited and it should be clearly stated whether the profit and attendance items in the contract bills will be allowed in addition or whether they are to be included in the tender. If these are allowed in addition the tender becomes directly comparable with that of other firms.

35.2.2 Clause 13 is incorporated into the sub-contract to govern the method of calculation of the prices of variations, but it is stated that the wording of clause 13 shall be held to be modified to refer to the sub-contract documents and not to the main contract documents. This preserves the prices in the sub-contract tender as the ones which form the basis of variation prices. No prices, or particular relationship of prices, in the contract bills will have any necessary significance in calculating sub-contract prices and the same may be said in reverse. Clauses 38.5.3 and 39.6.3 exclude such a sub-contract from the general fluctuations provisions: often it would be of short enough duration to be quoted for on a fixed price basis, but otherwise it should contain its own basis for fluctuations. The formula rules referred to by clause 40 imply a similar treatment.

35.2.3 The rest of clause 35 is excluded when the contractor's tender has been accepted. Anything else would be a nightmare. The work concerned therefore becomes normal contractor's work and subject to the body of the conditions (other than fluctuations), unless the tender contains any modification.

35.3 — DOCUMENTS RELATING TO NOMINATED SUB-CONTRACTORS

A number of 'Documents relating to Nominated Sub-Contractors' are listed with identification numbers. These documents are not part of the contract, being sub-contract, preparatory or collateral in status, but are referred to throughout clause 35 and within the documents themselves so that they constitute one system and are dependent upon each other for complete intelligibility.

They fall into two groups as considered in the preceding chapter. Those with the suffixes 1 to 4 are used for the nomination procedure of clauses 35.6 to 35.10, this being the more elaborate or 'basic' method. Those with the suffixes 2a and 4a are used for the less complex 'alternative' method of clauses 35.11 and 35.12, which arises out of clause 35.5.

They differ in comparative detail only from those with the suffixes 2 and 4 but unlike these latter do not depend on prescribed equivalents to those with the suffixes 1 and 3. The contents of all these documents are discussed in the chapters immediately following.

PROCEDURE FOR NOMINATION OF A SUB-CONTRACTOR

While clause 35.1 gives the architect both the power and the duty to nominate a sub-contractor in defined cases, it is counterbalanced by a number of provisions under this procedural section of clause 35 to ensure not only that a consistent sub-contract is achieved, but also that the contractor does not find himself with a framework and terms that he might not reasonably have expected. The main exchanges of documents under the 'basic' method may be followed in Figure 18.

35.4 — CONTRACTOR'S RIGHT OF REASONABLE OBJECTION TO PROPOSED SUB-CONTRACTOR

This clause deals with the right of objection as a procedure. The right is limited to objection to the person proposed and may be, for example, on the grounds of previous unsatisfactory dealings with the person. It does not extend to objection to terms offered or any withholding of terms. Under the 'alternative' method the contractor may not have seen these terms before nomination, and under either method a variation instruction may be sought to take up any discrepancy with the terms envisaged in the contract bills.

35.4.1 The first protection that the contractor has is that of 'reasonable objection' to a person whose nomination is proposed. To be effective the objection should be in writing. It must be made 'at the earliest practicable moment' according to each of the next two clauses, which also give final 'moments'. If the contractor's objection is sustained, the architect must then act under clause 35.23, to abandon the proposed sub-contract work or to make a fresh nomination.

35.4.2 When the 'basic' method is used, objection is to be made not later than completion of the contractor's last pre-nomination step of sending the agreed tender to the architect, who will then otherwise 'forthwith' nominate under clause 35.10.2.

35.4.3 When the 'alternative' method is used the contractor will not necessarily have been involved before nomination, and he therefore has seven days from nomination in which to object.

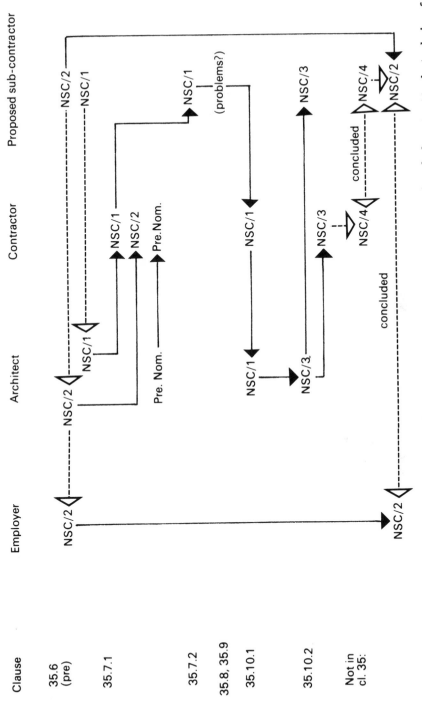

Figure 18: **Main exchanges of documents under 'basic' method of nominating sub-contractor, from preparation of sub-contract tender to placing of sub-contract**

35.5 — (SUPPLIED) SELECTION OF 'BASIC' OR 'ALTERNATIVE' METHOD OF NOMINATION

35.5.1 The 'basic' method relies on the procedure of using Tender NSC/1 and Agreement NSC/2 together and is to apply unless the 'alternative' method is stated to apply for any nominated sub-contractor. This is either to be given in the contract bills which then requires an endorsement of the individual prime cost sum, or is to be given in the instruction for a variation or the expenditure of a provisional sum that leads to nomination. If the 'alternative' method is stated to apply, it is further to be specified whether or not Agreement NSC/2a will be used under clause 35.11.1.

35.5.2 It is however possible for a switch to be made from either method of nomination to the other. Since the original method will have been stated either in the contract bills or in an instruction the switch calls for a variation instruction or further instruction. No switch may be instituted after the point at which the contractor has been brought into the procedure to start to treat with the sub-contractor, unless the nomination fails under clause 35.23 or there is renomination under clause 35.24. Like any variation instruction, one under this provision may carry with it financial consequences which will be covered by the broader terms discussed under main clause 13.1.1.1.

USE OF TENDER NSC/1 AND AGREEMENT NSC/2

35.6 — LIMIT ON NOMINATION

This clause states categorically and tersely that the 'basic' method is the only option other than the 'alternative' method although it gives no guidance as to when either method should be adopted. It also applies unless the 'alternative' method has originally been intended under clause 35.5.1.2 or (as that clause allows) has been substituted under clause 35.5.2.

35.7 — ARCHITECT'S PRELIMINARY ACTION PRIOR TO NOMINATION OF A SUB-CONTRACTOR — DUTY OF CONTRACTOR

35.7.1 The architect has to perform his first round of actions over securing a sub-contractor by obtaining a tender on Tender NSC/1 and provisional completion (by implication with the employer) of Agreement NSC/2. This may leave subsidiary details in Tender NSC/1 to be agreed between the contractor and proposed sub-contractor and so the architect is to forward Tender NSC/1 and Agreement NSC/2 under a preliminary notice of nomination to the contractor.

35.7.2 Upon receipt of these documents the contractor is to treat with the proposed sub-contractor and settle the outstanding details on Tender NSC/1 if he can. Meanwhile Agreement NSC/2 has been signed but is only effective under its own provisions. During this phase and until the architect finally nominates under clause 35.10.2 the sub-contractor is excused by Agreement NSC/2 from liability for any delay resulting in extension of time. Whether the contractor will incur liability or not may depend on whether he has taken all practicable steps to avoid or reduce such a delay under main clause 25.4.7, if that contentious clause can be construed as including a *potential* sub-contractor.

35.8 — CONTRACTOR AND PROPOSED SUB-CONTRACTOR — FAILURE TO AGREE — CONTRACTOR'S AND ARCHITECT'S DUTY

If agreement is not reached within 10 working days, the contractor is to notify the architect in writing of the reasons but he may not suspend negotiations. The architect then has to instruct the contractor further. His main options are to instruct the contractor to continue negotiations, to propose another sub-contractor, or to instruct the omission of the sub-contract work under clause 35.23. To accommodate the terms of a particular sub-contractor the architect may be prepared to give a variation instruction if, say, any of the attendance items in the contract bills do not agree with the tender or to allow some modification of the tender. This problem is discussed in greater detail in the section dealing with Tender NSC/1.

35.9 — PROPOSED SUB-CONTRACTOR — WITHDRAWAL OF OFFER

As the proposed sub-contractor's offer will not be accepted until after the final nomination under clause 35.10.2, the sub-contractor has the option of withdrawing until that point. This he may choose to do because negotiations with the contractor are leading towards too onerous an agreement, or for any other and perhaps less commendable reason, at the risk of losing goodwill. An intermediate option might be an informal approach to the architect to mediate on the lines suggested under clause 35.8 thus avoiding a withdrawal. If the proposed sub-contractor does withdraw, the architect again has to give instructions. As under clause 35.8, this could involve recourse to clause 35.23 or possibly it could be an instruction to resume negotiations after the architect has agreed to a modified tender. In any case the contractor is relieved of responsibility until he receives instructions. There is room for a number of finely balanced interactions here, but they are matters that cannot be resolved in advance in any contract.

35.10 — RECEIPT OF COMPLETED TENDER — ISSUE OF NOMINATION INSTRUCTION BY ARCHITECT

35.10.1 If all the foregoing obstacles are cleared, the contractor must send the now completed tender to the architect 'immediately', while Agreement NSC/2 requires the proposed sub-contractor also to notify his concurrence through the contractor. Under clause 35.4.2 this action ends the contractor's right to object to the nomination and thus in any way avoid the sub-contract.

35.10.2 The architect is then 'forthwith' to nominate the proposed sub-contractor to the contractor on Nomination NSC/3, with a copy to the sub-contractor. At this point the architect must proceed with the nomination, otherwise because of lack of instructions the contractor may be able to make out a case for extension of time under main clause 25.4.6, loss and expense under main clause 26.2.1 or determination under main clause 28.1.3.5. Until this point however the architect must not nominate, as the contractor and proposed sub-contractor are not known to be in agreement. Once the nomination has been made, the contractor must proceed with placing the sub-contract so as to avoid delay on his own part. Oddly enough, while the whole procedure assumes the use of Sub-Contract NSC/4 this is only mentioned in the list in clause 35.3 and in the other documents referenced. The contractor is not expressly required to conclude it as clause 35.12 requires the conclusion of Sub-Contract NSC/4a.

The final nomination of the sub-contractor and conclusion of sub-contract NSC/4 make the already signed Agreement NSC/2 effective in entirety without further action.

TENDER NSC/1 AND AGREEMENT NSC/2 NOT USED

35.11 — TENDER NSC/1 AND AGREEMENT NSC/2 NOT USED — USE OF AGREEMENT NSC/2a

The reference to clause 35.5.1.2 limits the use of this method, although it may be brought within the scope of that clause by a variation under clause 35.5.2 substituting the alternative for the basic method.

It can be inferred that the alternative method is intended for the simpler and smaller contract, so that questions of failure to agree and withdrawal of offer need not be dealt with at length. It is also inferred that the documentation will also be simpler although this does not necessarily follow. Only four documents are mentioned in this clause and the next, even obliquely.

35.11.1 The first two documents are the more precarious in standing. A tender will have been obtained in suitable unspecified form outside this contract (as with the parallel use of Tender NSC/1). If the tender has assumed the collateral responsibilities and financial implications of the optional Agreement NSC/2a, then the employer will enter into Agreement NSC/2a with the proposed sub-contractor.

35.11.2 As the third document, the architect is to issue a final nomination instruction to the contractor, the form to suit the situation again being left unspecified. While the clause is not precise on the point, this instruction should not be given until Agreement NSC/2a has been completed.

35.12 — SUB-CONTRACT NSC/4a

The fourth document is Sub-Contract NSC/4a, over which the contractor agrees under the present contract to 'proceed so as to conclude a sub-contract' with the proposed sub-contractor within 14 days of nomination occurring. This is an odd clause, as the contractor agrees to come to a satisfactory agreement with a third party who may not be entirely co-operative and who may not have been secured from withdrawal by such terms as those in Tender NSC/1 which limit the proposed sub-contractor's freedom. The contractor could then face responsibility if he were at fault for resulting delay, or for any later withdrawal of the sub-contract tender. If on the other hand the proposed sub-contractor is recalcitrant, the contractor is released by clause 35.23.3, although the present clause gives no hint of this and the question of blame in the case of failure to agree is in the nature of things difficult to allocate. The obvious lesson is that the architect should pursue his activities to the point where the operation of this clause is purely automatic.

PAYMENT OF NOMINATED SUB-CONTRACTOR

35.13 — (PART) — ARCHITECT — DIRECTION AS TO INTERIM PAYMENT FOR SUB-CONTRACTOR

This clause further promotes the position of nominated sub-contractors by regulating and protecting their payment in a way that is done neither for domestic sub-contractors nor for nominated suppliers. In spite of the heading it covers both interim and final payments.

35.13.1 With each interim certificate, the architect is required to 'direct the Contractor' on payments to nominated sub-contractors and so needs to calculate the net amounts after holding retention. He should ignore any deduction for cash discount, as this is mentioned only in the sub-contract. It arises if the contractor pays promptly and is retained by him and not passed on to the employer. In general amounts are to be based on the relevant sub-contract. Main clause 30.7 requires final payments to be made without retention deductions. To remove uncertainty, each nominated sub-contractor is to be informed by the architect of these amounts, by implication for his own sub-contract only. There is no need for a sub-contractor to notify non-payment other than indirectly through the 'reasonable proof' mechanism under the next certificate.

35.13.2 Under this sub-clause the contractor is obliged to make the payments directed and if he does not do so the events following on clause 35.13.3 take place. He must pay the nominated sub-contractor within 17 days of the issue of the architect's interim certificate in accordance with sub-contract clause 21.3.1.1 whether he himself has been paid or not less only the cash discount and any set-off under sub-contract clause 23. If the contractor has cash flow problems and the employer is a dilatory payer, the contractor should consider the implications very carefully. The contractor himself may be a dilatory payer and pay after the 17 days but in time to obtain proof of payment and may still choose to deduct the cash discount. If so he will be due to have the discount deducted from him and paid to the sub-contractor by the employer at the next interim certificate, since he will not have 'duly discharged' the payment under the terms of sub-contract clause 21.3.1.1, under which heading the point is further discussed. He must not however pay more than is certified or pay anything without the architect's direction, as the architect may have a particular reason for a seeming under-certification or complete withholding of payment.

The clause appears to be defective by its use of the term 'interim payment', whereas it must have been intended to say 'interim or final payment' or simply 'payment'. The contractor is still clearly liable to the nominated sub-contractors, but the wording breaks the chain of protection for them under these conditions, since clause 35.13.3 refers back to and depends on the present clause. Subsequent parts of clause 35.13 do not offer any solution. Therefore, unless the wording is amended the architect has no power to check on final payments to nominated sub-contractors, which is the reason behind securing payment under main clause 30.7 in advance of the final certificate.

35.13 — (PART) DIRECT PAYMENT OF NOMINATED SUB-CONTRACTOR

This clause refers only to direct payment made after the contractor has defaulted in passing on payments to the sub-contractor. There may also have been direct payments to the sub-contractor before nomination under the terms of Agreement NSC/2 or Agreement NSC/2a for design and fabricated work. The effect on the contractor's cash discount and profit in each case is considered under main clause 30.6.2.

35.13.3 In order that he may police the payment arrangements, the architect is to receive 'reasonable proof' from the contractor. This could be by way of formal receipts, letters or figures in regular statements of account, for instance. It is to be done before the issue of the following certificate, including the final certificate, and will begin as soon as a nominated sub-contractor has been brought into the picture. The clause is subject to the defect discussed in clause 35.13.2.

35.13.4 This clause is inserted to avoid the contractor being caught through no fault of his own between the upper and nether millstones of clauses 35.13.3 and 35.13.5. (It has the incidental effect of avoiding the sub-contractor being paid twice, a prospect which might otherwise encourage him *not* to provide proof!) If the architect is 'reasonably satisfied' that it is the lapse of a sub-contractor that prevents the contractor offering proof of payment then he must not operate the procedure for direct payment. This allows him to take oral assurances from the sub-contractor and, in the case of a contractor of sufficient standing, evidence from the internal accounting procedures of the contractor to show that payment has been passed through. It does not however allow him to accept any assurance that the payment is about to be made, as clause 35.13.3 requires 'proof of the discharge', not of the intention. Equally he may not accept a case of mixed responsibility: the sub-contractor's lapse must be the 'sole reason'. The architect must however take account of any set-off position under the provisions of sub-contract clause 23 and of the employer's deductions under sub-contract clause 21.3.1.2.

35.13.5 In the case of any nominated sub-contractor the employer has at least a discretionary right to operate direct payment if the contractor defaults. Agreements NSC/2 and NSC/2a and clause 35.13.5.1 make this obligatory where the agreements exist collaterally. There is however no right to make a direct payment to a sub-contractor without the contractor having defaulted (other than by mutual agreement between the employer and contractor). Any attempt to anticipate default and not to include an amount in an interim certificate for this, or any other reason, is a breach of contract. Whether or not the agreements are in use, the architect has to certify under clause 35.13.5.2 any case of lack of proof and the amount in question before the employer may act.

A copy of this must go to the sub-contractor as well as one to the contractor. Once this has been done, two actions follow under clause 35.13.5.3: future payments to the contractor are to be reduced by the amounts in default, and the employer is to pay the same amount direct to the nominated sub-contractor. If he does not follow this course of action when Agreements NSC/2 and NSC/2a apply, he faces the sub-contractor suspending work under sub-contract clause 21.8.1. He should not deduct cash discount when paying. The contractor has now foregone it and the nominated sub-contractor should receive it in recompense for the delay in payment, rather than the employer retain it as a windfall.

The former of these actions needs further comment: 'the future payments' to be reduced are those 'otherwise due', being either amounts 'stated as due' in interim certificates under main clause 30.2 or the 'balance due' in the final certificate under clause 30.8, but in either case 'after deducting any amounts due to the Employer from the Contractor under this Contract'. The full-scale sequence is thus: the architect certifies the unreduced (otherwise due) amount, the employer deducts any amounts that he may, and the reduced certified amount is then further reduced by the sub-contract amount in default. From this it follows that the employer makes the reduction as a reduction of a 'payment otherwise due', and that the architect must not make it as a reduction of an amount that he would otherwise state in a certificate under the provisions particularly of main clauses 30.1, 30.2 and 30.7. It would have been clearer if this clause like other clauses in the conditions had referred to the amounts as deductions made by the employer rather than as reductions.

Who makes the deduction and when may seem mere pedantry. There is another more important consequence, which follows from the order of deduction and reduction, when read with the proviso at the end of clause 35.13.5.3 that the employer is not obliged to pay out to nominated sub-contractors any more than he can retrieve from the contractor. This consequence is that the employer is entitled when monies are limited to recover his own contra-amounts in preference to making reductions and paying sub-contractors.

Clause 35.13.5.4 covers other qualifications to the employer's rights and duties. The first arises under clause 35.13.5.4.1 and covers the timing of a payment direct to a nominated sub-contractor. If there is still enough money for the contractor to receive some payment, the nominated sub-contractor is to be paid either at the same time or within the 14 days within which the contractor would have otherwise been paid. Thus the sub-contractor will be paid up to one month less three days behind the original schedule. The second is in clause 35.13.5.4.2 and states that where there is a release of retention due under a certificate, only the part that is contractor's retention is available for reduction. This is the clear intention of the split fund under main clause 30.4.2, but the present wording avoids possible pitfalls.

Having separated out the contractor and the nominated sub-contractors, the provisions go on in clause 35.13.5.4.3 to apportion payment between the several sub-contractors who may be involved. Where funds are inadequate the employer has two options: to share out the money available pro-rata to the outstanding amounts or to use his discretion and do something else that is 'fair and reasonable', or at least 'may appear' to be so. This gives the employer plenty of rope and perhaps allows little redress for an aggrieved sub-contractor. The spirit of the wording is for the pro-rata method to be the norm. The clause also refers to 'the amounts from time to time remaining undischarged' and thus envisages that in the course of a number of certificates all nominated sub-contractors will be paid completely, even if at uneven rates. If a fresh sub-contractor were to join the queue, it might well be reasonable for him to receive a less than proportionate payment compared with those of longer standing. The expression 'where the Employer has to pay' limits his activities at this stage to nominated sub-contractors who have entered into Agreement NSC/2 or Agreement NSC/2a, and whom he is obliged to pay, if possible, in preference to other nominated sub-contractors who depend on the 'may' of clause 35.13.5.1. The sub-contractor's right of suspension under sub-contract clause 21.8.1.2 (where it is discussed) if he is not paid direct 'the whole amount' is however something of a sword of Damocles over the whole procedure of apportioned payments. It could create severe problems for the employer and even force him to consider paying out more than he has in hand.

A particular problem may arise with the interim certificate under main clause 30.7 which finally pays off nominated sub-contractors, if the total of this certificate is greater than the balance remaining to be paid to the contractor under the final certificate. Here the employer must not pay out so much as to reverse the direction of indebtedness, as he would then be going beyond 'amounts available for reduction' and the contractor may well not be able to pay him in the circumstances. The situation can only be avoided if it is possible to pay off nominated sub-contractors progressively and at times when the amounts due to the contractor himself are greater than those due to sub-contractors. With a very high proportion of nominated sub-contract value in the contract this may not be practicable and the employer and the architect must simply do what they can. In any such case the employer will not incur any extra liability to nominated sub-contractors, even with Agreements NSC/2 and NSC/2a above.

The last provision is that clause 35.13.5.3 becomes inoperative if the contractor goes into liquidation or becomes bankrupt. (The footnote requires an amendment to be made when entering into the contract to relate to bankruptcy. It seems a pity that this clause does not provide for alternatives, as elsewhere in the conditions.) The employer must not then make any more payments, as is provided under main clause 27.4.2.2.

This clause gives the employer towards the contractor not only a right but a duty to pay nominated sub-contractors direct in the prescribed circumstances. Breach of this duty by the employer has two main effects on the contractor: delay and loss to himself and his responsibility for these elements to the sub-contractor. In the absence of express provision it is difficult to view the employer as liable to the contractor for failing in an activity that is only secondary as against the contractor's primary default. The conditions only allow extension of time to the contractor when he 'has taken all practicable steps to avoid or reduce' the sub-contractor's delay under main clauses 25.4.7 which he has not done in this situation. There is no provision for the contractor to recoup loss and expense from the employer under main clause 26 in these circumstances. It is therefore difficult to see why the clause obliges rather than gives the employer the right to pay direct, which he must do in furtherance of his obligations under Agreements NSC/2 or NSC/2a. This would avoid the threat of a possible suspension under sub-contract clause 21.8.1, if the employer lapses.

EXTENSION OF PERIOD OR PERIODS FOR COMPLETION OF NOMINATED SUB-CONTRACT WORKS

35.14 — (SUPPLIED) RESTRICTION ON CONTRACTOR — ACTION BY ARCHITECT

Most of the provisions on this matter are contained in Sub-Contract NSC/4 under which heading they are discussed. They are modelled closely on the provisions in main clause 25. The present clause simply incorporates these into the conditions.

35.14.1 The contractor is not empowered to grant any extensions of the sub-contract period or periods without the architect's consent. This is because an extension granted to the sub-contractor may result in an extension for the contractor as well, by virtue of main clause 25.4.7. The result may then be counterbalanced by the employer recovering from the sub-contractor under Agreement NSC/2 or NSC/2a.

35.14.2 The other side of the coin is that the architect must exercise his responsibilities. This carries over into the realm of the sub-contract where he is given particular duties and into the area of the contractor's programme and organisation, well beyond any design function.

FAILURE TO COMPLETE NOMINATED SUB-CONTRACT WORKS

35.15 — (SUPPLIED) CERTIFICATE OF FAILURE TO COMPLETE

This clause deals solely with the architect's certificate and the title for completeness should also include 'on time'. The question of damages is set out in the sub-contract, and discussed in chapter 18.

35.15.1 Failure of a nominated sub-contractor to complete his works as a whole or a due portion by a relevant date is to be notified to the architect by the contractor, so that if the architect is in agreement he may certify this fact back to the contractor. Before doing this he has to ensure that any extensions under clause 35.14 have been properly operated. Although he is responsible for granting them and although the sub-contractor joins with the contractor in requesting them, there is always the possibility that the contractor may try to conceal information if a particular extension would be contrary to his interests. Copies of the contractor's and the architect's documents are therefore to go to the sub-contractor for information and perhaps action.

35.15.2 To avoid undue uncertainty an upper time limit of two months is set between the two documents. Main clause 24.1 provides for no such time limit: implying that the architect acts at once. In the present case the architect is one step removed from the sub-contractor and needs time to make his checks under clause 35.15.1. Even so the architect's certificate is not final in effect, as under sub-contract clause 11.2.4 he still has until 12 weeks after practical completion of the sub-contract works to amend the completion date which is certified here as not having been achieved.

PRACTICAL COMPLETION OF NOMINATED SUB-CONTRACT WORKS

35.16 — (SUPPLIED) CERTIFICATE OF COMPLETION

As with the contractor, the architect is to certify practical completion of the work of the nominated sub-contractor as a whole and again on the same basis, his opinion. Under this clause he does not need to consult the contractor but reasonably would do so, especially if events under clauses 35.14 or 35.15 had taken place. Under sub-contract clause 14.1 the sub-contractor has the opportunity to warn the architect through the contractor of when practical completion is due, and this will alert everyone; in particular the contractor can then add his comments. An additional copy of the architect's certificate goes to the sub-contractor. It is a certificate with limited effects, directly affecting final payments to the sub-contractor and related matters under the following clauses, and this is why provision is made for only one certificate to cover the whole of the sub-contract works and not for a series of certificates for parts completed. Even so it may overlap with partial possession under main clause 18 if the whole of the sub-contract works comes within the part taken over by the employer, and in this case also the clause states that the certificate applies. If practical completion of the sub-contract and like completion of the main works occur simultaneously the provision becomes unnecessary. The clause has no direct role in relation to Agreement NSC/2 or Agreement NSC/2a, but is evidential on the question of programme for these agreements, and for any extension for the contractor under main clause 25.4.7.

FINAL PAYMENT OF NOMINATED SUB-CONTRACTORS

35.17 — (SUPPLIED) INTERIM CERTIFICATE

The architect may finally pay off a nominated sub-contractor at any time after his practical completion and must do so at the latest 12 months after this date. If this is before the contractor's practical completion, payment should be included in a convenient interim certificate, rather than be made through a special certificate on the anniversary of completion. If it is after the contractor's completion, the payment falls within the pattern of payments at irregular intervals or may come into the umbrella certificate to round up outstanding nominated sub-contract payments under clause 30.7. In the present clause there is no mention of credits to be allowed by the sub-contractor, as there should be to give the same effect as main clause 30.7 over payments made to the sub-contractor before nomination. There are four pre-conditions to this final payment. The first conditions which occur in this part of the clause are that either Agreement NSC/2 or NSC/2a applies and that their clauses 5 or 4 respectively remain in force unamended. These clauses complete the triangular relationship needed to apply clause 35.18.1.2 below.

35.17.1 The third pre-condition is that the sub-contractor has completed any remedial work to the satisfaction of both the architect and the contractor. The contractor's interest is that he will no longer have any amounts on which to draw, as he would otherwise up to the interim certificate under main clause 30.7. Any remaining defects might lead to consequential defects in the contractor's work for which he would be liable, or to further defects in the sub-contractor's work, affecting the position under clause 35.18.

35.17.2   Lastly, final payment is logically dependent on the nominated sub-contractor providing some of the necessary data, but this is made a precondition nevertheless. Sub-contract clauses 21.10.1.1 and 21.11.1 provide for the sub-contractor to act within 'reasonable time after (his) practical completion'.

35.18 — DEFECTS IN NOMINATED SUB-CONTRACT WORKS AFTER FINAL PAYMENT OF NOMINATED SUB-CONTRACTOR — BEFORE ISSUE OF FINAL CERTIFICATE

Once the final certificate is honoured, the contractor and nominated sub-contractors are in the same position in that, arbitration proceedings apart, no money is due to them from the employer. Before the final certificate and after a clause 35.17 final payment, the contractor is in an awkward position: he is still liable for defects on the whole works, but has paid off the sub-contractor under the terms of the contract. If the nominated sub-contractor (here called 'the original sub-contractor') honours his obligation to remedy defects, which sub-contract clause 14.3 places within the same time scale as that in the present conditions, all is well. If he does not do so, this clause gives the contractor some relief from action by the employer and so from liability.

35.18.1 Under clause 35.18.1.1 the architect is to 'issue an instruction nominating' (presumably under the 'alternative' method) a 'substituted sub-contractor' to do the remedial work and be paid by the contractor. The employer is required by clause 35.18.1.2 to act under Agreements NSC/2 and NSC/2a 'as may be reasonable' (thus including court action) to recover from the original sub-contractor the amount which he has paid or is due to pay to the substituted sub-contractor through the contractor. If he is fully successful accounts balance; if not, the contractor is to 'pay or allow' the difference so that the employer is not out of pocket. In the extreme case of the original sub-contractor going out of business, the contractor would have to meet the whole amount, as he would also have to do in the absence of this clause. This is subject to the contractor having agreed to the substituted sub-contract price before nomination. If he reasonably did not agree there would need to be a further nomination at a lower price. If he were instructed to accept the nomination in spite of a reasonable objection to the price, then under the strict wording of this clause he would not be obliged to make any payment or allowance to the employer. If he did not agree in advance however, the option of later arbitration over whether *he* was 'reasonable' is always open.

35.18.2 Nothing in clause 35.18 is to affect clause 35.21, which annexes certain matters to rest between the employer and a nominated sub-contractor.

35.19 — FINAL PAYMENTS — SAVING PROVISIONS

Paying off a nominated sub-contractor does not change liabilities for loss and damage.

35.19.1 These remain with the contractor until the usual time of practical completion or 'when the Employer takes possession of the Works', which presumably is intended to cover partial possession or sectional completion. The liability of the contractor to the employer is not at the same level as for the works in general, while the liability of the sub-contractor to the contractor has been almost extinguished by sub-contract clause 8.3.3. It is not clear why 'materials and goods' are mentioned in relation to completed sub-contract works.

35.19.2 In particular, there is to be no change in the position over insurance or otherwise of the works.

POSITION OF EMPLOYER IN RELATION TO NOMINATED SUB-CONTRACTOR

35.20 — (SUPPLIED) EXCLUSION OF EMPLOYER'S LIABILITY

Privity of contract lies between the contractor and the nominated sub-contractor and, although there are situations under clause 35 where the employer may intervene on the sub-contractor's behalf, this clause under-lines the fact that the employer is not contractually liable to a sub-contractor. It acts more as a defence against the contractor seeking to step aside from liability than against claims by the sub-contractor directly against the employer. If the employer, or the architect on his behalf, steps beyond the provisions of the contract in the course of day-to-day dealings, then some other and more direct relationship might well arise.

The corollary of this position is that nominated sub-contractors are not directly liable to the employer. Both of these positions are affected by whichever of Agreements NCS/2 or NSC/2a are in force.

CLAUSE 2 OF AGREEMENT NSC/2 OR CLAUSE 1 OF AGREEMENT NSC/2a
— POSITION OF CONTRACTOR

35.21 — (SUPPLIED) EXCLUSION OF CONTRACTOR'S LIABILITY

Since the agreements establish certain links between a nominated sub-contractor and the employer, this clause is necessary to avoid the possibility of the contractor incurring liability through the nominated sub-contractor for certain matters about which he knows no more than the prime cost sum on which he tenders. These involve design and specification undertaken by the sub-contractor and any work, whether of that nature or by way of fabrication, for which the sub-contractor is paid directly by the employer before nomination. The intention is not to remove the overall responsibility of the contractor for the work of the sub-contractor and the last sentence in the various provisions of the clause affirms this. This produces some overlap, since both the clause and the agreements talk about materials for instance, and variously include them all or exclude some of them from the contractor's responsibility. It is likely that the specific terms of the agreement would be so interpreted by the courts as to remove any responsibility of the contractor under the general term of this clause. This would support the intended effect in the area of overlap.

If neither agreement is in use for a nominated sub-contractor, this clause still gives the contractor the same protection over liabilities such as design. However, in the absence of an agreement the employer will lose his rights, unless corresponding terms are duly agreed with the sub-contractor.

RESTRICTIONS IN CONTRACTS OF SALE ETC — LIMITATION OF LIABILITY OF
NOMINATED SUB-CONTRACTORS

35.22 — (SUPPLIED) LIMITATION OF CONTRACTOR'S LIABILITY

Under sub-contract clause 2.3 the nominated sub-contractor may be required to enter into a sub-sub-contract or contract of sale in which the other person seeks to exclude some liability to the nominated sub-contractor. If the architect and the contractor accept the exclusion, then the nominated sub-contractor in turn is relieved of the same measure of liability. The present clause extends the same relief along the contractual line to the contractor.

Main clause 36.5 gives a parallel relief in relation to a nominated supplier, but here there is one less link in the contractual chain.

There is no equivalent in relation to a domestic sub-contractor or a domestic supplier, the main point of the provision being to allow for the unusual use of materials or perhaps the use of new materials, or for equipment that is complex or supplied as a standard item with standard conditions of sale.

POSITION WHERE PROPOSED NOMINATION DOES NOT PROCEED FURTHER

35.23 — (SUPPLIED) ARCHITECT'S ACTION

This clause gives three cases in which the architect must choose whether to instruct the omission of work under a proposed nomination or to start the nomination process with another person in view. They all occur in the course of arranging the sub-contract and between the selection based on tendering and the procedure under clause 35.4 onwards. It is difficult in most instances to see how the architect can simply omit work, so presumably some addition is envisaged that will not fall to be nominated work.

35.23.1 The contractor's reasonable objection to the person proposed has already been discussed.

35.23.2 The failure to agree particular conditions under the 'basic' method procedure which takes account of the present clause has also been discussed. There are points in question which are mentioned under that procedure. The 'reasonable time' limitation under this and the next case must be construed in the light of the margin of 10 working days from preliminary nomination given in clause 35.8.

35.23.3 The same may be said of the 'alternative' method procedure, except that it does not refer to the present clause in any way. The reference here in the opposite direction is however adequate.

CIRCUMSTANCES WHERE RE-NOMINATION NECESSARY

35.24 — (SUPPLIED) CIRCUMSTANCES FOR AND ACTION OVER RENOMINATION

A totally different situation exists when a sub-contract which has been entered into does not proceed to completion of the work. The clause sets out three circumstances that may lead to renomination; all are related to the usual situation which is determination of the sub-contractor's employment and not to determination of the sub-contract itself that occurs uniquely in clause 35.25.

35.24.1 The sub-contractor may be so in default under his sub-contract that the contractor has a right to determine against him for reasons almost identical to those giving the employer a right under the present contract. It is necessary for the contractor to inform the architect, forwarding any comments from the sub-contractor and for the architect to agree with the contractor that determination should take place.

35.24.2 The sub-contractor may become insolvent.

35.24.3 The sub-contractor may determine against the contractor on the grounds that the contractor has suspended work or seriously affected the sub-contractor's progress. The architect has a responsibility to state his 'opinion' under the Sub-Contracts NSC/4 and NSC/4a on these matters and also to give his consent under clauses 35.14 and 35.15 over smaller matters of delay. He is thus drawn into affairs quite deeply.

These three clauses do not necessarily lead to a determination, other than in the third situation. The sub-contractor has no right to determine because of default of the employer or because of non-payment, whether it is the employer or the contractor who is holding back the money, but simply to suspend under sub-contract clause 21.8.

For each of the three circumstances a distinct set of procedures and provisions is given.

35.24.4 There are three steps when the sub-contractor is found to be in default in the circumstances discussed under Sub-Contracts NSC/4 and NSC/4a, where points relevant to this clause emerge. The contractor is to give the formal notice of default to the sub-contractor under clause 35.24.4.1 and this may be followed by determination, if the sub-contractor does not cease the default. But the contractor may only issue notice if instructed by the architect, who may add a rider that a further instruction must be obtained before determination becomes final. Secondly, under clause 35.24.4.2 the contractor is to notify the architect whether or not the determination has followed on the default notice or confirm that he has determined after the further instruction, if any. Thirdly, when the contractor has confirmed that determination has occurred, the architect is to make a fresh nomination under clause 35.24.4.3.

There is a proviso to the last step, which applies if determination is due to the sub-contractor's refusal or neglect to carry out remedial work. It is for the contractor to have the chance to agree the substituted sub-contract price 'as provided in clause 35.18.1'. The latter deals with default over remedial work, but only after final payment of the sub-contractor whereas in contrast clause 32.24.4 may be invoked at any stage and, because it deals with determination of *employment*, is effective only before practical completion and final payment. In this instance the contractor is not likely to be concerned over the substituted price level, since clause 35.24.7 absolves him from responsibility for any part of it. The employer in turn will be able to proceed against the sub-contractor under Agreement NSC/2 or Agreement NSC/2a if in use, which obliges the sub-contractor not to default so as to lead to such a determination. The employer may also be able to recover any loss and expense under the provisions of sub-contract clause 29.4, although that position is confused in several respects, and the whole question of recovery is discussed there. There appears to be a drafting error here: it would seem the proviso could well be deleted.

35.24.5 In the case of a sub-contractor's insolvency the architect is to make a fresh nomination. This is the situation which gave rise to the case of *North West Metropolitan Regional Hospital Board* v. *T. A. Bickerton & Son Ltd.* If however the architect has 'reasonable grounds for supposing that the receiver or manager' can and will carry the work through, then the architect may wait and see if this happens. He has a duty to look to 'the interest of the Employer, the Contractor or any Sub-Contractor whether Nominated or Domestic engaged or to be engaged'. This offers wide scope for possible actions under both contract and tort.

35.24.6 When the sub-contractor chooses to determine because of the contractor's default, the architect must make a fresh nomination without apportioning blame for the determination, but treating it as a matter of fact. The contractor is not entitled to be consulted over the level of the substituted price and, while the employer will pay the new sub-contractor the full price through the contractor, the employer will recover any excess by deduction from the amounts due to the contractor under the same interim certificates. The architect should have regard both to technical matters and to the necessity of avoiding delay for the employer, with this if necessary overriding the consideration of price. If the contractor considers that the sub-contractor has determined unreasonably, and thus incurred him in unwarranted extra expense, this is a matter strictly between them.

In all these three circumstances if the original sub-contractor is the only person able to perform the balance of the sub-contract works in such a way as to match the part already completed this presents an acute practical problem. In a critical case it might be necessary to remove work already done and substitute alternative work with serious consequences in time and expense. Only where the sub-contractor or the contractor is *prima facie* in default is there a hope that the employer may recoup any of his losses. In such circumstances he effectively does not pay the excess amount of the sub-contract price and has the possibility of taking legal action over further expense. Where the contractor is in default he also has the option of suing for liquidated damages for delay. The option of deducting as of right from monies due is not given by the conditions and this could happen only if the contractor agreed. Clause 35.24.6 limits deduction to 'any extra amount . . . resulting from such further nomination' and does not include anything resulting from the determination itself. The immediate clause therefore excludes the cost of renomination itself, and other loss and expense.

35.24.7 As a tailpiece, this clause states that the 'amount properly payable' to a sub-contractor when there is a renomination is to be included in payments to the contractor, in the first two circumstances discussed. It might as well have said all three as clause 35.24.6 provides for separate deduction of the excess which must therefore have been included initially. The comment under 35.24.4 relating to this clause should also be noted.

The clause says nothing about the 'amount properly payable' to the original sub-contractor and a rational policy must be evolved from the sub-contract provisions. When the contractor determines against the sub-contractor for default or there is automatic determination for insolvency, the contractor is not due under sub-contract clause 29 to make any further payment to the sub-contractor until the sub-contract works are completed, when the architect and the quantity surveyor become involved. The procedure is discussed under the heading of that clause. An amount included in an interim certificate issued just before but payable after determination should not be paid by the contractor. It should then be excluded by the architect from the next interim certificate and the sub-contractor notified accordingly, rather than be deducted by the employer as would happen if the sub-contractor were to be paid direct.

When the sub-contractor determines against the contractor under sub-contract clause 30, no further amount should be included in an interim certificate at all, since sub-contract clause 30 leaves final settlement between the contractor and the sub-contractor only, whether it be for work already executed but not paid for or for disruption expenses. If however an amount is already in an interim certificate not yet met by the employer, it should be paid by him and then by the contractor accordingly, as it would fall into the final settlement in any case. All this is a rational enough policy deduced from the rather non-committal wording of sub-contract clause 30, as long as the amounts paid through interim certificates for the original and substituted sub-contractors total at least as much as would have been payable had the original sub-contractor completed his work. The employer ends up paying what he expected and the contractor carries the rest.

If however the two sub-contractors' amounts are less in total than the hypothetical amount, the employer stands to gain the difference as there is no provision requiring him to pass it on to the contractor. While they will usually *not* be less because of the costs of renomination, they may on occasions be less due to pace of work in the preceding month, and the timing of the interim certificate and the determination. The sub-contractor could in fact arrange matters to penalise the contractor, or give the employer a bonus. Even collusion is possible. At best the provision is hit and miss, and perhaps the courts will construe matters against the employer who puts forward the conditions.

DETERMINATION OR DETERMINATION OF EMPLOYMENT OF NOMINATED
SUB-CONTRACTOR — ARCHITECT'S INSTRUCTIONS

35.25 — (SUPPLIED) DETERMINATION OF NOMINATED SUB-CONTRACT

The expression used here and nowhere else in the conditions is 'determine any Nominated Sub-Contract', that is bringing the sub-contract itself to an end, and not just the employment of the sub-contractor. The distinction is discussed in introducing main clause 27. The contractor must not act in this way without an instruction from the architect despite 'any right' he may have, otherwise he may extinguish liabilities of the sub-contractor to him and leave himself liable to the employer without back-up from the sub-contractor.

35.26 — (SUPPLIED) DETERMINATION OF EMPLOYMENT OF NOMINATED SUB-CONTRACTOR

The expression used here is 'the employment of the Nominated Sub-Contractor is determined under clause 29 of (the) Sub-Contract'. This relates to the cases in which the sub-contractor is in default or is insolvent, and the contractor determines. The present clause mentions only the value of work and materials by the sub-contractor and this amount is to be included for payment as and when instructed by the architect, as would have been the case had the sub-contract run to completion. If an amount included in an interim certificate has not been paid at determination, the contractor must withhold payment and wait until 'the Architect shall direct', that is until the financial position is finalised after completion of work by the substituted sub-contractor. There is a different pattern in sub-contract clause 29.4.

This clause does not cover the situation in which the sub-contractor determines due to the contractor's default, since clause 35.24.6 prevents the employer from being out of pocket and all other financial issues rest between the contractor and the sub-contractor only.

CHAPTER 17

Nominated sub-contract documents: the tender, the agreement with employer and the nomination

The interrelationship of the documents taken in this chapter and of their several parts has been considered in Chapter 15 and they are therefore dealt with here severally and with the minimum of cross-reference. Their close relationship must again be stressed and the earlier chapter should be kept under review.

Tender NSC/1: standard form of nominated sub-contract tender and agreement

This document is for use only in the 'basic' method of nomination. Under the 'alternative' method no standard form is provided, so that the architect will use his own document to suit his chosen procedure. As a considerable amount of sub-contract information is embodied in the schedule, the whole of the present tender document becomes part of the sub-contract and cross-reference is made to it from various parts of Sub-Contract NSC/4. This arrangement therefore differs from that under the main contract where the tender form has only a passing significance, and is most akin to that under the GC/Works/1 and the ICE forms. The four parts of the document are described below.

(A) THE TENDER AND AGREEMENT PROPER

This contains the usual information about the sub-contract works and reference numbers for annexed sub-contract documentation on the one hand, counterbalanced by the sum for the works (expressed in one of two forms to suit Sub-Contract NSC/4 under article 2 and clause 15, where the options are discussed) and daywork percentages. The appropriate sum and the percentages include $2\frac{1}{2}\%$ cash discount for the main contractor, which is provided for under Sub-Contract NSC/4 clause 21.3.1.1, although the main contract is silent on this matter.

Three signatures are required in all. The sub-contractor signs first when he submits the tender, but this gives an offer 'upon and subject to the stipulations' discussed under (B) below. When he approves the tender at this stage, the architect signs next on behalf of the employer and sends to the contractor the whole document with a preliminary notice of nomination and a copy of Agreement NSC/2 as completed by the employer and the sub-contractor. There then follows the period allowed under main clause 35.7.2 for agreement between the contractor and the sub-contractor of schedule 2 discussed under (D) below. If all goes well the contractor signs last 'subject to a nomination instruction' and returns the completed document to the architect under main clause 35.10.1. The architect then issues his nomination instruction on Nomination NSC/3 under main clause 35.10.2 and the contractor and the sub-contractor (it must be inferred under that clause) then conclude Sub-Contract NSC/4.

While there is no mention of it in the actual tender and agreement, Sub-Contract NSC/4 in its fifth recital provides that the signatures of the contractor and the sub-contractor indicate that they have agreed to use Sub-Contract NSC/4 'unamended', which is how it is also referred to in schedule 1 following. This peculiar arrangement is discussed in Chapter 18.

No mention is made here or anywhere else other than in Agreement NSC/2 of any design or specification work by the sub-contractor, whether undertaken before or after tendering, as may be required if the sub-contractor's work is of a particularly specialised nature. 'Annexed hereto' are to be 'the drawings/specifications/bills of quantities/schedules of rates' and these may have been prepared and completed wholly by the architect, quantity surveyor, or sub-contractor, or shared by these persons prior to completion of the tender. What must be clearly stated in these documents as a whole is whether or not further design or similar work is to be performed by the sub-contractor and approved by the architect. If so, it must then be clear if the work is in development of 'any performance specification or requirement' or if it involves 'the selection of materials and goods' by the sub-contractor as Agreement NSC/2 envisages in clauses 2.2.1 and 2.2.2 respectively. In either of these cases no change is to be expected in the sum payable, unless the extent of this work cannot reasonably be forecast. Confusion may arise in at least two places, one being when the design parameters are ill-defined and the architect and the sub-contractor disagree subsequent to nomination over what the sub-contract or tender sum reasonably covered. The other case is that in which payment is based on a schedule of rates and design by the sub-contractor could result in completion of a blank cheque ultimately by the employer, unless the quantitative aspects of the design are closely examined. Subject to these cautions, the tender mechanism does allow flexibility to accommodate the many permutations that can arise.

(B) THE STIPULATIONS

All five are on the part of the sub-contractor at the time of tendering and all lapse at the latest when the architect issues Nomination NSC/3. They relate to various uncertainties and potential hazards in the interim that cannot fairly be covered in the tender.

Only the first and last of these need comment. Under the first, while the sub-contractor will complete Agreement NSC/2 soon after he learns his tender is under favourable consideration, he is not bound by Agreement NSC/2 until the architect has given the second signature on the tender and the employer also has signed Agreement NSC/2. Under the last, if there is a withdrawal related to the other stipulations the employer is under no liability except to pay for design and work similar already performed under Agreement NSC/2 which otherwise lapses.

The other stipulations allow the sub-contractor to withdraw his tender for stated reasons: if he finds that a previously unknown main contractor is undesirable (it would appear, for any reason at all), if he cannot agree schedule 2 (again no reason is given) and if nomination does not proceed within a period from the date of tender which he himself has inserted.

(c) SCHEDULE 1 — PARTICULARS OF MAIN CONTRACT AND SUB-CONTRACT

Here are to be inserted the names of the employer, the architect, the quantity surveyor and (if known) the contractor. These are to be followed by details of both sub-contract and main contract conditions, including the selection of alternative provisions and insertions in the main contract appendix. The comments about importing main contract conditions given under sub-contract clause 5 may be noted. Any changes to the printed main contract conditions are also to be given, but the sub-contract conditions are described in item 1 as 'unamended'. This latter point ties rather tacitly with the fifth recital of Sub-Contract NSC/4 where the parties agree by virtue of having signed the tender that 'the provisions of Sub-Contract NSC/4 shall apply unamended'. If this is not what is wanted then both documents must be amended.

In addition the schedule requires details of order of works, location, access, obligations and restrictions imposed by the employer and 'other relevant information'. A note suggests attaching a copy of the main preliminaries bill to cover some of this. It may cover it all, but any subsidiary level of detail necessary to the sub-contract should be considered.

Sub-schedules allow for alternative fluctuations data. For this purpose the notional date of tender has to be inserted and this may well differ from the date on which the sub-contractor signs the tender.

(d) SCHEDULE 2 — PARTICULAR CONDITIONS

These are all matters to be finally agreed by the contractor and the sub-contractor between preliminary and firm nomination. The architect is to insert the period or periods for working on the site when issuing the tender invitation and the sub-contractor is at the time of tendering to insert suggestions for other programme time (including drawing time) and for attendance other than general attendance which he will require from the contractor. In both these cases there is space for inserting what is finally agreed and there is also space for other items to be agreed or clarified (without prior suggestions by the sub-contractor) over insurance, labour conditions, working hours and so on. If there is disagreement on any of these matters the sub-contractor has the option of withdrawing his tender under the third stipulation already noted. There is no provision for any negotiation of a revised tender, although there might be circumstances in which this might make sense in either commercial or even ethical terms. Revision of the sum will require the agreement of the architect.

The only place where there is scope for negotiation is over the attendance items. The list of items in the present schedule comes from the Standard Method of Measurement and for conciseness the significance of particular items in it are discussed under sub-contract clause 27 in relation to general attendance. The main contract bills of quantities or other documents may well have set out which items the contractor has to provide free to the sub-contractor in a particular instance, basing this on whatever information or judicious forecast was available. If the sub-contractor is adamant that he needs more than the bills allow, then the contractor may reasonably ask for a variation instruction over changes in specified provisions so that he is reimbursed for the extra cost. Alternatively a provisional sum will have been given and the instruction to expend it will cover whatever is needed. These approaches do not give the sub-contractor a blank cheque; he has to declare his proposals when tendering (obviously as maximum figures) and the extra cost when added to his tender may put him out of the running if tenders are close.

Agreement NSC/2: standard form of employer/nominated sub-contractor agreement

This document is for use only in the 'basic' method of nomination and the very similar Agreement NSC/2a (considered later in this chapter) is provided for the 'alternative' method. The purpose of both documents is to overcome the problems created for the employer by the lack of privity of contract between him and the nominated sub-contractor. The employer will be without redress against the sub-contractor and unable to proceed against the contractor who is not responsible for certain matters in the peculiar circumstances of nomination. A collateral relationship is set up, as indicated in Figure 17 on page 174.

At either end of the document there is space provided for inserting the names of the works and parties, and for signing or sealing. The date of the agreement is to be the date on which the architect signs Tender NSC/1 and the agreement does not become binding until then under the stipulations of Tender NSC/1, which also allows later withdrawal in circumstances already discussed. The remainder of the document comprises the recitals (headed 'Whereas') and the clauses of the body of the agreement.

(A) THE RECITALS

These cover several matters of fact: they record that the sub-contractor has tendered on Tender NSC/1, that the architect has been appointed, that he has approved the tender and intends to make the nomination when the contractor and the sub-contractor have agreed their particular conditions, and end with a disclaimer that nothing in the agreement or tender 'is intended' (an odd expression if ever the Courts try to interpret it) to make the architect liable to the sub-contractor. The most likely area of concern here is the possible sharing of design responsibility between the architect and the sub-contractor; but, while the disclaimer purports to avoid liability it says nothing about indemnity. Other such areas may include the situation where the architect has a duty to act under the agreement over matters of payment for which the employer assumes a special duty and the architect acts as his agent. Here possibly the architect may be in an even more vulnerable position by virtue of the extension of his role.

(B) THE CLAUSES OF THE AGREEMENT

The main aims of the several clauses are two-fold.

Firstly there is the special question of 'design, materials, performance specification' covered by clause 2 as a whole, where liability cannot be transmitted through the contractor whose contract does not envisage him doing design and related work. This question breaks down into three issues. One is an obligation on the sub-contractor under clause 2.1 to 'exercise all reasonable skill and care' in whatever such work he has to do. This again raises the question of any division of responsibility if design work is shared, so that the sub-contractor's responsibility may range from merely specifying the quality of a component material to a position almost equivalent to that of a consultant. Each case needs careful analysis to avoid possible later confusion. (The related need of care in defining what has to be done in relation to the amount of the tender has already been discussed above.) The second issue in clause 2.2 is payment for design work and materials which may be ordered under this agreement before nomination. Payment in this situation is to be made direct by the employer but credited under the sub-contract if the nomination proceeds. (See main clause 30.7, but also main clause 35.17). Because of copyright such payment does not allow the employer to use any design, as distinct from material, which becomes his property, other than for the sub-contract works. The last issue under clauses 3.1 and 3.2 is delay in design work by the sub-contractor, which, under main clause 25.4.6, 26.2.1 and 28.1.3.5, is strictly a lapse on the part of the architect so far as the contractor's contractual relationship goes. As between clauses 3.1 and 3.2 the watershed is whether the architect has made the nomination on Nomination NSC/3: the sub-contractor is liable only after such nomination for claims by the contractor against the employer for extension of time or loss and expense, and also for the employer's loss due to a termination by the contractor. This is a very onerous position. Clause 3.2 at least affords relief to the architect, as it enables the employer to proceed against the sub-contractor.

The other main aim of the clauses is to counterbalance some of the effects created in the main contract by the inclusion of nominated sub-contractors. Clause 3.3 therefore requires the sub-contractor not to provoke determination of his own sub-contract by his own default, which does not include justifiable suspension on his part. If he does the employer will have the right of action against him and, under clause 6, to recompense for the expense of renomination. Clause 3.4 similarly requires him not to delay in such a way as to lead to the contractor being granted an extension of time under main clause 25.4.7. (In this situation, as distinct from the design delay situation mentioned above, no parallel loss and expense claim by the contractor can arise.) Under clause 5 the sub-contractor undertakes in return for early final payment for his work (that is ahead of the main retention releases and final certificate) to remain liable for defects, and in particular to have an additional liability to the employer. In each of these cases, under the main contract, the employer is in danger of being put to expense and delay which is not the liability of the contractor and again over which the employer has no redress against the sub-contractor. The present agreement thus outflanks this problem by making the sub-contractor directly responsible to the employer. At the same time this arrangement does not upset the philosophy of the main contract that the contractor is not liable in these matters for his sub-contractor. Main clauses 35.20 and 35.21 underline this position.

Several relatively subsidiary aims may be dealt with together. In clause 1 the sub-contractor undertakes to press ahead with the agreement of the particular conditions of the tender. This is only an undertaking that he will 'forthwith seek to settle' and he is hardly likely to incur any liability. In clauses 4 and 7 the architect and the employer are given the duty to operate the main contract payment provisions in favour of the sub-contractor. The most important point to note is that when Agreement NSC/2 is in force, the employer is obliged to make payments to the sub-contractor if the contractor defaults in his payments, although this is not an absolute protection to the sub-contractor in the circumstances of main clause 35.13.4.3. The sub-contractor may therefore enforce direct payment by the employer if necessary, and also has a right of suspension under sub-contract clause 21.8.1 which appears even to override the limitations of main clause 35.13.4.3.

Clause 8 leans on the sub-contractor to expedite the procedures under sub-contract clause 2.3 for approval of restrictions in contracts of sale. Clauses 9 and 10 respectively provide that in the case of a conflict between the tender and this agreement, the agreement shall prevail and sets up an arbitration procedure that allows for the reference to be joined with another under the main contract or sub-contract, or both, where appropriate.

Agreement NSC/2a: standard form of employer/nominated sub-contractor agreement

This document is for use in the 'alternative' method of nomination, and is almost identical to, but on a few points less precise than Agreement NSC/2. It is not in conflict with that document and could be used in its place.

The major distinction is the lack of any reference to the fairly detailed Tender NSC/1; instead the recitals refer to a tender that would be based on whatever documentation the architect considered suitable and 'on the basis . . . (of) Agreement NSC/2a'. As a consequence, the recitals and the clauses also do not refer to Nomination NSC/3 but to 'an instruction under clause 35.11 of the Main Contract Conditions nominating the Sub-Contractor'.

There is no reference to agreeing the particular conditions of the tender, as with Tender NSC/1. In so far as there is a need to formalise any of these in this simpler approach, the conditions should still be set out for agreement in the tender. There is no reference to the agreement prevailing if there is conflict with the tender; it is likely that the courts would reverse the situation on legal principles as the tender is the specially written document so care should be taken to avoid conflicts arising out of terms inserted in the tender at any stage in its completion.

Nomination NSC/3: Standard form for nomination of a sub-contractor

This document is for use only in the 'basic' method of nomination and, at this point, all is simplicity. The architect nominates the sub-contractor, referring to his preliminary nomination under main clause 35.7.2 and for present purposes to main clause 35.10.2. There is no instruction to enter into Sub-Contract NSC/4; this follows automatically upon the reference to that document in the sub-contractor's original tender on Tender NSC/1 and the contractor's signed acceptance at its foot, subject only to the nomination now being made.

No document is prescribed for the 'alternative' method, but the need for a suitable one is recognised there, as mentioned under Agreement NSC/2a.

CHAPTER 18

The nominated sub-contracts

Two sub-contract forms are considered in this chapter, these being for use with whichever method of nomination is being employed for the individual sub-contract concerned. The patterns into which they fit and the circumstances of their use are set out in Chapter 15. The two forms are:

(a) Nominated Sub-Contract NSC/4: for use with the 'basic' method of nomination.

(b) Nominated Sub-Contract NSC/4a: for use with the 'alternative' method of nomination.

These forms are intended to give identical practical and legal effects when in use, so their format and wording is identical wherever possible, and that is on most points. (The domestic sub-contract considered in Chapter 20 is also very similar.) The differences in format and wording are simply those needed to take account of the difference between the rigidly prescribed 'basic' method tendering documents (other than technical documents) and the document employed in the less constrained 'alternative' method. These differences may be summarised as follows:

(a) Sub-Contract NSC/4 is related to and incorporates Tender NSC/1 (inclusive of any annexed documents, such as drawings and specifications) into the sub-contract, and requires it to be appended. Sub-Contract NSC/4a is related to an undefined collection of other sub-contract documents and also accommodates subject matter corresponding to that in Tender NSC/1 itself either in the enlarged articles of agreement or in an additional appendix.

(b) As a result of this the two documents differ in the cross-references given in over 20 clauses.

(c) Clauses 16 and 17 differ between the forms in detail in providing for daywork valuation.

This chapter deals only with the last of these points of difference and all other comment is phrased with direct reference to Sub-Contract NSC/4. Where suitable, comparison has been made with corresponding clauses in the main contract conditions to save repetition, these being accordingly referred to as 'main clause'. Treatment is more detailed where there are substantial differences or where extra clauses have been inserted into the sub-contract, although only significant parts of each clause have been thus considered.

The sub-contracts are drafted for use with any of the six editions of the JCT main forms and also the prime cost form, although there is no reference to this on the face of the documents. Tender NSC/1 specifies the main contract conditions in its own particulars. The term 'Architect' is defined to cover

'Architect/Supervising Officer' to suit the local authorities editions, while the 'fair wages' clause applies only with those editions. There is however no provision for determination on the grounds of corruption. The sub-contracts themselves envisage quantities, approximate quantities and no quantities as alternative bases, but not prime cost. No attempt is made to introduce nominated sub-sub-contracts, although this is not uncommon in highly specialised industries and clause 2.3 makes limited provisions about sub-sub-contracts that the sub-contractor may be 'required to enter into' by the sub-contract. Normal sub-letting at the sub-contractor's option is however covered.

The forms adopt the order of clauses in the main contract only to a limited extent. Differences occur both for historical reasons and as a result of differing clauses. The forms are none the better for it.

Articles of sub-contract agreement

These articles follow the same general form and, where suitable, the same wording as the main contract. The preambles need no comment. There are seven recitals covering the history prior to the sub-contract becoming effective, and these are noted here in their NSC/4 form, the NSC/4a variants being self-explanatory.

1 The sub-contractor has tendered on Tender NSC/1 and the documents referred to in it, in relation to a specified main contract. This stage did not involve the contractor.

2 The tender has been 'duly completed and signed'. This is the stage at which the contractor has agreed the schedules and other documents with the sub-contractor. The total result is defined as now being 'the Tender'.

3 Copies of the tender have been distributed and one is appended to the sub-contract. As there are several references to the tender in the sub-contract, so that the sub-contract is incomplete without it, this is a sound practical point.

4 The sub-contractor is aware of the main contract provisions by means of Schedule 1 of the tender. Again there are a number of references to the main contract in the sub-contract. In particular, clause 5 leans heavily on the provisions for its effect.

5 By signing the tender the contractor and the sub-contractor have agreed that the present sub-contract shall apply 'unamended'. Tender NSC/1 does not make this effect of the signatures explicit, although schedule 1 does refer to 'Sub-Contract NSC/4 . . . unamended'. It may thus be wondered whether the signatures are sufficient to bind the parties to make no amendments when, later, Sub-Contract NSC/4 is itself signed and imposes this meaning on the first set of signatures. As the sub-contract (including recitals) is readily available as published, this seems to give rise to unnecessary and perhaps misleading circularity. If any amendment to the sub-contract is intended simply to clarify it or remove its conflicts, in order to be safe both the tender

and the sub-contract should at this point be amended.

Beyond this, while it is not stretching legal ingenuity to amend these two 'unamended' references and thus introduce valid amendments into Sub-Contract NSC/4, such action is fraught with danger. Agreement NSC/2 leans on Sub-Contract NSC/4 and the main contract leans on both, for completeness in particular circumstances. (The provisions over delay of and direct payments to sub-contractors are cases in point.) While it is common for contractors and sub-contractors to agree special clauses, the present arrangement could put them in severe difficulty, all the more so if both employer and architect are unaware of this position, and of the modification possibly introduced into the main contract. Oddly, neither main clause 35 nor Nomination NSC/3 expressly require Sub-Contract NSC/4 to be entered into at all, as main clause 35.12 requires with Sub-Contract NSC/4a.

6 Nomination has taken place.

7 The status of the sub-contractor, the contractor and the employer for the purposes of clauses 20A or 20B over tax matters is established.

After these recitals there are three articles, dealing variously with the sub-contractor's obligation, with the sub-contract sum or the ascertained final sub-contract sum, defined in clause 15, and with the arbitration provisions. Only this last recital needs any comment.

It is modelled on the main contract article, but the scope of arbitration is limited to matters arising out of the sub-contract, although the detail is not prescribed. It thus excludes the 'construction' of the sub-contract itself from arbitration, unless the parties agree otherwise. In view of the sub-contractual relationship and the similar wording of the documents, it is as well to leave it so and to rely on arbitration on the main contract construction if it becomes a live issue. The joint arbitration provision of article 3 may be invoked unless this optional provision has been deleted from the sub-contract by the corresponding deletion in the tender referred to in the article.

Unless the parties so agree, arbitration may not start until after practical completion or abandonment of the main contract works except over a few issues, so there could be considerable delay, of particular consequence to the sub-contractor. The matters for early arbitration include questions of payment: the withholding or irregularity of payment, whether there is practical completion of the sub-contract works (which affects solely payment of retention) and dispute over a set-off by the contractor. Others are disputes over instructions and extension of time. To neglect any of these issues would probably compound the matters in dispute.

There is the same footnote as in the main contract about amendment if the 'proper law' is not to be that of England. The proper law for the sub-contract should be the same for that of the main contract to avoid legal confusion, so any amendment should be as in the main contract. The case of *James Miller and Partners Ltd* v. *Whitworth Estates (Manchester) Ltd* is indicative of the type of problem to avoid.

Clause 1 — Interpretation, definitions etc

This clause fulfils the same purpose with the same format and general content as in the main contract. 'Variation' (as main clause 13.1) is here defined in alternative ways to allow for a 'Sub-Contract Sum', that is a lump sum in advance, or a 'Tender Sum' that is a sum to be recalculated by remeasurement. The main contract, the contract conditions and the main contract works are each distinguished.

Clause 2 — Sub-contract documents

The sub-contract documents are defined in clause 2.1 as the tender with referenced attachments on the one hand (as discussed in Chapter 17) and the present sub-contract on the other. If there is any conflict between them clause 2.2 establishes the sub-contract as prevailing generally over the rest. But it also establishes in particular that those terms of the main contract given in schedule 1 of the tender are to prevail over any other version elsewhere in the contract documents. This would include the present conditions, should the documents conflict to such an unlikely extent. What is lacking here is an equivalent to main clause 2.3 to deal with the resolution of conflict within or between the sub-contract documents other than this sub-contract. It would seem to be the intention that clause 5.1.1 should bring in main clause 2.3, but this provision is perhaps too weak to be effective.

The sub-contractor is protected by the present clause 2.3 over any restrictions in sub-sub-contracts of sale when he is obliged to enter into them. This corresponds with the protection given the contractor under main clause 36.5 over a contract of sale where there is a nomination, but not otherwise. Main clause 35.22 extends protection to the contractor in relation to the present case. Clause 2 does not operate as part of a nomination procedure and the sub-contract does not elaborate elsewhere on what restrictions may be acceptable here.

Clause 3 — Sub-contract sum — additions or deductions — computation of ascertained final sub-contract sum

This clause is equivalent to main clause 3, covering the inclusion of adjustments to or progressive calculation of the sub-contract sum.

Clause 4 — Execution of the sub-contract works — instructions of architect — directions of contractor

This clause in its heading indicates in outline the main functions of the three participants. The sub-contractor is to execute his works as sub-contractor, while observing the architect's instructions over his product that come to him through the contractor, and also complying with the contractor's directions aimed at securing harmonious interaction, particularly on the site. The clause corresponds in order to main clauses 2.1, 10 and restructured main clause 4.

The clause is a classic example of the system established of the architect not dealing with the sub-contractor once he is nominated, but only through the contractor who passes on any main contract instruction 'affecting the Sub-Contract Works' under clause 4.2. Failure to follow this pattern is one of the easiest and most common ways of producing confusion on the site. (No mention is made of the clerk of works, as he is even further down the chain of communication.) The sub-contractor is then to comply under clause 4.3, subject only to the instruction being in writing under clause 4.4 and to his right to challenge the architect's authority under clause 4.6. There is however no direct authority within the sub-contract for the architect's instructions to have effect there. Instead, under clause 4.6 as the equivalent of main clause 4.2, the reference is to 'the provision of the Main Contract which empowers the issue of the said instruction'. While under clause 5.1.1 the sub-contractor is to 'comply with all the provisions of the Main Contract', this does not give the architect direct standing here and in any case is imprecise in reference, as is discussed under clause 5. There appears to be something of a contractual lacuna here.

It is not immediately clear, for instance, that the architect may validly instruct in what is an 'entire' (sub-) contract, as there is no equivalent to main clause 13.2, 'The Architect may issue instructions requiring a Variation'. That the sub-contractor is to comply with any variation validly required is another issue. Furthermore, there is no direct power to bring about postponement of the sub-contract works.

Clause 4.4 deals with written confirmation of architect's instructions or contractor's directions in similar terms to main clause 4.3.2, including the same seven-day period to confirm and to dissent. This is tidy so far as the contractor's directions go, but in the case of architect's instructions there will be a time-lag before the contractor's own confirmation reaches the architect. The architect may then dissent at the last minute from the contractor's interpretation, by which time the sub-contractor will have a valid and binding instruction between him and the contractor. Even if the architect issues a countermanding instruction, there could be difficulties if the sub-contractor has acted quickly after waiting a total of 14 days.

Clause 4.5 takes the case of the sub-contractor failing to comply (in this case when he 'does not begin to comply') with the contractor's directions. It parallels main clause 4.1.2 by allowing the contractor to employ others after giving notice and obtaining the architect's permission. The reference is solely to 'a direction of the Contractor' which would not usually require the concurrence of the architect. The omission here of 'an instruction of the Architect' passed on to the sub-contractor by the contractor robs the clause of much of its point, and could lead to difficulty in applying the main contract provision of employing others to perform sub-contract work.

Clause 4.6 has already been mentioned. It contains one of the joint arbitration provisions discussed under article 5.5.

Clause 5 — Sub-contractor's liability under incorporated provisions of the main contract

Clause 5.1.1 has been mentioned under clause 4. It requires the sub-contractor to 'observe, perform and comply with' two sets of provisions. The first set is comprehensive: 'all the provisions of the Main Contract as described by or referred to in the Tender, Schedule 1 . . . so far as they relate and apply to the Sub-Contract Works'. These provisions are not limited to the main contract conditions and the reference is not only to *all* the main contract conditions via item 5 in the tender schedule, but also to all that is stated in items 1–14. Supporting this is the phrase on page 1 of the tender 'Sub-Contract NSC/4 which incorporates the particulars of the Main Contract set out in Schedule 1', which again is an omnibus term.

The second set is specific and incorporates the following of the main contract conditions (several titles are abbreviated) which are mentioned 'without prejudice to the generality of the foregoing':

Main clause 6   Statutory matters
Main clause 7   Levels etc
Main clause 9   Royalties etc
Main clause 16   Materials and goods
Main clause 32   Hostilities
Main clause 33   War damage
Main clause 34   Antiquities

This device saves the repetition of clauses which would need amending only in ways which may clearly be inferred, whereas other clauses are paralleled in the present conditions but changed in ways that may not be so inferred. One such example is in the detailing of the relevant events under clause 11.2.5. This is broad and effects a great economy of words. In many practical situations this approach may be acceptable, but in cases of legal conflict it could be anything but precise. Any wording in the main contract which is unusual in itself or which may produce unusual results by virtue of the nature of the works, main or sub-contract, should be reviewed carefully. But even in the absence of unusual wording, the problem of exactly how far the main contract conditions should 'relate and apply' arises. There could for instance be uncertainty over a point such as the architect's power to resolve discrepancies mentioned under clause 2 or to instruct, mentioned under clause 4. The cases of *Brightside Kilpatrick Engineering Services* v. *Mitchell Construction (1973) Ltd* and *Dunlop and Ranken Ltd* v. *Hendall Steel Structures* are illustrative in this area.

Clauses 5.1.2 and 5.2 (the marginal heading for the latter is mispositioned) deal firstly with the indemnity provided to the contractor by the sub-contractor in respect of the sub-contractor's breach or default and secondly with the relief of the sub-contractor from liability for default by the employer or the contractor, or those for whom they are responsible.

Clause 6 — Injury to persons and property — indemnity to contractor

Clause 7—Insurance—sub-contractor

Clause 8 — Loss or damage by the 'Clause 22 Perils' to sub-contract works and materials and goods properly on site

Clause 9 — Policies of insurance

These clauses are modelled closely in many places on the corresponding main contract clauses, subject to the omission of the elements not required and additions discussed here. The broad effect is that the sub-contractor indemnifies the contractor (while the contractor in turn indemnifies the employer under the main contract) and then insures against his liabilities, there being a limit in the case of property as detailed in the tender. There is no obligation under clause 7.1 for the sub-contractor to ensure that *his* sub-contractors also insure, a departure from the main contract pattern. The provisions appear to be adequate against the contingencies that led to the case of *City of Manchester* v. *Fram Gerrard Ltd.*

The other important differences occur in clause 8. When main clause 22A applies over the 'Clause 22 Perils' then the contractor insures for loss and damage both to his own and to the sub-contractor's work, materials and goods and so the sub-contractor does not insure against any of the risks. When either the main clause 22B or 22C applies the sub-contractor does nothing, as the employer carries the insurance or the uninsured risk, according to which edition of the main contract clauses is in use. Clauses 8.1.1.2 and 8.1.2.2 provide that within the sub-contract neither the contractor nor sub-contractor is responsible for the relevant loss or damage or for any insurance against them.

Clause 8.2 carries through the question of reinstatement and payment, so that the contractor receives proper recompense. But it introduces unnecessary possible complications in so doing by changing the bases of settlement by comparison with those in the main contract. Thus when main clause 22A applies and the contractor insures, the sub-contractor's extra payment is 'to be calculated as if . . . in accordance with instructions of the Architect . . . (over) a provisional sum', whereas the contractor is being reimbursed at the same time on the basis of a direct settlement with the insurer. This will include the sub-contractor's amounts and will not necessarily be at contract and sub-contract terms, and will not involve the quantity surveyor in his contract role, so that the contractor may gain or lose. If main clause 22B applies and the employer has insured new works, all is simple; both contractor and sub-contractor are paid as though the reinstatement 'were a variation required by an instruction of the Architect' and the quantity surveyor will be involved in settling with both of them. This gives the sub-contractor a similar mechanism for payment to that in the main clause 22A case, although there the basis is a provisional sum rather than a variation. If main clause 22C applies and the employer insures the alterations and extensions the sub-contractor is to 'receive such share of the monies paid to the Contractor in accordance with clause 22C.2.3 of the Main Contract Conditions as may be properly attributable'. This sounds like a share of the negotiated insurance settlement, whereas the clause in fact is based on valuation of a variation, as is main clause 22B. With imagination this provision can be used to obtain a fair settlement, but it looks like an example of incorrect drafting.

Clause 8.3 takes all causes of loss or damage to the sub-contract works, materials or goods by such risks as theft, vandalism and general damage during construction as are excluded from the 'Clause 22 Perils'. The clause divides progress into three stages: before incorporation of materials or goods, between incorporation and practical completion, and after practical completion by the sub-contractor. At the first stage the sub-contractor assumes responsibility for unfixed materials or goods in all cases other than loss or damage caused by the contractor or the employer or those for whom they are responsible. At other stages the sub-contractor is responsible only if he, or those for whom he is responsible, cause the injury. As with the comparable shift between liability over persons and property in clause 6 and main clause 20, liability for injury not caused by either of the parties as such passes from one to the other. At no stage is any obligation laid on the sub-contractor to insure, prudent though this may be.

In the first two stages, liability relates to materials and goods including, in the second stage, those incorporated, while in the last stage it relates to the sub-contract works. This appears to leave liability for labour and the like in the second stage open, but it would more validly lie with the relevant party under clause 6.2.

There are two postscripts. The sub-contractor is to observe under clause 8.4 all relevant conditions in the 'Clause 22 Perils' policy, rather more than the contractor himself is asked to do under the main contract. He might otherwise in any case find himself being proceeded against by the insurer. Clause 8.5 affirms that the sub-contractor's responsibility for defects remains, as would be expected, but presumably this relates especially to the unsatisfactory clause 14.4.

None of these clauses directly requires the contractor to take out insurances against his liabilities to the sub-contractor, except where he is liable for the 'Clause 22 Perils'. Some of his insurance obligations under the main contract will incidentally make him do so, while usually his all-risks policy will provide sufficient cover. Any hints of cross indemnity are thus avoided. Clause 9 allows for production of evidence of insurance by either party and for insurance by the contractor in the event of default, just as in the main contract.

Clause 10 — Sub-Contractor's responsibility for his own plant, etc

The principle of this clause is to leave its subject matter, which includes materials 'not properly on site for incorporation', at the sole risk of the sub-contractor except for the negligence of the contractor and those for whom he is responsible. Whether the sub-contractor insures is expressly left to his discretion and the clause thus aligns itself with the main contract, where only the works and unfixed materials and goods are to be insured.

Clause 11 — Sub-contractor's obligation — carrying out and completion of sub-contract works — extension of sub-contract time

Clause 12 — Failure of sub-contractor to complete on time

These also follow closely the wording of main contract clauses 23, 25 and 24, in that order. Clause 11.1 deals with the programme which has been set out in the tender and may well be in parts. The obligation is not to 'regularly and diligently proceed' but is to proceed 'reasonably in accordance with the programme of the Main Contract Works', following notice to commence.

The wording of clause 11.2 on extension of time needs comment only on a few of the points of difference from the main contract. As the sub-contractor only appears on the scene part way through the contract period, the reference in clause 11.2.1.1 is to delay in 'commencement, progress or completion' and not simply to progress. The sub-contractor is to give notice to the contractor so that it may be forwarded to the architect, and he is to 'identify in such notice any matter . . . within clause 11.2.2.1'. Such matters include the relevant events, which are worded to cover delay to the contractor or to the sub-contractor, and which in scope are as the main contract, except that they exclude delay on the part of *this* sub-contractor, but include his 'valid exercise' of the right of suspension under clause 21.8.1 for non-payment. The use of the same term 'Relevant Events' as in the main contract (where they lead to extension of time and therefore exonerate from liability for liquidated damages) would seem to infer that relevant events are matters leading to extension of time not only for the sub-contractor, but also where appropriate for the contractor under main clause 25.4.7 since here also they are not his fault. This may be contrasted with the other group 'act, omission or default of the Contractor' and his sub-contractors and others, where the contractor has to concede an extension while not himself receiving one. This distinction between the two groups is in general fair but it may cause problems over the question of suspension and the discussion on clause 21.8.1 and main clause 25.4.7 is relevant. The architect is to take account of all these matters, which may be closely linked, when consenting to a revised period or periods being fixed by the contractor. Under main clause 35.14.1 the contractor may not grant any extension to a nominated sub-contractor in accordance with the present clause without the architect's consent.

Final fixing of the period or periods is to be not later than twelve weeks from the date of practical completion of the sub-contract works or of the main contract 'whichever occurs first'. How the sub-contract date can ever be the later is a mystery. Fixing an earlier final date may produce more complications over any refund of payment as discussed under clause 12, but this is inevitable and the outcome is fairer.

It is the contractor who immediately and strictly grants any extension. Because the architect has to consent to it he effectively becomes adjudicator between the employer and the sub-contractor if there is a relevant event. Here the contractor is an interested third party, as his own extension position is likely to be affected by the knock-on effect. The architect similarly becomes adjudicator if there is default by the contractor. This places a heavy and difficult responsibility on the architect, especially if there are several nominated sub-contractors involved in the same or related relevant events or defaults. It also bring the architect into matters of detailed programme and site organisation that do not otherwise come within his ambit. If the sub-contractor is granted an extension on either count he is then exonerated from liability to the employer under Agreement NSC/2, by clause 3.1 of that agreement. If the extension is due to the contractor's default, then the contractor will have to absorb it or face liquidated damages for delay.

In the case of failure to agree, clause 11.3 contains a joint arbitration provision.

Clause 12.1 deals by implication with delay due to the sub-contractor's default and simply provides for such delay to be notified to the architect when the sub-contract works overrun the original or duly extended period or periods, with a copy furnished to the sub-contractor. This sets in train any action between the employer and the architect: if the contractor 'has taken all practicable steps to avoid or reduce' the delay then he will receive an extension, while the employer can seek redress against the sub-contractor under clause 3.4 of Agreement NSC/2 for then having to concede it. If the contractor has not taken such steps or has been in collusion with the sub-contractor, then the architect takes no action over any extension, but certifies the sub-contractor's failure back to the contractor under clause 12.2. The contractor and the sub-contractor then settle on a sum based on what has occurred and not on a liquidated damages provision. Since the contractor's loss may vary greatly according to the timing and extent of the sub-contractor's delay in relation to the on-going works, this is by far the fairest arrangement.

Clause 13 — Matters affecting regular progress — direct loss and/or expense — contractor's and sub-contractor's rights

Clause 13.1 follows the form of main clauses 26.1 and 26.2, while it gives the contractor the right to 'require the Architect to operate clause 26.4 of the Main Contract Conditions' to ascertain any loss and expense for the sub-contractor. It does not include anything corresponding to main clause 26.3 about stating extension of time granted to either the contractor or the sub-contractor. Among the matters leading to loss and expense, clause 13.1.2.3 limits itself to 'any discrepancy in or divergence between the Contract

Documents and/or Contract Bills'. It therefore excludes the sub-contract drawings or bills of quantities, whether they conflict within themselves, with each other or with the main contract documents. This is a difficult area as some of the contract documents may well have been prepared by the sub-contractor himself. Clause 2.1 of Agreement NSC/2 meets the general difficulty, but a lot will depend on what the sub-contractor knew when he produced the design or specification and how carefully the architect checked to eliminate discrepancies. While it is unfair to the sub-contractor not to mention the documents, the unqualified expansion of the clause would be equally unfair to the employer. Each situation needs care, but many cases will warrant an amendment to the clause to introduce some reference to sub-contract documents.

Clauses 13.2 and 13.3 respectively deal with the situation where there is 'act, omission or default' of the contractor which affects the sub-contract works and of the sub-contractor affecting the main contract works. In each case the parties are to settle between themselves, without the architect or the employer being concerned. In the former case the sub-contractor may claim from the contractor for loss and expense due also to other sub-contractors while in the latter case the contractor may claim from the sub-contractor on behalf of other sub-contractors. Obviously all the various sub-contractors may appear in a number of roles, according to which sub-contract is under examination.

The same reservation of rights as in the main contract appears in clause 13.4.

Clause 14 — Practical completion of sub-contract works — liability for defects

While the architect under main clauses 17.1 and 35.16 appears to notice practical completion of both the main contract works and the sub-contract works for himself, this clause gives the sub-contractor the opportunity under clause 14.1 to warn the architect through the contractor when 'the Sub-Contract Works will have reached practical completion', presumably suitably in advance. The operative date under clause 14.2 is still of the architect's own fixing and, by supplying evidence of the length of delay, is related to the question of failure to complete on time under clause 12.

Under clauses 14.3 and 14.4 the sub-contractor's liability to remedy defects is worded to keep him in step with the contractor as 'a similar liability to any liability of the Contractor'. This avoids the need to spell out the defects liability period or schedule of defects particulars, but it is made subject to main clause 18 over partial possession, the operation of which cannot be foreseen but must be accepted by the sub-contractor. On the other hand he will have had notice of the Sectional Completion Supplement when tendering and will have realised how it affects his own liabilities. Moreover, the sub-contractor is to be excused the cost of his making good when the architect instructs under the main contract, thus repeating the offending riders from main clauses 17.2 and 17.3 (see discussion under those headings.) At practical completion of the sub-contract, liability for frost damage passes to the contractor.

An additional issue between contractor and sub-contractor is the sub-contractor's responsibility to tidy up when he has finished and this is given in clause 14.5, while in the main contract conditions it is inferred. The specific matter of rubbish is dealt with in clause 27.1.

Clause 15 — Price for sub-contract works

Two versions are referred to here. There may be a 'Sub-Contract Sum' which will be based either on drawings and specification or on firm quantities. There may likewise be 'Tender Sum subject to complete remeasurement', apparently being based on approximate quantities rather than an unquantified schedule of rates. This does not precisely fit the wording here and does not give a 'Tender Sum' at all, although it is sometimes a useful approach in practice and is mentioned in clause 17.3. Clause 18.1.1.3 tucked away at the end of a clause dealing with other matters is the equivalent of main clause 14 and defines the two sums as based on the bills of quantities, firm or approximate.

The possibility of a sub-contract based on prime cost is not expressed in this clause, rather it is discounted. However clause 17.3 perhaps allows this alternative. If it is required, the sub-contract documents should be so drawn up as to contain the controls against over-expenditure that are discussed in Chapter 23.

Whatever the basis, either clause 16 or clause 17 contains the associated valuation rules, while the present clause aligns itself with Tender NSC/1 by referring to the two sums as 'VAT exclusive'. Value added tax is dealt with as an additional matter under clause 19A or clause 19B.

Clause 16 — Valuation of variations and provisional sum work

This clause deals with the adjustment of the firm sub-contract sum of clause 15.1. As discussed under clause 4, the present clause deals only with valuation and lacks the equivalent provisions to those in main clause 13.2, 'The Architect may issue instructions requiring a Variation' and in main clause 13.3, 'The Architect shall issue instructions in regard to the expenditure of provisional sums' and is apparently defective as a result. The clause operates by valuing the variations and the expenditure of provisional sums on the same basis as far as suitable as in main clauses 13.4 to 13.7. Its mainstream provision is therefore for measured additions and omissions supplemented by daywork. To this end clause 16.3.3.1 refers to bills of quantities which are then further described in clause 18. Clause 16.3.4 dealing with daywork is the only clause in the two sub-contracts differing substantially in wording. In

Sub-Contract NSC/4 it simply refers to the daywork definitions and percentages given in the tender, in which the percentages are stated to include an allowance for cash discount. In Sub-Contract NSC/4a the clause assumes that no such provision has been made elsewhere in the sub-contract documents and therefore stipulates the same definitions as in the main contract with the percentages given in the appendix, adding in the clause that the percentages 'take into account' the cash discount. It would perhaps have been better to put the appendix entries in the same form as in the tender, thus allowing for more flexibility in daywork definitions and emphasising the cash discount requirements at the point at which the percentages are set down.

Two slightly different approaches are covered in clause 16.2, although their purpose must be assumed. Firstly, possibly where the sub-contract sum is based on drawings and specification without quantities, there may be 'a schedule of rates or prices for measured work' to be used in lieu of 'any rates or prices . . . which would otherwise be applicable', a meaningless expression when none are defined and therefore none may be excluded. Secondly, whether there are bills of quantities or drawings and specification, it seems, there may be a special 'schedule of daywork prices' presumably for specialist work to be used in lieu of any of the standard definitions given in the clause.

The clause resolutely does not acknowledge that there may be a drawing and specification sub-contract without such apparatus for valuing variations. This it is to be hoped will be an infrequent occasion especially for the many sub-contracts large enough to warrant the 'basic' method of nomination and therefore using Agreement NSC/2. There are however sub-contracts involving work such as plant and equipment for which 'measured work' or even a numbered list of items is meaningless. In such cases, the present clause should be deleted and a clause substituted setting out a principle of lump sum valuation of variations on a fair and reasonable basis.

Clause 17 — Valuation of all work comprising the sub-contract works

This clause deals with the complete valuation of 'all work executed' when the tender sum of clause 15.2 is the sub-contract basis. Its wording follows that of clause 16 very closely and its mainstream provision assumes bills of approximate quantities as the basis for remeasurement without explicitly stating this fact, this time also assuming as does clause 15.2 that the tender sum is based on a quantified basis. The calculation of the anticipated final sub-contract sum follows from all this quite tidily.

Clause 17.3 assumes the same categories of schedules for measured daywork as clause 16.2 (the non-correspondence of numbers is due to different positioning of the 'Sub-Contractor's right to attend measurement' provision for unknown reasons). While this is intelligible enough for daywork, it is still difficult to follow for measured work. If 'schedules of rates or prices' means an unquantified schedule rather than a bill of approximate quantities, it will not be possible to apply the criterion in clause 17.4.1 'does not significantly change the quantity' unless drawings and the like have been sufficiently indicative at the tender stage.

Clause 18 — Bills of quantities — Standard Method of Measurement

This clause deals with contents and corrections of bills of quantities in the same way as main clause 2.2. It applies to bills of quantities as sub-contract documents whether they are firm in relation to clause 15.1 or approximate in relation to clause 15.2. The clause has no bearing on bills or quantities prepared by the sub-contractor when building up his tender for, say, a drawings and specification sub-contract. These will not form part of the sub-contract documentation, unless they are amended to form a schedule of rates only. The clause still has no bearing on such a schedule or on any other schedule of rates. When a schedule has been produced as 'builder's quantities' this is reasonable, but a schedule emanating from the quantity surveyor should have a defined basis and the Standard Method of Measurement is often the best starting point. An appropriate reference to this clause in the schedule may close the gap.

The clause also establishes that the sub-contract sum or sub-contract tender sum is based on the qualities and the quantities in the bills of quantities, rather than this being mentioned in clause 15 and so repeating the main contract pattern.

Clause 19A — Value Added Tax

This clause operates along broadly the same lines as main clause 15, with the major difference that it contains all the provisions as part of the sub-contract and does not refer to a supplemental agreement. The clause itself therefore provides for the sub-contract sum, tender sum or ascertained final sub-contract sum as the case may be to be exclusive of tax and for it to be paid as an extra under the sub-contract, for interim payments and finally. No tax is payable on cash discount, whether or not the contractor has to pay it to the sub-contractor.

The sub-contractor is to provide the provisional assessment at least seven days before payment is due from the contractor. The contractor is then responsible for calculating and making interim payments of tax, as these will not be included in the sums certified by the architect in the main certificate. Clause 21.3 makes no reference to the tax, although there is a reference to that clause here to fix the time scale for payment. The contractor in his turn will recover any tax that he pays here from the Commissioners as input tax. There are provisions about tax receipts, corrections of amount and late issue of receipts.

Clause 19B — Value Added Tax — special arrangement — VAT (General) Regulations 1972, Regulations 8(3) and 21

This clause is the alternative to Clause 19A and, in accordance with the footnote, 'can *only* be used when the Contractor . . . has been allowed to prepare the tax documents in substitution for an authenticated receipt issued by the Sub-Contractor'. Clause 19B.4.3 is the central difference and the rest of the clause essentially parallels clause 19A.

Clause 20A — Finance (No 2) Act 1975 — Tax Deduction Scheme

Clause 20B — Finance (No 2) Act 1975 — Tax Deduction Scheme — sub-contractor not user of current tax certificate

These two clauses relate to main clause 31 and complement the procedures there. They are alternatives and cover, as their titles indicate, the respective cases in which the sub-contractor has and has not a current tax certificate.

Clause 21 — Payment of Sub-Contractor

This clause covers interim and final payments as clause 21.1 indicates and relates itself to main clause 30 by its references. It also parallels that clause closely in a large part of its wording over the rights and duties of the contractor and sub-contractor, as equating to those of the employer and the contractor in that clause. The obligations of the contractor to the employer over payments to nominated sub-contractors are given in main clause 35.13. Clause 21 also contains extra provisions entirely between the contractor and the sub-contractor.

Clause 21.2 deals with three preparatory matters. The sub-contractor may put forward his own figures for inclusion in interim certificates under the main contract, which is reasonable as his work may be specialised and he is one step removed from the architect. (The reference to clause 30.2.3.3 should be to clause 30.2.3.2). The contractor must then pass on 'any written representations' from the sub-contractor to the architect. Lastly the sub-contractor is obliged to observe main clause 30.3 in so far as it affects payment to him for off-site materials and goods.

The main obligation to make payment is in clause 21.3.1.1. This refers to interim certificates under the main contract but in such a way as to cover both interim and final payments to the sub-contractor, the latter by the references to main clauses 35.17 and 30.7. Payments relate to 'the amount' further 'included in the amount stated as due'. This is in all cases inclusive of cash discount, but for interim amounts is net of retention and previous amounts in accordance with clause 21.4. The main contract makes no mention of cash discount since this does not affect the employer's payments, but it is here provided that the contractor may deduct for prompt payment. If he deducts after paying late, he does not 'duly discharge his obligation' as in any other case of inadequate payment. In return for being paid, both adequately and on time, the sub-contractor is to provide the 'reasonable proof' for the contractor to produce to the architect and this should identify deductions made by way of set-off under clause 23 or for other contractually justifiable reasons. In the absence of this proof the employer is obliged to pay direct to the sub-contractor the amount by which the contractor is in default including cash discount improperly deducted or risk the sub-contractor suspending work under clause 21.8.1, at least when Agreement NSC/2 is in force. This is also the case under the procedure of main clause 35.13, which has the fault in wording discussed under main clause 35.13.2. If the employer does not honour an interim certificate by paying the contractor within 14 days, there is no provision in either main contract or sub-contract entitling the contractor not to pay the sub-contractor within the further three days stipulated. Rather, the obligation under main clause 35.13.2 is for amounts to be 'duly discharged' under the present sub-contract, which echoes the obligation in clause 21.3.1.1.

As a rider, clause 21.3.1.2 allows the contractor to deduct from payments to the sub-contractor any relevant amounts which the employer has deducted from him. These will not have been deducted in the architect's certificate calculations. They are quite distinct from any deductions which the contractor may be entitled to make over matters entirely between him and the sub-contractor, which are dealt with by clause 23.

When the sub-contractor is finally paid under an interim certificate of the main contract, clause 21.3.2 provides for him to indemnify the contractor against defects and the like, while liable to the employer for them under Agreement NSC/2. This triangular arrangement is only effective if clause 5 of that Agreement is 'unamended in any way' and the agreement is 'in full force and effect'. While the present conditions are intended to be used strictly and solely on this basis, this clause allows the contractor not 'duly to discharge any amount certified' if there is any gap in operation. This is at first sight an extraordinary provision. It is not intended to allow the contractor to pocket any amount due to the sub-contractor, but presumably to permit him to go on holding retention for a while longer if the architect has operated main clause 35.17 when he should not have done. That clause clearly provides that it is based on the same 'clause 5 of Agreement NSC/2 . . . (remaining) in force unamended'. Otherwise it is a dead letter. So that at second sight the provision looks like a patched-up job. Whether it can be operated in this extraordinary manner especially given the wording of main clause 35.13.2 remains to be seen, perhaps in the courts.

The calculation of amounts due in interim certificates under clause 21.4 follows the main contract pattern, with provision that amounts due to be added under clause 3 shall have 'one thirty-ninth' added to allow for cash discount deduction. These include particular loss and expense amounts and fluctuations adjustments under the traditional method. The rules about retention are delineated even more precisely as being those in the main clauses 30.4 and 30.5. They are followed in clause 21.7 by the joint arbitration provision.

A distinctive feature of the sub-contract is the right given to the sub-contractor in clause 21.8.1 to suspend work when the contractor has already defaulted over payment to him and the employer does not pay him direct under main clause 35.13.5. Both stages present problems. A right for the contractor to 'set off against any money' including retention exists under clause 23.1, subject to several safeguards, if the sub-contractor is in default. This is related in clause 21.8.1.1 to 'any payments to the Sub-Contractor as hereinbefore provided' so that the contractor may deduct amounts as mentioned under clause 21.3.1.2 without risk. It is not clear about other rights and obligations to make deductions, such as under the tax deduction scheme of clause 20A or clause 20B, and exercise of these could lead to a suspension on a strict interpretation. On the other hand, a deduction of cash discount after the prescribed 17 days would be a failure to discharge on the part of the contractor. The employer's default may be in not operating main clause 35.13.5 at all when he should, and here the position is straightforward. But it may also lie in a failure to pay the sub-contractor 'the whole amount' of the contractor's lapse by only paying some portion. This becomes a clear lapse on the employer's part when there are adequate funds available, but when there are not, in the circumstances given in main clauses 35.13.5.3 or 35.13.5.4.3 the employer is only obliged under the main contract to pay what is available, if necessary apportioned between the various sub-contractors concerned. As the present clause talks of not paying 'for any reason' it is in open conflict with the main contract, and might produce consequences that could damage the employer severely if the sub-contractor operates the right to suspend which is clearly given here. The sub-contractor is also protected from the employer seeking direct redress by the provision under clause 5 of the Agreement NSC/2 that suspension is not a default.

In any case when both conditions are fulfilled, the sub-contractor may suspend work after 14 days written notice to both the contractor and the employer (since both are in default and both will be affected by the suspension), running from 35 days after issue of the interim certificate originally containing the amount. The outline timetable of latest dates resulting from a comparison of this provision with others in the sub-contract and in the main contract is:

Action	Earliest/latest days
Interim certificate 'X', including amount 'A' for the sub-contractor, issued under main clause 30.1.1.1	0
Contractor paid on interim certificate 'X' by employer under main clause 30.1.1.1	14
Contractor defaults in paying sub-contractor under sub-contract clause 21.3.1.1	17
Contractor fails to provide 'reasonable proof' to architect under main clause 35.13.3	18/30

Interim certificate 'X + 1', possibly including amount 'B' for the sub-contractor, issued under main clause 30.1.1.1, depending on length of month	28/31
Sub-contractor gives notice of suspension under sub-contract clause 21.8.1	35
Contractor paid on interim certificate 'X + 1' by employer under main clause 30.1.1.1 and employer does/does not deduct amount 'A' for the sub-contractor under main clause 35.13.5 (he must not deduct amount 'B' and he does not yet become liable to pay it)	42/45
Employer defaults in paying sub-contractor amount 'A', whether or not he has deducted it when paying the contractor, under sub-contract clause 21.8.1.2	42/45
Sub-contractor suspends work under sub-contract clause 21.8.1	49

The pressure point here is the sub-contractor's notice on day 35 and this is 7/10 days before the employer need have paid him. The issuing of notice at this point therefore suggests either a sub-contractor who is trigger-happy or one who has learned what to expect from the experience of past months.

The suspension ends when either the employer or the contractor pays and it must never start if either of them pays within the fourteen days that the notice runs. The sub-contractor's right of suspension replaces the right of determination available to the contractor under the main contract, but does not replace 'any other right or remedy', such as legal action, open to the sub-contractor. It is no defence for the contractor to say that he has not been paid, since he is obliged to pay whether he himself has been paid or not, as mentioned under clause 21.3.1.1. When the next interim certificate comes along the sub-contractor is therefore entitled to invoke the present clause, although his action would probably be pre-empted by the contractor giving notice of determination under main clause 28.1.

Assuming that suspension occurs, clause 21.8.2 deals with responsibility for delay, by stating that the sub-contractor *is not* liable (while clause 11.2.5.13 gives suspension as a relevant event leading to the extension of time) and that the contractor *is* liable to the sub-contractor for 'loss, damage or expense'. The corollaries that the contractor *is* liable to the sub-contractor over delay, while the sub-contractor *is not* liable for any contractor's loss, are valid. This leaves the liability of the employer to be considered, remembering that he has himself defaulted but subsequent to the contractor's default. In relation to the sub-contractor, Agreement NSC/2 requires the architect to 'operate the provisions of clause 35.13.1 . . . (and) in clauses 35.17 to 35.19 of the Main Contract Conditions' which cover the basic systems of interim and final payment. The Agreements then further require the employer to 'operate the provisions in regard to the payment of the Sub-Contractor in clause 35.13 of the Main Contract Conditions'. These clauses create a clearly enforceable liability towards the sub-contractor. The employer's liability to the contractor is much less clear, as discussed under main clause 35.13.5.

The contractor's fiduciary interest in the sub-contractor's retention is dealt with in clause 21.9, while main clause 35.5.2 distinguishes the nominated sub-contract retention from the contractor's retention. If the contractor wishes to use the sub-contractor's retention as a security, say for a loan, under clause 21.9.1 he must establish a separate bank account himself to hold the equivalent of the sub-contractor's retention. This account is then whittled down as the retention is released. When the sub-contractor's retention has once been released to the contractor by the employer, whether or not the previous arrangement applied, the contractor may have some good reasons for holding on to some of the sub-contractor's retention, say in relation to a set-off under clause 23 which is being disputed under clause 24. If so, under clause 21.9.2 he must similarly keep this retention in a trust account until it is paid over or he properly has recourse to it. In the normal course of events the sub-contractor's retention passes through the contractor's bank in a matter of a few days, and no special accounting is called for. It is only in this period that the retention may be considered at risk.

Two versions of the final payments provision are given: clause 21.10, where clause 15.1 for an adjustable sub-contract sum applies; clause 21.11, where clause 15.2 for a completely summated ascertained final sub-contract sum takes the place of the original tender sum. Each follows the general philosophy of main clause 30.6 in terms of the detailed components of the final sum, but only the first version allows for deductions in the nature of the case, although fluctuations could conceivably give a net credit with the second version. Some items such as measured work will have included an allowance for cash discount in the sub-contract documents, and so will include it automatically in the final sum. Others do not and so one thirty-ninth is to be added, a different arrangement from that in the domestic sub-contract. Those items listed are statutory fees and charges, setting out loss and expense accounts and fluctuations (whether deductions or additions), although others may arise under the 'any other amounts' provision. Clause 21.10.2.11 is in error by omitting wording in parentheses similar to that in clause 21.11.2.6, thus allowing cash discount to be included twice when formula fluctuations apply. There are one or two other faults of drafting in the clause.

The sub-contractor's documentation necessary for preparing the final account and a copy of the complete account are to be exchanged in the manner of the main contract, although only under clause 21.10.1.2 is a statement of variations given to the contractor and sub-contractor. The equivalent document would be just as useful in the case of remeasurement. The timing of events is set to allow settlement so that final payment of the sub-contractor is achieved at the latest in the umbrella interim certificate of main clause 30.7. Otherwise it may be made earlier under main clause 35.17. While much detail will be agreed directly between the quantity surveyor and the sub-contractor, it is important that at least the spirit of the clause is observed and that the architect and the contractor are involved at all critical points (as clause 21.11.3 omits to involve the contractor) over the inclusion or exclusion of amounts which may be disputed by one or another. This arises out of the triangular relationships, responsibilities and liabilities introduced by the structure of nomination.

Clause 22 — Benefits under main contract

In general the sub-contractor cannot sue the employer direct, having no contract with him. Only in a limited range of matters is there a direct contractual relationship under Agreement NSC/2. The intention therefore is that the contractor is prepared to proceed against the employer on the sub-contractor's behalf, where the employer is in default. This is obviously in the contractor's interest and is the alternative to proceeding against the employer to recoup the loss already suffered through being sued by the sub-contractor.

Clause 23 — Contractor's right to set-off

This clause gives the contractor a right 'to deduct from any money . . . due' to the sub-contractor where the amount has been either agreed by the sub-contractor or finally awarded in proceedings under the sub-contract. It also gives a right to deduct where the amount has not yet been agreed, subject to three provisos:

(a) There is an architect's certificate under clause 12.2.

(b) The amount 'has been quantified in detail and with reasonable accuracy'.

(c) The contractor has given proper notice, which may lead to the invoking of clause 24.

This clause is clearly related to *Dawnays Ltd* v. *F. G. Minter Ltd and Another* and also to *Gilbert-Ash (Northern) Ltd* v. *Modern Engineering (Bristol) Ltd* in its intent and detailed wording. It expressly excludes reliance on any right of set-off not covered by the conditions, while being itself without prejudice to final agreement of any amount or to any proceedings over such an amount.

Clause 24 — Contractor's claims not agreed by the sub-contractor — appointment of adjudicator

Without this clause the sub-contractor would be unable to appeal effectively against the contractor withholding an amount until arbitration becomes possible, upon the ending of the main contract works. This clause provides for an adjudicator, named in the sub-contract, to whom the parties are to submit their cases, upon the sub-contractor initiating a detailed procedure set down in the clause. The adjudicator has to give a decision in what is a matter of weeks from the original dispute over set-off arising, rather than what might otherwise be years. He is to decide whether the whole or part of the amount is to be retained by the contractor or paid to the sub-contractor or, for security, deposited with a trustee-stakeholder named in the sub-contract. In any of these cases, the decision is simply there to tide over affairs until arbitration comes about, when the whole of the matters at issue remains open.

Clause 25 — Right of access of contractor and architect

This clause deals with the right of access which main clause 11 requires the contractor to secure in all types of sub-contract, and thus saves special action by the contractor. Access is 'to any work which is being prepared' and therefore by implication is to any place. The architect at his discretion may waive the right for himself and the contractor. 'Reasonable grounds' for doing so would include confidential processes, production line work rendering inspection meaningless or inconvenient, or situations where other client's items or batches would be unduly on display. If loss of access might impede the contractor or lead to danger of mismatches of fabricated work, the architect must weight the factors to decide where 'reasonable' lies.

Clause 26 — Assignment — sub-letting

This clause carries both matters down into the sub-contract realm and, paralleling the main contract, is more stringent over assignment by the sub-contractor. This requires the consent of both architect and contractor, with no rider about unreasonably withholding. There is no requirement for the contractor to obtain the sub-contractor's consent before assigning the main contract. Such a restriction would be quite intolerable for him, faced with the employer on one side of him and an array of sub-contractors on the other. Again for sub-letting the dual consent is needed, but here it is not to 'be reasonably withheld' (presumably the missing 'un' is a mistake in drafting) with the architect's opinion prevailing.

Clause 27 — General attendance — other attendance etc

Clause 27.1.1 requires the contractor to provide 'general attendance . . . free of charge to the Sub-Contractor'. It defines it in wording identical to that in the Standard Method of Measurement of Building Works (Sixth Edition) clause B.9.2, although clause 27.1.2 then qualifies this by requiring the sub-contractor to remove his rubbish 'to a place provided on the site' and to maintain clear access to his works. Clause 27.2 then refers to 'other items of attendance' also provided free and as agreed in the tender. These are set out there in identical terms to those in SMM 6 clause B.9.3.

The general attendance definition restricts free use to 'standing scaffolding, standing power operated hoisting plant', that is what the contractor happens to have there at the time for his own use. While this is the generally accepted meaning of 'standing' there is room for doubt over what is 'standing plant'. It appears to include a barrow hoist, it perhaps includes a tower crane as 'standing' if this is the same thing as 'erected', but excludes a mobile crane and also a gin wheel as manually operated. Conceivably it includes a crane on rails. The likelihood of the contractor happily allowing a sub-contractor to operate any crane is remote. The definition is also restricted to 'temporary roads, pavings and paths' which by implication are those laid for the works at large, although perhaps not only those which the contractor needs for himself. The 'other attendance' list covers 'special' and 'additional' scaffolding, roads and hardstandings required solely by the sub-contractor, and hoisting and the like to whatever extent has been agreed in the tender. This latter will usually be restricted to 'significant items', but to the extent that it applies it makes the contractor and not the sub-contractor responsible for the plant, labour and operation and so erodes the contractor's obligation under general attendance. The tender adds to the SMM 6 definition the significant words '(to be at the risk of the Sub-Contractor)'. For items expensive to replace or with long delivery periods this unqualified expression is an insurer's nightmare.

The general attendance definition is embracing rather than restrictive over the provision of temporary lighting and water supplies and also use of mess rooms and so on. In the case of supplies, this must include charges and services and means any general site network that the sub-contractor needs. The 'other attendance' list covers lighting and power to any accommodation which the contractor provides for the sub-contractor and also power supplies in general. Both the definition and the list can be construed to exclude power supplies within accommodation which the sub-contractor supplies, while they leave doubt about provision of lighting in such accommodation. These elements should therefore be dealt with in the tender under '(g) Any other attendance' to avoid conflict.

The general attendance definition is also embracing over the use of mess rooms and the like. Since the extension of such facilities is determined on a per capita basis, the contractor's obligation here is to provide anything needed for the sub-contractor. For other accommodation and storage, the contractor is only required as general attendance to provide space, any such accommodation coming under the other attendance list. If it is not listed, clause 27.3 places the whole expense on the sub-contractor, although 'the Contractor agrees to give all reasonable facilities', presumably at a charge if not covered by general attendance. The sub-contractor has a right of 'reasonable objection' to the siting offered to him by the contractor in the 'provision of space' under general attendance. This should allow him to object to his huts and storage space being sited in a remote corner.

Clause 27.4 returns to the question of scaffolding and gives the contractor and sub-contractor and others on the site mutual rights of use of erecting scaffolding. These others strictly exclude the employer and persons doing work under main clause 29, as they are not operating 'for the purposes of the Main Contract Works'. The proviso excludes liability over the state of the scaffolding and so seeks to make the user responsible for checking its condition. This is adequate against gross overloading or other negligence, but may not cover hardly discernible weaknesses such as a single loose but critical coupler. The intention of the clause, judging by its antecedent in the 'Green Form', is presumably to cover situations in which persons use scaffolding in, for instance, the manner provided under the general attendance of clause 27.1.1. Its term 'any erected scaffolding' embraces also scaffolding provided as other attendance via clause 27.2 where a 'warranty or other liability' of some sort is created, at least as to 'suitability' and probably as to 'fitness' and 'condition'. On this issue the two parts of the clause are in conflict.

There is no attempt under the sub-contract to introduce any further exclusion of liability affecting any other plant or facilities provided under this clause or elsewhere and the position would be regulated by the wider law.

Clause 28 — Contractor and sub-contractor not to make wrongful use of or interfere with the property of the other

The first part of this clause is clear and is summarised neatly in the title. But, in addition, the parties are both bound not to contravene any Act, byelaw or the like, presumably in respect of the works in general and possibly in respect of the other party's property in particular. Nothing is said to clarify this: in this case the parties would be expected to observe the legal requirements affecting construction. But the clause ends with a proviso that its earlier parts are not to prejudice either party in their statutory or contractual duties. This part is quite mysterious; perhaps it means 'in an emergency use the other fellow's tackle and argue afterwards'.

Clause 29 — Determination of the employment of the sub-contractor by the contractor

Determination may be forced on the sub-contractor by any of four causes. Clauses 29 and 30 deal respectively with the cases of the contractor and the sub-contractor determining against each other. Clause 31 then caters for the two situations where the employer and the contractor determine against each other and so end the sub-contract from above. In this first clause, the pattern followed is similar to that of main clause 27 in which the employer determines against the contractor. The detailed wording is very similar, but several points demand comment.

Clause 29.1.3 extends the non-removal of defective work as a cause for determination to include non-rectification of defects. This is a reasonable extension. The original cause is qualified by 'the Works are materially affected' and relates to what is clearly wrong at the time of performance. The addition is not so qualified and is put into the same terms as clause 14, that is defects appearing at any time. This is thus fairly drastic and it is unlikely to be used except in major instances, lest it be done 'unreasonably and vexatiously'. It becomes a rather pointless weapon after practical completion.

The whole procedure may only be used by the contractor when he has warned the architect under clause 29.1 and the architect has instructed him under the main contract. Renomination by the architect is then needed to secure the new sub-contractor under clause 29.3.1. The discussion on renomination under main clause 35.24 is relevant here.

In clause 29.4 some of the same elements enter into the final settlement with the defaulting sub-contractor as occur in the main contract version, but they are deployed differently and with other elements. The sub-contractor is not to be paid anything further until completion of the sub-contract works by the substituted sub-contractor, but is then to be paid through an interim certificate any amount for work and materials not previously covered. The employer, but not the architect, may deduct in paying the certificate 'the amount of the expenses and direct loss and/or damage' which have been calculated by the architect for the quantity surveyor. 'Expenses' seems to bear the same interpretation as in main clause 27.4 and thus includes, amongst other things, the *whole* amount of the substituted sub-contract account. This may be far more than the *extra* amount of the substituted sub-contract account especially if determination occurs early in the sub-contract works. The extra amount is what would be expected to give a similar arithmetical effect to that in the main contract. It would seem likely that the wording given might often be set aside as punitive by the courts.

In the context of the sub-contract, to which the employer is not a party, this option to deduct can be read only as a statement of fact and not as a provision binding on the actual parties. It derives its force from clauses 3.3 and 6 of Agreement NSC/2 which place an obligation on the sub-contractor not to default, and requires him to indemnify the employer for 'any direct loss and/or expense' in the case of default. This is a somewhat different term, but adequate to cover what the employer can expect to recover. Agreement NSC/2 is silent as to how the employer may effect this recovery, while the main contract conditions are silent on the whole question of recovery, or indeed on any settlement with the original sub-contractor, providing simply for the substituted sub-contractor to be paid. The architect has to include the amount due to the original sub-contractor without making any deduction. There is thus doubt over precisely how much the employer may recover, and whether he may deduct the amount when paying the contractor on an interim certificate. If the employer has a right to deduct, then the contractor may deduct in paying the sub-contractor in accordance with clause 21.3.1.2.

When all this is said, the amount that the employer may wish to deduct may be larger than the amount due the sub-contractor, so that the employer will need to recover by direct action under Agreement NSC/2 in any case. Whatever the amount reaching the contractor, the clause provides for him in turn to deduct his own 'direct loss and/or damage' as well as cash discount. This is 'without prejudice to any other rights' and his deduction also may be greater than the amount available in outstanding monies, while he may also have other claims remaining against the sub-contractor not related to determination.

Delay to the main contract works will be almost inevitable in the case of a renomination which flows from the circumstances that this clause envisages. If this delay is not to be construed as 'on the part of' the sub-contractor under main clause 25.4.7 (and this is quite possible, as discussed under that clause), then payments to the contractor will be subject to a deduction for liquidated damages, so that the contractor in his turn must deduct for these when paying the sub-contractor to recover his loss. If however the delay *is* to be construed in this way, there will be an extension of time. This will relieve the contractor of paying damages, so that the employer will need to deduct an equivalent amount for loss from the sum that he pays through the contractor for the sub-contractor's account. Either way, the contractor may deduct for any costs he has incurred as a result of disruption to his programme.

Clause 30 — Determination of employment under the sub-contract by the sub-contractor

After the intricacies of the last clause, it is some relief to find that the present clause is modelled more directly on main clause 28 and presents no fresh problems in its wording. Its provisions relate entirely to actions, inactions and settlement between the contractor and the sub-contractor. The architect is mentioned only as receiving a copy of the notice of default, but not strangely enough the notice of determination. He can do nothing formally under the sub-contract through the contractor to help or hinder the determination. All his actions over renomination and the employer's position with the contractor over finances are dealt with in main clause 35.24.6 and do not affect the sub-contract. The contractor has to settle with the outgoing sub-contractor in the manner of main clause 28 but without the architect or the quantity surveyor becoming involved, as that clause at least implies. Here there will be no further payments for the sub-contractor through the mechanisms of interim certificates as the nomination has come to a premature end. The comments under main clause 35.24.7 are however relevant. Innocuous though the present clause is in itself, it is part of an overall picture of uncertainty as between the employer and the contractor.

Clause 31 — Determination of the main contractor's employment under the main contract

While the parties to the sub-contract may determine against each other, so also may either party to the main contract against the other. Whichever way this happens, it is probably in no way the sub-contractor's fault (the contractor would already have used clause 29.1). The key provision in either case is for the sub-contractor's employment also to determine automatically.

When the main contract determination is against the contractor, the contractor is at fault and clause 31.1 brings in the preceding clause 30.2 as the formula for settlement. It is conceivable that both employer and sub-contractor could determine against the contractor at the same time. Clause 31.1 covers the case of the contractor's insolvency which is quite additional to clause 30.1. In the circumstances covered by this clause, main clause 27.4.2 gives a right to the employer to require the contractor to assign sub-contracts. The present clause takes no account by way of a proviso for this, or of a reinstatement of employment should it happen, which could cause a hiatus.

When the main contract determination is against the employer, the employer is put at fault and the settlement runs accordingly in the main contract. The present clause 31.2.1 recognises the financial complexities that may flow down the contractual line and simply provides for the sub-contractor to receive his share of the cake, defined formally as 'the proportion fairly and reasonably attributable'. The only specific statement is about loss and/or damage, where further evidence will be needed. As it is the main contract cake that is being shared out the involvement of the architect and the quantity surveyor is inevitable.

Except in the case of the contractor's insolvency, clause 31.2.2 safeguards under a clause 31.2.1 determination the payment to the sub-contractor of any amount in the interim certificate pipeline before determination and thus avoids the doubt obtaining under clause 30. (The architect himself even has a date of issue under the wording.) In the case of clause 31.1 such doubt remains.

Clause 32 — Fair wages

This clause is included as a standard provision in the sub-contract. The main contract clause gives it only in the local authorities editions. Where the present sub-contract is used in relation to a private edition this clause could be deleted, although its presence causes no difficulty and has little effect. Both parties bind themselves to observe the wages and conditions prescribed. If the one party suffers due to, say, a strike brought on by a failure of the other to observe this clause, the right to reimbursement would arise under the indemnity given here.

Clause 33 — Strikes — loss or expense

Clause 33.1 provides for loss and/or expense resulting from a strike or similar industrial action to rest with the party incurring it. Thus, for instance, if the sub-contractor's 'workmen' strike, they may cause loss to the contractor as well as to the sub-contractor or indeed to another sub-contractor through the nexus of the contractor. None can claim against the other directly or indirectly. However the parties may not abandon work on the slightest pretext; if practicable the contractor is to keep the site open and the sub-contractor is to keep on working.

As a rider clause 33.2 keeps open 'any other right' of either party. This includes most commonly the right to extension of time for the sub-contractor under clause 11.2.5.4, but in an extreme case could cover frustration of the sub-contract and perhaps the main contract also. Either of these would lead to a determination, even if not one foreseen in the determination clauses.

Clause 34 — Choice of fluctuation provisions — tender, schedule 1, item 2

Clause 35 — Contribution, levy and tax fluctuations

Clause 36 — Labour and materials cost and tax fluctuations

Clause 37 — Formula adjustment

The first three of these clauses follow hard upon the wording of main clauses 37, 38 and 39 and differ only in essentially non-significant elements such as clause references. In no place is the effect changed.

Clause 37 also follows main clause 40 quite closely, but with a number of differences to take up matters of significance in the sub-contract. Thus reference is made under clause 37.1 to the distinct set of formula rules applying to nominated sub-contracts. This clause treats the same area as main clause 40.4.1, which appears to be superfluous. There is a gap in the wording of clause 37.1 in that it refers to the formula adjustment of 'The Sub-Contract Sums' (sic) 'or amounts ascertained under clause 17 as the case may be'. This strictly excludes adjustment to the sub-contract sum arising, for instance, under the variations and provisional sums procedures of clause 16. To give completeness the latter part of clause 15.1 from 'or such other sum' onwards should be added here.

Clauses 37.2.3 to 37.3.2 contain extra materials. The first of these requires valuations to be made for the purposes of fluctuations if the main contract itself is not subject to formula adjustment. This clause does not say anything about when the valuations are to be made, but clause 37.3.1 requires the contractor to ensure that adjustment is made 'in all Interim Certificates to which clause 21 applies'. This does not oblige the main contract dog to be wagged by the sub-contract tail. So long as the valuations follow a rigid timetable to give the necessary accuracy under the formula rules, the resulting adjustment amounts can be included in the next interim certificate in each case, even if the timing is a little out of step.

No reference is made to anyone as making these valuations under clause

37.2.3, the inference being that the sub-contractor and the quantity surveyor would be involved, with the contractor acting strictly as middleman, as he is named in clause 37.5 over the 'power to agree' methods and procedures. However the sub-contractor under clause 37.3.2 has a right for his representations on any valuation to be passed on to the architect by the contractor. Presumably they would then seep through to the quantity surveyor so that action could be taken before the next interim certificate was prepared.

As there is only one version of Sub-Contract NSC/4 or NSC/4a to go with the JCT main forms, clauses 37.3.3 and 37.3.4 contain on a conditional basis stipulations about the non-adjustable element in local authorities contracts. These follow the equivalent provisions in the main contract concerned as touched on in Chapter 21.

CHAPTER 19

Nominated suppliers in the main contract and in the related documents

The elements covered here are main clause 36 and the form of tender, which incorporates a warranty. In essence they are scaled down versions of the documents for nominated sub-contractors and the provisions of the latter documents may be viewed as having duly limited relevance to the present documents.

Main clause 36 — Nominated suppliers

36.1 — DEFINITION

36.1.1 While the following clause deals with an exclusion, clause 36.1.1 gives the positive definition of a nominated supplier. Its core is that the architect nominates (although in two of the variants this may be a 'deemed' nomination) leading to supply for fixing by the contractor. It is not unknown for the contractor subsequently to sub-let fixing to the supplier, but this is a separate issue and does not affect the present definition.

There are four variants. The first is the usual situation where a prime cost sum is inserted in the contract bills, and the supplier is named either there or at the time of nomination. This differs from the provisions for nominated sub-contractors, where main clause 35.1 envisages the possibility of naming in the contract bills without including a prime cost sum. Clause 36.1.2 specifically excludes this option over suppliers. The second variant is that of expending the whole or part of a provisional sum by way of a specially designated prime cost sum and a named supplier. This creates a position similar to the first, but two observations may be made. Firstly the materials or goods may be of a type covered by a previous nominated supply in which case they are better treated as an extension of that supply than as a fresh nomination. Secondly the provision does not expressly exclude the use of a nomination arising from a provisional sum to cover further materials or goods of a type already 'specified in the Contract Bills to be fixed by the Contractor'. (Clause 36.1.2 uses this expression, but does so to avoid the substitution of materials from a nominated supplier for those provided by a supplier of the contractor's choice.) To use nomination in this way is contrary to the spirit of the conditions, as the comparable provisions relating to nominated sub-contractors in main clauses 13.1.3 and 35.1.3 suggest, and would entitle the contractor to an overall level of reimbursement equivalent to that on the original measured basis. It would also create problems in such areas as extension of time and defects liability.

The last two variants bring in a 'deemed' nomination. The third is rather like the second in that it arises out of a provisional sum, but covers the case of only one possible supplier. Likewise, the fourth covers a similar supplier, but arises out of a variation instruction or sanction. Both of these must then be treated as nominated. This would not be the case if there were extra materials or goods from a supplier as envisaged by clause 36.1.2 in which case main clause 13.5 would apply. Since both of these variants become nominations only at the time of the instruction, it is unlikely that a formal tender will have been obtained on a similar basis to the standard form considered later in this chapter. Thus complications may occur over price and other provisions spelt out later in this clause. It is therefore better to avoid a 'deemed' nomination whenever possible.

36.1.2 This clause spells out the requirement for a prime cost sum for materials or goods 'which are specified in the Contract Bills to be fixed by the Contractor' as a necessary precondition. Restricting choice to a sole supplier, whether by naming or by lack of alternative choice, does not in itself create a nomination. Usually in the former case measured items will be of a 'fixing' nature only, while in the latter manufacturer's references or full technical specification will be given. If in this case the contractor is faced with an 'exclusion clause' of the type envisaged in clause 36.5.1, he should raise the question of restricting his own liability to the employer when tendering, rather than pricing higher than his competitors might to cover the risk. This clause is complementary to several of the points mentioned under clause 36.1.1.

36.2 — ARCHITECT'S INSTRUCTIONS

The present clause makes it mandatory upon the architect to 'issue instructions' (referred to only in clause 36.1.1) 'for the purpose of nominating a supplier'. This wording is wide enough to include the 'deemed' variants under clause 36.1.1. Read in conjunction with that clause, it also means that the contractor not only need not, but also must not act without the architect's prior instruction over any relevant materials or goods. The precise form of the instruction will depend on which variant under clause 36.1.1 applies.

36.3 — ASCERTAINMENT OF COSTS

This is the first part of clause 36 also to be included bodily in the Standard Tender. It covers matters relating to final accounts and could well have been placed at the end of the whole clause.

36.3.1 This covers those elements payable to the supplier himself as part of 'the total amount paid or payable', which will consist otherwise of the price of the materials and goods themselves. The first two of these may not be distinguishable in the supplier's price or prices, but may have been included in the calculations. They are 'any tax (other than any VAT . . .)', defined in the same way as in clause 39.3.3 for fluctuations, under which heading there is comment, and 'packing, carriage and delivery'. The latter is defined as 'the net cost . . . after allowing for any credit or return of any packing' — the word 'net' is not intended to imply that the 'cost' does not include a cash discount allowance.

The third element is 'any price adjustment', that is fluctuations. There are no rules for determining this, either in these conditions or given in detail in the Standard Tender, but space is left there for the architect or the supplier to complete as appropriate. As production is off-site and often in a factory, this approach best allows for the wide range of possibilities.

Cash discount is a different percentage from that for nominated sub-contractors and is to be included in 'the total amount' which is defined here as including the three elements discussed above. The discount may therefore be allowed to the contractor on those elements and be deducted by him in payments, as supported by clause 36.4.4. Only in the case of price adjustment is the point made explicit, but this should not be interpreted as excluding an allowance in the other cases. In any case these elements may not show in the supplier's pricing, but are only mentioned here to clarify financial responsibility as between the supplier and the contractor.

The total amount is to exclude all discount obtainable, other than the 5 per cent cash discount. In obtaining tenders the architect, or the quantity surveyor on his behalf, should ensure that such extra discounts are excluded, to avoid any claim for their inclusion later. Annual discounts for bulk buying will clearly not show on any quotation, or even on an invoice; they fall within the definition 'any discount' and should be deducted if detected. Alternatively an amendment of the clause at this point to leave annual discounts in the contractor's pocket would save any excessive enquiry on the point.

36.3.2 The usual arrangement is for the supplier to deliver and for the contractor to unload and be responsible for later handling, as assumed by clause 36.4.3 and as provided for by fixing items in the contract bills. If a departure from this procedure is known in advance, the contract bills may provide for the contractor to be reimbursed for the extra expense of say collecting at works, so that he is 'reimbursed . . . otherwise under this Contract' rather than through clause 36.3.1 which covers only payments to the supplier. If there is no such provision, the contractor is reimbursed under this clause after written authorisation, as discussed under main clause 3. In the reverse case, in which provision is made in the bills, the supplier's tender also includes for delivery and a variation instruction should be issued to amend the contract bill provision. The Standard Tender assumes, rather than states, in schedule 1 that delivery will be by the supplier while allowing for a specific statement about returnable packings, so that both the architect and the contractor should check insertions in this or any other tender form before they are committed.

36.4 — SALE CONTRACT

These provisions are set out to apply between the employer and the contractor, mainly over mutual benefits and liabilities, and to limit the power of the architect to nominating a person who will accept the provisions as being also sale contract provisions between him and the contractor. If such a person is not forthcoming or is not the most suitable in other ways at the stage of tendering for the supply, the architect must agree any consequent adjustment with the contractor as a prelude to nomination. Beyond this, the term '*inter alia*' recognises that there may be other provisions entirely between the contractor and the supplier, although clause 36.4.9 must be observed. The provisions do not afford the contractor any right of objection to the person nominated on more general grounds, as in the case of nomination of a sub-contractor. This is reasonable, since the supplier does not operate on site and so his contribution can go wrong in fewer ways than that of a sub-contractor.

36.4.1 The quality and standard of materials and goods are generally given in the same terms as in main clause 2.1. In addition schedule 3 of the Standard Tender gives a warranty to the employer, thus affording protection to the architect over matters of design and specification undertaken by the supplier.

36.4.2 The contractor has considerably wider protection here than is normally afforded by most suppliers' contracts of sale. The nominated supplier has to pay, for example, for cutting out defective materials and building in the new which he supplies. 'Expenses' qualified by 'as a direct consequence' may well be a wide enough term to allow the contractor to recover, in addition, the cost to him of the resultant delay. It should be compared however with the term 'direct loss and/or expense' in main clause 26.1 and with the comments made there, although this term has no direct bearing here.

There are three qualifications to the contractor's protection. One lies in the phrase 'which appear . . . Defects Liability Period' which places a limit on the supplier's liability to the contractor over direct replacement but not in any other case similar to that of the contractor for his own work. Then, under clause 36.4.2.1, the contractor's protection is lost after the materials or goods are fixed if he has not checked for patent defects before fixing, as he should have rejected them at once. Lastly any defects due to damage and the like after supply reasonably do not lie with the supplier, although the contractor may have redress elsewhere.

36.4.3 The Standard Tender allows for stipulations to be made over 'any delivery programme'. The contractor may otherwise give 'reasonable directions'. Beyond inserting the original stipulations, the architect does not become involved in these matters, whether the programme is maintained or not. This provision is clearly vital to the contractor's interests, since he will be quite unable to enter into a contract with a firm which could not comply with his programme. There will obviously also be terms in the quotations to cover minimum delivery times from receipt of orders and delivery of part loads, to give protection to the supplier.

36.4.4 The payment terms allow the contractor between one and two month's credit from delivery. Whether the contractor will himself be paid before or after he is due to make payments to the suppliers will depend on how the delivery is related to the dates of interim certificates. The term 'a discount . . . on all payments' in conjunction with clause 36.3.1 means what it says, no element of the account is free from discount. There is substantial repetition of this clause in clause 36.4.6.

36.4.5 This arrangement does not go so far as that for domestic sub-contractors for sub-let work under main clause 19.4 or that for nominated sub-contractors under main clause 35.24, in both of which the sub-contractor's employment is determined. Here the contract of sale remains but deliveries are suspended, thus permitting resumption, if necessary, or assignment to the employer under main clause 27.4.2.1.

36.4.6 This provision obliges the contractor to pay within the period given in clause 36.4.4 and could more logically have preceded that clause, or even have been conflated with it. Payments are in no way contingent upon the issue of the architect's certificate, as in the case of nominated sub-contractors, and the contractor must pay in accordance with the terms stated, whether the sums due have been included in a certificate or not. No retention money is to be held, which is in line with the policy over suppliers generally. This is the only provision in the series which places a liability on the contractor alone and he may therefore be at least indifferent about whether the supplier includes it. It involves him in no further obligations to the employer who can take no action if he fails to pay unless the supplier suspends deliveries or breaks off the contract of sale, and so causes delay and perhaps the need to renominate. None of these options is considered in the clause, and there is no provision for protecting nominated suppliers by direct payment if the contractor defaults.

36.4.7 The express passing of ownership to the contractor upon delivery to him or to others at his order, is a protection to the contractor, and also affords some protection to the employer on determination against the contractor by preventing the supplier from recovering the property as his. It applies whether the contractor has paid or not. The extent of protection to the employer is governed by main clauses 16 and 30.3 and the wider legal position (see cases under 'Insolvency of contractor and title to goods'), and depends on whether the materials or goods are off-site in the possession of the contractor or a sub-contractor, on site and unfixed, or fixed.

36.4.8 The special provisions for 'joint arbitration' under article 5.1.4 of the articles of agreement are grafted in here, subject to the rider in article 5.1.5.

36.4.9 The foregoing clauses by virtue of the introduction to clause 36.4 as a whole are to be amongst those which the contract of sale 'provides'. This clause guards against the possibility that, having 'provided' them, the contract of sale will then mutilate them by the addition of naive or devious extra clauses. This clause therefore mutilates any such potential provisions in turn. Broadly, this is a 'discrepancy provision' after the manner of main clause 2.2.1 asserting the pre-eminence of the conditions but worded more stringently as it includes 'affect in any way whatsoever'.

The effect of this clause in the face of a clear overriding provision such as 'clause 36.4.7 shall not apply in this contract of sale' is to nullify the overriding provision, in spite of the agreement of the architect and the contractor and the complicity of the supplier. To make the overrider effective, it will be necessary also to amend the present clause so that it remains operative except in respect of the overrider.

36.5 — CONTRACT OF SALE — RESTRICTION, LIMITATION OR EXCLUSION OF LIABILITY

36.5.1 Clause 36.4 permits the architect and the contractor to agree to the nomination of a person whose contract of sale excludes some element of the terms listed in the clause, (although this is subject to the problems introduced by clause 36.4.9) so it is reasonable to insert the present clause relieving the contractor of the corresponding obligations to the employer over the materials or goods in the same way that main clause 35.22 does for nominated sub-contractors. If, for example, some material from a nominated supplier is fixed by the contractor and then develops defects the architect cannot give instructions for its removal under main clause 8.4 and expect replacement and reinstatement to be carried out by the contractor without charge. (See *Gloucestershire County Council* v. *Richardson*). The instruction will be under main clause 13.1.1.2 and extra payment will fall to be made to the contractor under main clause 13.4.

36.5.2 This clause emphasises the change in the basic intention by making prior written approval or amendments obligatory.

36.5.3 Even when written approval is forthcoming, there is nothing either here or in clause 36.4 that can force the contractor to accept such a non-standard nomination if he does not wish to, whatever the inducements offered for him to do so. It applies only when he 'agrees' to it.

Standard form of tender by nominated supplier

This document is not required to be used with main clause 36, but its use is highly desirable as it meshes closely with that clause and something equivalent would otherwise need to be provided.

The form of tender is similar to but simpler than Tender NSC/1. Its main features are: the contract of sale is conditional upon both the architect's nomination instruction and the contractor's acceptance; the tender remains open for acceptance for a period as inserted, and subject to satisfaction over the identity of the contractor; the warranty agreement (if any) will operate collaterally, once the contract of sale is effective.

The tender has three schedules appended.

Schedule 1: This lists the variable features of the contract of sale for completion by the architect or the contractor as appropriate. These include the description and the quantity of materials or goods, programme dates and fluctuation provisions, most of which have either been alluded to under main clause 36 or need no comment. Important elements of the main contract affecting the nominated supplier's potential liability if he defaults such as the completion date, the defects liability period and whether the extension of time provisions have been amended, are also given. The schedule, rather than the preceding tender, gives the pricing either as a lump sum (without a defined means of variation) or as a schedule of rates. There is no provision for titling and signing the whole schedule, but it is prudent to do this for the purposes of identification.

Schedule 2: This is a simple recital of main clauses 36.3 to 36.5 so that the appropriate provisions become part of the contract of sale. The intention is clear enough, although the wording reads slightly oddly in places by virtue of its origin. Main clause 36.3.2 is not relevant to the supplier and it is difficult to see the relevance of main clause 36.5 other than as tendering information.

Schedule 3: This embodies the warranty agreement to be provided with the tender and concluded with the employer, if so required. This schedule or a separate form may be used for the actual agreement. It contains similar provisions concerning design and specification to Agreement NSC/2, and others concerning performance of the supply that are basically similar to those in Agreement NSC/2. This latter indemnifies the employer against loss of damages for delay by the contractor and payment of the contractor for direct loss and/or expense, when the responsibility lies with the nominated supplier. The amount of liquidated damages in the main contract conditions is to be stated. Beyond these provisions, the agreement simply contains a statement that nothing in the tender is to reduce the standard liability under the various warranties and it concludes with a joint arbitration clause, but not one for independent arbitration.

CHAPTER 20

The NFBTE domestic sub-contract

The document considered in this chapter is endorsed for use when the contractor is appointed under any of the four JCT standard forms, with and without quantities, and then sub-lets work by choice or as a contract requirement, under the provisions of main clause 19. It would be equally suitable for use with either of the JCT approximate quantities main forms. It should also be suitable for use with the JCT prime cost contract when this appears in its 1980 related edition, so long as the work sub-let is *not* itself to be paid for on a prime cost basis, which the sub-contract does not accommodate.

The contract is issued in two documents which are equivalent to either one of the nominated sub-contracts, NSC/4 or NSC/4a (these are nearly identical) and Tender NSC/1. One of these two documents contains the conditions while the other contains the articles of agreement and the tender elements. In spite of this rearrangement, the documents are very similar to the nominated versions in their subsidiary structure and in most clauses, in detail over matters of substance. The use of this domestic form is not obligatory and the main forms do not refer to it, even as an option. Its size and complexity make it something of a sledgehammer in relation to the nut of any small parcel of sub-let work.

This chapter should be read with Chapter 18 for completeness. It takes only the important differences between the form and the nominated versions (so that some clauses are not mentioned) and these are sometimes grouped under topics for easy discussion, although mostly the order of the form is followed. References elsewhere are given as to 'nominated clauses' and 'main clauses'.

The architect and the quantity surveyor

The quantity surveyor does not appear at all in the conditions as, strictly, he deals only with the contractor. The architect is seen in the shadow of the contractor in a few clauses, such as clause 4.2 over directions in general. In the main the contractor takes the place of the architect, because all directions and information come from the contractor and quite possibly will be in a different form from the corresponding data reaching the contractor from the architect. This reflects the fact that no 'special relationship' exists with the architect when there is no nomination. In addition privity of contract exists only between the contractor and the sub-contractor. The sub-contractor is just a part of the contractor in all respects under the main contract, while the architect almost becomes part of the contractor under the sub-contract. If a contractual matter is passed down the line there is a stronger reference, as when under clause 4.4 the contractor is to grant the sub-contractor the same relief over remedying of defects as he himself is granted by the architect over those same defects.

Arbitration

Among the articles of agreement there is an arbitration article which includes a similar joinder provision to that in the nominated article. However, it restricts itself to related disputes between the contractor and the employer, rather than also including nominated firms and other domestic sub-contractors. This does not exclude the possibility of an agreed joinder over and above the enforceable contract provision. Elsewhere in the conditions themselves there is no mention of a joint arbitration, since the sub-contractor has no relationship with the employer at the points concerned.

Clauses omitted from the domestic sub-contract

Several clauses in the nominated form are absent in the domestic sub-contract. The effect is usually self-evident, so that comments are not needed. The clauses in question are:

Clause 2.3   Restrictions in contract of sale etc
Clause 4.1.2 Sub-contractor's person-in-charge
Clause 4.6   Architect's instruction, authority therefor
Clause 14.5   Sub-contractor's obligation to clear up etc (this appears instead as clause 27.1.3.2)
Clause 16.4   Sub-contractor's right to attend measurement
Clause 17.2   Sub-contractor's right to attend measurement
Clause 23.2.1 Architect's certificate as condition of set-off

In addition to these omissions, clauses 23.1 and 23.2 omit reference to the contractor's fiduciary obligation over retention. Some of the differences discussed hereafter also involve a measure of omission.

Clause 2 — Sub-contract documents

Clauses 2.1 and 2.2 here follow the nominated clauses in principle, but quote different references. In clause 2.2 there is one major difference in that if there is any conflict between the main contract and the sub-contract, then 'the terms of the *Sub-Contract Documents* shall prevail' (italics supplied). As sub-letting commonly gives rise to more varied documentation than does nomination, this is a more reasonable approach that for the main contract to prevail. In these circumstances it is better to rely first upon the documents nearer to hand. But it does mean that whichever party does not draw up a particular document must read it carefully before welcoming it into the sub-contract, since the JCT conditions and procedures cannot be assumed if there is any clash.

Clause 2.3, not included in the nominated sub-contracts, consequently provides for the sub-contractor to give notice to the contractor over discrepancies and divergencies and to receive the contractor's directions. Whether the contractor needs to obtain the architect's instructions is not the concern of the sub-contractor, as he is entitled to financial recompense under clauses 16 or 17 as the case may be.

Clauses 4 and 5 — Execution of the works, and sub-contractor's liability

These clauses approximate to their counterparts. In particular, clause 4.1 over the basic obligation to carry out and complete carries the full reference to the opinion and satisfaction of the architect over quality and standard. The main reference in clauses 4.2 and 4.3 is to the contractor's directions and the clauses differ here in wording with no significant difference in meaning. The omission of two clauses has already been mentioned.

Clauses 11 and 12 — Completion, extension of time and failure to complete

Both these clauses are closely modelled on the nominated clauses although clause 11 is given different sub-clause numbers. However, in both, any reference to the architect over the effects of delay is excluded. Responsibility rests entirely on the contractor, subject of course to the possibility of arbitration. The architect is mentioned only as a possible cause of delay in the relevant events, in the same way as in the nominated form.

Clauses 11.4 and 11.5 are concerned with the mechanics of granting an interim extension of time and correspond to parts of nominated clause 11.2.2, but are arranged in the reverse order for drafting reasons. Of substance though, is the substitution of 16 weeks within which to grant an interim extension under clause 11.4 and similarly a final extension under clause 11.7, which gives the contractor a minimum of four weeks after being granted any extension of his own by the architect. This reflects the absence of the architect from dealings in this case, in contrast to his involvement with nominated sub-contractors over extension of time.

Clause 13 — Regular progress, loss and expense

Nominated clause 13.1 dealing with matters as given in the main contract affecting progress and nominated clause 13.2 dealing with act, omission or default of the contractor, are here conflated into clause 13.1 which includes procedural clauses 13.1.1 to 13.1.3 to cover both sets of matters in this instance. Clause 13.3 lists as 'Relevant Matters' the same matters as in nominated clause 13.1.2. Clause 13.2 is additional and requires the contractor to give the sub-contractor information about extension of time on the lines of the main contract provision. This is needed as the architect is not involved here either in granting extensions or in settling loss and expense, as he is under the nominated sub-contract.

Clause 13.4 deals with loss and expense suffered by the contractor and caused by the sub-contractor. It thus corresponds to nominated clause 13.3, but omits the reference in parenthesis to loss and expense caused to other sub-contractors. As the meeting of such amounts by the contractor will still be 'direct ... expense', this omission could well have been made in the nominated clause. Clauses 13.4.1 to 13.4.3 are inserted as extra, giving similar procedures when the alleged indebtedness is from contractor to sub-contractor. Such procedures do not occur in the nominated clause.

The proviso about 'other rights and remedies' still follows as clause 13.3.

Clause 14 — Practical completion

This clause follows nominated clause 14.1 by requiring the sub-contractor to give notice when in his opinion there is practical completion, but differs by requiring some agreement between the contractor and the sub-contractor. If the contractor does not dissent within 14 days, the sub-contractor's date holds under clause 14.1. If the contractor does dissent, then the next stage, under clause 14.2, is that practical completion is deemed to take place on any date then agreed. If agreement cannot be reached then, as a third possible stage, the date of practical completion is deemed to be that for the main contract works; and it can be no later. This is a rather curious arrangement, which can only benefit the contractor against the sub-contractor. It also by its 'deemed' and therefore automatic third stage date in default of agreement appears to exclude the possibility of arbitration over the date.

In view of the retention provisions in clause 21.4 which hinge on this date and on the main contract certificate of making good defects, both parties need to consider the effects of agreement or non-agreement carefully.

Clauses 16, 17 and 18 — Valuation of variations and of all work: bills of quantities

The procedures under these clauses, but not the principles of valuation, are affected by the absence of the quantity surveyor. The contractor is not substituted for the quantity surveyor, so that the inference is that the contractor and the sub-contractor proceed together through any stages of measurement and valuation to agreement, without either being able to set the pace. This explains the omission of the 'right to attend' clauses already noted.

In the two valuation clauses 16 and 17 the simple mention of 'direction of the Contractor', without a reference to the backing instruction of the architect to the contractor, makes the provisions wide enough to cover any direction which originates with the contractor, as is common enough in the circumstances of sub-letting. In clause 1.3, the definition of 'Variation' in most of its parts also omits reference to the architect and so ties in with the present position.

There is a difference from the nominated clauses in the daywork details in that the percentage additions 'take into account any cash discount specified in the Appendix', thus allowing for the individual negotiation of terms that frequently occurs.

The omission from clause 18 of the words 'subject always to clause 2.2', which appear in the nominated clause, produces no change as clause 2.2 has an overriding effect by virtue of its own terms.

Clause 21 — Payment of sub-contractor

While this clause follows the general flow and in many places the detail of nominated clause 21 it differs significantly in several ways, due to the almost complete absence of reference to the architect and total absence of reference to the quantity surveyor. Moreover no explicit connection is made between the payments provision of the sub-contract and the main contract.

Clauses 21.1 and 21.2 cover the timing of payments, which are termed first, interim and final. They thus correspond to nearly all of the more extensive nominated clauses 21.1 to 21.3. The due date of the first payment is to be 'not later than one month' from commencement of work, but at no particular time in relation to the main contract certificates and payments. Interim payments are 'due at intervals not exceeding one month' with the first payment setting the timing, so that once again the main contract rhythm is not in view. However this will be of concern at least to the contractor. Payment is to be made within 17 days of the due date. The final payment is only briefly referred to at this stage.

The amounts of the first and interim payments depend on clauses 21.3 to 21.5, the effect of which is broadly similar in terms of retention, discount and previous payments to that of nominated clauses 21.4 to 21.6. Clause 21.3 sets out the overall pattern of gross valuation and deductions while clause 21.4 deals with the elements in the gross valuation, both running quite close in terms to nominated clause 21.4.

Clause 21.3.2 gives the contractor the right to deduct from the amounts in clause 21.4.1 whatever level of discount for prompt payment is given in the appendix, this being $2\frac{1}{2}$ per cent unless some other percentage is inserted. These deductions are made from work, materials and goods, but not from the other elements of extra expense and fluctuations set out in clauses 21.4.2 and 21.4.3, a different position from that under nominated clause 21.3.1.1 where all the elements are subject to discount. Clause 21.3.2 is defective, however, in relation to its assumed intention of allowing the contractor to deduct discount on the total of payments made. It refers only to deduction of 'discount . . . in respect of the amounts . . . which have not previously been paid', so that each interim payment will see the contractor passing over to the sub-contractor the discount deducted a month before. His other deduction of 'the total amount previously paid' is not inclusive of previous discount and so does not reinstate the position (nominated clause 21.4 is able to refer, as the present clause is not, to deducting the previous 'total amounts stated as due' and so avoids the anomaly). Further clause 21.5 is silent about the contractor deducting discount when releasing retention, while clause 21.9 perpetuates the problem as mentioned there. No contractor should enter into the sub-contract without amending the wording.

In dealing with payment for off-site materials or goods, clause 21.4.1.3 refers to the architect exercising his discretion when including amounts. In the case of such materials or goods therefore, the contractor is not required to include their value when paying the sub-contractor until after the date of the corresponding main contract interim certificate (but not necessarily until after payment), although he may be obliged to pay for work and on-site materials and goods before the equivalent main contract certification.

The provisions about retention in clause 21.5 break into the same three stages as in the nominated sub-contract, that is those produced by the two dividing events of practical completion of the sub-contract works and the certificate of making good defects of the main contract works. The first of these events will not necessarily be at a time corresponding to that under a nominated sub-contract, because of the terms discussed under clause 14.2. The clause also envisages a possible difference in the level of retention: while 5 per cent is given as the norm in the appendix the option is given of 'a different rate', not just 'a lower rate' as the nominated sub-contract produces by its dependence on the main contract. Lastly, the retention provisions do not establish any fiduciary interest by the contractor acting as trustee for the sub-contractor, nor do they require any special banking account, so that there is no equivalent to nominated clause 21.9. The employer will hold the main contract retention in this way, but this does not protect the sub-contractor's amounts that are within it if the contractor fails in any way.

Clause 21.6 moves on to the question of the contractor failing 'to make any payment' which *inter alia* will encompass him deducting discount if clause 21.3.2 has not been amended. It is a version of nominated clause 21.8 on the right of the sub-contractor to suspend work, simplified because of the absence of any elements relating to the employer's failure to pay direct, which is not possible here. Four points may be made, the first being that this clause must be used in the absence of any equivalent to nominated clause 21.7 on arbitration, if the sub-contractor is dissatisfied over payments. Secondly, and counterbalancing the last point, the sub-contractor has to wait only a simple period of seven days after giving a very prompt notice before he may suspend work, whereas the nominated clause provides for the long and cumulative period of some 32 days, both from the due date. Thirdly, the present clause is 'without prejudice to any other rights and remedies' and one of these is an additional right of determination in a severe case under clause 30.1, which may be exercised over and above or instead of the present clause. Lastly, the right to suspend is related to failure over 'any payment . . . as herein provided'. Where 'herein' is may be conjectured; if it embraces the whole of the sub-contract then it is to be hoped that the present clause may be construed as 'subject to clause 23' over set-off, as is expressed in nominated clause 21.8.

Clause 21.7 deals with the final adjustment of the sub-contract sum as one of the alternatives for settlement and is very close in structure and effect to nominated clause 21.10, although inevitably the detailed wording differs in places. While the present clause requires the sub-contractor to send documents for the adjustment to the contractor, it does not then provide for the sub-contractor to receive back a complete final account before, or even at, final payment under clause 21.9. In keeping with this no specific times are given, even as targets. This reflects the common practice of the sub-contractor himself producing an account that then goes no further than the contractor.

Omitted from the domestic clauses are the two provisions for adding 'one thirty-ninth' to the elements of extra expense and to fluctuations, calculated on the traditional basis, whether themselves additions or omissions. This is not because of a possible different rate of discount, but because the contractor is not entitled to discount on them at all in this sub-contract, as clauses 21.4.1 and 21.9.1 establish. While the contractor will settle his own extra expense items with the architect and the quantity surveyor and thus possibly recoup the deficiency, under the main contract, the main contract fluctuation provisions give him no leeway for anything but net reimbursement. He must therefore view his original contract pricing accordingly. Under formula fluctuations a discount is envisaged, although this is provided in the defective clause 21.3.2. Additional provisions allow for the deduction and addition of 'any other amount' so required by the sub-contract. These do not affect the question of discount, but are intended for special elements written into the other documents in the sub-contract.

Clause 21.8 deals with the alternative of the completely ascertained final sub-contract sum and as such follows nominated clause 21.11 with differences limited to those discussed above.

Two completely additional clauses are needed here to deal with the final payment, as it is not possible to rely on the main contract provisions. Clause 21.9.1 treats the amount of the final payment as being the total amount calculated under clauses 21.8 or 21.9, as the case may be, less two elements. One element is any discount applicable, if the payment is made promptly. The reference to clause 21.4.1 rather than to clause 21.4.2 means that extra expense and fluctuation amounts do not suffer deductions of discounts at this stage, any more than they have done earlier. However deduction of discount on other amounts generally is only authorised 'provided that such amounts have not previously been paid'. The other element to be deducted is 'the total amount previously paid' which has been net of discount. The combined effect of these two elements, both of which exclude earlier discount, is that the contractor pays over a large slice of discount at this final stage. This perpetuates the anomaly already discussed. Unless the contractor amends this clause as well before entering into the sub-contract, his only hope is for the first and final payments to be one!

Clause 21.9.2 provides for the final payment to be due within seven days of the main contract final certificate and to be made within 14 days of becoming due. To be a final payment, in fact, it will be dependent on the sub-contractor providing the information and possibly a final account, and on the parties having come to an agreement. Even if any of these are missing, it would seem permissible and necessary that the contractor should make a 'final payment' so named, but subject either to continuing negotiations or to arbitration. This is because of the evidential effects of the final payment under the next clause.

It will often be the case, not that the main contract final payment gives an embarrassingly early date for the final payment, but that it leads to an uncomfortably late one for any sub-contract work finished early in the main contract period. There is no early time limit on the making of the final payment, but equally no pressure on the contractor to make it, although he will have to have made interim payments up to the full entitlement of the sub-contractor. He will also have to make one under clause 21.5.3 at least at the end of the monthly period in which the main contract certificate of making good defects is issued, so that the balance of sub-contract retention is released. The sub-contractor should weigh carefully the effects of the aggregated payments provisions on his cash flow position.

The evidential effects of the final payment under clause 21.10.1 are two-fold. One is that where quality or standards are to be to the architect's reasonable satisfaction under the main contract, they are so for the sub-contract purposes. Since the architect does not declare his satisfaction until the main contract final certificate, it follows that if the contractor makes the final payment ahead of the final certificate he will be signing away any redress he may need against the sub-contractor, even though the scope of the architect's reasonable satisfaction may be fairly limited, as discussed under main clauses 2.1 and 30.9.1.1. The other evidential effect is that the final payment is conclusive that effect has been given to all sub-contract terms, that is the sub-contract is properly wound up on the lines of the first part of main clause 30.9.1.2.

Clause 21.10.2 contains statements that the final payment is not conclusive over errors within it and that it is subject to arbitration or other proceedings started at the latest within 10 days after the final payment is made. The final payment itself may be made up to 14 days after it is due.

Clause 26 — Assignment and sub-letting

The two parts of this clause reproduce the two parts of the nominated clause, but without any reference to the architect's consent in either case and therefore, in the case of sub-letting, without reference to the architect's opinion prevailing. The position is thus that the contractor cannot sub-let work, and then enter into the present sub-contract if he wishes, without the consent of the architect. Once this is done, the architect is excluded from any further control. While the contractor must not 'unreasonably' withhold his consent in the case of sub-letting, he cannot point to the architect as a reasonable cause. Indeed, he may not wish to, and it would be possible to manipulate this clause to secure by assignment or sub-letting someone on site whom the architect has already rejected. The contractor is not in breach of main clause 27.1.4 at this point, as he has complied with main clause 19 and it is only at a later step that the snag (for the architect) has arisen.

The only case in which the contractor may be in breach is if there have been 'persons named in a list' under main clause 19.3.1 by whom the work 'must be carried out'. In this case the contractor is obliged to see that one of these persons performs the work and so, it may be inferred, must withhold consent to an assignment or sub-letting. Even here the further provisions in main clause 19.3.2 may be used to outflank this position, if they are invoked to introduce other persons who have not been 'named in a list'.

Clause 27 — Attendance

In keeping with its terse title this clause does not define any attendance as 'general' or as 'other' and differs in several other points of content from nominated clause 27, while covering a range of attendance matters. In general it is framed to take account of the direct interaction of the contractor and the sub-contractor in the tendering stage, without any prior action by the architect, so that some simplification is possible. This should not lead to lack of precision over specifying non-routine items to be provided.

In clause 27.1.1, the equivalent to general attendance is given as including 'all reasonable hoisting facilities, water, electricity and watching'. This is more comprehensive in terms of the items covered. There is no limit, other than 'reasonable', to the extent or categories of provision, whereas nominated clause 27.1.1 excludes, for example, power supplies. While the present clause also includes storage space and use of messrooms etc, it omits any specific mention of 'roads, pavings and paths'. All of this suggests that the smaller non-specialised type of work is being sub-let, so that the sub-contractor can fit in fairly simply with the contractor, using the same range of items without undue expense or disturbance. If the sub-let work is substantial or if it involves considerable hoisting or power loads, for instance, it may be prudent either to substitute wording from nominated clause 27.1.1 or to define requirements explicitly under clause 27.2 which refers to the appendix for details of 'particular items of attendance'.

An extra clause 27.1.2 takes over the question of scaffolding and requires the contractor to 'provide and erect all necessary scaffolding and scaffold boards for work over 11 feet high (or the metric equivalent thereof)', without charge to the sub-contractor. The pioneering attitude of the construction industry to metrication is recalled in passing. For work below the specified height the sub-contractor is to provide his own scaffolding at his own expense. While this excludes any concept of 'standing scaffolding', clause 27.4 repeats nominated clause 27.4 over mutual availability of scaffolding between the contractor and the sub-contractor and so *inter alia* allows the sub-contractor to use the contractor's scaffolding.

The overall effect of these scaffolding provisions is that the contractor is responsible for providing major scaffolding. This is a case in which his detailed knowledge of what he is sub-letting and the absence of need for the sub-contractor to know should result in a reasonable outcome. Meanwhile the sub-contractor provides the items below 11 feet (or the metric equivalent thereof) or pays the contractor to provide them, if they are not already there. This gives rise to the picture of neither contractor nor sub-contractor hurrying to erect at a time and place of mutual interest, but waiting to see who gives first. The 'standing scaffolding' arrangement is of course open to the same abuse; the present clause is just more explicit about the sub-contractor putting up scaffolding.

The height differentiation over scaffolding is expressed in terms of the height of the work, rather than the scaffolding, and gives a 'one lift' dividing point. Like all rules of this type it has its anomalies. Who, for instance, erects or shares the erection of scaffolding for wall coverings on a gabled wall varying between eight feet and 14 feet in height (or of course, the metric equivalents thereof)?

Clause 27.3 about workshops etc is identical with its opposite number, except for the addition of the word 'move' in the initial list of operations, and some elaboration at the end of the clause. This could well have occurred in the other clause, but here at least the sub-contractor will need to keep his right of 'reasonable objection' in view if disturbance is more than might have been anticipated.

Clause 29 — Determination by the contractor

Because the architect is not mentioned in this clause, its provisions are more direct in several places, two of which need mention. Notice of default and determination under clause 29.1 both go straight from the contractor to the sub-contractor, and the period for continuing default is 10 days rather than 14 days. Then under clause 29.3.1 the contractor himself or his sub-contractor or agent may complete work by using what the sub-contractor has left behind. This takes account of the possibility that the contractor may neither wish nor be able to sub-let to another person. If he does sub-let again, the wording still allows him to make the items available to the new sub-contractor.

There are two other differences. If the sub-contractor becomes insolvent, determination is not automatic but the contractor must give written notice under clause 29.2. Also the provision about financial settlement in clause 29.4 refers to 'any cash discount specified' in line with the terms in clause 21 and discussed there.

Clause 30 — Determination by the sub-contractor

The provisions here are mostly as in nominated clause 30. There is the addition of a further cause of determination: if the contractor 'fails to make payment in accordance with this Sub-Contract'. The architect does not certify the amounts payable to a domestic sub-contractor and these do not bear a fixed time relationship to the main contract payments. The unit prices for the contractor in respect of the same work will almost invariably differ and the quantities and so forth need not be the same. This extra safeguard therefore gives the sub-contractor more contractual muscle in the absence of any knowledge by the architect of what is happening and of any power of the employer to pay direct.

As this safeguard is additional to the right to suspend work under clause 21.6, the present clause establishes a time interval between them. If the sub-contractor gives a notice under clause 21.6 which allows him to suspend work after seven days, he must then wait until 17 days from that notice before issuing a notice under the present clause, thus giving 10 days of actual suspension to provoke the contractor into paying. The determination then becomes effective as soon as notified, rather than after 14 days as in the nominated clause. This follows clause 29 in its notice related to any of the causes there.

There is however no bar in the various clauses to the sub-contractor using the right of determination without having first suspended work. Whether he would wish to escalate the conflict so rapidly is a matter for his judgement in the light of all factors both within and outside the scope of the sub-contract.

The other difference is the omission of a clause 30.2.2.6 about payment of direct loss and expense. There is no apparent reason for this and the fact that the clause occurred in a draft version and that clause 30.2.2.5 ends with a semi-colon suggests that this omission was not intended. Its reintroduction may therefore be advisable in the interests of fairness.

Clause 31 — Determination of the contractor's employment

This clause treats the two cases of determination of the contractor's employment identically so far as the sub-contract is concerned and consists of the wording of nominated clause 31.1 only, with the incorporation of a reference to determination under main clause 28. As the settlement will be independent of what happens under the main contract, this is sensible and likely to give the same practical result as the more complex nominated provision.

PART 4

Other JCT Forms and related contracts

CHAPTER 21

The other editions of the JCT main form of contract

The private edition with quantities of the JCT form has been considered in detail in Parts 2 and 3 of this volume. The other five variants of that form differ for reasons that are apparent from their titles and that lead to differences of comparative detail in documents that are structured alike and have a great bulk of identical material and even identical clause numbers where possible. The aim of the present chapter is to highlight the more important of these differences and their broad effects, without going into the detail attempted in Parts 2 and 3 or covering every area of difference. An initial classification of the root causes of differences is as follows:

(a) The three financial bases: quantities (firm by implication), approximate quantities or no quantities (that is, reliance on drawings and specification).
(b) The two types of client: private or local authorities.

The combination of these produces the total of six forms already introduced in Chapter 1, of which five remain to be considered here. While the client types lead to a greater number of differences in wording in the forms, these differences are not so fundamental as those due to the financial bases. In the case of these bases, the use of approximate quantities does however cause more differences than the simple omission of quantities. The sequence of this chapter is therefore to deal with the private forms first, but to grasp the nettle of approximation before the simple lump sum case. The local authority forms are then dealt with fairly easily.

The Private Edition with approximate quantities

At the time of writing this form has not yet been published, but its precise wording may be deduced from the JCT Guide which lists all the differences from the with-quantities edition.

An explanatory note precedes the articles of agreement of this form as follows: 'This Form is for use where the Works have been substantially designed but not completely detailed so that the quantities shown in the Bills are approximate and subject to remeasurement.' While this note is not intended to form part of the contract (and could be deleted in practice to avoid doubt), it does signal the intention to remeasure quite clearly and also indicates that the drawings are still being developed. In itself it says nothing about the status of either bills or drawings as definitions of the work in the contract, or how these definitions are to be clarified later so that the precise works can actually be produced. It may be assumed that the money eventually passing between the parties is contingent upon these three elements of design, communication and quantification, plus the fourth element of pricing. The thread that links the elements may be traced in the aspects of the contract that are now discussed.

THE PREAMBLE TO THE ARTICLES OF AGREEMENT

Two differences are significant here. Firstly there is the expression 'Drawings and Bills of Approximate Quantities showing and describing, and intending to set out a reasonably accurate forecast of, the quantity of the work to be done'. The structure of this expression is such as to establish both drawings and bills as showing and describing the work, which accords with the with-quantities edition and introduces no change in concept. The words in parenthesis make both drawings and bills also forecast the quantity of work, which is not the position under the other with-quantities editions. There the bills alone set out (precisely) the quantity, and the drawings serve to indicate the broad character and arrangement of the works. So long as the works have been 'substantially designed' as stated in the introductory note, and so long as the quantities do reasonably represent the works shown on the drawings, there should be no difficulty — and this is the situation that the form has been drafted to meet. The quantities, being approximate, may well not correspond precisely with the drawings and, even more than firm quantities, they may well include items not to be discerned on the limited number of drawings usually included in the contract. These two factors do not clash with the expression 'reasonably accurate', indeed the second helps to achieve it.

Misunderstanding could conceivably arise if the drawings and bills diverged greatly. While clause 13.1 is clear that the quantity of work in the tender price is that in the bills, there is the possibility of a tenderer forming an inaccurate opinion of the scale of the works and thus, say, mispricing his preliminaries over major items of plant. Clauses 14.5.1.2 and 25.4.13 provide means of adjusting finance and time respectively in these various cases, as is discussed under these clauses. If it is intended to use this form of contract as the best available even where the works have not been 'substantially designed', it would be desirable to amend the present wording and give warning of this in the bills, amplifying matters with some definition of how each set of documents is to serve as the basis of the forecast of scale. This is difficult to do since precision is being sought where things are imprecise, the more so the more rudimentary the design is. Most things are possible here, not so many are prudent however, although other commercial considerations may lead to such an arrangement and the risks it may entail.

The second difference in the preamble is that the contract bills embody 'the

Tender Price' rather than 'the Contract Sum', since the works are to be remeasured and a final sum calculated on this basis rather than by adjustment of the contract sum, in accordance with the second agreement. The tender price is the priced total of the bills and is recorded in this preamble to avoid uncertainty as to the correct set of prices embodied in the contract. It does not appear in the agreement that follows and is not used as a total in the post-contract stage. Its contents are significant for several purposes though.

THE SECOND AGREEMENT IN THE ARTICLES OF AGREEMENT

In the with-quantities editions this agreement records the contract sum and gives it, as adjusted later under the conditions, as the employer's consideration. Here the consideration is not given in figures but is 'such sum or sums as shall become payable' with the total defined as 'the Ascertained Final Sum'. This reflects in particular the concept of complete remeasurement of the works.

CLAUSE 2 — CONTRACTOR'S OBLIGATION

Since the contract drawings and the contract bills are likely to differ in quantity shown owing to the partial development of the design and the approximation in measurement, the contractor's duty to report any differences to the architect under clause 2.2.2.2 is here limited to reporting differences of description, while under the other editions there is no express limitation. Effects flow from this difference in clauses 25, 26 and 28 in particular.

CLAUSE 4 — ARCHITECT'S INSTRUCTIONS

The wording here is identical with that under the other editions, including clause 4.1.2 under which the architect may bring in other persons to carry out work which the contractor has failed to perform as and when instructed. To operate this provision in a case in which the work concerned represents a measurable addition to the total extent of the work, and is not for instance remedial work, the work should be measured and valued and included in certificates and in the ascertained final sum. The total and usually different costs incurred by the employer should then be deducted from these sums. In clause 2.2.2.2 '(error) in quantity' has been omitted as not relevant here, while the effect of major inaccuracies in forecasting quantities is taken up in clauses 14 and 25.

CLAUSE 5 — CONTRACT DOCUMENTS

Except for the introduction of 'approximate' to qualify the quantities, this clause reads just as in the with-quantities editions. Since the contract drawings may well be 'approximate' also, clause 5.4 dealing with further drawings to 'explain and amplify' does not necessarily cover all cases, and the discussion under clause 14 about variations should be noted.

CLAUSE 6 — STATUTORY OBLIGATIONS, NOTICES, FEES AND CHARGES

Under clause 6.2 of the other editions the amounts of particular statutory fees and charges 'shall be added to the Contract Sum unless' they happen to be in particular categories already included in the contract sum. In the present clause the words 'shall be included in the calculation of the Ascertained Final Sum unless they are included in the Sub-Contract Sum or Tender Price' have been substituted. The present wording strictly means that such fees and charges as were covered in the contract bills by, for instance, a directly priced item or as part of a prime cost sum would not be recoverable by the contractor at the end of the day as part of the ascertained final sum. Since the ascertained final sum is defined in clause 30.6.2.6 as the aggregate of various items including these fees and charges, there plainly exists a conflict between the two clauses, with the present clause in the wrong if strictly interpreted. It reads better with 'unless . . .' deleted. The contractor would be on strong ground in asking for the discrepant conditions as printed to be construed in his favour.

CLAUSE 13 — CONTRACT BILLS

This clause is repositioned, renumbered and renamed from being 'Contract Sum' to act as an introduction for clause 14. There are two differences from clause 14 of the with-quantities editions. In clause 13.1 'Tender Price' is substituted for 'Contract Sum': this leaves the bills in the same position as stating the quality and quantity included in the contract. The importance of quantity being included is that it gives a defined basis from which to operate parts of clauses 14 and 25. The use of the term 'reasonably accurate forecast' in the articles of agreement has already been discussed and links with this clause. The other difference is the omission of any clause 13.2 containing parallel wording to that in clause 14.2. This is because the prohibition on the tender price being 'adjusted or altered' is not relevant. It also means that the positive statement about errors in computation being accepted by the parties has also been lost. Although this reflects normal practice, inserting such wording in the preliminaries of the contract bills will avoid argument.

CLAUSE 14 — MEASUREMENT AND VALUATION OF WORK, INCLUDING VARIATIONS AND PROVISIONAL SUMS

This is in many ways the key distinctive clause of these conditions, as it provides the essential authority for complete remeasurement. Its wording follows the with-quantities pattern and detail to a great extent, and much of the comment that is needed flows from the difference in operation.

Some care is needed on the architect's part in interpreting and working to clauses 14.1 to 14.3 covering definitions and instruction of variations etc. The only difference in wording is that in the definition of variations in clause 14.1.1 here the references to alteration of quantity which appears in the other editions is omitted since all quantities are approximate. 'Modification of the design' as used in this and the other editions would appear, in any case, on a broad interpretation to embrace a variation that changed quantity without changing quality or other aspects of specification. Under the parallel versions of the contract, the tacit position is that there exists alongside the contract drawings a further series of details in harmony with the contract set, and waiting to be issued during progress to amplify them under clause 5.4. The present clauses do nothing to dispel this idea, and clause 2.1 and the articles of agreement do not help. Only in the non-contractual note preceding the articles is the reality made clear.

In working to the clauses, therefore, the architect needs to take account of the position outlined and also of the realities of the design. If the contract drawings are correct so far as they go, even if incomplete, then he can proceed to supplement them under clause 5.4 and to vary them under the present clauses. Whether a particular drawing is a supplement or a variation may be a somewhat academic point and he should err on the safe side and use a variation when in doubt. If the contract drawings are substantially incorrect because the design has developed in a different direction, it may be best for the first variation order to say something like 'omit all contract drawings and start with the fresh set enclosed'. If this is done, all drawings subsequently issued are strictly variation drawings and should be covered by orders accordingly, since no contract drawings remain to be supplemented.

The danger area lies somewhere between correct and incorrect drawings where patch-up modifications may be attempted. The risk then is that the contractor may not correctly distinguish between instructions to be followed and those which have been superseded. Again if in doubt a clean sweep is advisable.

Clauses 14.4 to 14.6 focus attention on the quantity surveyor dealing with the 'Measurement and Valuation of Work' which is the substituted title of clause 14.4 in particular, while no clause 14.7 is needed in this edition. The provisions here are fundamental to the approximate-quantities arrangement, as indicated by the amended wording in clause 14.4.1 'All work carried out in accordance with clause 2.1 and . . . instructions issued under clauses 14.2 and 14.3'. The three references cover the works as in the contract documents, variations and expenditure of provisional sums, so that complete valuation of the works as executed is required.

The valuation rules of clause 14.5 are those of the with-quantities edition with only minor drafting changes in the main. More importantly, in the place of the earlier expression 'significantly changes the quantity' the reference in clause 14.5.1.2 is to 'Where the quantity of the work was not reasonably accurately forecast (in the Contract Bills)'; while in clause 14.5.5 the non-execution because of an instruction of 'work shown on the Contract Drawings and included in the Tender Price' may lead to an amended valuation of other work, the surrounding conditions but not the substance of which are changed as a result. These two expressions are linked to that commented on in the first recital of the articles, where both drawings and bills are intended to give the forecast. The former expression refers only to the bills in relation to quantity, while the second refers to the drawings and to the bills via the tender price, in relation to conditions. This is a fair distinction but, as discussed under the articles, there is a problem here if the content of the drawings and the content of the bills do not tally closely enough.

In principle these provisions give the same flexibility under remeasurement as is given under variations and, as has been commented, restraint is also needed in making use of them in the present case. The uncertainties inherent in tendering on approximate quantities and the extent of changes likely during construction do however increase the justification for using these powers.

'Clause 14.5.2 (Number not used)' marks the obvious, that there is no need for a provision for valuing omissions under this contract.

CLAUSE 25 — EXTENSION OF TIME

An additional clause, 25.4.13, is the sole difference here and introduces a distinctive cause for extension of time where the quantity of work was not reasonably accurately forecast and delay has resulted from performing extra work or work of a different character. This clause ties in wording with the articles of agreement and also relates to the statement in clause 14.1 that the contract bills set out the quantity of work included in the tender price. It is distinct from the introduction of additional work by way of variations. The adjustment of contract prices provided under clause 14.5.3.3 is wide enough to permit a corresponding adjustment of preliminaries in this one case of extension of time. This novelty is balanced by the absence of any loss and expense reimbursement under clause 26 or of a right for the contractor to determine under clause 28, either of which would be contrary to the spirit of the contract whereby the parties accept some operating uncertainty.

There is no reference here to the inadequacy of the contract drawings as a forecast, which the articles of agreement set them up to be. Should they be inadequate as is discussed under the articles, the contractor would need to rely on the effects of architect's instructions to secure an extension, as clause 25.4.5.1 provides. There is also no provision for advancing the completion date if too much work has been forecast, not even by reducing an existing extension.

CLAUSE 26 — LOSS AND EXPENSE CAUSED BY MATTERS MATERIALLY AFFECTING REGULAR PROGRESS OF THE WORKS

The lack of any mention of quantity of work in clause 2.3 as an area of discrepancy means that the reference to that clause here does not lead to any reimbursement arising out of inaccurate forecasting of quantity, this being covered in various ways by clause 14.5. Inaccurate forecasting is not likely in any case to affect regular progress.

CLAUSE 28 — DETERMINATION BY CONTRACTOR

The omission just mentioned also prevents the contractor from seeking determination for suspension of the works in any way related to inaccurate forecasting of quantity. If the contract drawings were particularly inaccurate, delay in issuing revisions or even the effect of variations to them might lead to suspension and thus to determination in some extreme case, but this would be a quite distinct cause. Only if there is severe misrepresentation might the contractor have a quite distinct ground for seeking to determine.

CLAUSE 30 — CERTIFICATES AND PAYMENTS

This clause differs in substance from the with-quantities editions in two ways only. One is that clause 30.1.2 makes interim valuations obligatory for ascertaining amounts due, as there are no firm quantities.

The other is in clause 30.6.2 dealing with the ascertained final sum. This lists the elements which are to be aggregated, mostly corresponding with those for additions in with-quantities clauses 30.6.2.6 to 30.6.2.16. The first is 'the amount of the valuation of the work' to take account of complete measurement and valuation, which takes the place of the two elements in the with-quantities clause for valuations of variations and provisional sum expenditure. But there is also clause 30.6.2.9 to cover 'any amounts due to the Employer'. These are credit items, but can easily be taken into account in the aggregate mentioned. Oddly though, the items are insurance premiums paid by the employer on the contractor's default under clause 22A.2 and the excess costs to the employer of further nomination under clause 35.18.1.2 and renomination under clause 35.24.6. These are as likely to occur under the with-quantities contract, but are not mentioned in settlement as that contract (like the present document) legislates for their recovery in other ways, as discussed under clause 30.6.2 and the other clauses quoted. There is no explanation for this difference.

Probably the main practical problem in this contract, where everything has to be aggregated rather than adjustments made, is the difficulty of having the whole final account in the hands of the contractor within the six-month period usually named, in those cases where something like a major loss and expense amount under clause 26 cannot be properly calculated unless the rest of the account is at least approaching completion.

CLAUSES 39 AND 40 — FLUCTUATIONS

Three differences of detail are introduced by comparison with the with-quantities editions. One is that 'the prices in the Contract Bills' (rather than the 'Tender Price') and not 'the Contract Sum' are deemed to have been calculated in the manner given: the reason for this needs no elaboration. A second is that clause 40.2 about mandatory interim valuations is omitted as unnecessary, due to the different wording of clause 30.1.2. The other is that an additional clause 40.8 gives a number of 'deemed amendments' to the formula rules referred to elsewhere in clause 40.

There are points of detail, such as clause numbers, to make the rules dovetail with the present conditions.

Of more substance is the omission of the alternative of clause 38 providing for fluctuation adjustment based on costs and limited to statutory effects. This is the result of the contract's philosophy that, where the quantity of work is uncertain, it is not reasonable to restrict the scope of fluctuations and thus introduce another uncertainty. It would be possible to introduce clause 38 without undue complication, but this should be considered only in the case of quantities that approximate closely to accuracy and in highly stable market conditions.

The Private Edition without quantities

The title of this edition indicates that no contract bills are included in the contract documents. More positively, the specification is included in the list of documents under clause 2.1. The schedule of rates mentioned later in the conditions is not named as a contract document, but becomes part of the contract in many cases, as is discussed.

Underlying these arrangements is the implied intention that this contract is for use primarily for projects not warranting quantities as part of the contract. Such projects will usually be modest in scale, such as a single house, or may be those rather larger but of an essentially simple type, such as a plain shed-like building. It is therefore disconcerting to find that the present conditions are as long as those envisaging quantities, because they are identical at every possible point. They include, for instance, the full rigour of the two methods of nomination of sub-contractors, where it is hoped that the 'alternative' method will be used when possible. There are some areas, such as indemnity and insurance, where fulsome wording is inevitable. This said, there appears to be a need for an intermediate contract form for suitable simple, and probably small, projects. All of this is something of a warning that in many cases the present form may qualify for the sledgehammer and nut award! In view of its content, it does have the virtue of needing only very selective comment here.

THE SPECIFICATION

This is referred to throughout the conditions in place of the contract bills, with particular effect in parts of clauses 2, 5 and 14, dealing respectively with the contractor's obligations, the contract documents and the contract sum.

These elements are interlocking. Clause 14.1 establishes the specification and also, in this case, the contract drawings as respectively describing and showing 'the quality and quantity of work included in the Contract Sum', while still leaving the conditions paramount. Clause 2.2.2 deals with the question of error and omission from the specification and the contract drawings and introduces possible uncertainty into the present contract. In the with-quantities editions the broad philosophy is that the contract drawings show the arrangement of the works contracted for, and the contract bills show the quality and also the quantity. If the two leave uncertainty as to what is to be done, an architect's instruction is to be sought under with-quantities clause 2.3, and if the drawings are at fault they will be corrected under that clause. If the contract bills are in error or deficient, they are to be corrected in the final account as a deemed variation under with-quantities clause 2.2.2.2.

The position under clause 2.3 remains clear in the present edition. In the case of clause 2.2.2 and 14.1 there are two doubts. One is the subject-matter of error or omission: there are no 'quantities' in the two documents and clause 14.3, discussed below, specifically excludes any 'supplied to the Contractor' from the contract. What then is an 'item' that might have been omitted? At best it can be a clause for the specification or a complete piece of work for the drawings that may have been left out without the omission being apparent. This is troublesome in view of cases like *Williams* v. *Fitzmaurice* which indicate that the contractor must include in his price for work shown in only one document, leading to the presumption that the contractor has priced anything shown in this way but, obviously, has not included what he has no means of knowing about. Apart from price, there is the question of action: if something is in one document and not the other, is it always clear that it is required at all and that it has not been included by mistake? If it is erroneously in both or in neither how can the contractor safely either leave it out or put it in without being covered by an architect's instruction under clause 2.3? The second doubt really underlies the first: it is that the relation of the two documents is not defined and therefore the contractor, in carrying out the works and for that matter the quantity surveyor in valuing them, has no unambiguous working guide lines. It would seem that the appeal must always be to clause 2.3 and not to clauses 2.2.2 and 14.1.

Since the contractor, under this without-quantities edition, must tender as well as build on the basis of the specification the latter must be a full document and not the supplementary document that it is in the with-quantities editions. It must, equally, not require supplementing if it is to fulfil both purposes. There is reference in clause 3(2) to the architect supplying the contractor in the post-contract stage with 'any descriptive schedules or other like document', which is disquieting, because unless they arise out of variations he should not be receiving any in the first place.

THE SCHEDULE OF RATES

Without the schedule of rates, variations could prove difficult to value under this contract, since there is no analysis of the contract sum. Clause 5.3.1.3 allows for the schedule to be provided by the contractor after signing of the contract, if it has not already been provided. It is far better for it to be provided and agreed at the tender stage, to avoid argument later as to whether, with no quantities to act as a bridge, it reflects the same level of pricing as the tender. It is best constructed by taking the contractor's build-up of his tender and using as many of the rates in that as are considered necessary, while ignoring the quantities for contract purposes. Alternatively an unpriced schedule can be sent out to tender for completion then, although this may need careful assessment of the level of prices.

Clause 14.3 is extra in this edition and emphasises the contractual status of the schedule of rates as against 'rates and prices and anything contained in' bills of quantities or the like supplied to the contractor for tendering purposes. There is little virtue in such bills of quantities, since the contractor is unable to rely on their accuracy or completeness and has no redress if they are wrong. It is far better for him to come to his own conclusions by his own methods.

The schedule of rates is referred to throughout clause 13.5 as the basis for variations. It should also contain daywork terms as the clause requires, and details of profit on nominated sub-contractors and suppliers to permit final adjustments in accordance with clauses 30.6.2.1 and 30.6.2.9.

CONTRACT DRAWINGS

The general position of the contract drawings under this edition is quite clear, while the problem arising under clause 2.2.2 has been mentioned in relation to any divergence from the specification. Clause 5.4 however repeats the with-quantities clause, so that the architect provides any 'further drawings and details . . . to explain and amplify the Contract Drawings', among other things.

Since the contractor needs all drawings and details for pricing purposes in the absence of bills of quantities, any serious use of this clause can be regarded only with concern. No architect should consider using this type of contract unless he can provide full drawing information with a detailed specification.

SUB-CONTRACTORS

There are two odd quirks here, resulting from too close similarity to the with-quantities edition that might give rise to doubt. Clause 19.3.1 dealing with persons named as possible domestic sub-contractors refers to 'work described in the Specification' and this would appear adequate for delineation, since such work cannot be construed as nominated work. The clause continues with 'and priced in the Schedule of Rates', which will only be true if the schedule of rates is comprehensive. To avoid debate because *both* conditions have not been fulfilled, the precaution is obvious: have it 'priced'.

Clause 35.1 contains the same last sentence as does its with-quantities counterpart referring to the Standard Method of Measurement. This does not form the basis of the specification in any way and is not incorporated into the contract by reference. The sentence is therefore strictly meaningless, and there is no need to include any reference to the Standard Method in the specification as its absence does not lead to any deficiency in definition.

FLUCTUATIONS

Clause 40 does not appear in this edition as there are no contract bills to supply the necessary data for formula adjustment. The schedule of rates is unsuitable and no other bills of quantities could be used as that clause envisages.

THE QUANTITY SURVEYOR

The articles of agreement and conditions refer to the quantity surveyor in the same way as the with-quantities editions. Frequently there will not be a separate quantity surveyor appointed for the small job based on this present edition. If for instance the architect intends to agree the final account himself his name should be filled in to the articles of agreement as being the quantity surveyor. There is no legal objection to this, since the use of the title is in no way restricted.

The Local Authorities edition with quantities

ARTICLE 3 — THE ARCHITECT OR SUPERVISING OFFICER

This article recognises two points of difference from private practice. First, the appropriate chief officer of a local authority may or may not be a registered architect; there are therefore alternative versions of the article to allow for either possibility. One of these versions must be deleted, but once this has been done, the related footnote to the article states that it is unnecessary to delete one of the terms 'architect' or 'supervising officer', which are both used throughout the conditions and which, thanks to the footnote, will be interpreted in whichever way is appropriate.

Secondly, where a local authority employs its own chief officer rather than appoint an outside architect it becomes unsatisfactory for the contractor to be able to object to any successor and this part of the article is to be deleted.

ARTICLE 4 — THE QUANTITY SURVEYOR

The second difference from private practice mentioned in connection with Article 3 also applies here.

ATTESTATION CLAUSE

This clause is left blank for detailing by the parties. Under the Corporate

Bodies Contract Act 1960 a local authority is not obliged to contract under seal, although many will still do so to secure the advantages that this brings, particularly that of a longer limitation period.

CLAUSE 19A — FAIR WAGES

The first six sub-clauses of this clause repeat the House of Commons' Fair Wages Resolution of 1946, with a few amendments to make the wording appropriate to a contract. Clauses 19A.7 and 19A.8 deal with the question of proof that the earlier clauses are being observed. They contain no means of enforcing observance, but an addition to clause 27.1.4 permits the employer to determine if there is a breach. This could be quite onerous, since the contractor is made responsible for sub-contractors under the present clause and he may have little evidence available to him. The only consolation is that wages and so forth are hardly likely to be 'less favourable' than those quoted!

CLAUSE 22 — INSURANCE OF THE WORKS AGAINST CLAUSE 22 PERILS

Clause 22B transfers the specified risks to the employer, but then differs from the private edition by not requiring insurance against those risks. A local authority may thus elect in effect to become its own insurer.

Clause 22C however requires the employer to insure, which seems inconsistent with the foregoing. It then provides no right for the contractor to check that this has been done or to act if he somehow finds out that it has not. This in turn is inconsistent with the private edition, although the contractor is not put at any real risk in this case.

CLAUSE 27 — DETERMINATION BY EMPLOYER

As mentioned under Clause 19A, breach of that clause becomes a cause for determination under clause 27.1.4 after a warning. An additional clause 27.3 is included in this edition. This provides for determination in the case of corruption; there is no period of notice and a single occurrence is sufficient, but the power to determine is optional. The clause is particularly onerous, since it covers 'any gift or consideration' without limit as to its value, so long as it is intended to corrupt and whether it was accepted or not. The clause becomes quite unjust however by making the qualification 'whether with or without the knowledge of the Contractor'. It does not extend to sub-contractors, which is some consolation to the contractor. The whole clause arises out of the model standing orders to which local authorities are subject, but it is no more palatable for that.

CLAUSE 28 — DETERMINATION BY CONTRACTOR

Clause 28.1.4 of the private edition, which provides for determination on the insolvency of the employer, is omitted here for obvious reasons: the ratepayers are always at hand.

CLAUSE 30 — CERTIFICATES AND PAYMENTS

Two clauses are omitted here: clause 30.5.3 requiring a separate trust account and clause 30.6.2.14 concerning reimbursement of the contractor for insuring on the employer's default. Clause 30.8 does not have a fixed period of three months from the end of the defects liability period to regulate the issue of the final certificate. Instead the period is to be inserted in an additional space in the appendix, where it is required by a footnote that the period should not exceed six months. A period of three months will apply if no insertion is made. This flexibility is presumably to allow for audit. The employer may not, however, seek to delay the issue of the final certificate beyond the period named on the grounds that the audit has not taken place; the certificate should be issued and the contractor is entitled to full payment. Any matter raised by audit should be dealt with under clause 30.9.1.2 and the sums recovered from the contractor, or conceivably, passed to him.

CLAUSES 38, 39 AND 40 — FLUCTUATIONS

The clauses follow the private edition throughout. There is however a provision in the appendix for the 'non-adjustable element' not to exceed 10 per cent, in respect of clause 40.1.1.1, which is the introduction to the formula adjustment provisions. The non-adjustable element is defined in the formula rules and means that the gross amount of fluctuations calculated is subject to a reduction of up to 10 per cent without any discrimination between work categories.

The Local Authorities edition with approximate quantities

This edition differs from the private edition with quantities by the sum of the distinctive features of the two obvious editions already considered in this chapter and thus calls for no further comment of its own.

The Local Authorities edition without quantities

The remarks under the last heading apply equally here.

CHAPTER 22

The JCT form with contractor's design

The document discussed in this chapter is titled the JCT Standard Form of Building Contract 'With Contractor's Design' 1981 Edition. It differs from most of the JCT contract forms in that it is in its first-ever edition. It also differs from *all* the other JCT forms and the other forms considered in this book in another and more significant way: the contractor accepts all design liability as well as construction responsibility after the employer's initial briefing. This goes much further than a provision for, say, some design work to be carried out by a nominated sub-contractor as a supplement to the architect's work. As a result, the form does not make express provision for an architect, nor for a quantity surveyor.

The principles of the form

While other contract forms of such an all-service or package contract are by no means unknown or novel, some introductory comments on the principles of this particular form are needed before its clauses are examined. JCT Practice Notes CD1A and CD1B also expand on several of these points.

(a) The needs of public sector housing in particular underlie the introduction of the form, although this has not influenced its drafting. It is available in one version to suit private and public employers, with options within it to take account of the type of employer.

(b) Like all other contract forms considered in this book, the form is a modified entire contract. It is based upon drawings and a specification and the financial basis is a lump sum, although with a supporting analysis. The contract sum covers remuneration for both design and construction.

(c) The nature of the employer's brief and invitation prior to the contract is left quite open. In the words of the practice note, there 'may be little more than a description of accommodation required, or may be anything up to a full "Scheme Design"'. The brief may be simply a gleam in the employer's eye or take the form of detailed proposals with drawings by the employer's consultants. Only delineation of the site is expressly required of the employer. The method of selection of the contractor, whether competitive or negotiated, is also not basic to this form, any more than it is to any of the others. What is important is that what are termed 'the Employer's Requirements' must be embodied in the contract in full. The whole brief must be given, including any preliminary and conditioning design work and such elements as planning permission obtained in full or part. The brief may have been modified during the pre-contract proceedings, while its effect may be further modified by the next item.

(d) The nature of the contractor's design and specification is left equally open. So far as its extent goes, this is inevitable because it interprets and supplements the very variable contents of the employer's requirements. The necessary degree of explicitness of these 'Contractor's Proposals' will depend on factors such as the complexity of the work and whether or not system building is used. The conditions do not assume that design has been finalised in all respects when the contract is entered into, or that statutory approvals have been obtained. Work not performed by the employer becomes the responsibility of the contractor and this approximates broadly to that assumed by the architect in the other forms. Again, the whole of the contractor's proposals must be included in the contract, so that it is clear precisely what has been done and agreed and what remains to be completed in design and so on.

(e) The breakdown of the contract sum is termed 'the Contract Sum Analysis'. It is obligatory in the evaluation of design changes and when formula fluctuations apply. It is also useful, but not obligatory, for calculating interim payments under one of the contract alternatives. Its form will vary according to the nature of the project, although the practice notes include possible divisions and also a suggestion that design work before and during construction should be distinguished and that both should be kept separate from construction costs.

(f) During progress of the works several matters follow from the pattern established: the contractor carries through construction along with any development of the design and obtaining of consents and produces 'as-built' drawings; the employer keeps a watch over progress and quality and may initiate changes in the design; the parties agree between themselves the resolution of discrepancies, programme changes, valuation of changes and amounts of fluctuations, or in the absence of agreement resort to arbitration or the like. A choice of patterns for payments on account is provided. The absence of an architect or quantity surveyor to hold the balance may be noted. If the employer engages these or other consultants, they will be present solely to safeguard his interests. They 'are' the employer as far as the contract goes, where there is limited reference to the employer's agent, who may be one of them so designated, or some other inspector such as a clerk of works.

(g) There is no provision for any nomination of either sub-contractors or suppliers. Simple approval of sub-letting proposed by the contractor alone is included for both construction and design. In some cases in a developed scheme design, it would be possible for the employer's requirements to stipulate particular firms to whom sub-letting was restricted. Such action would need care to avoid incongruities in a contract approach that does not encourage it.

The usual pattern of comment follows, but the foregoing points should be kept in mind, partly because they draw attention to silences in the conditions.

Clauses are compared with the JCT Private With Quantities clauses where appropriate, these being referred to as 'quantities clauses'. Clauses are mentioned only where differences arise, unless these are minor and predictable effects of other changes, needing no comment. The clauses not discussed here are:

Clause 3   Contract sum — additions or deductions — adjustment — interim payments

Clause 10 Person in charge

Clause 13 Contract sum

Clause 14 Value added tax — supplemental provisions (although the practice note covers practical detail here)

Clause 19 Fair wages (option applying only when the employer is a local authority)

Clause 20 Injury to persons and property and employer's indemnity

Clause 24 Damages for non-completion

Clause 31 Finance (No 2) Act 1975 — statutory tax deduction scheme

Clause 32 Outbreak of hostilities

Clause 33 War damage

Clause 34 Antiquities

Articles of agreement

Prefacing the articles is a note to the effect that the form is intended only for use when the contractor is responsible for complete design of the scheme based upon the employer's requirements, and that if only a portion of the works is to be designed by the contractor then the 'Contractor's Designed Portion Supplement' is available instead (See chapter 23).

The articles follow the usual pattern and need only selective comment. Neither they nor the conditions define the contract documents precisely, but these appear to be the articles, the conditions and the three appendices and also the employer's requirements and contractor's proposals referred to in article 4 'as stated in Appendix 3 and the Contract Sum Analysis'. This reflects the variations in content of the requirements and the proposals from project to project. In the third recital it is stated that 'the Employer . . . is satisfied that (the Contractor's Proposals) appear to meet the requirements of the Employer'. The conjunction of 'satisfied' and 'appear to' is strange and possibly contentious; the contractor, at least, might be happier without the latter. It is suggested in a footnote (which therefore does not form part of the contract) to the recital that any divergence accepted by the employer should be regularised by amendment of the employer's requirements. It is implicit in the form that any other divergence between the requirements and the proposals which has originated from the contractor has been accepted by the employer, errors apart. If this is so, then 'appear' would appear, equally, to mean that the proposals correctly interpret the requirements, which are themselves accepted and contractually binding. Clauses 2.3 and 2.4 expand on such issues. The practice notes explain that 'appears' is intended to mean that the two elements do 'correspond' on their faces, but this is not to erode the contractor's liability to produce final designs and specifications that in fact fulfil the employer's requirements over quality and performance. It would lead to more certainty in legal interpretation if the recital itself actually said this.

The contractor's obligation is given in article 1 as including that he 'will complete the design' (a point discussed under clause 2.1), while the contract sum is qualified in article 2 by 'or such other sum as shall become payable' to take account of later provisions. The employer's agent may be named under article 3 and the employer may also name 'such other person' later. From the wording of the clause such other person is obviously intended to act instead of but might conceivably act in addition to the employer's agent, if his function is clearly distinguished. The article allows of the agent acting for such purposes of communication as 'the Employer shall specify by written notice'. Such notice may be given or changed when the works are under way.

An important addition to article 5 is that early arbitration is permitted over 'whether either party has withheld or delayed a consent or statement' in cases in which the conditions include the usual criterion of reasonableness. In the absence of the architect, this is needed to avoid possible deadlock over the flow of information and the incorporation of design changes, for example. It underlines the potentially greater scope for arbitration in a contract on this basis.

Clause 1 — Interpretation, definitions, etc

This clause fulfils the same purpose as quantities clause 1. While it contains a few extra definitions, such as the date of tender, it also omits several appearing in that clause. The significant ones are covered under related clauses. Clause 1.2 supports the suggested list of contract documents put forward under the articles.

Clause 2 — Contractor's obligations

This clause is central to the differences under these conditions, while it follows the general framework of quantities clause 2. Clause 2.1 makes the contractor responsible for carrying out the works in accordance with the apparent contract documents mentioned again by name. As stated above in paragraphs (d) and (e), design and specification may not be complete when the contract is signed. There is a tension in the pre-contract stage: the employer prefers to know precisely what he is getting before he is committed, while the contractor does not wish to do too much work before he is sure of obtaining the contract, unless he has been assured of payment should the project be called off. Both parties will be constrained by the impending contract sum which will be adjustable only in ways similar to those given in the quantities clauses. If as a result there is fuzziness in the post-contract stage, only the provisions over divergences in clause 2.3 and discrepancies in clause 2.4 may be looked to for help.

It is however clearly provided in clause 2.1 that the contractor is to complete the design and to select materials, goods and workmanship 'so far as not described or stated in the Employer's Requirements or the Contractor's Proposals'. This design and specification is left to the contractor's discretion, although it is tempered by his design warranty under clause 2.5. It may be noted that while an architect may seek to protect himself by keeping standards high (subject to not exceeding the project budget) as he does not meet the extra cost himself, the contractor has to balance this consideration against the fact that he *does* meet the extra cost without being able to recover it from the employer. Thus the better developed the design, the smaller and more precise will be the design contingency that the contractor needs to include and the smaller will be the risk of the employer paying in the fixed contract sum for this hidden contingency without receiving a full return for it. The value of the design warranty here is limited. A particular material for instance may *not* represent a design fault but may still have a shorter life or higher maintenance cost than an initially dearer alternative.

Clause 2.2 makes the usual point that the other documents do not override the articles, the conditions and (this time) the appendices. Presumably this last has to be read as 'elsewhere in the Appendices', since in Appendix 3 are listed (if not actually contained) the employer's requirements and the contractor's proposals.

Clause 2.3 deals with divergences and clause 2.4 with discrepancies within either the employer's requirements or the contractor's proposals, but not as between the two. Recital 3 of the articles and its footnote seek to eliminate any differences between the two sets of documents. As mentioned under the articles, the position taken by the conditions is that in any conflict the proposals will prevail, so the employer needs to be well assured of his position before committing himself. The contractor has the clear advantage of the last word!

Under clause 2.3.1 divergences from the employer's side are considered only between his requirements proper and the post-contract definition of the site under clause 7. Since the contractor will have based his proposals on the requirements, any divergence now arising gives occasion for a change (the term used in this contract for a variation). Any other divergence is not considered and can only be treated as a discrepancy under clause 2.4.1.

For the purpose of clause 2.4.1 the employer's requirements are enlarged to include any change under clause 12.2. This done, it is stated that the contractor's proposals are to prevail over discrepancies *within* the employer's requirements, so that the alternative chosen by the contractor within his proposals is binding and the contract sum is unchanged. This is straightforward in the case of the original employer's requirements, but in the case of extra requirements as changes it is more difficult. If there is a discrepancy between an original requirement and something assumed as the basis for a change (such as to substitute 'A' for 'B', when in fact 'C' is in the contract and not 'B'), the contractor can act logically and fairly. If there is a discrepancy entirely within the change requirement itself, the contractor's proposals can prevail only if the change is ignored in so far as it is in conflict. Neither this approach nor the contractor constructing his own interpretation can be construed as reasonable. The contractor should rather refer back the change for clarification.

Clause 2.4.2 allows the employer to choose, without extra cost to himself, between alternatives thrown up by discrepancies in the contractor's proposals. In effect this parallels clause 2.4.1, under which the contractor is held to have made his choice between discrepancies in the employer's requirements when putting forward his proposals. This is an intriguing quid pro quo. In the present case, the choice has still to be made and this should be done reasonably, as there is a possibility of abuse. For this reason the contractor must first inform the employer of his proposed solution, so that the employer has notice of the contractor's views. But ultimately the choice lies with the employer.

Both clauses 2.3.2 and 2.4.3 require the party discovering the divergence or discrepancy to notify the other at once. Whichever set of documents contained a discrepancy, it is the position that the resolution must comply with statute. This may effectively override the earlier provisions about which document is to prevail in a conflict, by invalidating its content.

Clause 2.5 takes up the critical issue of the contractor's responsibility as designer, with the mainstay in clause 2.5.1. As some design may have been carried out by the employer and some development control requirements satisfied and embodied in his requirements, the contractor is responsible only for those remaining. The contractor's responsibilities fall into three categories: any outstanding to meet the employer's requirements, those arising from his own proposals, and any resulting from a change in requirements.

For this whole area of design work the contractor is liable to the employer in the same way as 'an architect or . . . other appropriate professional designer' acting in a separate contractual relationship with the employer. This embraces the exercise of discretion by the contractor in respect of the nature of the finished works and not just how they are achieved physically, as under the other conditions. Some implications of this have been mentioned under clause 2.1. But also it opens a whole avenue of responsibility that is beyond the present discussion of the conditions themselves (see cases under 'Design liability of contractor'), but that clearly needs a contractor to take out appropriate indemnity insurance, even if he is employing consultants on his own behalf who may have such insurance. In particular, clause 30.8.1 which establishes the final account and the final statement as equivalent to the final certificate under the quantities clauses in no way diminishes the contractor's liability running for the usual period. There is no direct requirement under the conditions to take out such an insurance, but the practice note expands on the issues at stake.

Whether or not the employer has his own consultant acting for him as agent under article 3, it is vital that neither the employer nor any such person acts in any way that could transfer responsibility for design from the contractor to the employer, or that might divide responsibility. While the employer's requirements may provide specifically for inspection of the contractor's proposals and of their later development by the employer or the agent, this should be couched in such a way and be so carried out in practice that any suggestion of approval or other positive endorsement is avoided. It is better to adopt some formula that is neutral or almost negative, such as that the contractor's design is accepted 'as meeting the requirements of the Employer' (similar to the expression in recital 3 of the articles) but that this acceptance is not to diminish the contractor's warranty under the present clause.

For his part the contractor should ensure that he does not, via the employer's requirements or otherwise, accept responsibility for the employer's prior design work or groundwork, such as obtaining approvals, unless he is fully able to check the work. Apart from design responsibility, there may be unexpected expense in overcoming problems and loss of right to extension of time or payments for loss and expense. It must be very clear in the employer's requirements or in their expansion what has been done and what is still to be done over such matters as statutory permissions.

Clause 2.5.2 is a rider applying when the subject of the contract is the design and construction of one or more dwellings, when the Defective Premises Act 1972 applies unavoidably. The Act imposes obligations as to fitness and so forth upon the contractor as vendor and as performer of the work and upon the employer also if he sells later. This is therefore an extension of straight design warranty, despite the title of clause 2.5, and includes a warranty as to the quality of the product. Under Section 2(1) of the Act an 'approved scheme', such as the National House Building Council Scheme, imposing a higher level of obligation upon the contractor initially may be substituted for the stated minima. In such a case, the present clause requires both the contractor and the employer to do their respective parts in seeing that a 'document of a type approved' (as the Act has it) is issued for 'the purposes of Section 2(1)(a)'. The approved scheme is to be given in Appendix 1.

Clause 2.5.3 is an alternative rider when the work does not comprise dwellings 'to which . . . the Act . . . applies'. The Act still applies to the work, though under its Sections 3 and 4. It is not against the statute to limit the contractor's liability here, and this should be done by entry in Appendix 1.

As this liability covers not just 'loss of use (and) loss of profit' for the employer, but also 'other consequential loss' which could arise in respect of third parties in tort, the amount entered should be assessed realistically high. The term 'limited to the amount, if any, named' is perhaps ambiguous, but the more likely construction is that if no amount is named then there is no liability, so that an entry is needed to activate the clause. The clause ends with a proviso that liability here cannot be construed as absorbing any liability which the contractor may incur to pay or allow liquidated damages. Under the present contract these might arise out of a delay due to late or faulty design, as well as late or faulty construction. Such lapses will occur during the construction period, which is not the primary reference of the clause. 'Other consequential loss' may however occur during that period and should be allowed for in assessing the limit.

Finally clause 2.5.4 defines the contractor's design as including any design 'prepared or issued by others'. The contractor should therefore ensure that those preparing designs are warned of and covered for their share of liability. In the case of design issued by others there is the situation where the contractor takes a ready prepared design, such as a standard system. In this case he may find that he is not only directly, but also solely liable for a design which he should have checked as being adequate for his purposes.

Clause 4 — Employer's instructions

This clause follows quantities clause 4 in both structure and detail. It therefore gives the contractor a right of reasonable objection to the same types of changes under clause 12.1.2 as are referred to as variations under the other clause. Clause 12.2 widens this by requiring the contractor's positive consent to other changes.

The range of employer's instructions under these conditions is substantially less than under the various conditions where the architect is named.

Clause 5 — Custody and supply of documents

With some substitution of documents, this clause follows the quantities clause 'Contract Documents' in pattern. It conflates into clause 5.3 quantities clauses 5.3 and 5.4 about provision of descriptive schedules and drawings or details, adds information on setting out (there being no other clause on this) and places the responsibility for production of all these on the contractor. No reference is made to the contractor's master programme.

Instead of quantities clause 5.6 on return of documents, there is clause 5.5 requiring the contractor to supply the employer without further charge with 'such drawings and information . . . as may be specified in the documents named in clause 5.1'. These cover the works as built with any installations and maintenance and operating instructions, but only to the extent given in the employer's requirements and the contractor's proposals, so that the parties must be specific. While clause 5.6 places the usual limit on the use of documents provided under clauses 5.1 and 5.3, it does not mention this important category under clause 5.5. The law on copyright would however apply.

There is no clause about certificates, as none are issued under these conditions.

Clause 6 — Statutory obligations, notices, fees and charges

While having a similar framework, this clause differs in a number of significant ways from quantities clause 6. The most onerous addition is that the contractor is made responsible under clause 6.1.1 for complying with development control requirements as well as other statutory requirements, so reflecting his design role. If there is a divergence between any of the larger body of statutory requirements on the one hand and either the employer's requirements or the contractor's proposals on the other, the contractor becomes entirely responsible under clause 6.1.2. He is to propose a solution for the employer's consent. This produces a rather similar effect to that of clause 2.4.2 in that there too the employer may choose between options, subject to compliance with statutory requirements. The similarity extends to financial liability in that the contractor must carry out work entirely at his own cost save as provided in clause 6.3. This latter under clause 6.3.1, allows financial adjustment if there is a change in statutory requirements after the date of tender. This whole pattern adds force to the terms of clause 2.5 that the contractor should check the employer's requirements carefully as well as his own design. In the present case he will be responsible for any divergence from statutory requirements whether he accepts wider responsibility for any design by the employer or not.

Clause 6.3.2 reverses the situation in dealing with amendments to the contractor's proposals due to permission or approval based on development control requirements. Here the issue is simply whether the permission or approval has been given after the date of tender and not, as in clause 6.3.1, whether the over-arching requirements have themselves been changed. This reflects the more variable position in this area of statutory. requirements. If therefore some matter is unsettled at the date of tender, the employer should be as concerned as under the other JCT forms: the primary responsibility in terms of cost, if not the onus of obtaining consents, is still his rather than the contractor's. In particular there may be time between tender and acceptance to take account of a consent granted in the interim, so that the contract sum may be amended accordingly. The responsibility for complying with development control requirements in specific respects may be transferred by insertions in the employer's requirements. In this case the closing proviso of clause 6 prevents a 'Change' being made.

Clause 6.2 covers liability for fees and charges by providing that there will be no adjustment of the contract sum for them, so that the contractor must include for them unless they arise out of an employer's change. The only other possibility is for them to be given as a provisional sum in the employer's requirements. This should reasonably be restricted to cases of major uncertainty; if the employer does not then include a sum, the contractor should ask for one to go into the employer's requirements. A sum included in the contractor's proposals is not strictly open to adjustment under the conditions, as clause 12.3 also suggests.

Despite the apparent rigidity of the foregoing, the contractor may be entitled to related extension of time under clause 25.4.7 or payment for loss and expense under clause 26.2.2.

Clause 7 — Site boundaries

This clause may be quoted in full: 'The Employer shall define the boundaries of the site'.

This laconic statement takes the place of quantities clause 7 over levels and setting out. The employer may choose to define the site by a fence or pegs or, in the manner of the other clause, 'by way of accurately dimensioned drawings'. Either way the definition should enable the contractor then to perform his own setting out, as his own responsibility. If the definition as given diverges from the employer's requirements, clauses 2.3.1 and 25.4.13 allow a change to apply under clause 12.

Clause 8 — Materials, goods and workmanship to conform to description — testing and inspection

The provisions here differ from the quantities clause in two places. There is an expanded clause 8.1 providing for materials, goods and workmanship to be as in the employer's requirements or, failing anything there, as in the contractor's proposals or his specifications issued under clause 5.3. The contractor may substitute in any of these cases only with the employer's consent, which is not to be unreasonably withheld. This arrangement generally gives the employer a control over standards. The weak point is clause 5.3 where the contractor may introduce materials etc without consent, in furtherance of his responsibility and right to design and specify outstanding elements under clause 2.1. The contractor's actions under clauses 2.1 and 5.3 may not however change anything in the requirements or the proposals, unless conceivably this happens in some marginal way in the course of design development. The last sentence of the clause about the limited effect of the employer's consent exemplifies the point made under clause 2.5 about caution in appearing to give approval.

The other difference is the lack of an equivalent to quantities clause 8.5 about excluding persons from the works. The point of this is not clear, and it might even extend if present to an architect or a quantity surveyor engaged by the contractor!

Clause 9 — Copyright, royalties and patent rights

The difference between this clause and quantities clause 9 is indicated by the heading above: the contractor's indemnity of the employer extends to infringements of copyright. The only exceptions are over drawings or models provided by the employer.

Clause 11 — Access for employer's agent etc to the works

This clause substitutes the employer's agent or anyone else authorised by the employer or his agent for the architect under quantities clause 11 as having access to the works or workshop. It does not cover the employer himself, unless perhaps the agent authorises him. For access to sub-contractor's workshops the reference is to 'the Employer and his representatives', with no mention of an agent.

There is no clause corresponding to quantities clause 12 about the clerk of works and such a person will be covered by the present clause. Neither he nor the employer's agent can give any instructions or directions.

Clause 12 — Changes in the employer's requirements and provisional sums

A 'Change in the Employer's Requirements' or simply a 'Change' is defined in clause 12.1 in the same way as a variation in quantities clause 13, so that both design changes and changes in obligations and restrictions are covered. Clause 12.2 extends the parallel by giving the employer power to instruct changes. When these are design changes the contractor must give his consent, which is not to be 'unreasonably delayed or withheld'. (Clause 4.1.1 gives the contractor a right of reasonable objection to the other type of change.) Delay here by the contractor might lead to his plea for extension of time under clause 25.4.5.1 being overruled, or at least to a smaller extension. While the JCT practice note hopefully recommends that only 'unavoidable' changes will be instructed, clause 12.2 still contains the provision that 'no Change . . . shall vitiate this Contract'. There is no need for reference to the employer sanctioning changes already introduced by the contractor.

Clause 12.3 empowers the employer to instruct the contractor on the expenditure of provisional sums within the employer's requirements. The conditions do not allow for provisional sums within the contractor's proposals and even when they are included in the employer's requirements, they should relate to complete parcels of work or other contingencies so that there is no overlap with what the contractor has designed and priced. The instructions for expenditure should in any case require the contractor to perform any necessary design.

The valuation of changes and provisional sum expenditure is authorised by clause 12.4 in similar terms to quantities clause 13.4, with the addition of a reference to adding or omitting related design work. The rules for valuation in clause 12.5 are simplified by comparison with quantities clause 13.5. The main statement is that 'valuation . . . shall be consistent' in level with the values in the contract sum analysis. There are the usual riders about character, conditions of execution and quantity, and that otherwise 'a fair valuation' shall apply. This is wide enough to take in whatever form the contract sum analysis assumes and whatever further rules for valuation it may set out. The values of omissions are to be taken from the analysis, and allowance is to be made for provisions included in the nature of the preliminaries, although the term is not used. Full provision in the usual form is made for daywork.

The definition of the contract sum analysis under clause 1.3 is that it has been prepared in accordance with the employer's requirements, even though clause 2.1 refers to it as annexed to the contractor's proposals. It is therefore the employer who determines its form, having regard to the nature and scale of the works and to the state of development of the design at the time the contract is formalised. It may vary from a number of lump sums to a bill of quantities, or even be part and part. Even if the changes are intended to be minimal, the analysis should be realistic in detail. A few small changes will not warrant a lot of effort in producing the analysis in the first place, but a multitude of small changes may be more trouble without this detail than a few large changes of similar total value that can be priced from much coarser data.

The particular form of the analysis may be such that the cost of design work is not shown separately but is spread over the sums, unit prices or percentage additions in daywork. It may therefore be suitable for the parties to agree that a simple adjustment of these amounts under clause 12.4 will fairly reflect design changes. If however the design changes represent disproportionate additions or omissions it would be reasonable to introduce a suitable adjustment by invoking the last sentence of clause 12.4.

The rest of the clause follows its quantities equivalent except that the contractor, who is responsible for preparing the final account is not required to give the employer (or even his agent) the opportunity to be present at measurement. Only in the case of daywork does the employer necessarily receive advance information. Under clause 30.5.1 he simply checks the final account when complete. The point is discussed further under clause 30.5.

Clause 15 — Unfixed materials and goods

This clause corresponds to quantities clause 16.1 only and so does not relate to materials and goods off-site. The present conditions do not contain a parallel to quantities clause 30.3, although clause 30.2B.1.3 gives the employer a 'discretion' to include such items in payments. The latter clause refers to appendix 2 which includes a clause equivalent to quantities clause 16.2.

Clause 16 — Practical completion and defects liability period

The absence of an architect causes a number of differences in drafting here, most of which need no comment — any more than does the unrelated omission of a parallel to quantities clause 17.5 about frost damage.

Clause 16.1 uses the simple term 'When the Works have reached Practical Completion' and does not substitute the opinion of the employer or the contractor for that of the architect, although the contractor will usually take the initiative. Thus the expression 'which statement' (that of practical completion) 'shall not be unreasonably delayed or withheld' is included to safeguard the contractor's position. A retrospective stated or amended date will right most injustices of delay other than those affecting cash flow matters, especially as 'alleged Practical Completion' will allow an immediate reference to arbitration.

Clause 17 — Partial possession by employer

This clause follows quantities clause 18 closely. Clause 17.1.1 requires the contractor to 'issue an itemised estimate' as the equivalent of the architect's certificate under the other clause. As the contractor is a party to the contract, there is a significant change here. The employer is given no right of objection and the matter is not to be one for early arbitration. Any inaccuracy affects retention, as clause 30.4.1.3 refers to this, while it also affects the contractor's residual insurance of the works and liability to meet liquidated damages. In the case of insurance, a serious inaccuracy could lead to difficulties for the employer.

Clause 18 — Assignments and sub-contracts

The provisions for sub-letting differ here, and clause 18.2.1 consists of an amalgamation of quantities clauses 19.2 and 19.4, requiring the employer's consent to sub-letting of 'the Works' (which here do not include design) and the provision for automatic determination of a sub-contract if the contractor's own employment is determined. The term 'Domestic Sub-Contract' is not needed in the present conditions.

Clause 18.2.2 governs the sub-letting of design in a similar way. There is no provision for automatic determination of any sub-contract for design, in the hope that some sort of continuity can be obtained in this critical matter. When sub-letting does occur, the proviso ensures that the contractor's design liability under clause 2.5 is not removed. There is little problem if the contractor is performing most of the design in-house and just wishes to sub-let a specialised facet of design. But it may be that he wishes to sub-let the whole of the post-contract design development, which may be extensive, or that he has already sub-let the pre-contract work and is logically committed to the same person or persons for the post-contract phase. Again, design and installation may be inextricably linked when someone gives 'a scheme and a price', for instance for a lift installation. Here, with installation costs included, the amount involved may be considerably higher than in a 'design only' case, because of quite different quality and performance considerations flowing from the choice of one sub-contractor rather than another. This question is not unimportant to the employer either. In any such critical case, the employer is advised to ask in his requirements for information about the persons and, if appropriate, the product. Even if the employer does not do this, the contractor should prudently clarify the position in his proposals before the contract is formalised.

Clause 21 — Insurance against injury to persons and property

Apart from the substitution of the employer for the architect at various points, this clause is almost identical with quantities clause 21. Three comments are needed here on clause 21.2 concerning the special insurance in joint names against injury to property which may apply in the contract.

The first of these is the only significant point of difference in the whole clause and occurs in clause 21.2.1. This is the omission of the introductory wording 'where a provisional sum is included in the Contract Bills' and the inclusion of a direct reference to the employer's requirements. If the insurance is required at all, therefore, the contractor must include a non-adjustable amount in his tender. As a consequence there is no equivalent of quantities clause 21.2.3 permitting any adjustment of the contract sum. It should be easier for the contractor to forecast the risk as he is responsible for the design, but even so the extent of his extra responsibility if the insurance is needed should not be underestimated.

The second comment is that clause 21.2.1.2, about omission from the insurance of damage due to errors or omissions in design, does *not* differ from the quantities clause. Such damage will be a matter for cover by professional indemnity insurance. The employer will not be so concerned under this form of contract with whether the contractor's execution was faulty or not, so long as it is clear that either design or execution is at fault. It is up to the contractor and his insurers to allocate these matters, and from this point of view the contractor may be advised to extend his public liability insurance, if this is possible, and so limit the number of potentially contending insurance companies. Professional indemnity insurance is bound to be separate.

The final comment is that clause 21.2.1.3 over damage 'which can reasonably be foreseen to be inevitable' also does *not* differ from the quantities clause. This is reasonable in respect of the insurer, but may point to the necessity of clarifying between the employer and the contractor the question of by whom the inevitability should 'reasonably be foreseen'. In general the employer should point out the risk in his requirements, so that the contractor may state in his proposals whether he is satisfied that he can design so as to overcome the problems and thus take the risk. He will then need to ensure that he has not created problems over his professional indemnity insurance.

Clause 22 — Insurance of the works against clause 22 perils

This clause contains the same three alternatives as the quantities clause and the only difference in substance in the wording is the addition in clause 22A.1 of 'the costs of the design work of the Contractor' to the reinstatement value, while there is the usual percentage otherwise covering 'any professional fees incurred by the Employer'. The percentage must obviously be agreed by the parties.

Clauses 22B.1 and 22C.1 contain no reference to 'the Contractor's design work' to supplement the wording repeated from the quantities clauses and this does not ease interpretation. In the case of the quantities clauses, the employer is responsible to the contractor for insuring the physical element, but whether or not he insures for his fee element is his own concern. In the present clauses the position is the same over these two elements, leaving the contractor's design apparently floating. It may be suggested that if clause 22B.1 or 22C.1 is read alone and not in comparison with other clauses, the terms 'work executed' in the one or 'the Works' in the other includes the design element, as does the contract sum and its analysis.

Under these present clauses there is simply the statement that the elements given are 'at the sole risk of the Employer', and the insurance required of him (even, be it noted, if he is a local authority) must take account of the liability. This is a distinct position from clause 22A.1, where the insurance is for 'the full reinstatement value' of the physical element, and also the cost of design. While therefore the present clauses might appear to cover both design and construction, the wording does not make the point clear to an unwary employer and is equivocal in the light of other clauses. An employer's requirement is needed, so that one party *does* insure.

Clause 23 — Date of possession, completion and postponement

This clause is straightforward. It includes the power for the employer to instruct postponement of design work.

Clause 25 — Extension of time

This clause substitutes the employer for the architect in the procedures sections of quantities clause 25, and excludes any reference to the employer's estimate or opinion in playing his part. The inference is that he does what is right, possibly with more negotiations. In the end, he still 'fixes' to make the clause work and cannot accept the contractor's estimates etc by default. It is even easier in this case for a lay employer to lose his right to damages by oversight in not fixing an extension date.

The contractor still has to use 'his best endeavours' and 'do all that may reasonably be required' to keep going. These terms have the same limited application as in the quantities clause. No question of redesign for speed is implied — unless the employer successfully instructs a change.

There are four differences from the quantities clause in the list of relevant events in clause 25.4, in addition to the automatic disappearance of references to nominated firms. Firstly clause 25.4.5.1 on employer's instructions in its reference to clause 2.3.1 is much narrower than its parallel clause. It allows only a divergence over the site boundary to lead to an extension. Responsibility for all other divergences and all discrepancies may lie somewhere between the parties and is therefore excluded here. Secondly clause 25.4.6 refers to delay by the employer over 'necessary instructions, decisions, information or consents' which he is obliged to give, and puts the employer in a role of passive reaction similar to that of the architect under the quantities clause. This is more often inevitable in the present case where the contractor is designing and so more acceptable. It specifically includes a decision by the employer under clause 2.4.2 over a discrepancy in the contractor's proposals.

The procedure there is that when either party finds a discrepancy the contractor suggests a solution. The employer then gives his decision (as in this clause) which may or may not be favourable. The contractor must accept the decision either way, so that the timing of his application for a decision must allow for the inherent risk of the employer opting for a solution which calls for a longer time scale. It is possible to read the qualification 'for which he specifically applied . . .' which is identical to the quantities clause wording as referring only to a clause 2.4.2 decision, and it would be better to put the words 'including a decision under clause 2.4.2' in brackets.

Thirdly, delay in receiving statutory permission or approval when 'the Contractor has taken all practicable steps to avoid or reduce' it is an extra relevant event under clause 25.4.7. This gives an equivalent position to that sometimes underlying quantities clause 25.4.6, where such a delay may mean that the architect is unable to supply design information to the contractor.

Lastly, another additional relevant event occurs in clause 25.4.13, or, rather, there are two related relevant events which link with that just discussed. These comprise the two cases discussed respectively under clauses 6.3.1 and 6.3.2 of changes in statutory requirements and of amendments due to development control requirements. The comments under those clauses are relevant, the additional point here is that the contractor has to take 'all practicable steps' as usual to mitigate the effects.

The unchanged clause 25.4.10 may need care in its references to 'the Contractor's inability for reasons beyond his control' to secure labour, goods or materials. If the contractor elects to develop the designs so as to introduce a fresh and scarce category of any one of these elements, this may well be within his control and so not warrant an extension.

Clause 26 — Loss and expense caused by matters affecting progress of the works

This clause differs in substance from quantities clause 26 only in one item in the 'matters' affecting progress, although the order is also slightly different. Quantities clause 26.2.3 referring to discrepancies and divergences is omitted completely here, although one category of divergence is permitted as a relevant event under the present clause 25.4.5.1. In place of discrepancies and divergences is delay in 'permission or approval for the purposes of Development Control Requirements', provided 'the Contractor has taken all practical steps' as usual. The philosophy here is similar to that underlying clause 25.4.7 also, but the scope is far more restricted than in that clause.

Clause 27 — Determination by employer

There are two differences here in the reasons for determination. Clause 27.1.2 dealing with failure to proceed regularly and diligently refers to 'the performance of (the Contractor's) obligations under the Contract' rather than just 'the Works' because of the matter of design. The corruption provision in clause 27.3 is included as applying only in local authorities contracts.

In the provisions for proceeding after determination in clause 27.4 the question of design is also implicated. There is an additional clause 27.4.1 requiring the contractor to provide the employer with information on the works 'as-built' to date to satisfy clause 5.5. This includes copies of 'drawings or details or descriptions . . . prepared or previously provided' which covers information not previously passed to the employer, while not requiring the contractor to carry out further design, reasonably enough. The clause further requires transmission of 'drawings and information relating to the Works completed before determination' which may introduce tautology, but does rub the point in. Clause 27.4.2 parallels quantities clause 27.4.1 over employing others with the insertion of 'the design and construction of' into 'complete the Works'. While clause 27.4.3.1 over assignment of agreements does not differ in words from the quantities clause, its effect is also to cover design by 'any work'. If the contractor has been employing outside consultants, the opportunity to secure continuity of approach will have an obvious appeal for the employer.

Clause 28 — Determination by contractor

The differences here lie in the grounds for determination, the procedures following being unchanged. The first difference is the omission of quantities clause 28.1.2 over interference with or obstruction of certificates, as there are no certificates under this form. The other is the serious omission, when there is a private employer, of determination when he is insolvent. This must be a mistake and should be remedied.

Clause 28.1.2 corresponds to quantities clause 28.1.3 over reasons for suspension. Its introduction substitutes 'the construction of the Works' for 'the uncompleted Works' and so excludes suspension of design alone, a distinction not precisely introduced into clauses 25 and 26. Interruption of design work may occur for the stated period without construction being similarly affected. The delay is likely to work its way through to site in due course, but its effects may be diluted there. Only if this is not the case will the clause be activated. In the extreme case of interruption of design before possession of the site, the contractor can precipitate matters if he so wishes by pressing for possession by the due date, so that suspension of construction becomes possible.

The causes of suspension follow those in the quantities clause. That relating to clause 22 perils is restricted to 'where clause 22A or 22B applies', with a footnote cross-referencing to clause 22C.2 containing the other set of determination provisions. The causes relating to employer's instructions and delays in receiving instructions and the like from the employer incorporate details as in the relevant events of clause 25.4, and may be linked with the design delay question discussed above. There is an additional cause of delay over development control requirements, identical with that given as a loss and expense matter in clause 26.2.2.

Clause 28.2 over rights and duties of the parties is expanded in three respects. Clause 28.2.2 gives the same provisions over 'as-built' drawings as in clause 27.4.1. Clause 28.2.3.1 includes the value of 'design work' in what shall be paid to the contractor. While clause 28.2.3.6 still allows direct loss caused by the determination, this is excluded when determination is due to delay related to development control requirements, presumably because the responsibilities of the parties may become blurred.

Clause 29 — Execution of work not forming part of contract

Predictably, this clause with an amended title deals with work which has, and work which has not, been adequately described in the employer's requirements in place of the contract bills of quantities clause 29. There is no change in principle but the practice of allowing any such work needs even more care when the contractor is designing and reasonably needs even more information to allow him to take it adequately into account. It is therefore possible that the criterion for adequate description may be even more severely interpreted.

Clause 30 — Payments

In the absence of certificates, this clause in its sections on payments on account requires applications for payment by the contractor, followed by interim payments by the employer.

Clause 30.1.1 provides a choice between two interim payment methods, as identified in Appendix 2, of which the second follows the quantities clause reasonably closely. In each case the formula set out in clause 30.1.2 for calculating the application is a gross value, paid less retention and the total of preceding applications. This formula is expanded for the alternative methods variously in clauses 30.2A and 30.2B, each of which is self-contained so that there is some repetition between them. Alternative A centres in a stage value, the details and gross values for which are in the appendix, adjusted under clause 30.2A.1 by the value of changes and the amounts of formula fluctuations, if applicable. There is no provision to add for materials on site, as these are included in the stage value. Alternative B centres in a valuation of work and design at the time concerned, adjusted under clause 30.2B.1 for changes and any formula fluctuations, with the value of materials and goods. These are 'on site' as standard, with any 'other than those' (and therefore off site) included at the employer's discretion as referred to in the appendix, where are rehearsed clauses corresponding to quantities clauses 30.3 and 16.2 in that order.

The central parts of both alternatives are subject to the addition under clause 30.2A.2 or 30.2B.2 and the deduction under clause 30.2A.3 or 30.2B.3 of amounts which are not subject to retention. These correspond with the quantities clause and are amounts adjusting the contract sum under clause 3, loss and expense and fluctuations amounts, calculated other than by formula.

Clause 30.3 regulates applications by the contractor and payments by the employer and so corresponds in purpose, if not in detail, to quantities clause 30.1 over interim certificates and valuations. Clause 30.3.1 deals separately with each of the alternative methods of application. For alternative A the stages are at times determined by physical progress rather than at fixed intervals. The main amounts payable at these stages are to be entered in the appendix and are adjustable only by the items mentioned above. Only one application is provided after practical completion, and this occurs at the later of two events: the end of the defects liability period or the making good of defects. This means that no topping-up payment can be made earlier to cover any miscellaneous adjustment amounts that arise. This pattern also corresponds with the times at which retention is reduced. For alternative B the provisions are the only ones to follow the quantities version closely, being modelled in principle on quantities clause 30.1.3 with the straight substitution of the differing terms needed.

The rest of clause 30.3 is common to the alternatives. Clause 30.3.2 requires applications to 'be accompanied by such details as may be stated in the Employer's Requirements', and this needs careful consideration in the light of the form of the contract sum analysis. Even in the case of alternative A the various adjustments may need elaboration. Payment is governed by clauses 30.3.3 and 30.3.4, which provide respectively that the employer is to pay within 14 days of the application, and that if he disagrees (in either direction) with the amount stated as due he is to notify the contractor why and 'pay at the same time' the amount that he sees as due. This could lead to uncertainty in the matter of retention, as mentioned in the next paragraph. While the 14 days is the same period as in the quantities clause from receipt of the architect's certificate, it is in effect tighter because the employer has to complete his checking of the application within this time. Clause 30.3.5 is a rider protecting the rights of the contractor still to seek redress over any amount considered to be incorrect.

Clause 30.4 deals with all matters of ascertainment and treatment of retention and equates to quantities clauses 30.4 and 30.5. It is lightened in content by the absence of the procedures relating to nominated sub-contractors, but otherwise quantities clause 30.4 is faithfully reproduced in clause 30.4.1. Clause 30.4.2 affirms the trustee position of the employer and contains the requirement of a separate banking account if the contractor so requests, as a provision when the employer is not a local authority.

Clause 30.4.3 affirms the employer's right of deduction from monies in similar terms to quantities clause 30.1.1.2. Here the clause ends, so that there is no requirement as in the other clause for the employer to issue a statement of the amount of retention to the contractor or to notify him of the amount of any deduction from the retention in particular, as distinct from notifying deductions in general under clause 30.3.4. The absence of these could lead to doubt over the level of retention in trust, in the further absence of an architect's certificate which at least states the full amount of the retention. The contractor's application will have shown this and be presumptive evidence, but the amount of payment may differ for reasons other than contra-amounts, including a reduction in the gross value of work under Alternative B, which would affect retention.

Clauses 30.5 onwards deal with the stage of final settlement.

Clause 30.5.1 gives the contractor the initiative and requires him within 3 months of practical completion to 'submit the Final Account and the Final Statement for agreement', a concept missing from the quantities clause. It follows from the absence of any provision in clause 12 for the employer's involvement in the earlier valuation of changes, such as by 'taking such notes and measurements as he may require', except when he receives daywork information. The contractor is to supply within an unspecified time 'such supporting documents as the Employer may reasonably require', suggesting documents that may accompany or follow the final account. In view of comment below about the overall time scale, the employer's requirements on a project of complexity and scale may advisedly embody items about 'notes and measurements' during progress and about documents that are to support and accompany the final account, without prejudice to asking for more under the present clause.

Clause 30.5.2 requires the final account to set out the contract sum and adjustments to it. These are listed in clause 30.5.3 and the pattern is similar to quantities clause 30.6.2 with appropriate differences in detail.

This leads to three clauses, equivalent to quantities clauses 30.8, on the issue of the final certificate. Of these, clause 30.5.4 requires the final statement to set out the amount of the final account, the amounts already paid and any difference between the two. Clause 30.5.5 deals with the period during which the employer may dispute either the final account or the final statement.

The final account and the final statement are already with the employer for approval and so the time limit set is that within which *he* must dispute any point, in default of which they become conclusive in the terms of clause 30.8.1. The latest of three possible dates applies: one month beyond the defects liability period, or beyond making good defects, or four months after the final account reaches the employer. Assuming a six-month defects liability period and the other activities happening promptly but not early, the whole matter could be wound up within little more than seven months of practical completion and four months of the employer receiving the final account. This adds point to the comment about the employer being involved progressively and early in the agreement of the final account. Clause 30.6 gives the remaining equivalent elements, covering the employer's right to make contractual deductions and payment of balance within 14 days.

Several delays are possible over the account itself. Firstly the contractor may not submit it within the three months allowed: if he fails it is strictly a breach, but hardly one on which the employer is able to act. It will not enable the latter to substitute a time at large for his four-month checking period; this will just be deferred by the extent of the delay. Another possible delay may be in the time taken by the contractor to supply supporting documents to the employer, so that the four-month period is overrun. This may be due to tardiness by the contractor, but it may also be due to a late demand for documents from the employer. Here the employer may have played for time, but it may only have been at a late stage of checking that he found the gap in information. Whether the 'may reasonably require' of clause 30.5.1 carries the implication of 'within a reasonable time' is doubtful. Whenever the employer receives information, he must then be allowed some time in which to deal with it and possibly to dispute it. Neither these nor any other delays in supplying information are considered in any part of clause 30, so that no fall-back date for the final account and final statement to become conclusive is provided. The basic trouble is that the order of 'information and then final account' that applies in the quantities contract is here reversed, while the timing centres on the actual account. The only remedy in this vague but variable situation lies in arbitration or other proceedings over whether one party was causing unreasonable delay, thus enabling a firm date to be fixed.

The other delay will occur if the employer and the contractor do not agree on a point disputed by the employer. Here the remedy again lies in proceedings, and the conclusive effect of the final account follows from this. Clause 30.8.2 deals with this and follows quantities clause 30.9.2 closely in effect: it differs only by not including words equivalent to 'before the Final Account and Final Statement have been issued', as proceedings on them cannot be instituted until they have actually been submitted to the employer.

Whenever the two documents become 'conclusive as to the balance due' under clause 30.5.3, they also become conclusive under clause 30.8.1 over quality and standards to the same extent as the final certificate under quantities clause 30.9.1.1. There is no equivalent to quantities clause 30.9.1.2. Clause 30.5.4.1 covers the first part of this, to the effect that the final account is conclusive evidence that all adjustments to the contract sum have been made, but the latter part excluding errors from the conclusive effect is nowhere reproduced. The basis for this is presumably that the contractor has prepared the account and it should stand against him if needs be. Whatever the reason the employer is also without redress and should therefore check the account all the more carefully while he may.

Clause 30.9 equates with quantities clause 30.10 by providing that no payment is conclusive evidence over 'design, works, materials or goods' being in accordance with the contract 'save as aforesaid': that is, save the final payment which evidences the employer's acceptance of the final account and final statement.

Clauses 35 to 38 — Fluctuations

The same range of options is provided here as in the quantities clauses, that is tax fluctuations, cost and tax fluctuations and formula fluctuations. As the structure and detail of the clauses are almost identical, only a few points need be picked out.

Fuels come within the scope of fluctuations under clauses 36.2.1 and 37.3.1 only if permitted by the employer's requirements. This corresponds with the quantities provision, but the contractor will need greater awareness to pick up an omission in documents that may vary more in structure, especially if prepared by someone unaccustomed to the task.

Substitution of the employer for the quantity surveyor in clauses 36.4.3, 37.5.3 and 38.4 which refer to agreeing amounts 'for all the purposes of this Contract' in ways other than those spelt out, leads directly to somewhat superfluous wording which has no discernible interpretation. The parties themselves may of course agree to any detail of adjustment. The provisions could have point if the employer's agent is introduced, but only if he is specifically given authority by both parties so to agree and exclude arbitration.

Definition of the date of tender is omitted from clauses 36.6 and 37.7, as it is covered in clause 1.3.

Clause 38.2 requires the contractor to 'provide any amplification of the Contract Sum Analysis' to allow allocation under the formula rules, and also to 'include a statement of the allocation' with his application for payment. This amplification is in the nature of things a post-contractual provision and could be a cause of contention if various elements in the monthly bulletins showed differing rates of change. If this possibility is foreseen, a more detailed contract sum analysis should be agreed before the contract is formalised, provided the state of design development permits it.

CHAPTER 23

The JCT contractor's designed portion supplement

The full title of the document considered in this chapter is the JCT Contractor's Designed Portion Supplement (1981) for use with the Standard Form of Building Contract With Quantities, Local Authorities and Private 1980 Editions. As this title indicates, it is intended for use in cases when an architect carries out the overall design function, and possibly the major share of the detailed design, and when bills of quantities are used for the share so designed, but when some part of the works is to be designed as well as constructed by the contractor.

The document is in the form of a supplement because it amends some clauses of the JCT with-quantities form (private or local authorities) and adds other and fresh clauses. In effect it grafts on many of the special provisions of the JCT with-contractor's design form (considered in Chapter 22), so that they apply to the designed portion of the contract, while leaving the usual provisions of the with quantities form to apply elsewhere. Being a supplement, the document obviously cannot be used alone and is not even intelligible when read alone. Indeed, employers using it frequently might well be advised to produce a consolidated version of form and supplement, subject to copyright. The application of the present supplement and that for sectional completion to the same contract is an exercise best left to the imagination!

This supplement picks a careful path between the design responsibilities allocated to architect and contractor. What it cannot do is to solve the practical problems and the supplement should be used only when there is a clear physical division of responsibility for various elements of the works. The basis is that the contractor puts forward his proposals as part of his tender and that he completes any outstanding part of the design when he has been awarded the contract. It should therefore be possible to clarify detailed design responsibility on receipt of the tender. Further, under the supplement the contractor does *not* assume the additional responsibility for satisfying development control requirements in the way that he does under the 'with-contractor's design' form, so that the architect retains a clear co-ordinating function.

Some element in the contractor's design may impinge upon the architect's design in such a way as to have financial consequences, by altering what is already contained in the contract bills. This possibility, as distinct from that of the architect's design altering that of the contractor, does not need special provisions in the supplement, but can be accommodated by an architect's instruction introducing a variation. If the effect produced by the contractor's design occurs at tender stage and is extensive, it may warrant amending the tendering bills before they become the contract bills. There is no specific reference to and nor does the supplement properly fit 'contractor-designed construction' of the category envisaged by the Standard Method of Measurement of Building Works, (that is work measured in quantity and described in performance terms in the contract bills). Such work might however be covered by the use of this supplement with amendments, particularly of references to the analysis introduced in the articles, while some marginal variations of other work might still be needed to achieve final settlement. Certainly without some form of supplementation the various main JCT forms do not cover *any* responsibility for design by the contractor.

Primarily, the intention is to use the supplement for complete buildings or other physically distinct entities. In principle, however, it may be used for even the smallest piece of work involving the contractor's 'design' right down to the selection of the last component which is left to his discretion. Clearly, there is a reasonable cut-off point on any project and use of the supplement is best restricted to work of some value and where a design failure would be critical. In other cases reliance is solely upon the usual statutory and contractual provisions, or even implied terms. It is possible to use the supplement for 'supply only' work with the fixing included separately in the contract bills, but such fragmentation has no advantages and can only be a potential source of problems.

While the supplement envisages the possibility of operation with sub-let work, it has no relevance to nominated work. Here Agreements NSC/2 and NSC/2a discussed in Chapter 17 and the Form of Tender by Nominated Suppliers discussed in Chapter 19 are the relevant documents to secure watertight arrangements over design responsibility. There is no possibility of nominating work within the designed portion. In essence, the supplement provides a means of obtaining specialist design from the contractor's side of the contract *without* nomination. It is not, however, suitable for inviting alternatives to, or detailed developments of, the architect's design of elements of the works.

The supplement may be adapted for use in contracts without quantities and with approximate quantities. Whether a contract of the former type is large enough to warrant it and whether one of the latter type is well enough defined to make it possible, are separate issues. In most cases a remeasurement basis for a contractor-designed portion would be undesirable for reasons of financial control. Any adaptation would involve problems of copyright — unless a 'supplement to the supplement' were produced in a nightmare moment!

Discussion below considers only the main areas of difference from the JCT forms with quantities and with contractor's design to which the supplement is related. Clauses in the other forms are referred to respectively as 'quantities clauses' and 'design clauses'. There are numerous points of drafting detail needing no special comment. The following clauses are not mentioned below although they *are* supplemented, in some cases by more significant material already covered under the form with contractor's design.

Clause 1   Interpretations, definitions etc
Clause 7   Levels and setting out of the works
Clause 14 Contract sum
Clause 17 Practical completion and defects liability
Clause 23 Date of possession, completion and postponement
Clause 24 Damages for non-completion
Clause 25 Extension of time
Clause 26 Loss and expense caused by matters materially affecting regular progress of the works
Clause 27 Determination by employer
Clause 28 Determination by contractor
Clause 38 Contribution, levy and tax fluctuations
Clause 39 Labour and materials cost and tax fluctuations

There is also a supplementary appendix allowing for additional entries along the lines of the design contract, and this too needs no comment.

Articles of agreement

The supplement firstly provides two pages of document which are to be taken out and substituted bodily for the with quantities equivalents down to and including article 1. The substitution allows space to describe briefly what is defined as 'the Contractor's Designed Portion'. It then uses the terms 'the Employer's Requirements', 'The Contractor's Proposals' and 'the Analysis' for elements fulfilling similar purposes for this designed portion to those under the design form. In the case of the requirements and the proposals, this similarity needs caution as it leads to *differences* of operation as discussed under clause 2.8. The analysis is of whatever sum is already included in or with the contract bills and so in the contract sum.

Article 1 requires the contractor to complete any design of his portion in accordance with the architect's directions', but not 'instructions'. These directions are solely for 'integrating such design with the design for the Works', that is with the architect's own design. These directions arise under clause 2.1.3, but are subject to clause 2.7, the procedure of which protects the contractor.

Clause 2 — Contractor's obligations

A substitute clause 2.1 expands the contract documents to include the employer's requirements, the contractor's proposals and the analysis. It still requires the contractor to carry out the works as a whole in accordance with the documents, but also includes a requirement under clause 2.1.3 for the contractor to complete any outstanding design and specification in the manner of design clause 2.1. This is followed by the mention of architect's 'directions' to secure integration, that also occurs in the articles. These directions do not produce a financial change and they do not allow the architect to affect matters inside the design itself, but simply permit him to co-ordinate the contractor's design with his own.

The extent to which the contractor has liberty in choosing materials and goods and workmanship in design development within his designed portion will depend on the nature of that portion and of the rest of the works. The employer's requirements will impose any restrictions (this also happens under design clause 2.1), but may well be shortened by phrases such 'as described in the Contract Bills'. This may be done in individual instances in the specification but it may also be done more widely by a blanket provision to cover anything relevant that the contractor may select. Two points need care here. Firstly, clause 2.1.4 read with clause 30.9.1.1 makes the architect liable for checking where his 'reasonable satisfaction' is the criterion and this provision thus takes his responsibility further into the designed portion than would otherwise be the case. This is particularly important if the contract bills have contained such an expression as 'all materials and workmanship not otherwise described are to be to the architect's approval'. This creates its own problems, but here may also lead to the architect being responsible for materials that he has not selected, and perhaps would not himself choose.

Secondly, the specification put forward in or by the employer's require-ments should not carry any implication that the architect is relieving the contractor of responsibility for selecting the correction option out of any given to form part of his total design, so that careful drafting is needed. Even more careful drafting is needed to keep design responsibilities clear if a specific requirement, say the use of a specific material, is imposed on the contractor.

Several modifications are provided in clauses 2.3 to 2.5 to take care of errors, discrepancies and divergences, and co-ordination, in view of the various origins of the contract documents. Where there is an error but there is no doubt as to what the parties intend, an additional clause 2.2.2.3 about the contractor's proposals and the analysis deals with 'errors in description or in quantity' and 'error consisting of an omission of items'. This is equivalent to quantities clause 2.2.2.2, but its effect is different. While such errors are to be 'corrected', there is to be 'no addition to the Contract Sum' on account either of the correction itself or of any resulting variation to the architect-designed work. This leaves open the question of whether there should be any omission from the contract sum. In the case of the designed portion, the analysis is provided only to support the contractual lump sum by giving a breakdown for the same purposes as does the contract sum analysis under the contractor's design form. Correction therefore should not alter the lump sum, but merely redistribute the breakdown. For the rest of the works, any variation omission should however take its effect in the usual way and produce a lower final settlement. It is fair to apply this principle by ascertaining whether there is a net omission and then making this adjustment only, rather than by ignoring gross additions but making gross omissions in respect of any correction.

Where there *is* doubt as to what is intended, a substitute clause 2.3 expands the list of documents to which the usual 'discrepancies and divergences' procedure applies to include the extra contract documents and the documents issued by the contractor later. As a rider to this, an additional clause 2.4 deals with discrepancies and divergences entirely within the contractor-produced documents. This permits the architect to issue resolving but not modifying instructions at his own discretion, although not until he has received the contractor's own proposals. These by implication he may adopt, modify or ignore. This gives an effect similar to that under design clause 2.4.2 where the employer may choose between options on matters of design without addition to the contract sum. Clause 2.7 will still apply, even though it is not mentioned here.

Under clause 2.5 the contractor must provide the architect 'from time to time' with drawings and specifications 'to explain or modify' his proposals. He must also supply levels and setting out dimensions for his design work. These are necessary as a minimum for the architect to co-ordinate the overall design and to check that the contractor is not departing from his proposals. In addition they permit the architect to watch for design defects under clause 2.8, so the contractor is obliged to provide calculations 'if required'. No approval procedure is given so that silence is taken to mean consent, but the contractor must wait 14 days after delivering these documents before beginning any work covered by them. The architect may request additional information at any time, rather than wait to be informed by the contractor.

The additional clauses 2.6 to 2.8 tackle responsibility for design of the contractor's portion. Clause 2.6 repeats design clause 2.5 to make the contractor responsible as professional designer. This has to be reconciled with the architect's responsibility to direct 'integration of the design' under clause 2.1.3 and to issue instructions generally. More particularly, he has to instruct over discrepancies and divergences under clause 2.4 and over variations under clause 13.2. In the one direction, clause 2.7 requires the contractor to give notice to the architect if, in his opinion, the architect's direction 'injuriously affects the efficacy of the (Contractor's) design'. If however the contractor does not give notice but passively accepts what the architect is requiring, then the responsibility remains with the contractor.

In the other direction, clause 2.8 requires the architect to give the contractor notice of 'anything which appears ... to be a defect of (the contractor's) design as referred to in clause 2.6.1'. The design in question is thus that 'comprised in the Contractor's Proposals and in what the Contractor's) design as referred to in clause 2.6.1'. The design in question is articles about supply to the employer of 'proposals ... for the design and construction' and the seventh recital that 'the Employer has examined the Contractor's Proposals and ... they appear to meet the Employer's Requirements'.

Here a consensus has been reached over subject matter of the contract, even though design may not be complete at the date of its formalising. It is only later in clause 2.8 and in sequence that the architect is mentioned, so that he may review any aspect of the contractor's design. In the case of any critical aspect, the contractor may wish to clear matters at the contract stage and have a suitable endorsement included in the contract.

Two factors relieve the contractor's position. One is that the architect, in spite of not being mentioned, will have checked at least the functional aspects of the design when the tender was received, while the present reference is to 'a defect'. The other is that under the clause the contractor does not necessarily have to take account of the architect's criticisms. Only if the architect gives an integrating 'direction' under clause 2.1.3 or instructs a variation to modify the employer's requirements under clause 13.2 must the contractor take notice and neither of these clauses relates to the question of design defects. If however the contractor does take notice of the architect under clause 2.8, he remains responsible for the design and should check that he is not absorbing any 'defect' on the architect's part. Equally he cannot rely on the architect to find defects and so plead 'want of notice' to excuse himself.

Clause 2.9 serves to exclude extension of time, payment for loss and expense, and determination by the contractor when the cause would be errors etc in the contractor's design or his failure to provide information to the architect, either on time or at all. As a result an appropriate rider is added to clauses 25.3.1.2, 26.2 and 28.1.3.

Clause 5 — Contract documents etc

Apart from prompting an exchange of documents, this clause introduces as clause 5.9 an 'as built' provision like that of design clause 5.5. It is widened by the addition of 'or as the Employer may reasonably require' to the description of what the contractor is to provide. The reason for the extra burden is not clear. It would be eased if the architect were empowered to require such technical information and thus could maintain a balance.

Clause 6 — Statutory obligations etc

A number of changes of detail and the addition of clauses 6.1.6 to 6.1.8 reflect the division of design responsibility. Thus if there is a divergence between the architect's design and the statutory requirements, the position remains as it is under the quantities clause. If the divergence is between the contractor's design and the statutory requirements, then under clause 6.1.6 the person discovering it notifies the other, the contractor proposes a solution and the architect may or may not accept this and instruct accordingly. This specifically is to be without extra cost to the employer and presumably no saving will accrue to him either. If however, there has been a change in statutory requirements since the date of tender, by virtue of clause 6.1.8 there is to be a variation with consequent financial adjustment. Clause 6.1.7 deals with emergency work on the designed portion in terms similar to quantities clause 6.1.4 for the rest of the works.

An additional clause 6.2.4 ensures that all fees and charges for the designed portion are deemed to be included in the contract sum.

Clause 8 — Materials, goods and workmanship etc

A substitute clause 8.1 combines quantities clause 8.1 and design clause 8.1 so that the 'kinds and standards' accord with the respective sections of the contract documents. Where these should be the same throughout the works, the employer's requirements should condition the contractor's proposals accordingly. The comments under clauses 2.1.2 and 2.1.4 are relevant here.

Clause 13 — Variations and provisional sums

Numerous additions of points of detail occur in this clause, to introduce extra provisions like the distinctive parts of design clause 12, here relating to the designed portion. In the earlier part dealing with authority for action, a substitute clause 13.2 expands the original version by the proviso that any variation to the designed portion 'shall be a statement of an alteration to or a modification of the Employer's Requirements', so that the responsibility for presenting a design solution remains with the contractor.

By comparison with the design clause, there is no reference here to the contractor's consent being needed for the introduction of a variation. When the designed portion is closely interrelated with the rest of the works, this may be the only practical procedure. In other cases, the contractor may be losing a reasonable right and so may wish to seek a pre-contractual modification of the wording here, rather than be forced to rely on the more tenuous provisions for vitiation. In the present clause the provision for subsequent sanctioning of variations (absent from the design clause) also covers the designed portion, while the addition of clause 13.3.3 covers expenditure of provisional sums included in the employer's requirements. The dubious nature of such provisional sums is mentioned under the design clause.

A substituted clause 13.4.1 also produces an expansion by pointing to an additional clause 13.8 covering valuation relating to the designed portion. In clauses 13.8.2 and 13.8.3 this repeats design clauses 12.5.1 and 12.5.2 for valuing additions and omissions, while clause 13.8.4 brings in preliminaries and similar matters.

Clause 19 — Assignment and sub-contracts

Clause 19.2 is renumbered 19.2.1 and an additional clause 19.2.2 covers sub-letting of design by the contractor in the same terms as design clause 18.2.2, except that the present clause does not mention a part only of the design. More importantly, the employer should reasonably be entitled to withhold his consent if the contractor proposes sub-letting to any of the employer's own designers. This would, as the practice note recognises, create a conflict of interests.

Clause 30 — Certificates and payments

No changes are introduced over interim payments. A stage payment system would tend to be unwieldy if applied to the designed portion alone, as it would be constrained by the normal timing of certificates and could therefore only lead to delay in payment of the contractor. It is accommodated, if needed, in quantities clause 30.2 by the words 'subject to any agreement between the parties as to stage payments' and could be used in suitable cases, preferably to cover the whole of the works. The analysis provided by the contractor for the designed portion would generally be used in the same way as under design clause 30.2B, but in conjunction with the procedures of the present clause.

A substituted clause 30.10 divides the question of architect's certificates as 'conclusive evidence' into two parts. Clause 30.10.1 covers 'any works, materials or goods to which (a certificate) relates', so that the wording is unchanged. Whether the significance is changed, so that the expression bears on the designed portion, will depend on the way in which the matters discussed under clauses 2.1.3 and 2.1.4 about the architect's 'reasonable satisfaction' have been handled.

Clause 30.10.2 covers the contractor's design under the designed portion, and this is the additional element. The effect here is that the architect's certificates are not conclusive 'save as aforesaid'. Since nothing to this effect is 'aforesaid' the certificates are not conclusive under the contract. This is a rather circuitous way of expressing the position and a separate clause 30.11 stating that the architect's certificates were not conclusive at all over the contractor's design would have made matters clearer. The statement is simply declaratory and reinforces article 1 and clauses 2.1.3, 2.7 and 2.8.

Clause 40 — Use of price adjustment formulae

The major adjustment here at the end of clause 40.1.1.1 is a list of modifications to the formula rules. As a result, the modified 'with-quantities' rules apply to the whole contract, rather than there being two sets of rules with the 'with-contractor's design' rules applying to the designed portion only. Many of the modifications are introduced to bring in a similar effect to the other set of rules by reference to the analysis of the designed portion. A difference in application is that the contractor is to 'indicate, when submitting the Contractor's Proposals' the allocation for formula purposes of each item in the analysis. This is then 'deemed' to have been agreed by the parties, whereas under design clause 38.2 the contractor provides 'any amplification' post-contractually. The present arrangement is the more satisfactory, if the design is far enough advanced to allow it.

CHAPTER 24

The JCT form of prime cost contract

The full title of the document considered in this chapter is the JCT Fixed Fee Form of Prime Cost Contract. The edition current at the time of writing is still that dated October 1976. It is dealt with here by considering its key differences from the 1980 JCT form private with quantities discussed in Parts 2 and 3 of this book. These latter two statements taken together mean that there are three broad ways in which it differs, which are dealt with as follows:

(a) Like other forms taken on a comparative basis, it has provisions relating to its particular purpose. These are the main burden of this chapter.

(b) In format, clause numbering order and system, general phraseology and 'common' provisions it compares most directly with the later revisions of the JCT forms, 1963 editions. It is to be expected when it appears as a post-1980 document, that it will be brought into line with the other 1980 documents in these respects so that, for instance, there will be an expanded extension of time clause that will differ only in minor drafting details from its counterparts. All clause and other references are made to the 1976 prime cost document; no attempt has been made to anticipate any post-1980 revised numbers or change in order. Other references to 'quantities clauses' are to the JCT forms private with quantities, quoting clause numbers in the revisions of the 1963 edition first and clause numbers in the 1980 edition second whenever both occur together.

(c) The document differs from the other 1963 documents even in points of substance, such as the absence of a clause dealing with the tax deduction scheme for sub-contractors (as with-quantities clause 30B/31). This chapter considers the 1976 prime cost document as it stands and, given the level of treatment of the subject, ignores such differences. It may be expected that they will be incorporated into the new edition and that they will need no special discussion.

This chapter must be read accordingly. While the discussion relates specifically to the existing contract, it should also be possible to relate it without undue difficulty to the revised contract when it appears. As always, there must be the caution that some differences of the type mentioned in (a) may be modified or fresh ones introduced. If the existing contract is used for a particular project, it should be checked for discrepancies of the type mentioned in (c) and amendments introduced into the 1963 forms where appropriate. Any attempt to revise the present contract by bringing in piecemeal any number of the points referred to in (b) would be laborious and likely to give rise to confusion. This means that related documents such as sub-contracts must be used in corresponding vintages.

The form consists of an agreement, conditions, an attestation, six schedules and an appendix. The conditions include part of what is in the articles of agreement of the other JCT forms. The contract is drafted to line up closely with the 1963 forms in their private editions and would need amending to suit local authorities. It also contains several italicised sections which apply only when the works are situated in Scotland. While a note on the front of the documents states this, it avoids confusion to delete these sections when they are not required. Should the works be situated in Scotland, but the contract be executed in England, it should be made plain which law is to apply and what happens to these sections.

The main difficulty in considering this contract is the closeness of its adherence to the main forms. There are places where the quite different philosophy of a cost reimbursement approach as against a lump sum, with or without quantities, appears to be inadequately reflected. This philosophy has three broad aims in most cases:

(a) To provide for works where the nature and perhaps the scope is uncertain before commencement, although the arrangement may be used for normally defined works.

(b) To pay the contractor for the costs which he actually incurs plus a profit margin, since any estimate of these costs in advance would be too inaccurate.

(c) To regularise the basis of payment in the interests of the employer and for the same reason to control the level of costs incurred.

The leading ways in which the contract is blurred in its philosophy are as follows:

(a) It is assumed that both nature and scope are clear from the beginning, as is discussed hereafter under clause 3 and its footnotes, under clause 26, and under the third schedule.

(b) The more vaguely the nature and scope are defined, to avoid the constrictive effect of (a) on the employer, the harder does it become for the contractor to insert his fixed fee in the second schedule and his estimate of the prime cost in the third schedule. The latter is of little financial consequence, except in calculating interim payments, although it may mislead the employer initially. The former will affect the contractor's profit level considerably however.

(c) The possibility of switching costs between sections of the first schedule, due to the effect of clause 13, and uncertainties within that schedule, can lead to the possibility of different payments for the same physical effort. There is also little bite in the conditions to regulate the actual physical effort to be reimbursed, as discussed under clause 7.

In what follows only the main points of difference from the main forms are noted, or the points where there reasonably could have been a difference. There are also other points of less consequence not considered and quite a number of verbal differences arising inevitably out of the different present-ation of the present contract. The following quantities clauses are not paralleled here owing to differences in philosophy:

Clauses 7/9	Royalties and patent rights.
Clauses 11/13	Variations and provisional sums.
Clauses 12.2.2 and 14.1	Contract bills.
Clauses 13/14.2	Contract sum.
Clauses 31/38, 39 and 40	Fluctuations.

Quantities clauses 11/13 appear to be implied in several clauses, so far as variations are concerned, but not otherwise. The absence of an equivalent to quantities clauses 12/2.2 and 14.1 means that the absolute supremacy of the conditions is not established and therefore a purpose-drafted specification or the like will take precedence if there is any conflict.

The agreement and conditions

THE AGREEMENT

This corresponds with the first part of the articles of agreement of the main forms and appears to establish the specification and any drawings as contract documents.

CLAUSE 1 — DEFINITIONS

These definitions include those given in the later part of the articles of agreement in the main forms, but not those in quantities clause 1 (1980). The definition of 'the Works' allows for variations, although the footnote emphasises that these must not change the nature or scope of the works. (See clause 3(1).)

CLAUSE 2 — CONTRACTOR'S GENERAL OBLIGATION

This clause corresponds to quantities clauses 1(1)/2.1, but there is no parallel to quantities clauses 1(2)/2.3 regulating action over discrepancies. The financial effect of these will be absorbed within the prime cost but the procedure for physical resolution is still needed.

CLAUSE 3 — ARCHITECT'S INSTRUCTIONS

While this clause largely parallels quantities clauses 2/4, it allows the architect to issue such instructions as he thinks fit. These will include changes in sequence and postponement of working and will perhaps affect even the contractor's own methods. This latter would be reasonable where delicate restoration work is going on, or where the contractor is not exercising proper economy, as clause 7(1) also considers. But under clause 3(1) the instructions may not change the nature or scope of the works and the footnote advises a separate or supplemental contract to achieve this. The contractor is under no obligation to enter into such a contract and deadlock could result at this point. The effect of clause 26 is also important in connection with the present clause.

The employer may employ others to carry out instructed work if the contractor does not do it. Although the contractor will not be paid for such work, the employer has no way of recovering any extra cost of having someone else do it, even if it can be ascertained in this case.

CLAUSE 4 — DRAWINGS AND CERTIFICATES

This clause corresponds to the relevant parts of quantities clauses 3/5. There is no definition of the contract documents.

CLAUSE 5 — STATUTORY OBLIGATIONS AND NOTICES

This clause repeats quantities clauses 4(1)/6.1 closely. It does not oblige the contractor to pay any fees or charges or give the employer any indemnity; these items are reimbursed to the contractor under Section C of the first schedule, however.

CLAUSE 6 — LEVELS AND SETTING OUT OF THE WORKS

Quantities clauses 5/7 are repeated here, except that the ambiguity over payment for the rectification of the contractor's errors is resolved. Oddly enough, it is resolved in favour of the possibility of the contractor being paid for such works, although this is solely at the architect's discretion. When the architect would choose to exercise such a discretion is a mystery.

CLAUSE 7 — LABOUR, MATERIALS, GOODS AND WORKMANSHIP

The clause obliges the contractor to provide all that is needed for the works, with qualifications over sub-letting and nomination. It rather vaguely provides that he shall not at any time make a greater provision than is reasonably required, except at his own cost. This gives some lever to the architect or the quantity surveyor, but could be amplified with advantage in the specification.

Otherwise the clause combines quantities clauses 6/8 and 8/10, although it omits any reference to the removal of defective work, materials or goods or the exclusion of persons. Clause 11(3) covers the former of these.

CLAUSE 8 — MATERIALS AND GOODS UNFIXED OR OFF-SITE

Quantities clauses 14/16 are here moved next to clause 7 of these conditions and this enables the several references to materials and goods to keep each other company.

CLAUSE 9 — ACCESS FOR ARCHITECT TO THE SITE

Quantities clauses 9/11 are paralleled here, with a minor change in title.

CLAUSE 10 — CLERK OF WORKS

Quantities clauses 10/12 are paralleled here.

CLAUSE 11 — PRACTICAL COMPLETION AND DEFECTS LIABILITY

Quantities clauses 15/17 are given here with three changes. In the present clause 11(3) instructions regarding defects and the like are not limited to those appearing within the defects liability period as in the main forms, but extend to those which 'at any time appear or are discovered'. This covers the gap in clause 7.

The other two changes are identical and occur in clauses 11(2) and 11(3). They provide that the cost of making good defects and the like which are the contractor's fault may be reimbursed to the contractor if the architect so instructs. While the ambiguity of the main forms is thus removed, the direction of change is as unexpected here as it is in clause 6.

CLAUSE 12 — PARTIAL POSSESSION BY EMPLOYER

The provisions of this clause have the same effect generally as quantities clauses 16/18. There is no reference to insurance, due to the difference in the present contract.

The reduction in retention is related to the retention percentage, which is held on the prime cost, but not the fixed fee, in accordance with clause 27(4).

CLAUSE 13 — ASSIGNMENT AND SUB-LETTING

The provision here over assignment is as in quantities clauses 17/19 and needs no further comment. So far as sub-letting is concerned, the position is more complex owing to the prime cost basis of the contract. Sub-letting here affects more than quality of work: it may introduce a different method of payment, perhaps even a lump sum or one based on quantities, and it certainly entitles the contractor to a profit margin additional to that within the fixed fee. This arises because the portion sub-let falls under Section D of the first schedule instead of Section A, B or C. The architect, in his consent to sub-letting, must therefore expressly approve the method of charge which may be quite out of step with the contract generally and this 'may be subject to such reasonable conditions as the Architect thinks fit.'

No principles are given to guide either the architect or an arbitrator in all this and they must do what they can, but in the end consent may not be unreasonably withheld to the prejudice of the contractor. Any payment which may be to the prejudice of the employer is not considered. Where labour-only sub-letting is in question the position may be particularly awkward; the rates per hour may be above those provided by Section A of the first schedule, even before the percentage under Section D is added. If consent to a sub-letting is withheld, the contractor may have a claim for extension of time under clause 19(j), on the ground that he cannot otherwise obtain labour. This is a very unsatisfactory position and it seems best to establish the extent and financial basis of any known sub-letting at the time of signing the contract.

CLAUSE 14 — INJURY TO PERSONS AND PROPERTY AND EMPLOYER'S LIABILITY

Quantities clauses 18/20 are repeated here and no further comment is needed.

CLAUSE 15 — INSURANCE AGAINST INJURY TO PERSONS AND PROPERTY

The broad scope and method of insurance here is as in quantities clauses 19/21. The premiums for the special insurances under clause 15(2) are separately reimbursable under Section C of the first schedule. Premiums for insurance under clause 15(1) however are not mentioned there or anywhere else in the schedules. They are therefore to be allowed for in the fixed fee in accordance with clause 26(2).

CLAUSE 15A — EXCEPTED RISKS — NUCLEAR PERILS, ETC

This clause corresponds to quantities clauses 19A/21.3.

CLAUSE 16 — INSURANCE OF THE WORKS AGAINST FIRE

Two alternatives, clause 16[A] for a new building and clause 16[B] for alterations or extensions to an existing building are given here: these correspond to quantities clauses 20[B]/22B and 20[C]/22C respectively. Both alternatives thus place both the risk and the insurance on the employer. There is no provision for the contractor to carry these two matters for a new building, although the footnote does suggest that this could be done by using a clause based on quantities clause 20[A] (1963). This is to be recommended, as discussed under the similar quantities clause 22A in this book, and it is puzzling that the present contract does not allow for it in its own drafting. If the contractor does have to take out any insurance upon the employer's default, he will recover the premiums under Section C of the first schedule.

CLAUSE 17 — POSSESSION AND COMPLETION

This clause corresponds to quantities clauses 21(1)/23.1. There is no reference to postponement, since this comes under the architect's instructions in clause 3(1). The contractor is held to a date for completion. There is some tension here, both because of the possible uncertainties inherent in much prime cost work and also because overtime and incentive payments are made subject to the architect's authorisation, if the contractor wishes to be paid for them under Section A of the first schedule. The same tension extends into clauses 18 and 19 as a result.

CLAUSE 18 — DAMAGES FOR NON-COMPLETION

This clause corresponds to quantities clauses 22/24. The comments under clause 17 should be noted.

CLAUSE 19 — EXTENSION OF TIME

This clause corresponds to quantities clauses 23/25 and again the comments under clause 17 should be noted. Architect's instructions as cause for extension under clause 19(e) are cast more widely and the contractor might often rely on 'the order . . . of work', 'the addition, omission or substitution . . . of work', and 'or the postponement . . . of work' to secure extension for unforeseen problems in alterations to existing buildings. While such happenings cannot be used in isolation (as in quantities clause 25 (1980)) to secure a shortening of the original or already extended time for completion, it is quite reasonable to off-set suitable ones to reduce the overall extension granted on a particular occasion. Also, in the context of prime cost work where the contractor is paid for what he reasonably does, the closing proviso that the contractor is to co-operate to minimise delay gives the architect an opportunity to instruct suitable measures, as he cannot under the main forms.

CLAUSE 20 — LOSS AND EXPENSE CAUSED BY DISTURBANCE OF REGULAR PROGRESS OF THE WORKS

While this clause corresponds to quantities clauses 24/26, it is difficult to see it having the same importance when so much of the contractor's expenditure is covered by the prime cost payments under the first schedule. All that is really left is the fixed fee which is referred to in this respect in clause 26(1). Here the fee as a whole may need to be increased to take account of any significant overall change in the prime cost and the element of supervision and overheads within the fee may call for a distinct increase in the case of some types of disturbance. In particular site staff, as distinct from foremen and timekeepers, are not mentioned in the first schedule and, being included in the fixed fee, will be dealt with in this way.

One cause, that of 'discrepancy or divergence' which figures in the main forms, is omitted here for some reason. To postponement, however, is added changes in the order of working instructed by the architect.

CLAUSE 21 — DETERMINATION BY EMPLOYER

This clause repeats quantities clauses 25/27 in full. It thus provides a big stick for the employer to use against unauthorised sub-letting among other things, although the weapon would be of little value unless the architect's decision against sub-letting under the rather different provisions of these conditions were upheld by an arbitrator and this would be doubtful in many cases. The calculation of the ultimate indebtedness of the one party to the other will involve several differences from that resulting from determination of a lump sum contract, but is quite practicable.

CLAUSE 22 — DETERMINATION BY THE CONTRACTOR

This clause in the main repeats quantities clauses 26/28. It introduces two changes: one is a different reference to architect's instructions, similar to part of that already noted under clause 19. The other is a difference in the formula for calculating the final payment to the contractor, which follows from the prime cost provisions in general.

CLAUSE 23 — NOMINATED SUB-CONTRACTORS

Except at its two ends, this clause follows quantities clause 27 (1963) closely and, in principle but not in detail, quantities clause 35 (1980). At its beginning the clause refers to the fourth schedule where the nominated sub-contract items are to be listed in the absence of any contract bills. In addition to these listed items, the subject-matter of the clause is also given as including substituted or additional items which the architect may introduce. These latter are the equivalent of items arising from provisional sums under the main forms. As in the 1980 clause, there is no reference to discount but this is covered in Section D of the first schedule.

At the end of the clause it is tersely stated that if the architect wishes the contractor to undertake any work of a nominated sub-contract character, and the contractor agrees, there should be a separate agreement. This is considerably more simple than the statement of the main forms, and at least as helpful.

CLAUSE 24 — NOMINATED SUPPLIERS

This clause parallels quantities clauses 28/36, but includes elements at its beginning of a similar character to those introduced in clause 23 above. In this case discount is covered in Section B of the first schedule.

CLAUSE 25 — WORK BY OTHER PERSONS

Here quantities clauses 29/29 are paralleled, although the vague term 'other persons' is used. The sixth schedule provides for the listing of their work and is itself referred to in the opening agreement. The employer is not thereby debarred from employing persons to do other unlisted work. In fact, the listing may make the items concerned 'part of the agreement' and thus remove them from the scope of the present clause.

CLAUSE 26 — PAYMENT

This clause has no strict parallel; its nearest equivalents are quantities clauses 13/14 'Contract Sum'. Its primary aim is to draw together the elements forming the payment to the contractor. These are (a) the prime cost of the works, which is defined in the first schedule and there includes nominated items listed in the fourth and fifth schedules and (b) the fixed fee, which is stated in the second schedule without any definition and may be adjusted only for disturbance elements under clauses 20 and 30(2).

The clause then emphasises the basic philosophy of this arrangement. This is that the first element has been defined in some detail to establish its content.

The second element is scarcely defined, so that it may be held to include all that is not spelt out in the first element; only the mention of insurance in the clause acts as a clear reminder of anything that needs to be included. Even here, some premiums are reimbursable under the prime cost as mentioned in discussing clauses 15 and 16. As mentioned under clause 20, site staff must be covered by the fixed fee.

The contractor should therefore determine the items to be covered in the fixed fee with some care, as he will be unable to recover their cost in any other way. Equally if the architect or the quantity surveyor needs to analyse the fee for purposes of later negotiation, comparable care will be needed.

Not only is the scope of the fixed fee thus made quite rigid by the contract, but also its amount can be changed only where there is a disturbance. The effect of clause 3(1) and its footnote is to make any change in 'the nature or the scope of the Works' require a fresh agreement and this agreement should include any addition to, or subtraction from, the fixed fee. No architect's instructions can lead to an adjustment: the fee is fixed, apart from the effects of disturbance already mentioned.

In passing, it may be noted that the estimated amount of the prime cost of the works given in the third schedule has no bearing on final payment, as already mentioned in the introductory part of this chapter. It could not be used to support a claim for adjustment of the fixed fee, for instance.

The last part of the clause requires the contractor to maintain full details supporting the prime cost. It will usually be helpful to incorporate more detailed definitions and procedures for this in the contract, to avoid lack of information or delay in its production. This will be vital not only to the final settlement but to the making of reasonably accurate interim payments, since there is no other evidence available.

CLAUSE 26A — VALUE ADDED TAX, SUPPLEMENTAL AGREEMENT

This clause repeats quantities clauses 13A/15 and introduces the supplemental agreement. As such it needs no further comment.

CLAUSE 27 — METHOD OF PAYMENT

With a certain amount of rearrangement in places, this clause holds quite closely to the pattern of quantities clause 30 (1963) and to the similar principles of quantities clause 30 (1980).

For the purpose of interim payment, it makes the contractor responsible for producing 'all documents necessary for the purpose of ascertaining the amount'. The architect is under no obligation to include in his certificate any sum to cover items not covered by the necessary documents, although some reasonable allowance is not precluded where, say, a substantial invoice is not rendered by a supplier. A proportion of the fixed fee is to be included without deduction of retention and here the estimate in the third schedule serves its only clear purpose, in the formula set out for calculating the proportion due. The discretionary payment for materials off-site is not satisfactory in

Scotland (see Chapter 26) and the footnote therefore requires deletion of the sub-clause concerned. References to it elsewhere need not be deleted: their effect lapses.

For the purposes of the final certificate, the contractor inevitably is given the responsibility of producing all the information required to calculate the prime cost, although the architect or the quantity surveyor then becomes responsible for the calculation itself. In practice the contractor will need to do a considerable share of the work himself to comply with clause 26. Usually the architect will check at most that no irregular items have been included in the prime cost, while the quantity surveyor will carry out the detailed checking.

CLAUSE 28 — OUTBREAK OF HOSTILITIES

This clause repeats quantities clauses 32/32 and needs no further comment.

CLAUSE 29 — WAR DAMAGE

This clause repeats quantities clauses 33/33 and needs no further comment.

CLAUSE 30 — ANTIQUITIES

This clause repeats quantities clauses 34/34 and also is the only clause, other than clause 20, leading to an adjustment of the fixed fee.

CLAUSE 31 — ARBITRATION

The modelling of this clause on quantities clause 35 (1963), and so its similarity to much of quantities article 5, calls on the whole for no comment. By its references to the first schedule it does put important elements of the prime cost within the scope of arbitration, not only during the progress of the works but also before the elements of cost are incurred. This is understandable, if once the hesitancy of the contract over defining these elements in advance is accepted. Whereas under a lump sum contract the contractor is paid for a defined finished product and not for the cost of producing it, he is under this contract paid for no more than the cost of producing the product. If that cost is unreasonable, he will be paid less. As a result the present clause puts the uncertain elements of overtime, incentives, travel and subsistence into the arena of early arbitration. If the works are not to be delayed, it will also need to be almost instant arbitration. This effect of the contract may not be unduly important in some cases, but the urgency of the works or the need to import labour may give it prominence. If this is so, the contract documents should modify the provisions of the first schedule to dispose of its vagueness.

The foregoing is in line with what has been suggested over sub-letting under clause 13. Here again a reference to arbitration is possible but, in default of agreement, only after practical completion or its equivalent; prior clarification therefore becomes even more desirable.

Attestation, schedules, appendix and supplementary agreement

THE ATTESTATION

Since the opening agreement runs into the body of the clauses, the attestation is placed after the clauses, but otherwise calls for no comment.

FIRST SCHEDULE — DEFINITION OF PRIME COST

This schedule is divided as follows: Section A, labour; Section B, materials and goods; Section C, plant, consumable stores and services; Section D, work sub-contracted and work sub-let.

The purpose of this schedule, as discussed under clause 26, is to set out every category of payment that is directly reimbursable as part of the prime cost. What is not specifically stated is deemed to be part of the fixed fee in accordance with clause 26. The sections are therefore quite detailed and this is particularly true of Section A and Section C. Within their detail there is some uncertainty over the payment arising out of sub-letting; the comments under clauses 13, 26 and 31 should be noted here.

By virtue of this schedule the 'prime cost' includes nominated suppliers under Section B and nominated sub-contractors under Section D, as well as the contractor's own direct work and sub-let work.

SECOND SCHEDULE — FIXED FEE

To accord with the detail and principle of the first schedule, this schedule has no detail at all and again clause 26 should be noted, along with the comment on the third schedule.

THIRD SCHEDULE — ESTIMATED AMOUNT OF THE PRIME COST

The contract is quite coy as to where this estimate originates. Its function under the contract is limited purely to interim payment calculations under clauses 12 and 27 and to that degree only a general accuracy is needed. It is however upon this estimate, presumably, that the contractor will base the calculation of his fixed fee. Since so little can be done to adjust the fee later, the accuracy of the estimate becomes very important, as does a knowledge of what proportion of it affords discounts to the contractor. This means that the estimate should either be prepared by, or be carefully checked by, the contractor. The practical difficulty with so much prime cost work is that the cost cannot be closely estimated in advance, even when the nature and the scope of the works are defined, and the contractor must come to terms with this as best he may.

Where the nature or the scope of the works cannot clearly be defined, it is equitable for the parties to define what they can and base the initial contract on this. The basis for one or more supplemental contracts can then be embodied in an appendix to the contract, so that clause 3 and its footnote may be observed and also so that some reasonable means of adjusting the fee may be to hand.

FOURTH SCHEDULE — ITEMS OF WORK TO BE EXECUTED BY NOMINATED SUB-CONTRACTORS

A simple, clear description of each of the various items will suffice here, the estimated value of these items in total being included in the third schedule. If the contractor agrees later to execute any of these items himself, then there is to be a separate agreement covering it, in accordance with clause 23(g).

FIFTH SCHEDULE — GOODS TO BE SUPPLIED BY NOMINATED SUPPLIERS

The position here is similar to that under the fourth schedule, except that no question of a separate agreement will arise. Whatever the source of supply, the contractor will be reimbursed under Section B of the first schedule and receive the same discount. If he becomes the manufacturer also, his quotation should take account of any allowance in lieu of discount.

SIXTH SCHEDULE — ITEMS OF WORK TO BE EXECUTED BY OTHER PERSONS

Again, only descriptions are needed; no question of payment through the contractor arises with these direct contracts and any attendance will form part of the prime cost. The omission of an item from the schedule will not preclude the employer from introducing it later; the wording of clause 25 follows that of quantities clause 29 (1963) more closely, where no initial schedule is required. In any case the distinctions between items listed and not listed, as in quantities clause 29 (1980), are not so critical here as the prime cost reimbursement will cover most expense, unless the effect is enough to disturb the 'fixed' fee by way of claim.

THE APPENDIX

The entries required here consist of items corresponding to those required by the main forms so far as they are relevant to this contract. No further comment is needed.

THE SUPPLEMENTAL AGREEMENT

This agreement repeats the agreement or provisions used with the main forms and needs no further comment.

CHAPTER 25

The JCT agreement for minor building works

The Agreement for Minor Building Works appears in the current edition of 1980. It is issued by the Joint Contract Tribunal as are the main JCT forms.

The document consists of an agreement and conditions, within which are spaces for insertions corresponding to some of those in the appendix to the main forms. There is also a supplementary memorandum issued separately. The purpose of the agreement is stated in the heading to the document itself, which reads as follows:

> This Form of Agreement and Conditions is designed for use where minor building works are to be carried out for an agreed lump sum and where an Architect/Supervising Officer has been appointed on behalf of the Employer. The Form is not for use for works for which bills of quantities have been prepared, or where the Employer wishes to nominate sub-contractors or suppliers, or where the duration is such that full labour and materials fluctuations provisions are required; nor for works of a complex nature or which involve complex services or require more than a short period of time for their execution.

The form is also not suitable for prime cost work and is specifically endorsed as 'not for use in Scotland'. It will be seen that clauses 5.4 and 5.5 make the contract suitable for local authorities use as well as for private work. To achieve its purpose the form sets out clauses which are essentially a condensation of the relevant points of the main form, although they differ in drafting.

The condensation inevitably produces less firmness of wording. Only in the case of injury, insurance, fluctuations, value added tax and tax deduction are the clauses relatively full. However, since the contract is intended only for work of the scale of a small public convenience, or a small extension to a house, this will usually be quite a reasonable arrangement.

Should the works be fairly substantial, while still not justifying quantities, the appropriate edition of the main forms should be used and not the present contract. Where work is of a specialised nature, and particularly where the contractor is responsible for aspects of design, the contract will also need adaptation.

The clause titles, and the corresponding clauses of the main form, are as follows. Those that are options or that need completion or selection within them are asterisked.

8	Supplementary memorandum	No equivalent
8.1	Meaning of references in 4.5, 5.2 and 5.3	No equivalent
A	Contribution, levy and tax changes	38
B	Value added tax	Supplemental provisions
C	Statutory tax deduction scheme — Finance (No 2) Act 1975	31

Some notes may be added on selected points within the various parts of the documents as follows:

ARTICLES OF AGREEMENT

These take the usual form. There is reference to both the architect and the quantity surveyor, the latter in case one is appointed, although he has no mention in and so no powers or duties under the conditions. The contractor is said to have priced one of three things: the specification (possibly itemised), schedules provided to him, or a schedule of rates provided by him. This makes them mutually exclusive as a basis, although clause 3.6 does not read accordingly. The only provision for the sum payable here is for a lump sum. Thus it would appear that what is intended is a single price based on the drawings and specification, but providing for variations by one of the three means named in the recital. A short arbitration clause is provided.

CLAUSE 2.2

Extension of time is to be granted simply 'for reasons beyond the control of the Contractor' and no time is stipulated within which an extension is to be granted.

CLAUSE 2.4

A certificate of practical completion is required, with effects similar to those in the main forms, but more restricted.

CLAUSE 2.5

Defects liability is stated as three months only, and this will apply unless an alternative is inserted.

CLAUSE 3.5

The power to employ others to carry out the architect's instructions if the contractor defaults is included, small though the works may be.

CLAUSE 3.6

The scope of variations is given as 'an addition to or omission from or other change in the Works', that is physical change in the finished product, and also

Clause of minor works form	Title of clause	Corresponding clause(s) of main form
1	Intentions of the parties	
1.1	Contractor's obligation	2.1
1.2	Architect's/supervising officer's duties	4.3, 5
2	Commencement and completion	
2.1*	Commencement and completion	23.1
2.2	Extension of contract period	25
2.3*	Damages for non-completion	24
2.4	Completion date	17.1
2.5*	Defects liability	17.2 to 17.5
3	Control of the works	
3.1	Assignment	19.1
3.2	Sub-contracting	19.2
3.3	Contractor's representative	10
3.4	Exclusion from the works	8.5
3.5	Architect's/supervising officer's instructions	4.1
3.6*	Variations	13.1, 13.2, 13.4 to 13.7
3.7	Provisional sums	13.3
4	Payment	
4.1*	Correction of inconsistencies	2.3
4.2*	Progress payments and retention	30.1, 30.2, 30.4
4.3*	Penultimate certificate	
4.4*	Final certificate	30.6, 30.8
4.5*	Contribution, levy and tax changes	38
4.6	Fixed price	14.2
5	Statutory obligations	
5.1	Statutory obligations, notices, fees and charges	6.1, 6.2
5.2	Value added tax	15
5.3	Statutory tax deduction scheme	31
5.4*	Fair wages resolution	19A
5.5*	Prevention of corruption	27.3
6	Injury, damage and insurance	
6.1	Injury to or death of persons	20.1, 21.1
6.2	Damage to property	20.2, 21.1
6.3A*	Insurance of the works — fire, etc — new works	22A
6.3B*	Insurance of the works — fire, etc — existing structures	22C
6.4	Evidence of insurance	2.1.1.1, 22A.2
7	Determination	
7.1	Determination by employer	27.1, 27.2
7.2	Determination by contractor	28

CLAUSES 6.1 AND 6.2

These clauses combine in each case the requirements over indemnity and insurance that are separately treated in the main forms. There is no limit placed on the insured liability in either case. An additional proviso protects a sub-contractor from incurring liability for negligence or breach by the main parties and others.

CLAUSES 6.3A AND 6.3B

These clauses do not provide for the option of the employer taking the risk, with or without insurance, for new works not involved with existing structures. The deletion of the first portion in brackets in clause 6.3B and a change in the heading would transfer the risk, while deletion of the last few words would further remove the question of insuring. This is an undesirable alternative, as commented under the main forms, but it can be achieved and may suit local authorities.

CLAUSE 7.1

This parallels only the first part of the procedure for determination by the employer under the main forms. There are no provisions about completing the works, with or without using the contractor's belongings; this may not be critical in view of the small scale of operations. But there is also no statement about settlement, by way of recovering any excess expenditure against what might otherwise be due or as a debt. There remains however the 'without prejudice' rider, pointing to action for breach in at least some situations. This is not much help when there is insolvency, although the amount is likely to be small. The clause does not cover corruption as a cause for local authorities: this under clause 5.5 permits the employer 'to cancel the Contract and to recover . . . any loss'.

SUPPLEMENTARY MEMORANDUM

Clause 8.1 is simply a cross-referencing clause. The three parts of the memorandum itself are as extensive as the corresponding clauses in the main forms etc. They may be brought into the contract as required, although in any case of doubt they should be included rather than excluded.

as 'or the order or period in which they are to be carried out'. This latter part is quite distinct from anything in the main forms, except postponement. It does not exclude the possibility of an advancement of the completion date, although the contractor could not be obliged to meet unreasonable demands. For all variations the basis of valuation is to be 'fair and reasonable' using the prices available 'where relevant'. Instead of this valuation, the price may be agreed in advance and this may be particularly useful for completely different work or for the programme changes mentioned.

CLAUSE 4.2

Payments are 'at intervals of not less than four weeks', rather than monthly, if the contractor requests them. The standard provision is for 5 per cent retention unless another level is given. As any defect is likely to form a relatively large element in the whole works, a higher figure may often be prudent.

CLAUSE 4.3

Correspondingly, the 'penultimate certificate' after practical completion intends the retention to be halved. The use of 'penultimate' indicates that no further payment is to be made until finality.

CLAUSE 4.4

The contractor is to 'supply within three months' information for the final account, unless another period is given. He is entitled to the final certificate within 28 days of supplying the data, so long as the architect has cleared defects liability, and payment is due within a further 14 days. No other effect of the final certificate is expressed, so that the contractor cannot rely on it to the same extent as under the main forms, unless the architect so provides in issuing it and this is accepted by the employer.

CLAUSE 4.6

This clause only affirms that no fluctuations provisions apply, unless adjustments for statutory changes under part B of the supplementary memorandum apply. There is no statement about errors, which the parties would be held to have accepted, unless such errors concerned the subject matter of the contract.

CLAUSE 5.2

Under this provision the inclusion of part B of the supplementary memorandum means that VAT payments are made through the contract, rather than as supplementary amounts.

CHAPTER 26

The Scottish building contract, building sub-contract and related documents

The substance of the majority of the various JCT documents is used in Scotland as well as the rest of the United Kingdom. The existence of a distinct Scots law does however lead to a number of variant points and these are taken into account by a series of documents issued by the Scottish Building Contract Committee. This is a constituent body of the Joint Contracts Tribunal and its own constituent bodies are as follows:

Royal Incorporation of Architects in Scotland
Scottish Building Employers Federation
Scottish Branch of the Royal Institution of Chartered Surveyors
Convention of Scottish Local Authorities
Federation of Specialists and Sub-Contractors (Scottish Board)
Committee of Associations of Specialist Engineering Contractors (Scottish Branch)
Association of Consulting Engineers (Scottish Group)

The range of Scottish documents at present leaves out several of the JCT documents and also the domestic sub-contract. Only the prime cost contract is so drafted as to suit use in Scotland in its own right. The documents issued fall into three categories:

(a) Brief documents which incorporate the conditions only of the JCT with and without quantities main forms (but not the 'with approximate quantities' form) and nominated sub-contract forms by reference:

Scottish Building Contract
Scottish Building Contract, Sectional Completion Edition
Scottish Building Sub-Contract NSC/4/Scot
Scottish Building Sub-Contract NSC/4a/Scot

The first of these is discussed in its parts in this chapter; the rest need no separate discussion. The second is very similar to the first, but incorporates within itself the amending provisions of the JCT Sectional Completion Supplement, which is thus rendered unnecessary. The other two are similar in principle to the first, but are for use with the 'basic' and 'alternative' methods of nomination respectively.

(b) Full documents superseding the equivalent JCT documents:

Tender NSC/1/Scot
Agreement NSC/2/Scot
Agreement NSC/2a/Scot
Nomination NSC/3/Scot
Nomination NSC/3a/Scot
Standard Form of Tender for use in Scotland by Nominated Suppliers, and Warranty
Standard Form for Nomination of Suppliers for use in Scotland

It will be noted that the second sub-contract nomination extends the JCT range, which only provides Nomination NSC/3. All of these documents differ only in drafting detail from their equivalents and need no comment.

(c) Full documents without JCT equivalents and called for by unique legal needs:

Contract relative to the purchase of materials and/or goods, between Employer and Contractor
Contract relative to the purchase of materials and/or goods, between Employer, Contractor and Sub-Contractor

These are discussed in the context of clause 30.3 of the Scottish Building Contract.

The rest of this chapter centres on the Scottish Building Contract, in which the principle used is that the building contract itself is signed by the parties as constituting the contract. The articles of agreement and appendix of the JCT form are not used at all and a special 'conditions only' printing of the form may be obtained for general reference, although this need not be physically included in the contract documents for an individual contract as it is incorporated by reference. The building contract and its own appendices between them perform the functions of the unused parts of the JCT form and also impart the specifically Scottish flavour. The whole document is so drafted that it may be used with slight amendment with any of the four editions of the JCT form mentioned.

Each section of the document is considered in this chapter, giving its headings and sub-headings and an outline of its main implications and the reasons for differences introduced. Otherwise the comments in preceding chapters should be taken into account here also.

The building contract

The contract itself is a very brief document of approximately the same extent as the JCT articles of agreement and serving the same purpose. It allows for insertions into its blank spaces to give the same information as the articles, except that the site is not identified (although it may be included in the space for 'the Works'), while the quantity surveyor is. The employer and the contractor are identified only by their signatures and their addresses are not given.

The wording provides alternatives so that one of four editions of the conditions of the JCT form may be incorporated, these being the private or local authorities editions, in each case with or without quantities. Also incorporated by the wording is the VAT agreement. There are also alternatives in the proviso about the contractor's right of objection to the nomination of a new architect or quantity surveyor. All this gives a similar intention to the articles of agreement and the wording has a close similarity in the main. The references to the two appendices of the contract also serve primarily to tie the various sections together and as such need no comment. It is however the first of these references that relates the JCT conditions to the law of Scotland by establishing that the conditions are 'amended and modified by the provisions contained in the Scottish Supplement forming Appendix No 1'. The matter of the law applying to the contract and to arbitration arose in *James Miller & Partners Ltd* v. *Whitworth Estates (Manchester) Ltd.*

Apart from a number of smaller points related to Scottish practice and the fact that the Arbitration Acts 1950 to 1979 do not apply in Scotland, there are few material points of difference in clause 4 on arbitration. There is no reference in the subjects of arbitration to 'the construction of the Contract' so that the arbiter (as he is termed in Scotland) is restricted to 'any matter or thing . . . arising', although usually this will be his practical limit. Early arbitration over a reasonable objection by the contractor under JCT clause 4.1 to a variation instruction under JCT clause 13.1.2 changing obligations or restrictions imposed by the employer is omitted from the provisions. The reason for this is not known and it could allow a very difficult situation to develop for the contractor, who might well press therefore for the inclusion of the provision when entering into the contract. The law of Scotland is to apply to all arbitrations, so that this automatically becomes so by the execution of the building contract. It is also provided for the arbiter to be remunerated and to recover his outlays!

For those many matters where arbitration may not be commenced until such a time as practical completion unless the parties agree otherwise, it is desirable to give written notice of intent as soon as possible. If not, it is possible that the Prescription and Limitation (Scotland) Act 1973 may lead to proceedings being time barred.

For cases in which the building contract is not being executed, clauses 4 and 5 on arbitration and law are repeated in Appendix No 1 as clauses 41 and 42 so that they may then be included in the contract by reference. This duplication will have no serious effect if left, but the second set of clauses could be deleted for clarity when the building contract *is* being executed.

When it is arranged for the conditions to accord with Scots law and for arbitration to be under that law, it is also necessary to ensure that the law then applies to the contract. This is done by clause 5 to establish the agreement of the parties on the point. Without this it would appear that English law would apply in the courts and in arbitration should the contract be entered into outside Scotland, even despite the use of the Scottish supplement as such. In accordance with Scottish practice the contract will be signed, but the option of sealing is not available as it is in England. A sentence, not noted as an option but which can easily be deleted, provides for registration of the contract which allows either party to follow a special Scottish means of proceeding against the other for recovery of money under the contract.

Appendix No 1 — Scottish supplement

The elements of this supplement serve three main purposes:

(a) To interpret certain expressions in the building contract and the JCT conditions in particular ways.

(b) To establish which of the alternatives within the various JCT conditions apply and thus to avoid using a set of conditions directly amended for each individual contract.

(c) To amend the JCT conditions in a number of respects.

Of these the first two are straightforward. The interpretations are given initially in a single section and redefine the articles of agreement and the appendix as the building contract and the present Appendix No 2 respectively, 'arbitrator' as 'arbiter' and so on. The other elements follow in a single set of references to the JCT conditions. References to each of the alternatives are listed to permit deletion of those not wanted. Some of the amendments to the conditions need more comment individually as follows.

CLAUSE 14 — CONTRACT SUM

This clause includes a rider to bring in the effect of clause 30.11 mentioned below.

CLAUSE 16 — MATERIALS AND GOODS UNFIXED OR OFF-SITE

Here clause 16.2 relating to ownership of off-site materials and goods is deleted, as later is the connected clause 30.3 relating to payment for them. The reason for this is that, while payment under clause 30.3 usually secures the employer a good title under English law, it does not do so under Scottish law. This is because a building contract is not a contract of sale or purchase which is needed to give the necessary effect. An amended clause 30.3 is included to deal with this.

CLAUSE 27 — DETERMINATION BY EMPLOYER; CLAUSE 28 — DETERMINATION BY CONTRACTOR; CLAUSE 35 — NOMINATED SUB-CONTRACTORS; CLAUSE 36 — NOMINATED SUPPLIERS

Amendments or addition to each of these make the changes necessary to match Scottish legal terminology and detailed practice over insolvency, while leaving the broad position much the same. The most important practical issue usually is that covered by the changes in clauses 16 and 30.

CLAUSE 30 — CERTIFICATES AND PAYMENTS

In this case the JCT clause 30.3 is deleted in favour of an alternative version, so corresponding to the earlier deletion of clause 16.2. The architect thus does not have an optional right here to certify payment for materials or goods not brought on site. This could become a dangerous right since the ownership of the materials or goods would not pass under Scottish law — hence the deletion of clause 16.2 as being ineffective in such circumstances as insolvency.

To provide an alternative route to the same objective of funding the contractor, and perhaps his sub-contractors, for extensive early outlay before materials or goods reach the site, a quite different clause 30.3 is introduced. This gives the employer the option to enter into a separate direct contract with the contractor or sub-contractor and to purchase the items concerned so that ownership will effectively pass to him under the law of Scotland. As with the procedure under the JCT clause, the exercise of this arrangement is optional in that it depends upon the architect's 'opinion' and is something which the employer 'may' do, while the contractor cannot insist on it. If it were intended by both parties at the time of entering into the contract that such contracts of purchase would be used in respect of known elements, the obvious policy would be to exclude these elements from the contract in the first place and provide for the contract of purchase from the outset.

When this separate contract is entered into the materials and goods are excluded from the present contract and the contract sum is adjusted by the amount of the contract of purchase, thus leaving fixing, profit, etc in the present contract and also any error in the amount included for the cost of the items in the contract sum. When the items are purchased from the contractor, the purchase price agreed may or may not be exactly what the contractor paid for the items with any addition for work performed on them, so long as it is a reasonable price to have paid in the event of his subsequent insolvency. This then protects the employer's interests. In the case of purchases from sub-contractors, it is clearly far tidier for the exact sum chargeable to be used. Clause 30.3.2 protects the contractor's right to 'any cash discount or other emolument' and thus balances clause 30.3.1 which requires his consent to a direct purchase from a sub-contractor, with the usual rider about such consent not being unreasonably withheld.

The two contracts of purchase are used to cover the two cases of items included in the contract originally for supply by either the contractor or a sub-contractor, whether or not nominated. In the first the employer agrees with the contractor to purchase the items direct as outlined above and to pay for them direct, at 95 per cent of value at once and the remaining 5 per cent at the time when the second stage of retention reduction will occur under the main contract. It is also provided that all clauses of the main contract other than those for payment will apply, and this is important to preserve the position over such matters as damage and insurance, which are expressly mentioned without excluding other issues. Covering instructions appended to the contract rehearse paragraphs very similar to those in the deleted version of clause 30.3, the main exception being omission of proof of insurance, to set out the precautions that should be observed before the use of the system is considered. There is an additional exhortation to obtain a receipt for the first stage of payment to complete proof. The second contract of purchase is almost identical, but involves all three persons. The contractor features simply as consenting to the employer and the sub-contractor carrying out the deal, while he still retains his responsibilities over damage and the like. In both contracts of purchase the levels and release of retention may differ slightly from those that would have applied if the items had been paid for through the main contract.

There is an additional clause 30.11 providing that 'Nothing in Clauses 30.6.2 or 30.9.2 shall prevent the Employer from deducting or adding liquidated and ascertained damages' (again, 'liquidate' is the Scottish term). This has been included to cancel the effect of the judgement in the case of *Robert Paterson* v. *Household Supplies* decided on the previous JCT contract. If that decision is wrong, as appears likely (see, for instance, the earlier *Port Glasgow Magistrates* v. *Scottish Construction Co Ltd*), the clause becomes as unnecessary in Scotland as it is in England.

Appendix No 2 — Abstract of schedule of conditions

This section is very similar to the appendix to the JCT form and provides the places for filling in those details, such as contract dates, which vary from project to project.

PART 5

Contracts for government and civil engineering work

General conditions of government contracts for building and civil engineering works

The form of contract generally used for government contracts goes by the same title as this chapter, but it is more commonly referred to by its official reference of 'Form GC/Works/1'. The edition discussed here is Edition 2 (Autumn 1977) with supplementary conditions mentioned at the end of this chapter. The form is in general use in government departments and among some government corporations and the like; in these latter cases it may appear under some other title and may have small differences in its contents. It is not suitable for adaptation for use by other public bodies or in the private sector.

Background to the form

The form originates in an interdepartmental committee representing all ministries concerned with construction; this body consults with the major employers' federations in the construction industry in producing amendments to the form. The main locus of responsibility is now in the Property Services Agency of the Department of the Environment.

There are other related forms for mechanical and electrical direct contracts, for minor contracts and for sub-contracts. The first exists to meet the fairly frequent practice of placing direct contracts rather than nominated sub-contracts where engineering services are of high value in relation to the building work. It differs from the GC/Works/1 contract in many more respects than can be explained by the difference in subject matter and has a number of unexpected omissions. The minor contracts form is suitable only for lump sums without quantities.

The form of what follows combines a summary of GC/Works/1 with a commentary on it. This present chapter seeks to do no more than underline key features, particularly where there is difference in principle from the JCT form with which comparison is made. (The term 'JCT form' usually refers here to the private edition with quantities which is discussed in detail in Parts 2 and 3 of the present work.)

Within the present limited treatment it is not possible to consider all the implications of the clauses discussed and where comments are made their comparative brevity precludes the greater precision that comes with fullness.

Some general points about the conditions contained in the form may be noted. One, which is evidenced by their title, is that they are intended both for building and for civil engineering work; they thus combine the purposes of the JCT form and the ICE form although the philosophy of their drafting is much more akin to that of the former. There are in fact none of the really distinctive features of the ICE form — and the conditions operate none the worse for that. Another feature is that they may be used with a variety of financial bases, as is discussed under 'Contract Documents' below.

There are a number of features peculiar to the present conditions. 'The Authority' (treated in the conditions as masculine singular), who here takes the place of 'the Employer', appears in a more active role than in either of the other forms, being able to make decisions and to give consents that may govern both parties. More than this, a number of important matters are withheld from arbitration and the decision of the authority is made final and conclusive. Some of these matters are peculiar in character to government contracts, although not all of them are; an indication of them is given in connection with the arbitration condition below.

'The Superintending Officer', abbreviated to 'the SO', takes the place of the architect under the JCT form. What is important is that he appears within the authority's organisation and not as an independent professional person standing between the parties. This is the contractual position even if outside consultants are engaged. The situation in which the authority will seek arbitration as a means of redress against the decision of the SO will therefore not arise.

The contract itself is evidenced by the tender on the one hand and a letter of acceptance on the other: there is no equivalent to the JCT articles of agreement. The form serving as invitation and form of tender also contains the abstract of particulars, which is the counterpart of the appendix to the JCT form. There can thus be no case of an English contract under seal and such a form in fact is not used by government departments.

While the conditions exhibit somewhat greater legal precision than the JCT form, and considerably more than the ICE form, they also include material which appears to be spelling out procedural points for the benefit of the SO or even perhaps of the authority. In practice 'the authority' may often be equated with the departmental contracts branch, which in the governmental system of balance of power exists alongside the professional departments, who in turn are enshrined in the term 'the SO', except for the quantity surveyor and any resident engineer or clerk of works.

To simplify discussion, the conditions are here considered under broad topics rather than their printed order, but the order is broadly that used for the JCT form. (Form GC/Works/1 uses the title 'condition' rather than 'clause'.) All conditions are noted in the discussion; a serial check will show that conditions 11, 54 and 60 are not mentioned: the reason is simple — these conditions do not occur in the form either. There are however conditions 5A, 5B, 11G and 28A to redress the balance. In addition, there are separately printed optional conditions, amongst them conditions 11A to 11F, commented on in the last section of this chapter.

Conditions similar to JCT clauses

A number of conditions may be considered as having a similar effect to certain clauses or parts of clauses in the JCT form and also not to need comment under later headings. This type of comparison must always be superficial, since there will often be differences of detail or even of effect that may not have been envisaged by the drafters. Also, the subject-matter of a condition or clause may be split between two or more clauses or conditions in the other document. Conditions that bear such reasonable comparison are listed below, with the JCT equivalent and some comments.

GC/Works/1 condition	JCT clause	Subject and comments
1	1 & 14	Definitions etc. There are also some equivalent matters in the JCT articles of agreement. Parts of this condition are discussed under the heading of 'Contract documents' below.
12	7	Setting out works.
13	8 & 11	Materials and workmanship to conform to description. This condition is more detailed about costs of testing and covers access for inspection.
15	9	Patent rights.
20	34	Excavations, and materials arising therefrom. This deals with the ownership and disposal of whatever may be excavated, including antiquities which are treated in the JCT manner.
32	17	Defects liability. This condition is less detailed over procedure and the time-tabling of remedial work.
36	8	Replacement of contractor's employees. There is a two-tier system, by grade of employee, as to whether the SO or the authority requires the replacement.

Conditions without equivalent in the JCT clauses

A number of the present conditions are not paralleled in the JCT form: some are considered under later headings, but those needing little comment are as follows:

GC/Works/1 condition	Subject and comments
2	Contractor deemed to have satisfied himself as to conditions affecting execution of the works.
17	Watching, lighting and protection of the works.
18	Precautions to prevent nuisance.
19	Removal of rubbish.
21	Foundations.

22	Contractor to give due notice prior to covering work. This applies generally (presumably for inspection) and to varied work under condition 9.
34	Daily returns.
43	Recovery of sums due from the contractor. This is a wide provision permitting recovery of such things as liquidated damages through other contracts, and indeed other government bodies.
49	Emergency powers. This allows the authority itself to carry out emergency work where it considers it necessary and to recover the cost from the contractor if appropriate.
52	Racial discrimination.
56	Admission to the site. This gives the authority wide control over the persons who may come on the site.
57	Passes. These are issued when public safety or security necessitates them.
58	Photographs. This empowers the authority to control photography and subsequent publication.
59	Secrecy. This is a sombre reminder of the Official Secrets Acts among others, with some echoes of JCT clause 5 over the reuse of information obtained.

There are two further conditions that are not paralleled in the JCT form under the private editions, although they are in the local authorities editions. These are:

GC/Works/1 condition	JCT clause	Subject
51	19A	Fair wages etc.
55	27.3	Corrupt gifts and payment of commission.

JCT clauses without equivalent in the conditions

A few clauses in the JCT form are not paralleled in these present conditions, as follows:

JCT clause	Subject and comments
21	Insurance against injury to persons and property. No insurance by the contractor is mandatory, as is considered under 'Risks and injury' below.
28	Determination by contractor. Unless the contractor chooses to forfeit the contract he has no remedy of this type open to him.
39 & 40	Fluctuations: while condition 11G is included to cover labour-tax matters, so paralleling the option in JCT clause 38, all other aspects are covered in supplementary optional conditions (considered at the end of this chapter).
33	War damage. While this is not dealt with as such, condition 44 'Special powers of determination' is cast in wide enough terms to give a similar effect.

Of the above, clauses 21 and 28 are particularly significant. The omission of an equivalent of clause 28 is typical of the bias of Form GC/Works/1 in favour of the authority.

Contract documents

The conditions corresponding to JCT clause 2.2, 5 and 14 are:
1   Definitions etc.
4   Specifications, bills of quantities, drawings etc.
5   Bills of quantities.
5A   The authority's schedule of rates.
5B   The contractor's schedule of rates.

These conditions cover substantially the same ground as the clauses. Condition 1(1) establishes the various documents as forming one contract and as complementary to one another, while condition 4 sets out that in case of discrepancy these conditions shall prevail. This is in the line of the JCT form. The present conditions are far more flexible as to what the contract documents need be, beyond the conditions and the drawings. In particular where there are bills of quantities, the specification is a contract document alongside the bills of quantities, which is contrary to the JCT form, although its relationship to the other documents is not defined and is therefore at the discretion of the persons drafting it. Usually it will contain positional information amplifying the drawings and details of materials and workmanship that would otherwise occur in the preambles of the bills of quantities.

Condition 1(2) defines the contract sum as 'the sum accepted, or the sum calculated in accordance with the prices accepted'. This allows for a financial basis that is a lump sum known in advance, whether or not related to quantities, or a set of prices from which the sum is calculated. It does not allow for prime cost and the contract in general is not intended for this approach. The alternative approaches envisaged are set out below.

(A) FIRM QUANTITIES

Conditions 5(1) and 5(2) run in a similar vein to the JCT with-quantities form. The method of measurement is to be that expressed in the bills, rather than that any one standard method applies unless otherwise stated.

(B) PROVISIONAL OR APPROXIMATE QUANTITIES

These two appear to be the same for practical purposes and are stated in condition 5(3) as though they are a variant form of quantities, so that the points about firm quantities will apply to them also. Once such quantities have been used for tendering, they become effectively a schedule of rates for remeasurement, as the condition implies.

(C) SCHEDULE OF RATES

This is used in one of two ways: for measurement of work as it is executed, or in support of a lump sum without quantities. Condition 5A refers to the former and to the authority's schedule in similar terms to those used in the provisions about approximate quantities. It does not however import the provisions about such matters as errors in descriptions or prices that are there, or any statement about the method of measurement.

(D) DRAWINGS AND SPECIFICATION

Here there is a lump sum without any quantities in the usual way. However a breakdown in the tender may be provided by the contractor, giving a schedule of rates for variations. Condition 5B covers this second way of using a schedule. The provisions mentioned as not being present in condition 5A are missing here also, but are not relevant.

Condition 1(1) is so worded that no amendment of the text of the conditions is needed to allow for any of these possibilities, although reference to the inclusion of either condition 5 or 5A will be made in the tender documents. If neither applies, condition 5B automatically does.

Local and other authorities' notices and fees (condition 14)

Like JCT clause 6, condition 14 provides for the contractor to give notices and pay all fees and to indemnify the authority. The big difference is that there is no provision for the amount of fees to be added to the contract sum: the contractor must therefore include them in his original tender in all cases.

SO's instructions and related matters

Several conditions may be taken here as broadly equivalent to JCT clauses, while being rather stronger in some respects.

CONDITION 7 — SO'S INSTRUCTIONS

This condition is the equivalent of parts of JCT clause 4 in that it obliges the contractor to obey the SO's instructions. There is however no right for the contractor to obtain any substantiation of the SO's authority to order any matter in doubt. On the contrary, the SO's decision here is final and conclusive. The condition lists in one place the subject matter of the SO's instructions, whereas the JCT form considers such matters only under the various clauses concerned. It therefore covers variations, clarifications and a number of wide ranging issues, while further the list is open-ended since its last item begins 'Any other matter . . .'. The specific inclusion of rights to instruct the contractor on the order of working, on hours of working, and on emergency action needed for security (whether of the works or the State is not defined), thus gives considerable scope to dictate matters which the JCT form leaves strictly to the contractor. The JCT form goes no further than allowing changes under clause 13.2 in obligations or restrictions already imposed by the employer in the contract.

The SO is required to confirm in writing any oral instructions, but it is not made clear whether or not the instructions are valid and must be obeyed if they remain oral. Certainly the condition forbids the contractor making any variation without the SO's instructions. There is no provision for the contractor to confirm oral instructions back to the SO so that they become valid after a waiting period. The next condition might just help here.

CONDITION 8 — FAILURE OF CONTRACTOR TO COMPLY WITH SO'S INSTRUCTIONS

This is equivalent to further parts of JCT clause 4, and like it allows other persons to be employed to carry out work arising out of instructions that the contractor has not implemented after a written notice requiring compliance. Presumably if the contractor were to wait for such a notice before complying he could obtain written confirmation of a sort this way, if his earlier request had for some reason not been met. This is something of a counsel of desperation, only to be thought of in abnormal circumstances.

CONDITION 16 — APPOINTMENT OF RESIDENT ENGINEER OR CLERK OF WORKS

While this condition makes any such person an inspector along the lines of JCT clause 12, it also gives him power to condemn work and allows the SO to delegate to him such other of his powers as he chooses, which will include the power of giving instructions. This seems far more workable for the SO than the JCT arrangement and is balanced by a requirement that the contractor be notified of the extent of delegation. Without this notification, the contractor may decline to receive such instructions or other matters.

CONDITION 33 — CONTRACTOR'S AGENT

This person is the parallel of the person-in-charge under JCT clause 10 and is to receive 'directions' (a sub-category of 'instructions'?) on the site.

CONDITION 35 — CONTRACTOR TO CONFORM TO REGULATIONS

This condition, which has no JCT equivalent, refers to rules and regulations of an individual establishment within which the works may be situated. These matters may vary considerably within the orbit of governmental activity and they are to be those 'described in the Contract'. Any beyond these would need to be notified under SO's instructions and might lead to modified payment.

The programme of the works

As in the last section, a number of conditions may be taken as covering similar ground to JCT clauses. However, the conditions relating to determination are sufficiently varied and detailed to warrant separate treatment in the next section.

CONDITION 6 — PROGRESS OF THE WORKS

This condition covers all the ground of JCT clause 23 and a little more. Possession or commencement is by notice, which means that the contractor does not have a fixed date known in advance. On the other hand the date for completion may well be a fixed date in the abstract of particulars, the implications of which do not need elaborating. The SO may give directions over the progression of the works which will include, but not be limited to postponement.

CONDITION 23 — SUSPENSION FOR FROST, ETC

Here the SO has a power, unparalleled in the JCT form to order a suspension of vulnerable work. There may or may not be requirements in the specification for the contractor to take particular precautions: the present power is over and above these requirements. Where the contractor has complied with the specification, he will be reimbursed for the expense arising from the SO's instruction, but otherwise not since he will be in default. Where the specification is silent he will be reimbursed, unless he is clearly not conforming with some blanket provision. There is some room for doubt here, but not over extension of time where the present causes are taken up in condition 28 considered next.

CONDITION 28 — DATE FOR COMPLETION — EXTENSIONS OF TIME

This condition starts with the equivalent of JCT clause 2.1 about the works being to the satisfaction of the SO, but specifically includes here that they are to be delivered up by the date of completion. This latter is defined in Condition 1 as being modified by any extensions of time. The main part of the condition is concerned with this theme and runs fairly close to JCT clause 25 over a decidedly more limited range of causes, but without such an elaborate set of procedures for granting extensions.

The condition includes any act or default of the employer as a blanket factor and weather conditions which stop work, without specifying them as exceptional, so that any such weather results in an extension. On the other hand there is no mention of shortages of labour or materials or of delay in any way to nominated sub-contractors. Delays due to circumstances wholly beyond the contractor's control are acceptable and could include labour and materials, but he is expected to foresee circumstances where possible and allow for them. Where the contractor is negligent or the like he receives no extension and any authorised omission may reduce an extension. This would not permit any reduction of the original or already extended time in the absence of an extension. Extension may be for 'delay in such completion which has been caused' or 'which . . . will be caused', so that it would appear that an extension after completion will be valid.

CONDITION 28A — PARTIAL POSSESSION BEFORE COMPLETION

The main effect of this condition is similar to that of JCT clause 18, when allowance has been made for such distinctive features between the two sets of conditions as the insurance provisions. The imminent occurrence of partial possession is however more clearly signalled here by a certificate of satisfaction from the SO, whose decision under the condition at large is to be final and conclusive. The certificate does give some precision to happenings in a way that the JCT form procedure does not, as is evident from the case of *English Industrial Estates Corporation* v. *George Wimpey and Co Ltd.*

There are also three sets of circumstances giving rise to the right of the authority to take possession. The first is an agreement in the contract for phasing to occur, which is an arrangement that can be accommodated in the JCT framework by the sectional completion supplement. The second is an agreement between the parties and this parallels the explicit JCT situation. Such an agreement would necessarily trigger off for the contractor only such things as a release of retention that are given in the condition. The third circumstance is an instruction by the SO for the contractor to give possession. This may arise quite contrary to anything that the contractor may wish and would rank for the possibility of extra payment, as with other instructions of the SO. It will be clear that between the second and third of these circumstances of agreement or otherwise there exists a twilight area, but the third does give the authority a valuable option to assume possession in a way that would be a breach under the JCT provisions.

CONDITION 29 — LIQUIDATED DAMAGES

The provisions here are in step with JCT clause 24. Condition 28 has maintained the right of the authority to damages, including where there has been 'any act or default of the Authority', and this position is reinforced in certain details here. In addition it is made explicit that damages may be recovered under the quite wide provisions of condition 43, a condition without equivalent in the JCT form. This may include the case in which the contractor has overrun the date for completion and in which an extension of time is not granted, so that a backlog of damages may arise. Recovery through withholding some part of advances on account is the obvious first choice and the procedural niceties under the JCT form are thus avoided.

Determination of the contract

The main conditions dealing with this subject are considered separately below. In each case it is the contract that is determined and not the contractor's employment under the contract, as in the JCT form. Properly such determination leaves the parties without apparatus for settlement and casts them back on a barter or court action. The conditions however provide their own apparatus for settlement and therefore, in effect, carry a similar meaning to JCT clause 27 in this respect.

As already mentioned, these conditions make no provision at all for the contractor to determine on the lines of JCT clause 28. All that he can do is forfeit the contract and fight out the result.

CONDITION 3 — VESTING OF WORKS ETC IN THE AUTHORITY. THINGS NOT TO BE REMOVED

While condition 3 relates to more situations than determination, it has particular significance in this context since it makes the contractor's plant and other items the property of the authority while on site and restricts the contractor in his rights of removal. When determination occurs these items are available to the authority under condition 46 in a way they are not under JCT clause 27. This cannot however cover hired plant, whether under hire purchase or otherwise.

CONDITION 44 — SPECIAL POWERS OF DETERMINATION

Condition 44(1) permits the authority to determine the contract at any time and apparently for any reason. It will not be invoked where the contractor is in default, when condition 45 will be used. Its most obvious uses are where there is some major policy or other outside cause affecting the desirability of proceeding, or where the works have suffered major damage.

Condition 44(2) covers various matters which the contractor may be directed to perform after the determination has otherwise become effective. Like that for SO's instructions, the list given is open-ended, as its last item also begins 'any other matter . . .'.

Conditions 44(3) to 44(6) inclusive cover the payment of the contractor for works and materials and require him to remove his plant and the like and determine any sub-contracts. There is no provision for the cost of premature removal or of other attendant circumstances of the determination to be met, except additional payments under sub-contracts and contracts of employment; there is however provision for the contractor to lodge a hardship claim under which he could include such matters. Such a claim is not subject to arbitration however. Payment as a whole under the condition is conditional only on coming to a settlement and not on completion of the works, as in the JCT form. The contractor may thus receive his money comparatively early.

CONDITION 45 — DETERMINATION OF CONTRACT DUE TO DEFAULT OR FAILURE OF THE CONTRACTOR

Condition 45 deals with the act of determination only; condition 46 governs subsequent matters. The majority of the cases on which the authority may act are similar to those under JCT clause 27, being the contractor's default in quality and progress and also his insolvency. Sub-letting without approval is not included, however. In the case of insolvency there is no automatic determination, but the difficulties of the employer determining unilaterally under the JCT form on this account will still apply for the authority here.

The other case for determination is a breach of security under condition 56.

The provisions of condition 46 follow on condition 45, but are not relevant to condition 44 which incorporates its own rules. The effect is similar to that of the JCT form, except that the authority may recoup loss that it stands to suffer by selling plant and the like which vests in it under condition 3. Any plant or monies remaining after recouping losses are however to be returned to the contractor. If the authority happens to have effected an overall saving as a result of the determination, all plant has to be returned to the contractor, as has any monies arising from sale of plant. Beyond this, the contractor is to be paid any outstanding sums for work done and for materials supplied and used by the authority, up to the amount of the saving. As a result of this arrangement, the authority retains any residual saving; this element also differs from that obtaining under the JCT form.

In place of an amount for 'direct loss and/or damage' recoverable under the JCT form, the present condition specifically retains liquidated damages as the amount recoverable.

Risks and injury

The present conditions differ from the JCT form in that there is no contractual obligation on the contractor to take out insurances either of the works or of matters over which the contractor is required to indemnify the authority.

While not requiring insurance, the conditions proceed on the basis of allocating to the authority certain risks of damage to the works, and the authority then bears the cost of reinstatement or of determination. As far as reinstatement is concerned, this parallels the position under clause 22B of the local authorities editions of the JCT form, where insurance is not required. The risks concerned are defined in condition 1 and are known collectively as the accepted risks. They are broadly similar to the JCT clause 22 perils but include also war damage.

Condition 25 (Precautions against fire and other risks) requires the contractor to 'take all reasonable precautions' against the accepted risks and to comply with any SO's instructions to further this end — presumably with reimbursement unless the contractor's own negligence leads to the instruction. The condition does not establish that the contractor shall carry the cost of any reinstatement where his own negligence has been established;

condition 26 points in the other direction and thus puts the authority in a position equivalent to an insurer.

Condition 26 (Damage to works, plant etc) leaves all responsibility for plant and other temporary items with the contractor and does the same with the works and materials except in two cases. One of these is to the extent that there has been neglect or default on the part of a servant of the Crown and the other is to the extent that any accepted risk has caused the loss or damage.

PERSONS AND PROPERTY

Condition 47 (Injury to persons: loss of property) applies to all cases except the works, which are covered by condition 26, and public roads so far as they are covered by condition 48.

A great part of the wording of condition 47 arises out of the special position of the Crown, particularly with regard to servants of the Crown. If these special matters be left aside, the main provisions of the contract are that the contractor is to make good property of the Crown or pay compensation and that he is to indemnify the Crown and servants of the Crown against claims from all quarters, including claims of servants against the Crown. The contractor is however liable only where neglect or default can be laid at his door or that of persons for whom he is responsible, which in the case of injury to persons means that the position differs from that under the JCT form. The onus of proof is however in all cases on the contractor to show that he is not liable.

Condition 48 (Damage to public roads) provides that the authority indemnifies the contractor against the particular case of claims and proceedings for damage to highways or bridges caused by extraordinary traffic of the contractor. This is made subject to the contractor taking all reasonable steps to prevent damage. If he does not do this then the authority, while still initially affording the indemnity, may recover its expense from the contractor.

Variations, remeasurement and extra expense

Several conditions need to be taken together here, but the overall effect is quite close to that under the JCT conditions, with a few important qualifications and some procedural differences. Of these latter only the more weighty are touched upon here.

CONDITION 9 — VALUATION OF THE SO'S INSTRUCTIONS

This condition covers much of the ground of JCT clause 13. It does not deal with provisional sums which come under condition 38.

Condition 9(1) relates to variations and covers the traditional formula for their valuation by the quantity surveyor using the usual range of measured alternatives or daywork. The latter is to be covered in the contract, so far as all its details of calculation are concerned. The quantity surveyor has the power under condition 9(3) to value work which should be measured but has been covered without him having the chance to see it; his decision is final and conclusive. There is no provision here to cover extra expense arising out of variation instructions and not taken up in the measured basis or daywork — simply a provision for measured variation prices on a contract or pro rata basis to be adjusted to a star rate basis in suitable cases. Condition 9(2) specifically excludes any application to variations in its own scope. Condition 53, however, takes up the wider expense that may arise.

Condition 9(2) deals with the reimbursement of extra expense arising out of other categories of SO's instructions. Probably owing to the more extensive scope of SO's instructions, there is a reasonable provision for the recovery of any possible saving in the contractor's expense. It is a condition precedent to payment of any increase, but not to the recovery of any saving, that the SO's instructions must be in writing. This gives considerable edge to the question of confirmation of instructions under condition 7, as discussed there. In addition it is a condition precedent that the contractor is to provide 'documents and information' as soon as possible. There is no requirement for him to give notice that he intends to make a claim, as the JCT form requires. Whether 'information' after the event is sufficient may be doubted. Where the contractor obeys oral instructions without confirmation, leaving all these arrangements deficient at root, it is normal departmental practice to hold that any expense incurred cannot be recovered under the terms of the contract. Payments for such expense are usually dealt with under a separate claims procedure on what is termed an 'extra-contractual basis', whatever the expression may mean.

CONDITION 10 — VALUATION BY MEASUREMENT

In the cases where the financial basis is related to rates rather than some form of lump sum, this condition provides for measurement and valuation of the works *in toto* using the rules in condition 9. This arrangement therefore covers the forms considered under 'Contract Documents' as provisional and approximate quantities and schedules of rates and dealt with in conditions 5 and 5A. Condition 5B also deals with a schedule of rates case, but this is a schedule provided for use in assessing variations and not as a basis for remeasurement and so is not covered here.

CONDITION 24 — DAYWORK

The matters covered here are procedural only, as the main provision is in condition 9.

CONDITION 37 — ATTENDING FOR MEASUREMENT AND PROVISION OF INFORMATION

The contractor is required to attend to accept the quantity surveyor's records and also to provide 'documents and information' in support of variations and other financial adjustments.

CONDITION 39 — PROVISIONAL SUMS AND PROVISIONAL QUANTITIES

Both categories of provisional items are treated here, rather than only the former as in the JCT form. They are to be dealt with over calculation of expenditure in the same way, that is by measurement and valuation under the main formulae. There is no mention of any part falling to be nominated expenditure and condition 38 is also silent on the point, as is considered there.

CONDITION 53 — PROLONGATION AND DISRUPTION EXPENSES

This condition parallels JCT clause 26 and has a primary provision under condition 53(1) for adjustment of the contract sum by the quantity surveyor to cover extra expense that is 'beyond that otherwise provided for in or reasonably contemplated by the Contract'. The causes given there and amplified by condition 53(2) are:

(a) Any SO's instructions.

(b) Damage to the works, in the same proportion as the authority is liable for the damage itself under condition 26(2).

(c) Work by direct contractors under condition 50.

(d) Delay in the SO providing design information, in the authority executing work or supplying items, and in the SO or the authority making nominations or performing other activities regarding PC items.

Condition 53(3) lists three conditions precedent to the contractor's entitlement to payment:

(a) The SO's instructions are to be in writing.

(b) The contractor has to give proper notice of information or action required from the SO or the authority.

(c) The contractor has to give immediate advance notice of any likely claim and has to provide 'documents and information' soon afterwards.

Other persons employed on the works

As with the JCT form, there are several conditions that deal with the various categories of persons who may be employed on the works. They cover substantially the same material, but are arranged somewhat differently and diverge at several important points.

CONDITION 27 — ASSIGNMENT OR TRANSFER OF CONTRACT

This most drastic way of the contractor shedding his work load is dealt with as in JCT clause 19.1, by severe control.

CONDITION 30 — SUB-LETTING

This condition parallels JCT clause 19.2 by requiring consent, but further requires certain provisions to be included in any sub-contract, including variation of price conditions. It does not parallel JCT clause 19.3 over selection from a specified list. There is no reference to nominated work in the condition and it is not drafted to take account of it; the comments under condition 38 should however be noted.

CONDITION 31 — SUB-CONTRACTORS AND SUPPLIERS

Three matters forming parts of JCT clauses 35 and 36 are covered here: the right of the contractor to make reasonable objection to a nomination (which includes a supplier nomination), his responsibility for a person once accepted and his liability to make good any loss or expense due to default of such a person. In the latter two matters the reference is to persons 'nominated or approved', that is it partly refers back to condition 30. Condition 38 also takes up one special type of default, as there discussed. 'Nomination' itself is defined in condition 40(7) but not here, oddly.

CONDITION 38 — PRIME COST ITEMS

This condition compares with further parts of clauses 35 and 36 but not all of the balance. The question of nomination, but not its definition, is covered as part of the contents of condition 31, while condition 40(6) deals with the withholding of payments and direct payments if the contractor defaults in payment of firms.

   The present condition refers to 'any work to be executed or any things to be supplied by a sub-contractor or supplier' and these persons are to be nominated by the SO or selected in such ways as may be directed. This last expression allows, for example, the SO to ask the contractor to obtain quotations from firms of his own choice from which the SO may make the final selection. It gives no clear authority however to make a nomination to cover expenditure under a provisional sum, although condition 7(1)(m) may perhaps be stretched to cover this. The openness of definition in the condition is otherwise of comparatively little moment since the bills of quantities of the specification will take care of most points, and it contrasts starkly with the JCT 'basic' and 'alternative' approaches. The crucial matter of cash discount is defined as common in all cases, with the level restricted to that obtainable and not exceeding $2\frac{1}{2}$ per cent. The contractor should therefore check the level of discount in any quotation before acceptance: he will lose any excess and cannot recover any deficiency. He cannot make reasonable objection under conditions 31(1), which covers the 'person' as such and not the terms offered.

   The condition is concerned with several matters of accountancy. It excludes any profit for the contractor on variation or price adjustments, whether they are increases or decreases, making a reference to condition 30(3) which apparently does not apply here on a strict reading of that condition. Its definition of 'fixing' is deficient by comparison with that of the Standard Method of Measurement, while not contrary to it.

   A significant provision of the condition is that the authority reserves the right to order and pay for prime cost items direct. This is an alternative to nomination under the condition, but does not entitle the authority to pay direct where the contractor has already ordered the work as a result of nomination. It is also distinct from direct payment when the contractor is in default, which is treated in condition 40(6). The provision here is important since, while the contractor will still be paid his profit on the amount of such work, it appears that he must lose his discount. This seems grossly unfair to the contractor; although the discount is ostensibly to be retained solely on account of prompt payment it also forms an important part of the profit margin of the contractor, and should not be spirited away without redress.

Lastly, a provision clearly taking account of the decision in the case of *North West Metropolitan Regional Hospital Board* v. *T. A. Bickerton Ltd* makes the contractor responsible for the completion of work where a sub-contract is terminated. There is no limitation as to the cause of termination and thus the provision is wider than the circumstances arising in the case. The contractor is either to find another sub-contractor or himself carry out the work, but whichever is done is subject to the approval of the authority and his reimbursement will be in the same sum as would have been payable had the original sub-contractor carried on. All this is in direct contrast to the position under JCT clause 35, where the architect only must renominate and where the employer pays the excess cost, unless the determination has been caused by the contractor.

The condition is silent over several matters mentioned in the JCT form. There is no reference to the form of sub-contract or to the provisions to be incorporated into a sub-contract; condition 30 deals with these for sub-letting but is not relevant to the present case. Again there is no reference to retention, called 'a reserve' in these conditions; apparently the contractor should pay sub-contractors in full while himself bearing retention on their accounts — a view which is strengthened by condition 40(6). Further, there is no consideration of damages, although the contractor is himself liable under condition 31(3). In each of these cases a prudent contractor will put forward his own conditions if the quotation offered to him for acceptance is also silent. Lastly, the position if the contractor tenders for a PC item is not considered, although this can be dealt with easily in practice.

CONDITION 50 — FACILITIES FOR OTHER WORKS

This is worded openly enough to allow other direct contracts of magnitude to proceed and thus denies the contractor the right to exclusive possession of the site during his own operations, without giving him any right reasonably to withhold consent, along the lines of JCT clause 29.2, if he did not know of these when entering into the contract. To take account of this, provision for reimbursement of extra unforeseen expense is included in condition 53. So far as the nature and extent of such direct contracts has been set out in the contract documents, the cost to the contractor should have been included and will not fall as an extra. For the purpose of damage to the respective works, there is mutual liability between the contractor and the authority for damage arising out of negligence and the like, with direct contractors ranking for this purpose as servants of the Crown.

Advances, payments and certificates

Conditions 40, 41 and 42 cover the ground of parts of JCT clauses 17 and 30, although with several important differences and less precision about certificates.

CONDITION 40 — ADVANCES ON ACCOUNT

Condition 40 is the equivalent of JCT clauses 30.1, 30.2 and 30.4. It only applies to affairs 'during the progress' and condition 41 takes up all later payments. It may be considered under its sub-condition references as follows:

(1) The reserve held on the work executed during progress is to be 3 per cent as a flat rate throughout.

(2) Materials on site are subject to their own reserve level of 10 per cent as a flat rate. There is no provision for materials off-site, as in JCT clause 30.3.

(3) Advances on account are to be normally at not less than monthly intervals and the contractor is responsible for making the valuation; extra expense amounts or corresponding savings may be taken into account under condition 9(2) and 9(3), provided that in the case of extra sums agreement has been reached on the amount. However, where the contract sum exceeds a modest £100,000 there may be an interim advance between any pair of main advances, but based on an approximate estimate only. The contractor has no remedy open to him if the authority delays in making payments on account.

(4) The credit value of old materials may be deducted from advances.

(5) Additional sums or savings under condition 9(2) and additional sums under condition 53(1) may be taken into account in advances. This is at the discretion of the SO and without prejudice to final settlements of the amounts or even the principle of any entitlement.

(6) The withholding from advances of amounts included in previous advances is permitted as an option to the extent that the contractor has defaulted in paying sub-contractors and suppliers.

There are several distinctions from JCT clause 35 here. Firstly, suppliers are included and indeed there is no limitation to nominated firms alone; this could lead to the most painful inquiries, although the SO is not obliged to inquire at all. Secondly, there is no mention of any reserve, as discussed under condition 38, and only a possible hint at contra-charges in the closing paragraph. Thirdly, the contractor is not due, for the purposes of this condition, to pay until he has been paid. Lastly, while there is a right in the case of nominated firms only to make direct payments up to the amount of default as in the JCT form, but entirely optionally, this right covers suppliers as well as sub-contractors in the present condition.

(7) The definition of nominated sub-contractor and nominated supplier is given for the purposes of the preceding sub-condition. It happens to be the

only definition in the conditions, although it is implied in the intentions of conditions 31 and 38 and might well occur in a more systematic relation to them. The definition itself is quite orthodox.

CONDITION 41 — PAYMENT ON AND AFTER COMPLETION

Three aspects of payment are dealt with here, explicitly or otherwise:

(a) Any underpayment or overpayment during progress: at completion the final sum is to be estimated and, since the balance of this sum outstanding is to be paid except half the reserve, any discrepancy will be resolved. There is no provision for further advances on account during the ensuing period as there is in JCT clause 30.1.3, so that some care is needed here.

(b) Reduction of the reserve: half of the reserve is released at completion, by reason of the formula stated in (a). The release of the second half is not mentioned distinctly, as discussed in (c), and it could well be held over until the final sum is agreed, or strictly not be paid at all. There is no equivalent to JCT clause 30.4.1.3 releasing it at any time related to the making good of defects. However the (masculine) authority may pay further sums from the reserve 'if he thinks fit'. It is hoped that he will.

(c) Payment of the final balance: this occurs upon agreement of the final sum and will be in whichever direction the indebtedness lies. The timing is not dependent upon whether the making good of defects is complete as in JCT clause 30.8. If, as is most likely, agreement follows the making good of defects, the amount paid to be the whole gap between past payments and the final sum and will therefore automatically clear the balance of the reserve. If however, agreement comes within the maintenance period, the reserve is maintained and only any further balance becomes payable at once. The payment of the rest of the reserve is not then provided for, but in practice will follow on the making good of defects. The third possibility of agreement coming after the maintenance period but before making good of defects is complete is not considered in an already cumbersome provision.

The quantity surveyor is responsible for preparing the final account and forwarding it to the contractor. If it is not agreed, it is subject to arbitration.

CONDITION 42 — CERTIFICATES

This is the only condition other than condition 28A dealing with certificates and the position is more open than under the JCT form. The certificates here mentioned are:

(a) Certificates of sums due under conditions 40 and 41: these parallel the JCT interim certificates and so the release of the first half of the retention, and also the financial part of the final certificate.

(b) Certificate of date of completion: this parallels the JCT certificate of practical completion and has similar consequences. Partial possession is covered under condition 28A.

(c) Certificate of the state of the works, at the end of the maintenance period: this is the equivalent of the JCT certificate of making good defects and of the expressions of satisfaction in the JCT final certificate.

(d) Final certificate for payment: this is alluded to in passing as modifying or correcting interim certificates but is otherwise unexplained. It appears as a special case of a certificate as mentioned under (a) and as equalling the other part of the JCT final certificate.

No guide is given as to who is to be the recipient of certificates. Interim certificates are not to be 'conclusive evidence' over quality or payment, and this is in accordance with the normal legal position established by case law. On the other hand the contractor's counter-right to dispute an interim certificate is excluded. This right exists in full over final certificates, whether of satisfaction or about finance. There is also no statement in the present conditions, here or elsewhere, that contracts out of the effects of the Limitations Act that would otherwise apply. This is quite distinct from the position under JCT clause 30.9 and leaves either party with a right of legal action if the need arises.

Arbitration (condition 61)

Condition 61 shares several similarities with JCT article 5. Reference is to be a single arbitrator, agreed between the parties or appointed through one of several professional bodies. The reference is not to take place until after completion or the like, unless the parties agree. The arbitrator's award will be final within the terms of the Arbitration Acts in England and of Scots law in Scotland. This latter is subject to the law of Scotland being the proper law of the contract under the last sub-condition of the condition and to such considerations as in the case of *Whitworth Street Estates (Manchester) Ltd* v. *James Miller and Partners Ltd.* There is no provision for a nominated firm to be joined in the same reference as in the JCT forms.

The great difference, though, lies in the scope of arbitration. Under the JCT form this is unlimited, although the parties may choose to agree a few particulars in such a way that arbitration is precluded. Under the present conditions a number of matters are made subject to the decision of the authority or even the SO and that decision is to be final and conclusive. Condition 61 specifically excludes these matters from its own scope, along with condition 51. Among the more notable exclusions, listed by condition reference, are:

3   The contractor's right to remove plant and materials from the site.
7(1)   The SO's power to instruct on any matter and thus affect the scope or performance of the works.
40(1)   The amount of interim certificates.
40(6)   Whether payment should be withheld due to the contractor's failure to pay others.

44(5) Hardship payment to the contractor where there is special determination.

Variation of price based on cost

This matter is the more traditional of the forms of JCT fluctuations under another name and dealt with through two main conditions that give a similar effect when they apply. Each of the conditions given includes the equivalent of the JCT clauses on sub-letting, general procedures and definitions, but there is no provision permitting a blanket percentage addition to adjustments.

CONDITION 11G — VARIATION OF PRICE (LABOUR-TAX MATTERS)

As a minimum this condition applies in the contract and covers the same range of matters as JCT clause 38, in so far as that clause relates to labour. The critical factor for adjustment is any change 'coming into effect after the date for the return of tenders' and there is thus parity with the JCT form in that no element of foreseeing is called for on the part of the contractor in arriving at his tender price.

SUPPLEMENTARY CONDITIONS 145 — VARIATION OF PRICE (CONDITIONS 11A TO 11F)

This condition is issued separately from the main body of the conditions into which it fits as the six sub-conditions with the distinct numbers as given in the margin of the main document, as well as having the overall supplementary number. There appears to be no profound significance in this particular oddity. The conditions apply in addition to condition 11G and correspond to the market price fluctuations parts of JCT clause 39 for labour and materials and the overall effect is mainly similar to that arising there. However alterations leading to variation of price are those 'coming into effect after' the date of tender and so, again, the contractor does not have to foresee any increases when tendering. This time, this is a major difference from the JCT arrangements over market fluctuations in the case of labour, although in step in the case of materials. A smaller difference is that there is no reference to timber used in formwork and so this is not open to adjustment. Some selectivity is possible in principle in these conditions in that, say, labour or materials could be deleted from the scope.

There are some additional points which may be noted:

(a) The authority may be able to examine suppliers' costs and reduce excessive charges, although the sub-clause is weakly worded.

(b) The general provisions are to be those incorporated in nominated supply and nominated sub-contract agreements where variations of price apply.

(c) Daywork is not mentioned and so it is necessary for the daywork terms (all defined in the bills of quantities or their equivalent) to state whether the rates used are to be those current when daywork is carried out or otherwise.

(d) In special cases, orders for materials subject to variation of price may incorporate the general provisions.

(e) The authority's decision is final and conclusive. There is therefore no arbitration here, in addition to the other excluded matters listed under condition 61 above.

Any adjustment resulting from the conditions is not to be made until completion of the contract, 'unless the parties otherwise agree'. There is therefore no obligation to add or deduct any sums in advances on account, although this is often done.

Variation of price based on work executed

This is the new method of adjustment under a formula method and corresponds to JCT clause 40. It is covered by 'Supplementary Condition 146: Variation of price (Formula price adjustment on building contracts)', which is issued separately from the main body of the conditions and is not referred to in any way in them. It will be incorporated into the contract therefore by means of the abstract of particulars.

The whole basis of this condition is close to that of the JCT clause and the effect is correspondingly close. There is no separately issued set of formula rules in the present case, since these are included in the condition. The condition allows for a 'productivity deduction' as does the local authorities edition of the JCT form, applied on a percentage basis. This similarity to the JCT provisions carries with it two main differences from the treatment of variation of price under the alternative conditions considered under the preceding heading: daywork is definitely not covered by the arrangement and amounts calculated monthly are payable monthly also through the regular advances after deduction for the reserve. No payment is to be made in the mid-month interim advance if any.

Value Added Tax

As with a JCT contract, the contract sum for a GC/Works/1 contract is exclusive of value added tax and the authority agrees to reimburse it under supplementary condition 139A. There is no direct reference to this condition or to the fact of reimbursement in the main body of the conditions, which when read alone make no mention of value added tax other than to state that it is excluded from a few matters such as labour-tax reimbursement. Strictly therefore the exclusion of value added tax from the contract sum is a matter of inference.

Reimbursement of the tax is made through the regular series of advances on account and final payment, since the supplementary condition forms part of the contract and does not act as supplemental provisions as in the JCT pattern. It is however the responsibility of the authority to calculate the amount of tax due on any payment, but of the contractor to supply the information needed to make the calculation; these elements are again in distinction from those in the JCT supplement. The contractor is to check amounts received as being the correct sums that he has to pass on to the Commissioners and then issue a receipt. This procedure takes account of the alternative definition of the tax point as being the date of payment preceding the issue of a receipt.

Otherwise the condition follows the general philosophy of the JCT provisions. There are paragraphs about adjustment of errors, reference of disputes to the Commissioners rather than to an arbitrator and the treatment of tax on sub-contracted work. Nothing is mentioned about the possibility of a change in tax status of a part of the work leaving the contractor liable to pay over tax, but unable to recover it, which eventually is covered by JCT clause 15.3.

CHAPTER 28

The ICE conditions of contract

This chapter title is that by which the documents under consideration are commonly known. Their formal title is 'General Conditions of Contract and Forms of Tender, Agreement and Bond for use in connection with Works of Civil Engineering Construction' and the edition considered here is the Fifth Edition (June 1973) (Revised January 1979). The three bodies responsible for the documents are: the Institution of Civil Engineers, the Association of Consulting Engineers and the Federation of Civil Engineering Contractors.

The form of what follows is a blend of summary of the documents and comment on them, as in the case of the GC/Works/1 contract. This chapter follows the aim of the previous chapter by underlining key features, largely by comparison with the JCT form. As before, the term 'JCT form' usually refers to the private edition with quantities of those conditions discussed in detail in Parts 2 and 3. Again it is not possible to consider all the implications of the clauses discussed and brevity precludes precision.

Of the conditions in general, little need to said. They are issued in one version only and that version is intended for public and private clients alike, although most clients will be in the public sector. The form of tender and form of agreement between them act as the equivalent of the JCT articles of agreement and appendix. The conditions are not intended for essentially building work, nor are they really suitable for such work. They are drafted to suit the larger and in some ways coarser scale of civil engineering works, with their heavy emphasis on ground works and the relatively high incidence of plant and cost of temporary works. The frequently scattered nature of these works also affects the conditions, as does the fact that parts of them will often be put into use before those parts are complete in every detail or finish. There are also differences arising out of the role of the engineer, who is architect and quantity surveyor all in one under normal civil engineering procedure. The employer fulfils an essentially passive role as he does under the JCT form.

While the principles of the conditions are affected by such consideration as these, their drafting also differs in character from that of the JCT form and the GC/Works/1 contract. The present conditions are more diffuse in tone and, while they follow an orderly pattern as a whole, they are often imprecise to the degree of ambiguity or meaninglessness and leave important issues to the imagination. This approach may have certain practical advantages, but it does not aid interpretation.

The clauses have individual titles and are also grouped in the conditions under major headings. The clauses have been considered under several of these major headings or broader headings and then either as groups or under separate sub-headings as seems appropriate.

Introductory matters

CLAUSE 1 — DEFINITION AND INTERPRETATION

This clause gathers together several definitions, as do the JCT form and the GC/Works/1 contract.

CLAUSE 2 — ENGINEER'S REPRESENTATIVE

The engineer's representative is defined in clause 1 as including a resident engineer, clerk of works or the like. Under the present clause the engineer's representative may be given delegated powers at the engineer's discretion but subject to the contractor's right of appeal to the engineer. This places him in a far different position from that of the clerk of works under JCT clause 12 and on a large contract may lead to him having considerable authority. There is also provision for engineer's assistants, who are allotted functions by the engineer's representative, as he chooses but more on points of detail in particular areas of the work. Again there is a right of appeal, this time to the representative. The representative may not receive delegated powers over the following major decision areas:

Clause 12(3)	Delay and extra cost due to adverse conditions
Clause 44	Extension of time
Clause 48	Certificates of completion
Clause 60(3)	Agreement of the final account
Clause 61	Maintenance certificate
Clause 63	Forfeiture and assignment
Clause 66	Settlement of disputes by the engineer.

These exclusions still allow the possibility of substantial delegation in matters of physical work and programme that will carry financial consequences with them.

CLAUSES 3 AND 4 — ASSIGNMENT AND SUB-LETTING

The position under these clauses is essentially similar to that under JCT clauses 19.1 and 19.2 only. Under clause 1 the employer's successors are mentioned, which implies the possibility of a novation. Since the employer will often be a public body liable to change this is not unreasonable.

CLAUSE 5 TO 7 — CONTRACT DOCUMENTS

These clauses do not state what the documents are. Clause 1 gives the 'Contract' as the conditions, specification, drawings, priced bill of quantities, the tender and its acceptance and the contract agreement — this last being optional. The documents are to be read under clause 5 as mutually explanatory and, if this fails, ambiguities or discrepancies are to be explained and adjusted by the engineer. The contractor can thus assume nothing about the relative status of documents, except presumably that the conditions will always hold legal priority. In particular, it is left to the specification and bills of quantities to define their own relative positions or the engineer to give instructions to remove ambiguities.

The remaining provisions are essentially administrative in their character, but also empower the issue of further drawings and instructions.

General obligations

Clauses 8 to 33 cover a wide range of matters relating to the tender and the execution of the works. Some of them which follow the broad pattern of the JCT form or are reasonably self-explanatory are:

9	Contract agreement: annexed to the conditions.
11	Inspection of site: by contractor when tendering.
	to the contractor on how to perform the work.
15	Contractor's superintendence: covers an agent or the like.
16	Removal of contractor's employees.
17	Setting-out.
25	Remedy on contractor's failure to insure: this is related to clauses 21, 23 and 24 discussed below.
26	Giving of notices and payment of fees: all such payments are reimbursable.
28	Patent rights and royalties.
32	Fossils etc.

Several other clauses call for no comment and cover such matters as bore holes, watching and lighting and clearance at completion that would otherwise occur in the specification or bills of quantities. Clauses of more consequence are dealt with below.

Of the clauses that follow, clauses 12, 13, 14, 27 and 31 contain provision for extension of time and extra payment to the contractor and refer to clauses 44, 52 and 60 that govern these matters in more detail. Discussion in the main is given under these latter clauses.

CLAUSE 8 — CONTRACTOR'S GENERAL RESPONSIBILITIES

The clause defines these as to 'construct complete and maintain the Works' with all that is needed to that end including, be it noted, what is 'reasonably to be inferred from the Contract'. These latter words are important in view of the different approach of civil engineering bills of quantities. The contract is thus an entire contract, with its rigours eased by other provisions, as happens in the JCT form. It is not a lump sum contract, since the contract price under clause 1(1)(i) is described as 'the sum to be ascertained' and this is in line with the use of approximate quantities as the sole financial basis given in clause 55(1) and with the provision for complete measurement given in clause 56(1).

CLAUSE 10 — SURETIES

This clause and the optional bond here provided for are mentioned at the end of this chapter, since the bond is given as an appendix to the conditions.

CLAUSE 12 — ADVERSE PHYSICAL CONDITIONS AND ARTIFICIAL OBSTRUCTIONS

The contractor is held under clause 11(2) 'Sufficiency of tender' to have made adequate financial provision for all his obligations under the contract and this must include matters relating to the site and its conditions, which the immediately preceding clause 11(1) deems him to have checked. Nevertheless, the present clause, which has no JCT parallel, recognises the possibility that there may be matters which 'could not reasonably have been foreseen by an experienced contractor' — and may not have been foreseen by the engineer either, it may be noted in passing. Experience suggests that such contingencies are well nigh inevitable and they have led to legal proceedings as in cases under 'Documentation and measurement'. The clause divides them into two categories, of which 'artificial obstructions' calls for no comment. The other is 'physical conditions (other than weather conditions or conditions due to weather conditions)'. Some physical conditions, such as rock, may call for separate treatment in the bills of quantities in any case and so they will be taken up in the measurement of the work. Where this is not the case, reimbursement can be made under this clause. There will be instances where weather may not cause the condition, but in fact makes it worse when it arises from some other cause. These instances would not properly come within the exclusion proviso of the clause and it would be reasonable for reimbursement to be made. Apart from reimbursement, there is the question of effect on the programme of any of these conditions that rank for payment (including those measurable under bill items), and here extension of time is permitted.

The procedure is for the contractor to give warning of the cause and likely effects as soon as possible, with a statement of his intended counter-measures, the effects covering money and time. The engineer may require a financial estimate from the contractor and may instruct any amended measures including suspension of work. In the end the contractor is paid the amount calculated under the terms of the contract, and not the amount of his estimate.

CLAUSE 13 — WORK TO BE TO SATISFACTION OF ENGINEER

This provision in its opening part is the equivalent of JCT clause 2 in expressing that the satisfaction of the engineer is the criterion of acceptability —a criterion which would be subject to arbitration as usual. It goes further in requiring his approval to the 'mode, manner and speed of construction and maintenance'. In view of the engineer's wider powers of control (although still related to obtaining only the contract works) and of the possible need to clarify the relationship of the contract documents under clause 5, there is again a provision about 'delay and extra cost' cast in similar terms to that in clause 12 so far as relevant. In addition the engineer's actions may lead to a straightforward variation.

CLAUSE 14 — PROGRAMME TO BE FURNISHED

Under a civil engineering contract a programme is particularly significant. It will show the proposed sequence of what may be quite scattered work and also the nature of temporary work. This latter may involve the contractor in extensive design and also form a relatively large proportion of the cost of work. It is therefore provided that a programme covering this information is to be furnished for approval, soon after acceptance of the tender, to cover the timing of sections of the works, and accompanied by method statements which include information about temporary works and plant. This programme and the statements will need amplifying as the contractor develops his planning and may need modifying as problems arise, especially over progress. Here the engineer may call for such data and at all stages must give his express consent to the proposals, without his consent relieving the contractor of his obligations. Since the engineer is entitled to furnish the contractor with 'design criteria' to achieve consent, there is the possibility that he may go beyond what the contractor could reasonably have foreseen, or at least that this will be asserted. In addition his consent may be delayed. In either case the contractor is entitled to lodge a 'delay and extra cost' claim. All in all, these provisions go considerably beyond the master programme provided 'for information only' under JCT clause 5.3.1.2.

CLAUSE 20 — CARE OF WORKS AND EXCEPTED RISKS

The contractor's obligation to make good damage and deliver up the works, come what may, without extra payment for repair work is made explicit in the first part of this clause, which includes temporary works in the obligation. It is made subject only to the excepted risks which consist mainly of such acts of human violence as war and insurrection, and the usual range of aerial and nuclear risks, but also includes damage caused by the employer after completion or damage due to faulty design. Damage arising from the excepted risks is still to be made good by the contractor should the engineer so instruct, but not otherwise; but he is to be paid for the cost. The effect of this is some diminution of the contractor's responsibility for both the works and the temporary works. Over a narrower range of risks it roughly parallels JCT clause 22B (local authorities edition) by making the employer his own insurer.

The obligation extends over the period of the works up to completion and to 14 days beyond. It is shortened in respect of any portion for which sectional completion occurs and is extended in respect of any work allowed to run over into the period of maintenance.

CLAUSE 21 — INSURANCE OF WORKS ETC

The contractor is required by this clause to back up by insurance his responsibility under clause 20 without limiting his responsibility, so that he will remain liable if the insurance fails and can recover no excess from the employer. The subject-matter of the insurance is widened beyond that of clause 20 to include materials and plant. It is to cover not only the period of construction, but also the period of maintenance so far as any cause prior to the period has effects during it.

The effect of this clause thus differs from that in JCT clause 22A in several ways. Where the JCT clause requires the contractor to insure, it requires him to do so against specified risks only; this clause requires him to insure against all risks other than those specified as excepted. The scope of the JCT clause is more limited: it covers the works and materials, makes no reference to temporary works — which are of less consequence in building work, but would be covered — and categorically excludes plant. Again, the contractor's insurance under the JCT clause ceases with practical completion. As an alternative to the contractor insuring, JCT clause 22B allows for the employer insuring and taking the risks or for him taking the risks without insurance.

CLAUSES 22 TO 24 — DAMAGE TO PERSONS AND PROPERTY AND INSURANCE

The contractor is to indemnify the employer under these clauses broadly as he does under JCT clause 20, but with a number of exceptions for which the employer gives an indemnity to the contractor. Clause 30 introduces a further exception, as considered below. The contractor is to insure against his liabilities on the lines of JCT clause 21 and the employer has rights of approval over the insurances. The amount of insurance cover is specified in the contract appendix, and the limit applies to both persons in the present case. While the policy is in the name of the contractor, there is a term entitling the employer to indemnity under it by the insurer.

CLAUSE 25 — REMEDY ON CONTRACTOR'S FAILURE TO INSURE

Should the contractor fail to produce evidence of insurance when asked by the employer in respect of the works etc, or in respect of persons and property, the employer may carry out the necessary insurances and recover the costs from the contractor.

CLAUSE 27 — PUBLIC UTILITIES STREET WORKS ACT 1950

The Act in question regulates the often complex position arising in a street where several authorities and undertakings may have jurisdiction and responsibilities. This clause sets out the relation of the contractor under the contract to this Act on the one hand and the works on the other. To come to any detailed understanding of the provisions of the clause, it should be studied alongside the Act.

CLAUSE 30 — AVOIDANCE OF DAMAGE TO HIGHWAYS ETC

Claims over damage due to extraordinary traffic on highways or bridges or the cost of precautions to avoid the damage are, under this clause, to be borne by the employer. If however the contractor fails to observe care in dealing with such traffic, he is to bear the amounts concerned. This clause arises from the heavier nature of civil engineering work and has no equivalent under the JCT forms, where the contractor is responsible under the indemnity provisions.

CLAUSE 31 — FACILITIES FOR OTHER CONTRACTORS

This is a wide-ranging provision as is the equivalent condition in the GC/Works/1 form. It mentions other contractors and statutory bodies and some of these could be performing work of some magnitude 'on or near the site'. Where possible, these activities should be identified in the contract documents in sufficient detail for the contractor to allow for them, although this is not specifically mentioned. The contractor becomes entitled to a 'delay and extra cost' claim if what happens is not 'reasonably to be foreseen by an experienced contractor', so that a solution like that under JCT clause 29 is available.

The clause needs to be read in the light of clause 42, which does not afford exclusive possession of the site to the contractor and allows the employer to be in breach of giving possession, without this being a fundamental breach of contract.

Labour, work, materials and plant

CLAUSES 34 AND 35 — LABOUR

These clauses rehearse the 'Fair Wages Resolution', as does the JCT local authorities clause 19A, and also appear to be aimed at securing harmonious labour relations on site and at giving the engineer a right to detailed labour and plant returns. In these latter respects they are thus additional to any provision made under the JCT form. Whether they would often give any right to damages for breach to the employer is doubtful.

CLAUSES 36 TO 40 — WORK, MATERIALS AND PLANT

These clauses cover similar ground to those in JCT clauses 8, 10 and 4.1.2 (in that order) about quality, testing, inspection, access for the engineer to the site, the removal of defective work and materials and the engaging of other persons to remedy the contractor's default if necessary. The effect is very similar regarding responsibility and costs. There is an additional obligation on the contractor not to cover up any work before inspection.

The clause about suspension of work has a similar effect to JCT clause 23.2 over postponement, but also allows the engineer to order suspension at the contractor's expense because of weather, contractor's default, or safety considerations. When suspension ordered by the engineer lasts more than three months, the contractor has the option of treating the part of the works concerned as omitted, or the works as abandoned if the whole has been suspended. This option will not apply if the suspension is contemplated in the contract or is due to the contractor's default.

When the suspension warrants it the contractor will be entitled to a 'delay and extra cost' claim.

Commencement time and delays

The heading of this group of clauses could well make reference to completion also, since it is covered here. While there is broad correspondence with JCT clauses 17, 18, 23, 24 and 25, several points in the clauses warrant consideration for the different effect that they produce.

CLAUSE 41 — COMMENCEMENT OF WORKS

The contract documents make no reference to a date for possession or commencement but this clause requires the engineer to notify the date reasonably soon after acceptance of the tender. The contractor in turn is to start on or reasonably soon after that date. This gives a little flexibility over programme, but not reasonably over costs such as work load, rises in prices or changed seasonal conditions. Contractors are advised to qualify their tenders as being related to commencement within a suitable stated period.

CLAUSE 42 — POSSESSION OF SITE — WAYLEAVES ETC

Due to the often scattered nature of civil engineering work, provision is made for possession to be progressive but for the contractor to be reimbursed for delay in receiving possession and to be granted extension of time. These remedies would not apply until a date or dates for possession had been established and clause 41 should be compared here. The JCT form does not contemplate phased possession, although it can be provided for in the Sectional Completion Supplement.

The contractor is here made responsible for any wayleaves and the like that he may require for accesses to the site proper, in respect of which the employer would be responsible in such matters.

CLAUSE 43 — TIME FOR COMPLETION

Phased completion is specifically contemplated here at the contract stage. In the case of the JCT form partial possession is agreed during progress (clause 18) and any prior arrangements are made in the supplementary clause. The time or times here will be determined in relation to the flexible date for commencement in clause 41.

CLAUSE 44 — EXTENSION OF TIME FOR COMPLETION

The clauses already considered include a number of references to this clause and need no further mention. In addition the clause points forward to variations under clause 51 and permits also 'exceptional adverse weather conditions' to lead to an extension. This establishes a broad parity with JCT clause 25 by giving a number of causes that stem from the employer or his engineer; the effect of these leading to an extension is to keep the right to claim for damages alive for the employer as well. Delay or other default of nominated sub-contractors (who include nominated suppliers) is not a cause for extension, except in the extreme case of forfeiture under clause 59B. Weather appears as a 'neutral' cause, but is alone in this respect — for instance, there is no reference to the excepted risks as such. There is, however, a reference to 'other special circumstances of any kind whatsoever' as leading to an extension. This is wide enough, to say the least, to accommodate the excepted risks, but is so broad as to be open to disputes without limit and is perhaps legally useless.

There are a number of matters concerned with the calculation of any extension. Firstly, there is the recognition of sectional completion and, secondly, the obligation on the part of the contractor to give particulars of any claim to extension as soon as he reasonably can, but not apparently of the original cause. The engineer is to act in a three stage way:

(a) Grant an interim extension as soon as he can.

(b) Review the position when the due or extended date arrives, and advise the employer and contractor as to whether he is proposing a further interim extension.

(c) Grant the final extension upon issuing the certificate of completion.

However once the engineer has granted an interim extension, he may not reduce it in the final extension. This arrangement goes part of the way to resolving the doubt that may well arise when an extension must be retrospective, although it clearly needs care in its application. It is probably not reasonable to try to get much closer to an ideal scheme.

CLAUSE 45 — NIGHT AND SUNDAY WORK

Both categories of work are generally prohibited, except where unavoidable or absolutely necessary and then only after notice. They are permitted for work where shifts are customary. Clause 46 affects this clause considerably.

CLAUSE 46 — RATE OF PROGRESS

Read with clause 45, this clause shows a difference of fundamental principle from the JCT form which is silent on how the contractor is to achieve the date for completion. Here the contractor may be notified if his rate of working appears to the engineer to be too slow to achieve this date. Presumably the engineer will take due account of the programme under clause 14. If the contractor ignores the engineer's representations there would appear to be a stalemate under this present clause: no other remedy is prescribed for the impending breach (and it is no more) until and only if liquidated damages fall due. If the contractor chooses to work night or Sunday work and the engineer permits this, the contractor may do so at his own expense.

CLAUSE 47 — LIQUIDATED DAMAGES

In overall terms this clause establishes a position similar to that under JCT clause 24, but it goes about it rather differently. It is related to the original completion date and any extensions due to the specified causes, so that the right to damages is maintained; it has an apparatus for relating the amount of damages to progressive handing over to the works; and it allows for deduction of damages from payments or for otherwise recovering them. It is in the second of these areas that the main difference comes by way of elaboration, and with the support of the contract appendix. The parts of the apparatus provided are:

(a) For the whole of the works — An overall sum for delayed completion which may be reduced in proportion to the values concerned if any part of the works is certified completed early. For this overall sum may be substituted (apparently before the contract is entered into) a sum representing the limit of the contractor's liability for damages. This seems to be an attempt to secure the contractor's agreement that the sum is liquidated damages and not a penalty: it may not be a valid attempt if tried in the courts.

(b) For designated sections of the work — individual sums for each section which again may be reduced proportionately. These sums in turn reduce the overall level of damages. However, each sum is dealt with in a two stage arrangement: the first being a sum for the loss to the employer if delay renders him liable to another contractor for damages (the other contract being held up), and the second being the employer's own overall loss due to delay and including any damages that the first stage sum represented.

This summary of the provision suggests that it needs careful assimilation and also that the amounts inserted in the appendix should be thoroughly assessed to give the desired effect. The various amounts could be related to overlapping elements of the works as between foreseen and unforeseen completion of sections and this aspect could cause problems during progress unless handled carefully. This is an area where it may be as well not to make too complicated a set of entries in the appendix, while trying to cover any major case where the simple use of the value of delayed work could lead to a calculation of damages on a proportionate basis that would be seriously in error. This could mean either an inadequate recovery by the employer or the repudiation of the sum as a penalty by the contractor. A reference in the clause to all sums as being liquidated damages and not penalties is without any force.

There is also a provision for the reimbursement to the contractor of any excess damages levied, should a review lead to a later completion date being granted. Interest is then payable.

CLAUSE 48 — CERTIFICATE OF COMPLETION OF WORKS

The effect of this form differs from JCT clause 17 in that it applies where the works have been substantially completed, which is a different conception from practical completion and less onerous, due to the nature of final operations such as landscaping, on a civil engineering contract which may well go on into the period of maintenance. The clause is more onerous in requiring the works to have passed any final test before certification.

The primary procedure is for the contractor to give written notice of completion of the works or of a section specified in the contract or arising by virtue of the employer occupying or using it. As a secondary procedure the engineer may take the initiative over a part of the works and certify it.

Maintenance, defects, alterations and property

CLAUSES 49 AND 50 — MAINTENANCE AND DEFECTS

Despite the different term 'Period of maintenance' used, the clauses have a similar effect to JCT clause 17 so far as liability is concerned, since fair wear and tear is excepted. There are however rights for the engineer to require the contractor to remedy defects and also to search for the causes of defects even where they may not be his fault. These faults are subject to a counter-right of the contractor to be paid if defects turn out not to be his fault. However since the contractor can be required to do the work the term 'maintenance' is appropriate here.

CLAUSES 51 AND 52 — ALTERATIONS, ADDITIONS AND OMISSIONS

The engineer is given wide scope to order variations in writing or otherwise and there is no right open to the contractor to question the validity of such orders, as in JCT clause 4.1.1. The provisions for the confirmation of oral instructions by either the engineer or the contractor are looser here and subject to no time limits. While orders for variation need not be in writing, the intention of either party to seek varied rates is to be notified in writing at an early, but imprecise date.

The definition of variations comprehends the same categories of physical change as does JCT clause 13.1.1 and also (corresponding broadly to part of JCT clause 13.1.2) includes 'changes in the specified sequence method or timing of construction (if any)'. To make sense the expression '(if any)' must be read as applying to everything from 'specified' onwards, while on a strict reading any changes in the sequence and so on proposed by the contractor under his own programme mentioned in clause 14 are not permitted here. On the face of things the present clause is therefore more limited than JCT clause 13.1, as it does not include all the categories in JCT clause 13.1.2. Clause 14 however permits the engineer to require changes in particular circumstances and in practice the distinction between these various changes becomes difficult to maintain, so that often the engineer may reasonably cover any category in and beyond JCT clause 13.1.2.

While the provisions for valuing variations will usually be interpreted along similar lines to those in JCT clause 13.5, there is not the same detailing of a formula. Instead other measured rates or daywork may be introduced where this is suitable in the opinion of the engineer.

In the case of changes in the quantity only of the work variation orders are not required, since such changes are covered by the procedure for complete measurement under clause 56. Orders are needed for all changes in the description of work.

Where daywork is permitted, its valuation will be at current rates when it is executed if the standard federation schedule is used. If this is not used, the conditions for daywork are to be set out in the bill of quantities and the contractor should check these so as to be clear about how his various expenses will be reimbursed and whether or not his overheads will be fully covered, and even his fluctuations in costs.

Items leading to claims are specified elsewhere in the conditions, but the present clause sets out the procedures to be followed. For this purpose the requesting of a higher measured rate by the contractor constitutes a claim, along with 'extra cost' matters as such. The key elements of procedure are early written notification of intent from the contractor, followed by the keeping of records in a manner approved by the engineer and available to him, and the presentation of accounts progressively. It will not always be practicable to put forward such accounts, given the nature of some claims. It is not appropriate to pro rata rates and some claims may need calculation after the event. The importance of keeping records in whatever form is needed cannot be overstressed and both engineer and contractor should look to these to avoid later difficulties, even though the claim may not even have been admitted in principle, as the clause recognises may be the case. The inclusion of a procedure for records is an advance over the JCT position where nothing is made mandatory. Should the contractor fail in any of his parts of the whole procedure, he will lose entitlement to payment to the extent that his lapse has prevented full assessment. Thus where there was doubt he might qualify for only a conservative amount. So far as a claim amount has been ascertained, it ranks for interim payment. This agrees with the JCT form, whereas the GC/Works/1 form only allows the inclusion of agreed claims.

CLAUSE 53 — PLANT ETC

While this clause produces a similar effect to JCT clauses 16.1 and 27.4.1 over the ownership of materials on site, whether paid for in interim certificates or not, it aims to introduce a different concept over plant to give the employer additional protection in the event of the contractor's insolvency or default. This concept centres in the words in clause 53(2) 'deemed to be the property of the Employer' which refer to plant on the site owned by the contractor. These words do not have the same precision and force as the words of the corresponding condition 3 of the GC/Works/1 contract and could well fail in themselves. In relation to hired plant, the clause makes some provisions designed to keep key plant on site to avoid constructional failure, and with hire charges taken up by the employer. This is an area where the law is full of pitfalls and it should not be lightly assumed either that the contractor has complied with the provisions or that, even when he has, they will be adequate in all situations.

CLAUSE 54 — VESTING OF GOODS AND MATERIALS NOT ON SITE

Unlike the corresponding JCT clauses 16.2 and 30.3, this clause operates only in respect of items listed in the contract appendix, but then operates as of right for the contractor, provided that he has observed the requirements given. These cover similar ground to JCT clause 30.3 in respect of physical identification and documentary evidence and the like; as a result they are likely to be as strong or weak as those provisions in the various circumstances that may arise. In particular they will be invalid in Scotland and the comment in Chapter 26 should be noted.

Measurement

CLAUSES 55 TO 57 — QUANTITIES MEASUREMENT AND VALUATION

Approximate quantities are the only basis of tendering envisaged under these conditions, with full re-measurement of the works as executed. No engineer's instruction is required under the conditions for an alteration in quantity alone and such a basis does not destroy the character of the contract as an entire contract. The form of tender provides for 'such sums as may be ascertained.' The present clauses, along with clauses 51 and 52 and the various scattered provisions for extra payment, are the appropriate authority for arriving at this. If the contractor does not attend for measurement when required, the engineer's measurements are to be taken as correct. This would be likely to hold in an arbitration, particularly as clause 66 does not give measurement, but only valuation, as open to review.

The Civil Engineering Standard Method of Measurement is incorporated into the bills of quantities by reference and there is thus a parallel with JCT clause 2.2.2.1. The method of measurement can be followed by producing very terse bills with some discretion as to what is included in the rates for other items. Unmeasured items are to be inferred from the drawings and specification and allowed for in tendering where it is reasonable to do so. In a contract that then requires complete remeasurement and allows the engineer some control over the contractor's methods and temporary works, the scene is duly set for quite an amount of discussion at least. Several cases under 'Documentation and measurement' are relevant and the need for the bills to be unambiguous is important over such matters, even though the principle of brevity of description and reliance on the other documents be adhered to as the standard method requires.

There are two qualifications to be read in this context. One is that errors and omissions in the bill are to be corrected and the effect taken up in the measurement and valuation, subject to the contractor holding to any estimating errors. The other is that where the final measured quantities differ sufficiently from those in the original bill, the unit rates may be adjusted up or down to take account of the change in such matters as plant use. These qualifications are paralleled in JCT clause 13.5, but are particularly important in a contract based on approximate quantities — often very approximate.

Provisional and prime cost sums and nominated sub-contracts

This group of clauses produces an effect similar to those in clauses 35 and 36, although there are some important differences of principle as well as in detail.

CLAUSE 58 — PROVISIONAL SUMS AND PRIME COST ITEMS

The main elements here are definitions which are less detailed than, but in line with, those in the JCT form, except that nominated sub-contractors include suppliers. There are procedures for the expenditure of the sums (which again equate with the JCT position and cover the principle of nomination without anything equivalent to the JCT 'basic' or 'alternative' methods), the contractor carrying out prime cost work and nominated work arising out of provisional sums. The case of items, (usually measured items) which include a prime cost element is specifically recognised.

A significant extra sub-clause requires any design element in a provisional or prime cost amount to be identified in the main contract and any sub-contract, so that 'the obligation of the contractor' may be limited to what is 'expressly stated'. Limitation though this may be, it in fact outflanks the general position under clause 8(2) that he is not responsible for the design of the permanent works. This element of design needs careful description if the contractor is to allow for any potential liability in any item other than the provisional or prime cost amount (which is subject to adjustment), and before that careful thought as to any overlap of responsibility between the contractor and the engineer in the case of a composite structure, for example.

The clause itself establishes no demarcation over indemnities and, as there is no standard equivalent to Agreements NSC/2 and NSC/2a, an adequate collateral arrangement should be considered for the protection of the engineer at least in vital cases. Indemnity for the contractor comes under the next clause.

CLAUSE 59A — NOMINATED SUB-CONTRACTORS, OBJECTION, RESPONSIBILITY AND PAYMENT

The contractor may object to the nomination of a sub-contractor in only a very limited range of cases, which amount to the person named, as such, adequate indemnity provisions (including over design as a 'serviee') and forfeiture arrangements. Nothing is required that comes close to the JCT use of Sub-Contracts NSC/4 and NSC/4a. When, however, his objection is accepted there are several courses prescribed as options:

(a) A fresh nomination.

(b) Omission of the work from the contract and its execution as a direct contract with the employer by others, concurrently or later, and by inference with those others being either the same firm as was proposed for the nomination, or another.

(c) Direction of the contractor to enter into a sub-contract with the original firm, but with some (unspecified) amendment of terms and relief for the contractor from his own obligations to allow for any remaining gap; this is an implied remedy in the JCT form.

(d) Arranging for the contractor to carry out the work; subsequent sub-letting by him is not expressly precluded, but might be as a condition of a particular arrangement.

Subject to any exclusions coming out of these arrangements, the contractor is held responsible for all sub-contract work (including any design, it would appear), as would be the implied legal position if not expressed. Lastly, the clause covers final payment, while leaving interim payment to clause 59C, oddly. This is straightforward, except for the matter of discount for prompt payment. This is limited to 'any discount obtainable' without there being any requirement that the terms of sub-contracts should include a given level of discount or any at all, and without there being any stipulation over discount in the provisions about prime cost items. A contractor has no right of objection on the ground that a quotation offers less than an adequate discount in his opinion, although he may well look for one based on the other grounds given earlier in the clause. He should therefore include an adequate allowance in his profit margin stated in the appendix to the form of tender to cover this hazard as far as is practicable.

CLAUSE 59B — FORFEITURE OF SUB-CONTRACT

This is a long, somewhat tortuously worded clause in so far as it provides for a number of the complex possibilities over termination and renomination that may arise in these circumstances, as for example in the case of *North West Metropolitan Regional Hospital Board* v. *T. A. Bickerton Ltd.* Within the present scope it is as well to summarise the position established as that responsibility in financial terms is placed as far as possible with the person 'at fault', so that the result is closer to that under the JCT form than to that under the GC/Works/1 form. In straight commercial terms, this will mean either the contractor, if he forfeits unreasonably, or the sub-contractor if his action or default leads to forfeiture. In the former case the contractor is to bear any extra expense and to receive no extension of time. In the latter case the contractor is to recover from the sub-contractor as far as possible (for there may be insolvency) his own and the employer's loss, and any 'irrecoverable costs and expenses' of so doing are to be shared 'as may be fair' between the employer and the contractor.

In the sense that the original nomination was the employer's 'fault' under the philosophy of the contract, he then bears the cost of making a fresh nomination, the contractor's loss due to delay and the like, any resulting extension of time and any higher price payable as a result, except to the extent that these excess costs are recovered from the defaulting sub-contractor or unless, as noted, the forfeiture was unreasonable on the part of the contractor. There may well be circumstances in which responsibility cannot be placed in such a single-minded way, and here the costs may need apportioning. It is because of such considerations and to allow for a number of other possible 'kinks' that the clause takes such a roundabout route to achieve its object with any precision.

CLAUSE 59C — PAYMENT TO NOMINATED SUB-CONTRACTORS

While the employer has the same right to pay nominated sub-contractors direct if the contractor defaults on payment, this clause explicitly makes the point, which the JCT clause covers by reference to the sub-contract, that the contractor may with reasonable cause hold amounts for contra-charges and the like. This reaffirms the common law position, as does the case of *Gilbert Ash (Northern) Ltd* v. *Modern Engineering (Bristol) Ltd.* All nominated sub-contractors, who will include suppliers, are subject to any retention 'provided for in the sub-contract'. Nothing is stipulated here about its level or it being proportionate to the contractor's retention or otherwise, so that the engineer must check the particulars of each sub-contract before he can safely certify a direct payment by the employer.

Certificates and payment

CLAUSE 60 — MONTHLY PAYMENTS, RETENTION AND FINAL ACCOUNT

Payments are to be made monthly, with the contractor forwarding a detailed statement to the engineer at the end of each month and the employer paying on the engineer's certificate within twenty-eight days of the contractor's statement. The elements to be paid for are permanent work, materials on site for permanent work and off site where covered by clause 54, temporary work and constructional plant. There is a provision for a minimum amount for an interim certificate, the amount being stated in the appendix. The retention formula allows for the holding of an initial 5 per cent with this reaching a ceiling which is 3 per cent of the *tender* amount for all but the smallest of contracts. This is held on everything except unfixed materials, which are not strictly subject to retention but are to be included as a percentage of value as given in the appendix to the form of tender. At substantial completion half the sum is to be released, with the rest following after the end of the maintenance period. Early release of $1\frac{1}{2}$ per cent of value is made where there is sectional completion, subject to this release not exceeding half of the aggregate of retention proper held, while a sum may be held after the end of the maintenance period to cover the value of work to be done. This last is the only point of principle over retention that differs from JCT clause 30, although the percentages differ and the details of sectional release are more complex.

Certificates are given here as to include nominated amounts, while the clauses elsewhere dealing with extra cost claims allow these amounts to be included in certificates. In view of the silence, these sums will carry retention, unlike their equivalents in the JCT case. The employer is entitled under the conditions to deduct from the amounts of certificates for liquidated damages, while the engineer is to deduct for any previous direct payments to nominated sub-contractors on the contractor's default.

Should a certificate not be paid on time due to the default of either the engineer or the employer, the contractor is entitled to interest on the amount outstanding. This is distinct from the JCT position where the contractor has the remedy of determination under clause 28 open to him instead, in respect only of the employer's default, although this does include interference before issue of a certificate.

For some reason the final account is dealt with in the middle of the clause. It is to be prepared by the contractor within three months of the maintenance certificate and within a further three months, subject to any supporting information being received, the engineer is to issue a final certificate of the amount. This certificate has no bearing on satisfaction with the work, which comes under the maintenance certificate in the next clause. Payment of the final balance is subject to any due counter amounts outstanding, but is due within 28 days of the certificate. If either engineer or employer falls down on this timetable, there will again be an entitlement of the contractor to interest. Preparation of the account is the bigger problem in sheer labour involved and it will usually be agreed progressively. However, if the *contractor* supplies it with all supporting information, time will then be tight before interest starts to accrue. The exact intention is a little unclear, since the *engineer* may act alone in the measurement stage if the contractor fails to attend 'to assist' under clause 56(3), while it is the engineer again who determines rates under clause 52(1) if there is disagreement. A reference to arbitration is always another possible source of delay or complication.

CLAUSE 61 — MAINTENANCE CERTIFICATE

This certificate deals with the engineer's satisfaction with the works and not with financial matters, as will be evident from clause 60. Release of retention is not dependent on the issue of the certificate either, although some retention will be held until it is issued. While there will be more than one period of maintenance when there is sectional completion, there is to be only one maintenance certificate issued after the last of these periods and when all making good and the like has been carried out. The effect of the certificate is not defined in such a way as to reduce the liabilities of the parties under the Limitation Act, as occurs under JCT clause 30.9.1. It does end the right of the employer to expect the contractor to return to remedy defects.

Remedies and powers

CLAUSE 62 — URGENT REPAIRS

If the contractor defaults in carrying out emergency remedial work during construction or maintenance, the employer may arrange for others to do it and charge the contractor if appropriate. This parallels parts of the provisions of JCT clause 4.1.2 for employing others.

CLAUSE 63 — FORFEITURE

The causes leading to forfeiture of the contract here are similar to those leading to determination of the contractor's employment by the employer under JCT clause 27. The employer's remedy is to give seven days' notice and then enter and expel the contractor, a somewhat boisterous sounding proceeding. He may then complete the works using materials and plant on the site, or engage another contractor to do so. At completion and settlement the amount of indebtedness in one direction or the other is to be met in the manner of the JCT clause, with the difference that the employer may sell any plant which he has held and take the proceeds into account. This means that any monies arising from the sale of plant that are not needed to recoup the employer's losses will be returned to the contractor.

There are two procedural matters covered. One is that the employer may act on the named causes only where the engineer certifies their occurrence, which parallels the architect taking the initiative in the JCT form; the exceptions are insolvency and assignment, where the employer may act without the engineer's certificate. There is no case of automatic determination or other effect as in the JCT clause. The other procedural matter is that the engineer is to carry out a valuation at the time of expulsion covering all work, materials and plant. This sort of valuation may be useful for evidential purposes at some later stage, but it has no direct usefulness in coming to a settlement under the clause.

Miscellaneous provisions

CLAUSE 64 — FRUSTRATION

If frustration occurs, that is a situation arises preventing any reasonable completion, the contractor is to be paid on the same basis as in the case of a determination under clause 65.

CLAUSE 65 — WAR CLAUSE

The clause provides for work to continue for 28 days if this is possible and, if then complete, to be settled without the contractor necessarily carrying out all maintenance work. If it is not then complete, only the employer has an option of determination at any time, whereupon the procedure for closing the site and paying off the contractor follows the pattern of JCT clauses 32 and 33. For any work following the outbreak of hostilities, a special variation of price clause applies.

CLAUSE 66 — SETTLEMENT OF DISPUTES

The pattern of this arbitration clause is generally very close to that in the JCT article in its key parts, although the wording of other clauses of the two sets of conditions vary their respective scopes somewhat. There is however a requirement that the parties submit their dispute to the engineer first and only go to arbitration if still dissatisfied. Seeing that the engineer will be a key figure in most disputes and thus already committed to a point of view, this seems to be a near pointless procedure.

CLAUSE 67 — APPLICATION TO SCOTLAND

The situation of the works is made the criterion as to which branch of law shall apply, rather than the addresses of the parties. The cast of *Whitworth Street Estates (Manchester) Ltd* v. *James Miller and Partners Ltd* is relevant however, and the present clause may not adequately settle the arbitration procedure.

CLAUSE 68 — NOTICES

All notices served on the contractor or the employer are to be served at their formal addresses. This would not be very satisfactory for day-to-day site notices to the contractor, but is limited to the few matters specifically termed 'notices' in the conditions.

CLAUSE 71 — METRICATION

In the transition stage between imperial and metric sizes for materials it was necessary to provide for the problems arising when items are specified in the one system but turn out to be obtainable only in the other. The clause still survives. The contractor is to notify the engineer of the problem and the engineer is to instruct a variation so that either the alternative available to the contractor may be used or some change in design is introduced to avoid the material.

Tax matters

CLAUSE 69 — TAX FLUCTUATIONS

This clause applies as a minimum in the contract and covers the same range of matters as that part of JCT clause 38 that relates to labour. The critical factor for adjustment is that rates are to be based on the levels of taxes payable 'at the date for return of tenders'. This gives parity with the JCT form by not requiring the contractor to foresee any increase in arriving at his tender. The position is also in line with the provisions of the GC/Works/1 form. The present clause does not specifically exclude value added tax from its ambit, although clause 70 excludes it from the contract in general. However, the reference is to taxes and so forth 'in respect of . . . workpeople', so that there can be no doubt. The clause is curtailed in its effect where the supplementary clause 'Contract price fluctuations' is used, as is there discussed.

CLAUSE 70 — VALUE ADDED TAX

The inclusion of this clause in the mainstream of the conditions is different from the arrangement under either the JCT form or the GC/Works/1 form, although the financial result is similar. The contractor is deemed not to have allowed for any tax in his tender and where there is a taxable supply to the employer he receives payment of the tax. The procedure is that he should provide alongside, but not as part of, any interim valuation statement affected an estimate of the value of taxable supplies so that the employer may calculate and pay the tax with, but distinct from, the payment on account. Here the procedure follows the GC/Works/1 form closely, as do the subsequent procedures for receipts, disputes and adjustment of errors. There is no mention of the effect of liquidated damages or of retention, but these are fairly obvious and little is lost here. There is a sub-clause about change in tax status of part of the work, such that it alters the amount payable by the contractor but not chargeable to the employer. This is similar to JCT clause 15.3, except that it envisages the recovery of any saving as well as the reimbursement of any loss.

Contract price fluctuations

A supplementary clause for price fluctuations in general is available which may be included in the contract as clause 72 or later, according to what other clauses may be inserted into the gap provided in the conditions as printed. A covering note states that it is 'for use in appropriate cases' and its effect is to extend fluctuations reimbursement beyond the tax matters of clause 69 into the field of 'full' fluctuations. It does this by a formula method as does JCT clause 40 and GC/Works/1 supplementary condition 146, but the formula differs in points of principle. Of these the most important is that a single set of index figures applies to the whole of the works, irrespective of the types of work by trade or otherwise that are included. This means that in any one month the fluctuations adjustment will be made by a single expression, the price fluctuation factor, applied to the effective value for that month. However the index figures used, that is the base and current figures, are compiled for each contract by weighting various figures published by Her Majesty's Stationery Office. These figures cover labour and plant as two inclusive categories and the main materials as separate categories. There is a provision in the clause for insertion of the percentages of each category that are used to achieve the all-in weighted index for the particular contract. In view of the fairly crude basis that this system produces, the contractor is well advised to check for himself the weightings inserted into the clause by the engineer before he accepts them as part of the contract. Equally this implies the need for care on the part of the engineer in arriving at the figures in the first place. The figures eventually agreed are in any case inclusive of an element that is non-adjustable to represent the productivity deduction.

In other respects the clause follows the JCT principle in allowing monthly adjustment and payment and in freezing the level of adjustment at the figure for the due date for completion. There is no provision to deal with any increase in the value of work thrown up in settlement of the final account and this needs some supplementing in framing the other documents. The clause incorporates its own formula rules, as does the GC/Works/1 form, but is still brief although clear in what it does say.

A subsidiary provision renders clause 69 'Tax fluctuations' inapplicable where the present clause is used except where there is adjustment of a matter not contained within the underlying official labour index.

A further supplementary clause for price fluctuations in fabricated structural steelwork is also available. This proceeds on a similar basis and with similar wording to the general fluctuations clause, and is intended to supplement the first supplementary clause in any case in which there is a significant element of steelwork. It provides for those parts of the works to which it applies to be listed by bill of quantities references in a table, so that there is no doubt as to its scope. Any additional work to which it might apply must therefore be decided during progress and dealt with as a prelude by appropriate negotiation.

Forms of tender, agreement and bond

FORM OF TENDER

In addition to the offer, the form of tender printed with the conditions also gives the appendix details. A separately printed form of tender would usually be sent to tenderers for return with their priced bill of quantities, in accordance with the recommendations preceding the conditions. The form of tender is said to constitute evidence of agreement until the contract is formalised. This would be so in any case.

FORM OF AGREEMENT

The general pattern of this form is like that of the JCT articles of agreement, although the contract price is not named on the face of the form, due to the nature of the contract basis. It is provided that it should be executed under seal as the normal arrangement and thus the 12-year limitation period is secured in England.

FORM OF BOND

The operation of a performance bond is far more common in the realm of civil engineering, although it is still optional within the contract. It covers the full range of the contractor's obligations under the contract, and not just completion, and binds him and his surety or sureties jointly to that end up to the sum inserted in the appendix.

Over completion in particular, the bond provides its own arbitration mechanism if there is a dispute between the employer and the contractor about the date given in the maintenance certificate. Clause 10 establishes that this date, as and however arrived at for the purposes of the bond, is without prejudice to any arbitration within the contract itself under clause 66.

Table of cases

These cases are of interest in relation to the forms of contract discussed in this book. Some are related to earlier editions of these forms, dealing with provisions that may be unchanged or that may have been modified in current editions. Other cases were decided on non-standard forms. All cases may be consulted to deepen the legal background of the commentary, but the specific wording of current editions may lead to different legal decisions based on the same underlying principles.

Cases are grouped under headings and followed by notes, to indicate their salient features for present purposes only. In some instances a case occurs more than once. The table acts as an index to references to individual cases or groups of cases in the commentary. Cases are also referenced where possible to the standard law reports and in particular to the readily available Building Law Reports (BLR). Unreported cases receive some comment in these reports or in textbooks given in the Bibliography.

Page

Arbitration

Scott v. *Avery* (1856) 25 LJ Ex 308   18
> Decision that a contract (not building) precluded initial court action: *not* so in standard forms

Dawnays Ltd v. *F. G. Minter Ltd & Trollope & Colls Ltd* [1971] 1   —
WLR 1205; [1971] 2 All ER 1389; [1971] 2 Lloyd's Rep. 192, CA; (pet. dis.) [1971] 1 WLR HL; 1 BLR 16
> Court action allowed ahead of arbitration to help cash flow

James Miller & Partners Ltd v. *Whitworth Estates (Manches-* 22, 218, 327,
ter) Ltd [1970] AC 572; [1970] 1 All ER 1202; [1970] 1 Lloyd's   350, 372
Rep 107, CA
> Whether proper law of contract was English or Scottish and relation to arbitration

Monmouthshire County Council v. *Costelloe & Kemple Ltd*   —
(1965) 63 LGR 429; 5 BLR 83
> Enforcement of arbitration in civil engineering contract

Documentation and measurement

Trollope & Colls Ltd & Holland, Hannen & Cubitt Ltd v. *Atomic*   —
Power Constructions Ltd [1962] 3 All ER 1035; 107 SJ 254;
[1963] 1 WLR 333
> Formalising of contract after work commenced

Delay and liquidated damages
(Some cases under 'Certificates and payments' also relate to
this theme and to the wider question of deductions from sums
due)

Page

Bibliography

The books named below may be consulted for further reading. It should be remembered that even the latest edition of a legal reference book may not be completely up to date, owing to revisions of the standard forms themselves or to new rulings by the Courts. Before taking decisions of consequence in a legal matter professional advice should be obtained.

The legal background

Introduction to English Law. Philip S. James (Butterworth & Co)

General Principles of Scots Law. E. A. Marshall (Sweet & Maxwell)

Outline of the Law of Contract and Tort. G. G. G. Robb and John P. Brookes (Estates Gazette Ltd)

Construction Law. John Uff (Sweet & Maxwell)

The Law and Practice of Arbitrations. John Parris (George Godwin)

Building contract law

Hudson's Building and Engineering Contracts. I. N. Duncan Wallace (Sweet & Maxwell)

Law and Practice of Building Contracts. D. Keating (Sweet & Maxwell)

Emden's Building Contracts and Practice, Vols 1 and 2. Bickford-Smith and Freeth (Butterworth & Co)

Building Law Reports. A series of volumes issued at intervals and reporting both new and significant past cases (George Godwin)

The standard forms

The Standard Forms of Building Contract. Sir Derek Walker-Smith and Howard A. Close (Charles Knight & Co)

Building and Civil Engineering Standard Forms. I. N. Duncan Wallace (Sweet & Maxwell)

Supplements to Building and Civil Engineering Standard Forms. I. N. Duncan Wallace (Sweet & Maxwell)

Further Building and Engineering Standard Forms. I. N. Duncan Wallace (Sweet & Maxwell)

A New Approach to the 1980 Standard Form of Building Contract. Glyn P. Jones (Construction Press)
A New Approach to the 1980 Standard Form of Nominated Sub-Contract. Glyn P. Jones (Construction Press)

A New Approach to the ICE Conditions of Contract. Glyn P. Jones (Construction Press)

Insurance for the Construction Industry. F. N. Eaglestone (George Godwin)

The ICE Conditions of Contract — A Study of the Principal Changes. Quantity Surveyors (Civil Engineering) Working Party of the RICS (Royal Institution of Chartered Surveyors)

A Report in connection with the ICE Conditions of Contract. Civil Engineering Committee of the IQS (Institute of Quantity Surveyors)

Practical aspects

Management of Building Contracts. National Joint Consultative Committee of Architects, Quantity Surveyors and Builders (RIBA Publications)

Handbook of Architectural Practice and Management. Royal Institute of British Architects (RIBA Publications)

Contract Administration for Architects and Quantity Surveyors. The Aqua Group (Granada)

Building and Civil Engineering Claims. R. D. Wood (Estates Gazette)

Price Adjustment Formulae for Building Contracts. Quantity Surveyors (Practice and Management) Committee of the RICS (Royal Institution of Chartered Surveyors)

Price Adjustment Formulae for Building Contracts. Building Economic Development Committee (HMSO)

Quantity Surveying Practice and Administration. Dennis F. Turner (George Godwin)

The last named volume contains an extensive bibliography that includes a number of references to meet the needs of others apart from quantity surveyors.

Other references

Practice Notes. Issued by the Joint Contracts Tribunal as guides to the use of the standard forms. Up-to-date sets are available from the RIBA, the NFBTE, and the RICS. Further notes are published from time to time and details of them are given in the trade and technical press.

Articles and Reports in the official journals of the RIBA, the CIOB, the RICS, the IQS and the NFBTE.

Articles and Reports in: *Building, The Architect's Journal, QS Weekly, The Estates Gazette* and other periodicals.

Index

The terminology of the JCT forms has been used generally where differing from the other forms: for instance 'architect' has been used to include 'engineer' and 'SO', while 'employer' includes 'authority'.

Legal cases are not given here, but are classified by topics and references to them are indexed in the Table of Cases beginning on page 376.

Chapter 1 lists all contract forms considered throughout the book. Chapter 15 contains a table acting as an index to the detailed steps involved in nomination and subsequent dealings. Some diagrams in the text act as indexes to their subject matter.

The GC/Works/1 contract and the ICE Conditions both have an index or list of contents attached to their texts.